Core Professional Responsibility

Learning through Multiple-Choice Questions

Ray Brescia
HON. HAROLD R. TYLER CHAIR IN LAW AND TECHNOLOGY
PROFESSOR OF LAW
ALBANY LAW SCHOOL

CAROLINA ACADEMIC PRESS
Durham, North Carolina

LCCN 2023942319
ISBN 978-1-5310-2609-7
eISBN 978-1-5310-2610-3

CAROLINA ACADEMIC PRESS
700 Kent Street
Durham, North Carolina 27701
(919) 489-7486
www.cap-press.com

Printed in the United States of America

Core Professional Responsibility

Contents

Introduction

Welcome and Overview

This guide is designed to supplement and build your knowledge around the topic of legal ethics and professional responsibility. It does so through multiple-choice questions designed to test and deepen your understanding of these topics through the concept of *deliberate practice*, which is work toward an obtainable but far-off goal, with constant feedback. As you work through the material in this guide, you will slowly build your understanding of the core concepts of legal ethics and professional responsibility and move on to the next topic area once you have done so. Use this guide to supplement a class on legal ethics, as preparation for the national Multi-State Professional Responsibility Exam (MPRE), or simply to brush up on or solidify your understanding of a lawyer's professional ethics. This guide focuses mostly on the Model Rules of Professional Conduct promulgated by the American Bar Association (ABA), and, to a lesser extent, the Model Code of Judicial Conduct, also promulgated by the ABA. As their names imply, these are model rules that are adopted, as appropriate, by the various states. In order to prepare for the national MPRE, one should study their application. They do not have the force of law in any given state, however. To consider a state's rules regarding a particular question of a lawyer's professional responsibility in a given state, one must consult that state's rules and accompanying authorities interpreting those rules. This guide is designed to give you a firm grounding in core concepts related to legal ethics and professional responsibility, but it cannot be used to answer a specific question about a particular practice in a particular state.

While many of the questions in this guide are a bit more complex and challenging than what one might find in a typical legal ethics exam, their relative difficulty will prepare you well to spot the key issues, identify the knowledge a particular question is testing, and select the correct answer in the sometimes more straightforward questions you might typically see in an ethics examination. Working with these questions will also facilitate your ability to read critically and effectively and train you to do so more quickly, which are all skills you will need in any examination.

In addition to the questions themselves, at the end of each chapter there is a Formative Assessment Quiz which helps you gauge your understanding of the material in that chapter. The answer key in Chapter 10 provides only the correct answer to each question in the book, whereas Chapter 11 provides an in-depth explanation for each answer. Those explanations contain not just the answer but also the sources for the answer, such as the Model Rules of Professional Conduct, the Model Code of Judicial Conduct, and relevant case law, as appropriate. Use these explanations not only to understand the questions you got wrong and identify the concepts with which you may struggle but also to ensure you are understanding the things you got right. Think of them as a coach along the way. This coaching is a particularly important aspect of deliberate practice.

You can use the Formative Assessment Quiz when you have concluded your work in a given chapter. You can also wait to take the Formative Assessment Quiz until you have finished a few chapters and then take a series of them collectively, and let them serve as a "midterm," to test your understanding of the issues at different points in the semester or during the course of your studies. Note that instead of a Formative Assessment Quiz, Chapter 9 contains a Summative Assessment Quiz. This is an excellent way to review the material contained in the entire guide and to prepare for a final examination as well as the MPRE.

This guide is structured by chapters devoted to different topics and sub-topics related to a particular chapter's broad subject matter. You can work through the material in each chapter and follow along with a course or bar review based on the topical sections in each chapter. You do not have to follow the order of the chapters. Only the Summative Assessment Quiz is cumulative.

What This Guide Covers, and What It Does Not

This text is designed to introduce the reader to the issues that are typically covered in a course on professional responsibility, which is taught in virtually every law school in the United States. Because of that, there are comprehensive chapters on core concepts such as forming the attorney-client relationship, conflicts of interests, and confidentiality. There are also chapters on attorney's fees, ethics in advocacy, and judicial ethics. This guide does not cover state-specific rules nor does it include a comprehensive analysis of all potential sources of authorities related to professional responsibility, like treatises or the ethics opinions of state bar associations or state disciplinary authorities. The information here is more a starting point than an end point in your understanding of legal ethics and professional responsibility. Nevertheless, it will give you a firm grounding in these topics to prepare you to take the MPRE and to assist you in understanding the core concepts related to these topics.

A Note to Students

This book is designed to be *modular*. You can follow along with whatever course plan or casebook your instructor may utilize, aligning your work in this guide with the structure and order of materials your instructor uses. Try to refrain from diving into material you have not yet learned in whatever course you are taking. The understanding and skills you will gain from working through this guide will occur through testing your knowledge of the information learned in a traditional course. It will also strengthen that learning. At the same time, it is no substitute for what you will learn in a traditional course.

First and foremost, you should use the information you learn from these exercises to deepen your understanding of the knowledge you are supposed to be developing. In addition, you can also use these exercises to gather information about *you*: how well you are absorbing the material, the effectiveness of your study strategies, etc. Use this second-order information to hone in on not only your strengths but also your weaknesses, so you can build on the former and shore up the latter.

One more important note: given the format of the answers, it is very difficult to take these questions and then look for the answer after each question. You will invariably see the answer to the next question. At a minimum, it is recommended that you take the questions in a particular section before looking up the answers.

Taking Multiple-Choice Exams

Multiple-choice questions are challenging. It is easy to get lost in the weeds of the fact pattern: you may think it is taking you in one direction, and then you find the question is completely different from what you were anticipating. Once you start on that other direction, certain facts and issues will seem important to you, and when you get to the call of the question, you find that you might have to read the question all over again. I am sorry to report that this is often the express design of the questions you will face. Figuring out how to sort out the signal from the noise is a critical skill you will need to develop. In addition, having potential answers available to you might give you some degree of comfort, but those can be deceptive, and just because the wording of a potential answer might seem *familiar* to you does not mean that it is *correct*. The key question to ask with every multiple-choice question is "What knowledge is this question testing?" There can be many false paths and potential mis-directions and distractions in a typical multiple-choice question. When trying to answer a multiple-choice question, you must identify the specific nugget of knowledge, regarding a very particular issue, that is the focus of the question. A question cannot cover every possible issue under the sun, and practically every question is trying to assess your understanding of a very discrete topic. In order to ensure you can focus on what knowledge a particular question is testing, use the following approach, one that I call, with a nod to popular culture, *using the F.O.R.C.E.*

F. *Find* the question:

Turn first to the call of the question to get a general sense of what the exam question is asking. It might require you to read the last sentence or two of the fact pattern if the question itself is opaque, such as when it says something like "Is the lawyer subject to discipline for their conduct?" Finding the question first helps you avoid turning down a distracting and diverting path in the fact pattern.

O. *Observe*:

What are the facts of the fact pattern and how do they relate to the call of the question?

R. *Re-Orient*:

This is the most important step. Once you have read the call of the question and understand the facts, you now ask yourself, "What knowledge is this question testing?" Once you can focus on that, it will likely make certain facts more salient and important than others. Then you can focus on the important ones and orient yourself toward the direction in which the question is truly going.

C. *Codify*:

Here, you are going to identify the applicable rule that addresses the question presented. It is the next logical step following Step 3. Once you have re-oriented yourself to understand what knowledge the question is testing, you can then align the question, facts, and the appropriate rule that governs the situation. And when we say "rule" in the context of a professional responsibility exam, sometimes it means a specific model rule, sometimes it refers to a more general principle, and sometimes it might mean a rule that derives from case law relevant to a particular setting. It can even come from the U.S. Constitution itself. For example, if the knowledge the question is testing is the limits placed on a lawyer's right to advertise or solicit clients (*see* Chapter 7), the "rule" to apply in that situation may be derived, at least in part, from the First Amendment to the U.S. Constitution as interpreted in case law. Whatever the situation, apply the correct and appropriate "small-r" rule to fact pattern and question presented. At the same time, sometimes the "small-r" rule may actually be a "capital r" rule: for example, answering a question might require that you apply Model Rule 4.2, which deals with the prohibition on a lawyer's contacting a represented party without the consent of the lawyer who represents that party, to a given situation.

E. *Execute*:

Finally, it is time to look at the potential answers offered to you. Here, you will choose the answer that best matches your identification of the knowledge tested in Step 3 and your codification of the answer in Step 4. Really try to figure out what the answer should be before you look at the potential answers. And be aware of "traps"—for example, you might see an answer with wording that sounds familiar and want to choose it as a result, but the answer might only be familiar because it relates to a legitimate rule in the pantheon of professional responsibility rules, not because it is actually the proper rule to apply in a given situation.

Once again, the most important step in this process is Step 3. Every multiple-choice question is testing specific knowledge. Once you can hone in on what specific knowledge a particular question is testing, the extraneous issues melt away, and the answer should become clear. It takes some practice to utilize this approach (deliberate practice, in fact), and you can experiment with it without time constraints at first. Eventually, it will become habitual. You will find that it actually makes reading less time-consuming (with less time spent re-reading the question), and your answering the question will go more quickly.

Using Multiple-Choice Questions to Deepen Your Learning and Prepare for Essay-Based Questions

First, while the questions in this guide stand on their own and you can utilize them to develop your understanding of particular issues at face value, you can also use them creatively to further deepen your learning. First, you can take apart a particular question and manipulate the facts to determine whether a change in facts might change the outcome. For example, when it comes to questions of confidentiality (Chapter 3), a client's consent to release particular information is likely dispositive: the lawyer can release it. But what happens if the client does not give such consent? Are there situations in which a lawyer might still be able to release particular information without such consent? Are these situations in which that release is permissive? Are there situations in which the lawyer is required to release it? What change(s) to the fact pattern might change the outcome? Which will not? You can play around with each of the fact patterns in each question to help you develop a deeper understanding of the application of the different rules in particular situations. This can also help prepare you for anything—any iteration of a range of general facts that dictate the results in a particular situation. Pull together a study group of your colleagues. Have each of you change the fact pattern of a few questions and then share those changed fact patterns within the group. (Study groups are highly recommended generally.)

On a related note, you will probably notice that for a small percentage of questions, the fact patterns appear very similar. That is by design. For a few questions, this guide uses this method to test your knowledge and understanding of the material, borrowing some facts from a previous question and changing them up a bit. The basic elements of the question may even come from a different chapter altogether. Do not be fooled into thinking the question is the same, and, as a result, the answer and outcome are the same as well. Sometimes the facts change, but it does not necessarily change the outcome. At other times, the facts will change, and it *will* change the outcome. If you develop an ability to identify these situations and determine what changes to the outcome, if any, may occur as a result of those changes, you are on the road to mastery.

Second, since many law school exams and bar examinations include essay questions, any one of the questions contained in this guide can be converted into an essay question. Just ignore the potential answers and ask yourself, "How would I answer this question if it were an essay?" You can elaborate on the given facts and expand the issues you want to address (or have a colleague do so), but you can certainly use these fact patterns as prompts for an essay-based question and answer. Again, pull together a study group to help expand your capacity to do this by tackling a number of questions in this way.

A Note to Instructors

The chapters in this guide are presented in a particular order, one commonly used in an introductory professional responsibility course. At the same time, as described above, the chapters and the sections found within them are modular. You can align them with your course syllabus and assign them by chapter and even section within specific chapters to correspond to the structure and order of your course. Students can use the Formative Assessment Quizzes that conclude each chapter as a way to chart their progress on a particular topic, or you could recommend that students group those quizzes together as a "midterm" of sorts. If, for example, after the first month or so of class, you have covered forming the attorney-client relationship, conflicts, and confidentiality, you can recommend that students take the Formative Assessment Quizzes at the ends of Chapters 1, 2, and 3 together, as a way to assess their progress and understanding of the material. The Summative Assessment Quiz (Chapter 9) can also serve as a good review prior to your final exam. Once again, I do not see the materials in this guide as supplanting anything you are teaching, or as a substitute for it, but rather as a way to supplement the important work you are doing inside and outside the classroom.

Acknowledgments

Since becoming a lawyer, issues of professional responsibility have been core to my practice, but they have also become central to my teaching. I first taught a course on professional responsibility in the early 2000s as an adjunct professor at New York Law School. But I have been teaching professional responsibility every year since 2007, when I began teaching full-time at Albany Law School. This teaching has been informed by the many mentors I have had along the way: professors in law school, my colleagues and supervisors in practice, and my academic colleagues today. While in law school, Harold Hongju Koh, Michael Ratner, Bob Solomon and Steve Wizner were incredible mentors and role models. Once in practice, Andrew Lehrer, David Weinraub, and Michael Bournas-Ney all taught me much, and well, as a young attorney. In more recent years, working collaboratively with colleagues at the Urban Justice Center helped me develop and hone my understanding of professional responsibility, including Wendy Bach, Molly Biklen, Madeline Garcia-Bigelow, Susan Hazeldean, Doug Lasdon, Harvey Epstein, Kim Hawkins, Carmen Huertas-Noble, Megan Lewis, Andrew Kashyap, Gowri Krishna, Annie Lai, Tony Lu, Serge Martinez, Anika Singh Lemar, John Whitlow, and Haeyoung Yoon.

Since joining the academy, even on a part-time basis, Richard Marsico (who, to my great fortune, is also my brother-in-law) helped to shape my early years teaching, and colleagues Connie Mayer, Patrick Connors, Sarah Rogerson, and Ava Ayers continue to develop my thinking on issues of professional responsibility. Former colleague Joe Buffington also helped to sharpen my approach to writing multiple-choice questions.

Most importantly, for more than the last thirty years, I have spoken constantly with Michael Wishnie on what it means to be a lawyer, and these conversations have probably informed my understanding of professional responsibility more than any other source or colleague.

In addition, Polly Boyle, Alice Broussard, Miller Fina, Paige Gottorff, E. Conor Graham, Eunice Lee, and Taylor Yensan offered editorial assistance with this guide, while my intrepid colleague Sherri Meyer offers tireless assistance in all of my work. Finally, the fantastic team at Carolina Academic Press has been wonderful to work with, including Carol McGeehan, Ryland Bowman, Jennifer Hill, and Scott Sipe.

More than anything, though, this guide is a product of countless conversations and mutual learning with students in my legal ethics class, who always teach me so much. This book is a small token of my appreciation for them and the many who I hope will follow in their footsteps.

Core Professional Responsibility

Chapter 1

The Attorney-Client Relationship

Probably the most important question in professional responsibility is, When does a lawyer's ethical obligations attach to a particular relationship, that is, when must a lawyer comport with their ethical obligations with respect to a particular client by virtue of the lawyer-client relationship? Relatedly, while most obligations of the lawyer arise once the lawyer has already become a member of the bar and is admitted to practice law by the appropriate jurisdiction, certain obligations arise in applying for bar admission, both for the applicant and the lawyers who assist the applicant in seeking admission. This chapter will start with questions surrounding admission to the bar and the formation of the attorney-client relationship. It will then explore some of the duties that apply to that relationship, including the following: the attorney's duty of care; communication with clients; the allocation of authority between lawyers and clients; the duties of supervisory and subordinate lawyers; the unauthorized practice of law; questions and the applicable rules related to forming partnerships with non-lawyers; and declining or withdrawing from representation. Like all chapters, it concludes with a formative assessment quiz.

1.1 Admission to the Bar

The ethics rules set forth requirements regarding applicants to the bar and those lawyers who support their applications. Model Rule (MR) 8.1 is mostly at play here, although there are sometimes related issues around confidentiality and even truthfulness to others (MR 1.6 and MR 4.3).

1. Lawyer has employed a law student intern in her office for the student's last semester of law school. During the internship, Lawyer learns that the law student has been a very active stock trader while on his "down time" in the office. One day, an investigator from the U.S. Securities and Exchange Commission (SEC) alerts Lawyer that there is suspicious stock trading occurring from computers at Lawyer's office. Lawyer investigates the matter and discovers that it is the law student's actions that have come to the attention of the SEC. Lawyer divulges this to the SEC investigator, and the investigator decides that the actions, though illegal, are not worthy of any action against the law firm or the student at this time because it appears to be a first offense and the dollar amounts involved in the transactions are quite small. Nevertheless, the SEC issues a formal notice to the law student to "cease and desist" from all such illegal action in the future. Lawyer believes, in good faith, that the law student stopped engaging in this behavior after the matter was brought

to the student's attention. When it comes time for the law student to apply for the bar, Lawyer is asked by the local committee assessing the law student's fitness to practice law to offer her impressions of the student, including whether she knows of any reason why he should not be admitted to practice law. The committee asks Lawyer specifically whether she has any knowledge that the law student ever engaged in any illegal or unethical conduct while he was employed by her. The law student's bar application, submitted under oath, states that he has not engaged in any illegal or unethical behavior while employed at Lawyer's office.

Is Lawyer required to inform the committee about the falsity of the law student's claims that he has not engaged in any illegal conduct while employed at Lawyer's office?

A. No, because Lawyer is under no obligation to respond to the committee's request for information, given that the SEC took no formal action against the law student.

B. Yes, because Lawyer is obligated to correct the statement of the law student on the bar application.

C. No, because the knowledge Lawyer possesses about the student's actions is subject to the attorney-client privilege.

D. Yes, because Lawyer must be honest and transparent in all of her interactions with the committee, regardless of the source of any information Lawyer may have learned about the law student's conduct.

2. Lawyer has employed a law student intern in her office for the student's last semester of law school. During the internship, the law student seeks the advice of Lawyer on a legal matter. The law student divulges that in his past career as a talent agent in the music industry, he sometimes took advantage of his clients by pocketing some of their royalties without telling them. The law student wants to "come clean" and reimburse all of his former clients, with interest, for any improperly obtained royalties. Lawyer agrees to assist the law student in this effort and provides representation to him throughout the process of resolving the disputes with his former talent agency clients. Lawyer prepares confidential agreements for the former clients of the law student to sign, through which they agree to accept these back payments, with interest, in exchange for releasing the law student from any liability for his actions. When it comes time for the law student to apply for the bar, Lawyer is asked by the local committee assessing the law student's fitness to practice law to offer her impressions of him, including whether she knows of any reason why he should not be admitted to practice law, because they have not unearthed any improprieties in his background.

Is Lawyer subject to discipline should she fail to correct the character committee's impression that the student has no questionable conduct in his background that would call into question his fitness to practice law?

A. No, because Lawyer is under no obligation to respond to the committee's request for information, given that all claims involving the former talent agency clients of the law student have been resolved to the satisfaction of those clients.

B. Yes, because Lawyer is obligated to speak truthfully to the committee and correct its misapprehension that there is nothing in the law student's past that reflects poorly on his fitness to practice law.

C. No, because the knowledge Lawyer possesses about the student's past is subject to the attorney-client privilege, and thus she is under no obligation to reveal it to the committee.

D. Yes, because Lawyer must be honest and transparent in all of her interactions with the committee.

1.2 Forming the Attorney-Client Relationship

Most attorney-client relationships are formed by a formal agreement between the lawyer and the client as to the terms of the representation, and even the fact of the representation. But there are also instances where the attorney-client relationship can arise based on the reasonable belief of the client that such a relationship has been formed, or even simply by overt action on the part of the lawyer indicating some provision of services to the client. This matters because the duties a lawyer owes to a client only arise when an attorney-client relationship is formed. As we will see in this section, such a relationship—and thus a lawyer's duties—can arise in a number of different contexts.

3. Lawyer is waiting in line at a local restaurant to pick up a take-out order. There is another group of patrons in line in front of Lawyer, and Lawyer can overhear their conversation. One of these other patrons, Pat, is talking about a recent injury she suffered on a public bus. Lawyer interrupts the conversation and says, "I'm sorry, I couldn't help but overhear your conversation. I have heard that the local government agency that runs the bus service tends to try to settle cases pretty quickly if you bring a lawsuit against them. You should probably talk to a lawyer about that, if this is something you might want to pursue and if those rumors about how the government treats people who bring claims against it are true. You can call the local bar association, and they can make a referral for you."

Has Lawyer created an attorney-client relationship with Pat? If so, why? If not, why not?

A. No, because no lawyer-client relationship could be formed in any instance without a formal, written retainer agreement.

B. No, because Lawyer dispensed no legal advice, and so it would be unreasonable for Pat to think that an attorney-client relationship had been formed by the communication.

C. Yes, because Lawyer engaged in the practice of law and thus created an attorney-client relationship by doing so.

D. Yes, because Lawyer's advice was unsolicited and Pat could reasonably rely on the advice given.

4. Lawyer is one of the most highly sought-after criminal defense lawyers in the country, but she has decided that she no longer wishes to engage in trials. The days of televised criminal trials are long over, and she feels that she no longer gets the same sort of attention from handling high-profile trials that she used to receive. Trials thus do not have the same thrill for her that they once did, and she is no longer interested in handling them on behalf of her clients. As a result, she continues to handle cases but always limits her representation to those that might resolve in plea agreements. Her standard retainer now contains an express limitation that she will handle a criminal matter only to determine if a plea agreement can be reached. If a plea arrangement cannot be reached, the retainer states that the client will need to obtain other counsel and Lawyer's representation will terminate automatically. Lawyer always ensures the following protections are made a part of any retainer she enters into with a client: (1) that there is separate trial counsel, pre-approved by the client, who is ready to take on the case in the event plea negotiations fail; and (2) that the substitute counsel has adequate time to prepare for trial in the event a plea cannot be reached. Lawyer is approached by Client, an individual charged with a serious criminal charge. Lawyer advises Client, in writing, on the nature of the limitations she imposes on her provision of services, which include the protections she typically includes in her retainers as described above. Client gives informed consent to the representation but is not advised by separate counsel in entering into the retainer. After a brief period of negotiations with the prosecuting author-

ity in Client's case, and well before there may be a trial in the matter, it is apparent that Client does not want to enter into a plea arrangement. Client insists Lawyer handle his case at trial. Lawyer indicates that the retainer agreement is binding and refers the matter to the substitute counsel who is available to assume responsibility for the Client's case.

Is Lawyer subject to discipline for imposing limitations on her practice in the manner in which she did in Client's case?

A. No, because the limitation on practice was reasonable and Client gave informed consent to the arrangement.

B. Yes, because the restriction on practice was unreasonable because Client was entitled to representation to the conclusion of the matter.

C. Yes, because Lawyer should have provided separate counsel to Client at Lawyer's own expense, at least for the execution of the retainer, if she wanted to place limits on the representation.

D. No, because a lawyer in a criminal matter is never obligated to take a case to trial, even if the client demands that they do so.

5. Lawyer has long represented Client, a sophisticated businessperson, who, it has been revealed, has been laundering money for a drug cartel. Client operates a chain of casinos in the jurisdiction. Lawyer's retainer addresses representing Client strictly to handle Client's dealings with the jurisdiction's Racing & Gaming Commission (RGC). Lawyer freely admits that he is not competent to handle criminal matters and Client agrees. The retainer between Lawyer and Client is expressly limited to RGC legal and compliance matters and states that Lawyer will not assist Client in any criminal matters, including those related to Client's casino holdings. Client personally reviewed the retainer and was advised of the fact that Lawyer would not handle criminal matters. Client indicates that he understands the terms of the retainer, consented to those terms, and signs it. Client is arrested by the local authorities on suspicion of money laundering and contacts Lawyer expecting Lawyer to appear at Client's arraignment. Lawyer refuses.

Is Lawyer subject to discipline for the limitation on the scope of the representation? If so, why? If not, why not?

A. No, because a lawyer is permitted to put any restrictions on a representation that are deemed appropriate by that lawyer.

B. Yes, because once a lawyer agrees to represent a client, that lawyer must do so zealously, despite potential inconvenience to that lawyer, and must see the representation in the matter through to its conclusion.

C. No, because the limitation on the representation is reasonable and Client gave informed consent to it.

D. Yes, because the limitation on representation was unreasonable under the circumstances.

1.3 The Attorney's Duty of Care

Generally speaking, a lawyer must provide competent representation to the client (*see* M.R. 1.1). What competence demands in a particular situation will vary, as the questions in this section show.

6. Lawyer works in a non-profit legal services organization that serves as assigned counsel on behalf of indigent criminal defendants in the jurisdiction. Lawyer is dedicated to her work and tries to take on as many cases as she can because she feels that some of the other assigned counsel in the community are not as dedicated as she is to the work. Because of these beliefs, Lawyer sometimes takes on more cases than she can handle competently. She holds a reasonable belief that she is still providing better service to these clients than some of the other assigned counsel might provide them.

Is Lawyer subject to discipline if she cannot provide competent services to all of her clients?

A. Yes, unless she has a reasonable belief that the clients will not receive competent services from other lawyers in the jurisdiction.

B. No, because a primary motivation for her work is non-pecuniary.

C. No, because Lawyer cannot refuse clients to which she is assigned by a court-operated assigned counsel program.

D. Yes, because a lawyer must manage their case load to ensure that all clients receive competent services.

7. Lawyer receives a call that Client, a recent immigrant to the United States, is facing imminent deportation from the country. Lawyer has been working with Client to set up a small business. Client, on the eve of being deported, reaches out to Lawyer for advice. Lawyer informs Client that Lawyer is not an immigration attorney and is not competent to handle actions to prevent deportation. Client is still desperate for any guidance Lawyer can provide. Lawyer asks if Client can consult with an attorney who is experienced to handle this sort of matter, and Client informs Lawyer that there is no time to do so. The immigration authorities anticipate that Client will be taken to the airport in the next hour and flown back to her home country. Lawyer gives some basic advice that a general practitioner might dispense about what to say to the authorities about Client's situation and what sort of legal defenses Client might consider asserting. Client follows Lawyer's advice. Despite saying what Client was told by Lawyer to say, Client is deported. An experienced immigration attorney, which Lawyer is not, would have known that Client had a viable defense that could have been asserted to delay the matter. If that defense had been raised, the immigration officials would have had

to at least provide Client with more time to mount a proper defense.

Did Lawyer engage in misconduct by failing to offer guidance to Client to enable Client to delay the deportation until a proper defense could be mounted? If so, why? If not, why not?

A. No, because Lawyer provided basic guidance in an emergency consistent with the level of care appropriate to the situation.

B. Yes, because Lawyer failed to offer basic guidance in a manner consistent with the level of care appropriate to the situation.

C. Yes, because Lawyer failed to provide competent assistance given the nature of Client's legal need.

D. No, because Lawyer made it clear to Client that Lawyer was not competent to provide guidance in the situation.

8. Lawyer handles mostly personal injury cases arising out of automobile accidents. She is afraid that, with the advent of autonomous (i.e., driverless) cars, she may be out of a career. She starts exploring whether she could branch out into another area of personal injury law and agrees to take a case involving a train accident, which covers similar principles and similar, but not identical, substantive law. Lawyer determines, correctly, that with a reasonable amount of preparation and research, she can become competent in this new area of law in a timely fashion, and she will not charge her clients for developing this new expertise.

Is Lawyer subject to discipline for taking on a case involving a train accident that she is not competent to handle at this time?

A. Yes, because a lawyer can only take on matters about which they possess the requisite competence and skill.

B. Yes, because a lawyer may not assume responsibility for a case without being competent to handle it at the time they accept the case for representation.

C. No, because a lawyer can develop the requisite competence and skill in a reasonable amount of time and in a timely fashion.

D. No, because the area of practice Lawyer wants to enter into is similar to one in which she is competent.

9. Client is a private garbage company that collects garbage from commercial establishments in the community. Lawyer represents Client in proceedings before the local environmental control board, which regulates the actions of such private companies. Client routinely faces fines for dumping trash in vacant lots, contrary to local ordinances. When Lawyer originally agreed to represent Client, the parties entered into a one-year retainer, with Lawyer saying, "Let's see how it goes." Despite the retainer's lapsing, Lawyer has continued to represent Client for over ten years without formally renewing the retainer. The practice between Lawyer and Client is that Client just forwards the summonses whenever he receives them and Lawyer handles the matter, appearing at the local control board to pay the fines on Client's behalf out of a fund set up by Client for this purpose. Lawyer begins to suffer pangs of conscience about representing this profligate polluter and no longer wishes to represent Client. Lawyer starts to ignore the correspondence from Client which transmits the summonses to Lawyer. Client faces several stiff fines for failure to appear in response to these summonses.

Is Lawyer subject to discipline for failing to appear at the hearings on the outstanding summonses?

A. Yes, because Lawyer was obligated to terminate the relationship in writing.

B. Yes, because Lawyer was obligated to communicate his desire to terminate the relationship with Client.

C. No, because the retainer between Lawyer and Client had lapsed, and Lawyer was under no obligation to continue representing Client.

D. No, because Client's expectation that Lawyer would continue to represent him was unreasonable.

10. Lawyer recently switched to a data management system that placed all of her office's data in a "cloud-based" system, operated remotely. Before moving her data to the cloud, Lawyer consulted with a cybersecurity expert so that she could understand any potential ramifications for her practice. The cybersecurity expert, who has years as a data security expert, informed Lawyer that moving her data to the cloud in this way would give her better security than the system she was using at the time, which was highly vulnerable to a cyberattack. The expert informed Lawyer, correctly, that many law firms were using the cloud computing system that Lawyer would ultimately use and that it was the state of the art, providing her the best available protection the industry has to offer. Despite moving her data to this system, Lawyer discovers that there was a security breach of her computer system, and it is likely that those responsible for the breach gained access to confidential client communications.

Is Lawyer guilty of professional misconduct for the breach of her data system containing confidential information?

A. No, because Lawyer made reasonable efforts to preserve her clients' confidences.

B. Yes, because Lawyer failed to act competently in preserving her clients' confidences.

C. No, because Lawyer was obligated to update her old data management system.

D. Yes, because Lawyer's failure to secure her clients' confidences means she is strictly liable for the breach that occurred.

11. Lawyer represents Client in a personal injury action against a local restaurant. Lawyer is friendly with counsel for the restaurant, and they both are generally very accommodating to each other's scheduling needs. Lawyer receives several requests from counsel for the restaurant to postpone the scheduling of the final pre-trial conference in the matter. Once that conference does occur, the court handling the matter will soon thereafter schedule the trial, and it is believed the trial will last no more than two days. Client learns from a friend that the restaurant is preparing to file for bankruptcy, which would effectively shield the restaurant from liability if a judgment is not rendered in Client's trial before the bankruptcy filing occurs. The attorney for the restaurant calls again to request another otherwise reasonable delay in the pre-trial conference. Lawyer understands that it is customary in the jurisdiction to grant such extensions of time in the schedule for these matters. If the Lawyer does not grant the extension, the attorney for the restaurant will have to seek it from the court, which, Lawyer knows, is likely to deny it.

Is Lawyer subject to discipline for granting the attorney for the restaurant's request to further delay the pre-trial conference in Client's matter?

A. No, because it is customary in the community to grant such extensions.

B. Yes, because it is not in Client's best interest to further extend the date of the pre-trial conference.

C. No, because the attorney for the restaurant can still seek an extension of time from the court.

D. Yes, if the attorney for the restaurant has reasonable grounds for seeking the extension of time.

1.4 Communication with Clients

A lawyer generally has obligations to communicate effectively with a client so that the client understands what is involved in the representation, can give proper guidance to the lawyer about the scope of the representation, and can give informed consent to certain matters when such consent is required. This section explores these and other questions and duties surrounding the obligation on the part of the lawyer to communicate with clients.

12. Lawyer is handling litigation on behalf of Client. Lawyer is aware that Client has health problems and sometimes must go into the hospital to deal with a chronic condition. Client has given Lawyer express, written permission to contact a family member of Client should Lawyer need to try to get in touch with Client in an emergency. Lawyer can also seek guidance from that family member on matters related to the representation should Client become incapacitated or unreachable. During the course of the litigation, Lawyer has an upcoming deadline by which he must respond to a settlement offer made by the opposing party's attorney. Unaware that Client has been admitted to the hospital again to deal with the chronic condition, Lawyer attempts to contact Client so that Lawyer can provide a response to the settlement offer. Lawyer believes the offer is a good one and that it is in Client's best interests to accept it. Lawyer attempts to leave a message for Client on Client's voicemail box, but the outgoing message says that the box is full. Lawyer has the information that would enable Lawyer to reach Client's emergency contact but chooses not to communicate through that channel to reach Client or otherwise get guidance on the case from the emergency contact. Lawyer does not respond to the settlement offer within the time frame set forth by Lawyer's adversary. When Lawyer is finally able to communicate with Client, Lawyer informs Client of the settlement offer and Client says to accept it. Lawyer contacts the adversary who says the offer is no longer available because the adversary has decided to take the case to trial and has begun preparing to do so.

Is Lawyer subject to discipline for not communicating the settlement offer to Client through the third-party contact Client provided to Lawyer? If so, why? If not, why not?

A. No, because Lawyer took reasonable steps to communicate with Client and it was Client's fault Lawyer was unable to reach Client.

B. Yes, because Lawyer had other means to contact Client on this important matter and failed to utilize those means of communication to do so.

C. No, because Lawyer was unaware of the reason why Client was not available and cannot be held responsible because Client was rendered unavailable.

D. Yes, because Lawyer was obligated to visit Client in the hospital to communicate this important information to Client in person.

13. Client presents information to Lawyer indicating that Client was the victim of a fraudulent scheme. Client is a sophisticated securities trader and investment fund manager who, nevertheless, was lured into investing in what was clearly an arrangement designed to defraud its investors. Lawyer is asked to seek compensation for the fraud, and Client reveals to Lawyer the amount Client claims was lost in the scheme, which is millions of dollars. Client wants all the money back, which will be difficult to secure, but Lawyer says he will do his best to pursue the perpetrators of the fraud, who have filed for bankruptcy. At the same time, Client informs Lawyer that she does not want it to become generally known that she was duped into investing in this scheme for fear that investors in the fund Client manages will think Client is not very good at her job, which involves identifying legitimate and lucrative investments for the investment fund Client manages. Lawyer informs Client that he could file a claim on Client's behalf in the bankruptcy proceeding for the amount of money Client says she lost in the scheme. Client is informed that such a filing will be public and that anyone who wants to review the filing will be able to do so. Lawyer says that in his experience, these filings rarely garner much attention, but, since this is a relatively high-profile matter, and Client is a well-known businessperson in the community, there is some risk that someone will take note of the filing and publicize it, especially now that there are "citizen journalists" who like to monitor bankruptcy filings and put interesting tidbits from such filings on social media. Based on this advice, Client approves of the filing despite these risks. Client says

she is all about risk, and that after calculating the risk involved, she is willing to take it. Lawyer proceeds to assert the claim in the bankruptcy court on behalf of Client. News of the filing makes it into social media and then, ultimately, into a highly critical and snarky column in a business journal, which many of Client's investors read. Some investors leave the funds Client manages as a result, which means lower income for Client. Lawyer knew that the filing could have been made under seal to protect the identity of Client, but Lawyer failed to advise Client of that option.

Is Lawyer subject to discipline for failing to advise Client of the option of pursuing a filing under seal? If so, why? If not, why not?

A. No, because Client was a sophisticated businessperson and never asked about whether filing the matter under seal was an option.

B. No, because Client expressly authorized Lawyer to reveal the information about Client's identity and losses.

C. Yes, because Lawyer should have advised Client about the option of filing the matter under seal.

D. Yes, because Lawyer's failure to file the matter under seal harmed Client.

1.5 Allocation of Authority Between Lawyers and Clients

Rule 1.2(a) provides that a lawyer "shall abide by a client's decisions concerning the objectives of representation and, as required by Rule 1.4, shall consult with the client as to the means by which they are to be pursued." Furthermore, a lawyer may "take such action on behalf of the client as is impliedly authorized to carry out the representation." Finally, the lawyer "shall abide by a client's decision whether to settle a matter. In a criminal case, the lawyer shall abide by the client's decision, after consultation with the lawyer, as to a plea to be entered, whether to waive jury trial and whether the client will testify." The contours of these questions are explored in greater depth in this section.

14. Lawyer is asked to represent Client, the adult child of Parents. Parents have agreed to pay the legal fees on behalf of Client, to defend Client against a charge of driving while intoxicated. Parents insist that Lawyer must share all information about the representation with them as a condition of their paying the fee. Client consents to share confidential information with Parents because Client is unable to pay the fees on his own. Lawyer takes direction only from Client, however, and does not let Parents direct the representation in any way. When it comes time to present a plea deal to Client, Parents are informed of the plea offer as well. Parents object to Client's accepting the plea deal and insist that Lawyer reject it. But Client wants to accept it, and so Lawyer informs the prosecutor's office that Client wishes to accept the plea deal, even though Lawyer agrees with Parents and believes it is not in the best interests of Client to accept the deal.

Is Lawyer subject to discipline for any of Lawyer's actions?

A. Lawyer is not subject to discipline for any of Lawyer's actions.

B. Lawyer is subject to discipline for sharing confidential information with Parents.

C. Lawyer is subject to discipline for accepting the plea deal when Lawyer believed it was not in the best interests of Client.

D. Lawyer is subject to discipline for accepting the plea deal over the objection of Parents.

15. Lawyer is involved in protracted litigation involving a dispute over commercial real estate. Lawyer believes that it would be beneficial to her case to notice and take the depositions of over one dozen individuals employed by the opposing party. Such depositions are likely to generate useful information for her case: she believes these individuals all have information relevant to the case and she knows the depositions will be costly to the opposing party, imposing financial strains on their ability to litigate the case. She also knows that taking this many depositions will likely delay the trial date considerably, which is contrary to Client's wishes. Lawyer and Client discuss the matter, and Client understands the ramifications of not taking these depositions. Client directs Lawyer to refrain from taking them. Client asks Lawyer to expedite the trial, even if it means not obtaining all of the information that might be helpful to the case, because Client wants the matter resolved as quickly as possible. Lawyer wants to proceed with the depositions because she believes in good faith that they are necessary to prosecute Client's claims competently.

Is Lawyer subject to discipline if she goes ahead with taking the depositions contrary to Client's wishes?

A. Yes, because Client's goal of an expedited trial will be frustrated.

B. Yes, because the depositions have no substantial purpose other than delay.

C. No, because Lawyer controls the manner in which the case should be litigated.

D. No, because Lawyer believes in good faith that she must proceed with the depositions to provide competent representation to Client.

16. Lawyer is a skilled negotiator but does not like litigation. She agrees to handle only cases that she thinks will settle. Client asks Lawyer to handle his case, which involves his being delinquent on his mortgage. The bank that made the mortgage loan to Client is threatening to sue him through a mortgage foreclosure proceeding. No court proceeding has been commenced to date, but one is reasonably anticipated unless the case can be settled without the need for litigation. Lawyer reviews the materials Client has supplied and believes it is a good case for a potential settlement. Lawyer provides Client with her standard retainer stating that Lawyer will handle any negotiations to resolve the dispute without resort to litigation, but if a case is filed and litigation commenced, Lawyer will not represent Client in such litigation. Such arrangements are common in the community. Client gives informed consent to this arrangement.

Is Lawyer subject to discipline for limiting the scope of the representation of Client in this way?

A. Yes, because Client is entitled to representation to the conclusion of the matter.

B. Yes, because Client may understand the scope of the representation but may not understand the limitations under which Lawyer will act.

C. No, because Client understood the limited scope of the representation.

D. No, provided the scope of the representation is reasonable and Client gave informed consent.

17. Lawyer represents Client in a dispute with her neighbor involving a disagreement over the property line between two adjacent lots. The dispute has become contentious because the parties do not like each other. Lawyer believes a resolution of the matter without trial is in Client's best interest, but Client refuses to negotiate. Client seems committed to taking the case to trial and will not accept any settlement, even though she stands a good chance of losing and the fees associated with the representation will only increase. Lawyer knows Client is having a hard time paying her fees. Without informing Client, Lawyer enters settlement negotiations on behalf of Client. Lawyer strives in good faith to obtain a fair settlement. Lawyer reaches a settlement that obtains more for Client than Lawyer believes he can obtain for Client were the case to go to trial. He also agrees to give Client a discount on the fees he charges for his work as a way to make Client feel better about the settlement.

Is Lawyer subject to discipline for his actions?

A. Yes, because Lawyer required the consent of Client to enter into the settlement agreement.

B. Yes, because Lawyer had an obligation to inform Client of his intent to enter into settlement negotiations on behalf of Client prior to doing so.

C. No, because Lawyer had an obligation to ensure that Client was not prolonging the litigation unnecessarily.

D. No, because the settlement was in the best interests of Client.

18. Lawyer has been representing Corporate Client in a drawn-out and complex antitrust matter before federal regulators that, to this point, has mostly involved negotiations over changes to Corporate Client's business practices that the regulators want Corporate Client to make. The negotiations break down and the federal regulators plan to commence legal action against Corporate Client. Corporate Client's leadership appreciates all of the work Lawyer has done for it, but the leadership also thinks it is time to retain new counsel, one that the leadership feels will be better able to handle the matter moving forward as it enters the litigation phase of the dispute. Corporate Client also knows that, under the terms of the retainer between Lawyer and Corporate Client, Lawyer will receive a higher hourly fee if the matter moves from negotiations into litigation, as it appears is about to happen. Corporate Client will also experience some material harm by switching attorneys at this time because any new counsel will have to get up to speed on the case, which will require Corporate Client to pay the new counsel for the time required to do so. Corporate Client is aware of this additional cost associated with changing attorneys and still goes ahead to terminate the relationship between Lawyer and Corporate Client. Corporate Client then retains new counsel that will handle the imminent litigation in the matter.

May Corporate Client terminate the relationship between Lawyer and Corporate Client? If so, why? If not, why not?

A. No, because Corporate Client will be harmed materially by the termination of the attorney-client relationship with Lawyer.

B. Yes, because Corporate Client may choose to terminate the relationship in this situation.

C. No, because Corporate Client is prohibited from terminating the relationship at the precise point that the fee arrangement will change.

D. Yes, but only because Corporate Client has good cause for terminating the relationship.

19. Lawyer has represented Client through a very difficult trial on a civil rights claim where Client won on some claims but lost on the overwhelming majority of them. The case raises very interesting issues of constitutional law. It is likely that after the appellate court now hearing the case issues its decision, it could be reviewed by the U.S. Supreme Court. Lawyer has always dreamed about arguing before the Supreme Court and believes this might be her chance to do so. When Client first came to Lawyer's office to see if Lawyer would represent him, Lawyer indicated that the case was really interesting and could lead to the development of new law that could protect not only Client in his case but also litigants like Client in other cases because of the precedent the case could set. Client understood that the case was a difficult one to win, but Client was willing to go ahead, no matter what the potential outcome. "We'll take it to the Supreme Court if we have to!" Client said to Lawyer, and Lawyer agreed. It is in part based on this statement that Lawyer agreed to take on the case for no fee whatsoever. While the appeal is pending before the Court of Appeals, the immediate step before the Supreme Court, the defendant makes an offer to settle the case. The offer is very generous, probably more than what Client will win even if he is victorious in the case, but it comes with a catch: the settlement offer will contain a non-disclosure agreement. Client informs Lawyer that Client is tired of fighting and nervous about whether he will win the case. Client directs Lawyer to accept the settlement. Lawyer refuses, saying that Client had agreed earlier to take the case to the Supreme Court if necessary.

Is it misconduct for Lawyer to refuse to accept the settlement offer? If so, why? If not, why not?

A. Yes, because it is in the best interest of Client to accept the offer.

B. No, because Lawyer agreed to take the case on as a volunteer.

C. Yes, because Client has the ultimate authority over whether to accept the settlement.

D. No, because Client agreed to take the case to the Supreme Court if necessary.

20. Lawyer represents Plaintiff in a personal injury case. Lawyer has conferred with Plaintiff about her demands in settlement. Plaintiff has informed Lawyer that Plaintiff is willing to settle the case for at least $100,000. Plaintiff hopes for more but will accept this figure in satisfaction of all claims. Plaintiff's case involves a number of arguments that are novel and creative. If Plaintiff succeeds on those claims, Lawyer and Plaintiff believe a trial of the case could generate a larger award for Plaintiff, one that could exceed $500,000. Indeed, even the threat of those claims going to trial should be enough to raise the stakes for the opposing party so that they might make a significant offer to Plaintiff to settle the action. If those more creative claims are dismissed, however, it is possible that a jury award would be far less than the $100,000 Plaintiff would accept to settle the case. However, Plaintiff does not wish to settle for less than $80,000. Plaintiff authorizes Lawyer to pursue $100,000 to settle all of Plaintiff's claims but directs Lawyer to not accept anything less than $80,000 through the negotiations. Defendant's counsel makes a motion to dismiss the more creative claims Plaintiff has interposed, and that motion is denied, meaning that the case will go to trial on these claims, raising the Defendant's risk for of a much larger payout than the $100,000 Plaintiff told Lawyer she would accept previously. After losing the motion to dismiss Plaintiff's creative claims, the attorney for Defendant in the action makes an offer to settle the case for $100,000, the amount at the higher end of the prior authorization Lawyer received from Client. Lawyer, believing it is in the best interests of Plaintiff to accept the offer, accepts that offer based

on the prior direction given by Plaintiff to accept a settlement offer of $100,000.

Is Lawyer subject to discipline for accepting the $100,000 settlement offer without consulting Plaintiff first? If so, why? If not, why not?

A. No, because Lawyer believed it was in the best interests of Plaintiff to accept the offer.

B. Yes, because of the material change in the circumstances related to the case. Lawyer was obligated to inform Plaintiff of the developments in the case involving the denial of the motion to dismiss, which might have changed Plaintiff's perspective on settlement.

C. No, because the settlement amount offered by the adversary was consistent with the amount Lawyer was authorized to accept according to the express direction of Plaintiff.

D. Yes, because it was improper to seek advanced guidance with respect to a potential settlement offer.

1.6 Duties of Supervisory and Subordinate Lawyers

Underlying the regulation of the legal profession in the United States is the idea that the profession should regulate itself: that lawyers are the first line of defense against misconduct of other lawyers, particularly in situations where a supervisory lawyer might oversee the work of other lawyers. This section explores the responsibilities of supervisory lawyers and the "subordinate" lawyers (as the rules call them) they oversee to ensure compliance with professional responsibility.

21. Lawyer has responsibility for supervising several newly hired attorneys at the firm. These attorneys both graduated near the top of their class at law school and, together, won a moot court competition while in law school. Having witnessed these attorneys when they were law students, because Lawyer served as one of the judges of this moot court competition, Lawyer has a general sense, based on Lawyer's "gut feeling" about them, that they are competent to handle several

difficult cases that the firm has agreed to handle. Some of these cases deal squarely with the substantive issue the students addressed so expertly in winning the national moot court competition. Lawyer is generally regarded as having a good sense of who is going to be an effective and competent practitioner. Every couple of weeks, Lawyer checks in on the progress of the subordinate attorneys to make sure they are serving the clients well. Occasionally, Lawyer will ask to review some of the pleadings and memoranda the attorneys are preparing, but basically allows them to proceed with very little guidance. A case the two subordinate attorneys worked on together is dismissed because they failed to file a reply to a summary judgment motion in a timely fashion. Lawyer is shocked that the subordinate attorneys failed to satisfy the simplest of instructions from the court, that is, to file an opposition to a motion for summary judgment on time. When confronted, the subordinate attorneys state that, like in school, they thought the deadlines were sort of "soft" deadlines and that they could likely file their opposition papers after the time set by the court.

Is Lawyer subject to discipline for the manner in which that Lawyer supervised the subordinate attorneys? If so, why? If not, why not?

A. No, because Lawyer had personally witnessed the subordinate attorneys' performance in a moot court competition and thus had sufficient reassurance that the subordinate attorneys were competent.

B. Yes, because Lawyer did not have reasonable measures in place to provide the firm with reasonable assurances that the subordinate attorneys were acting in a competent fashion.

C. No, because a supervisory lawyer is permitted to assume that any graduate of a law school would have sufficient knowledge of their obligations to comply with court deadlines.

D. Yes, because a supervisory lawyer is strictly liable for any failure on the part of a subordinate lawyer under their supervision to fail to act competently.

22. A relatively inexperienced law firm associate (Associate) is handling a real estate closing for a firm client. In reviewing the case with the senior lawyer at the firm, who is Associate's immediate supervisor, they discover two pieces of information related to the sale of the property. First, that the client (Seller), the owner of the property, has not paid real estate taxes for some time on the property, and second, that there is asbestos on the property which Seller has not revealed to Buyer. Associate has reviewed the correspondence in the file and noticed that the attorney for Buyer has sent a standard questionnaire typically used in a sale of real estate in the community. The questionnaire includes the following:

Question 2: Is Seller currently up to date on all real estate taxes?

Question 7: Has Seller become aware of the presence of any asbestos on the property over the last ten years?

Under applicable state law, sellers who fail to answer these questions truthfully can be subject to a damages action on behalf of the buyer after the sale if the buyer experiences any harm as a result of the misrepresentations on the form. The time limit under law to respond to the questionnaire will expire in five business days. There are also statutory penalties for submitting untrue statements on these forms, and a misrepresentation could lead to perjury charges because the statements are to be notarized and affirmed as true. Associate discusses the matter with the senior lawyer, who suggests the following course of action. First, Seller must pay all outstanding real estate taxes and fees so that Question 2 can be answered in the affirmative. Second, Seller should be instructed to remove all asbestos from the premises as soon as possible so that they can answer Question 7 in the negative. The senior lawyer says to Associate, "What Buyer doesn't know can't hurt him."

Is Associate subject to discipline for following either, both, or neither of these courses of action on behalf of Seller?

A. Associate is subject to discipline for following the planned course of action with respect to both questions.

B. Associate is subject to discipline for following the planned course of action with respect to the taxes but not the asbestos.

C. Associate is subject to discipline for following the planned course of action for the asbestos but not the taxes.

D. Associate will not be subject to discipline for following either course of action.

23. A second-year associate, Allie, working at a large law firm, has served as "second chair" in a number of high-profile depositions in the defense of a former bank president for white collar crime. Each of the depositions has been handled by a senior partner in the firm, Patty, one of the best trial attorneys in the area. On the day of the deposition of another high-profile witness, Walt, Patty informs Allie that she will be the lead attorney defending Walt's deposition. "You've earned it," Patty tells Allie. Patty sits in as second chair this time around but walks in and out of the deposition frequently, attending to matters on her smartphone. Allie makes several rookie mistakes in defending the deposition, as could be anticipated, because she has never been the primary attorney defending a deposition and has never received formal training in how to do so. Although Allie stumbles, Patty happens to be present in the room on each occasion where Allie makes these mistakes, and Patty is able to correct those mistakes in a timely fashion. The deposition is successfully defended without the deponent's making any revelations that might have damaged the firm's client. Nevertheless, the client hears that Allie handled the deposition and is furious. Client wants to file a disciplinary charge against Patty for letting Allie take first chair and not being present in the room the entire time the deposition was being taken.

If Patty is charged with unethical conduct for her actions, what will be the most important issue in assessing the propriety of that conduct?

A. What harm may have come to Client.

B. Whether Patty was able to correct all of Allie's mistakes in a timely fashion.

C. Whether Allie committed malpractice.

D. Whether Patty's supervision of Allie was reasonable under the circumstances.

24. Jane Lawyer (Jane) is a new associate at the Botts Law Firm (Botts). Botts prides itself on hiring new lawyers with lots of experience in clinical practice and internships when they were law students, and Jane fits the bill. By the time she starts at the firm, she has a great deal of experience handling worker compensation cases. Jane is supervised by Cynthia, an experienced worker compensation lawyer. Jane is involved in a worker compensation case in which Client was injured while at a worksite. Jane uncovers evidence that Client had a pre-existing condition that likely made the injury worse than it would have been had Client not had that previous injury. Such a pre-existing condition could limit the employer's liability. The lawyer for Client's employer conducts discovery seeking all information related to pre-existing conditions. Cynthia informs Jane that such information is immaterial and irrelevant to the proceeding and that Jane should not turn the information over to the employer's lawyer. Cynthia says no further action is required on Jane's part and she can just ignore the document request.

Is Jane subject to discipline if she does not turn over the information sought through discovery to her adversary?

A. No, because the information would be damaging to Client.

B. Yes, if she has a clear legal duty to turn over such information.

C. No, because Cynthia's approach is a reasonable resolution of an arguable question of professional duty.

D. Yes, because the opposing counsel has sought such information in discovery.

1.7 Unauthorized Practice of Law

This section explores questions related to the unauthorized practice of law. The entire system of professional responsibility breaks down if individuals who are not authorized to practice law do so, but such individuals are not subject to the rules of legal ethics. A lawyer can both engage in the unauthorized practice of law and assist others in doing so. When either occurs, the lawyer is violating the lawyer's professional obligations.

25. Lawyer provides representation to tenants in landlord-tenant proceedings in a jurisdiction in which Lawyer is admitted to practice law. In addition to representing individual tenants, Lawyer is also engaged in advocacy work in the community. As part of Lawyer's community work, Lawyer provides know-your-rights guidance to tenants, speaking at community forums and events at local schools. Lawyer offers only general information and does not provide individualized guidance to any specific tenant in light of a tenant's particular facts and circumstances. Lawyer also advises local community organizers who do not work for Lawyer's organization but who assist local tenants, tenant groups, and community associations. These community organizers sometimes go into court to assist tenants when Lawyer cannot do so. Lawyer knows that the information Lawyer provides to these tenant organizers, who are not attorneys, is used to provide individualized guidance to particular tenants. The assistance the organizers provide includes advising those tenants about their legal rights and assisting those tenants by having the organizers negotiate with the tenants' landlords to resolve the tenants' cases. Lawyer knows that these tenants will not receive any legal assistance otherwise—either from Lawyer or any other non-profit legal services provider—in trying to prevent their evictions. Lawyer does not participate in providing such guidance to these individual tenants directly.

Is Lawyer subject to discipline for any of Lawyer's community activities?

A. No. Since Lawyer is an attorney admitted to practice in the jurisdiction, all of Lawyer's efforts are permissible.

B. Yes, because Lawyer should not have given information to community members in community-wide forums where their confidential information might be exposed.

C. No, because Lawyer did not provide individualized assistance directly to individual tenants, and because the tenants would have no other legal assistance if the organizers did not assist these tenants.

D. Yes. By advising the community organizers in their work, Lawyer is assisting others to engage in the unauthorized practice of law.

26. Lawyer, admitted to practice in the relevant jurisdiction, has been asked to represent Family Friend to prepare a will. Lawyer informs Family Friend that he is not a trusts and estates lawyer and that, although he wants to help, it has been twenty years since he studied this area of law for the bar, so Lawyer does not feel competent to handle the matter. Family Friend states that she does not really know anyone else who can help her. Lawyer visits an online service that is available through a non-profit legal services organization that supplies straightforward forms individuals can use to prepare basic documents, like wills and power of attorney forms. This information is not individualized or specific to any particular visitor to the site. It is made available simply in an effort to help such visitors understand and protect their legal rights on their own. Those forms are not individually tailored to specific client needs; rather, the organization's website sets forth clear and accurate guidance on what those forms can and cannot be used to accomplish and the types of individuals who should and should not use those forms. Lawyer reviews the guidance provided through the online service and concludes, correctly, that Family Friend's relatively straightforward needs can be met by using one or more of these online forms. Lawyer directs Family Friend to the site, and Family Friend utilizes the services of the non-profit organization successfully, satisfying her legal needs.

Has Lawyer or the non-profit legal services organization engaged in the unauthorized practice of law?

A. Lawyer has engaged in the unauthorized practice of law, but the non-profit legal services organization has not.

B. The non-profit legal services organization has engaged in the unauthorized practice of law, but Lawyer has not.

C. Neither the non-profit legal services organization nor Lawyer has engaged in the unauthorized practice of law.

D. Both the non-profit legal services organization and Lawyer have engaged in the unauthorized practice of law.

27. Lawyer is admitted only in California and is not disbarred from practice in any other jurisdiction. Lawyer is retained to assist Client, whom she has served on several occasions in California for a real estate transaction in Oregon that is unrelated to other work Lawyer does for Client. Lawyer contacts her friend, Portia, an attorney admitted to practice in Oregon, to determine if Portia would be willing to hold the real estate closing transaction in a conference room in Portia's office in Portland, Oregon. In order to not inconvenience Portia, and to facilitate a successful transaction between Client and the party with whom Client wishes to transact business, Lawyer informs Portia that she does not have to do anything with respect to the transaction except to agree to host the closing in her offices.

Is Lawyer subject to discipline for handling the real estate transaction in Oregon?

A. No, because Lawyer cooperated with Portia, a lawyer admitted in Oregon, to host the closing conference in which the transaction was consummated.

B. No, because Lawyer regularly represents Client in other transactions.

C. Yes, because Lawyer is not admitted to practice in Oregon and Portia did not participate in the representation of Client.

D. Yes, because Lawyer did not obtain the consent of the other party to the transaction to the out-of-state representation.

1.8 Partnerships with Non-Lawyers and Rules Related to Law-Related Services

Just as lawyers cannot assist others in the unauthorized practice of law, neither can they enter into partnerships with non-lawyers except in circumstances set forth in the rules. These prohibitions and permissions are explored in this section.

28. Lawyer is a real estate attorney in the Capital Region of New York State. She enters into a partnership with a local real estate broker (Broker) to provide, as they call it, "full service real estate assistance, including legal and broker services." Lawyer will handle all of the legal matters and Broker will match willing buyers with willing sellers. Broker is licensed as a real estate broker but not as a lawyer. Lawyer is licensed in New York State to practice law but does not have a real estate broker's license. Broker and Lawyer are very careful not to mix their responsibilities or their fees and Broker cannot direct Lawyer in the provision of legal services. Lawyer is completely in charge of the legal work, and Broker is completely in charge of delivering real estate broker services. The partnership is very successful, and Lawyer and Broker turn a profit every year, though they never divide their fees. A legal fee is charged for each transaction and a separate broker's commission applies to each sale. Both fees are reasonable and consistent with the fees typically charged in the community for such services.

Has Lawyer acted unethically in this partnership arrangement?

A. Yes. Broker is not licensed to practice law, and thus the provision of services through the company is unethical, constituting the unauthorized practice of law.

B. Yes. Lawyer cannot enter into a partnership with a non-lawyer if any of the activities of the partnership are the provision of legal services.

C. No. Broker does not control the decisions of Lawyer.

D. No. Broker and Lawyer do not share fees for the separate services they offer and each is responsible for delivering separate professional services consistent with their respective professional licenses.

29. Lawyer provides an array of generally undifferentiated legal and legislative lobbying assistance to her clients, which are all large real estate developers. As part of Lawyer's work, she routinely serves clients in preparing formal legal comments to the proposed regulations put forward by state agencies and also lobbies state legislators when legislative matters come before those legislators that affect her clients, particularly matters that affect those clients' tax liabilities. When engaging in lobbying with the legislature for tax matters on behalf of her clients, which does not require Lawyer's legal expertise and does not entail the practice of law, Lawyer does not feel it necessary to avoid conflicts of interest or maintain her clients' confidences.

Is it professional misconduct for Lawyer to fail to provide her clients with the protections typically afforded a legal client when Lawyer is lobbying on behalf of her clients?

A. No, because Lawyer is not engaged in the practice of law when engaged in lobbying to obtain tax breaks for her clients.

B. Yes, because Lawyer's lobbying services are not distinct from her legal practice.

C. No, because Lawyer's clients are aware that some of the services rendered by Lawyer are not legal in nature.

D. Yes, because a lawyer is subject to the full range of professional obligations whenever they provide any service to a third party.

1.9 Declining or Withdrawing from Representation

Just as there are rules surrounding the formation of the attorney-client relationship, there are also important professional responsibility questions that emerge when a lawyer wants to decline such representation or feels compelled to withdraw from representation that has already begun. This section examines issues related to both scenarios, most of which are covered in MR 1.16.

30. Lawyer represents Client, an individual who engages in high-frequency trading and faces a potential indictment for his alleged participation in a massive fraud scheme. Client faces the prospect of twenty years in prison for the offenses that law enforcement has uncovered in its investigation. Prior to convening the grand jury in the action, or otherwise taking the matter before a tribunal in any way, Prosecutor offers to enter into an agreement through which Client will pay millions of dollars in restitution. Client is adamant that he is not guilty of any crimes. Still, Client is obviously very concerned about what will happen should he be convicted, in part because Client could be subject to a bar that will prevent him from trading stocks in the future, even if he enters into an agreement settling any potential charges with Prosecutor without the matter coming before a tribunal. In the retainer between Lawyer and Client, Lawyer agreed to represent Client up to and including any presentation of the matter to the grand jury, but the retainer is limited and leaves open only the possibility that Lawyer will represent Client after that point if Client is indicted. One day, while Lawyer and Client are preparing for the negotiations, Lawyer learns that not everything Client has been telling Lawyer is true, and that Client's conduct is far worse than Lawyer originally believed. Lawyer no longer wants to be associated with Client, and Lawyer wants to withdraw from the representation. Prosecutor agrees that they will suspend the negotiations to provide Client adequate time to retain new counsel. There is no tribunal from which Lawyer will need to seek permission to withdraw, so Lawyer sends notice to Client informing him that Lawyer will no longer represent him.

Is Lawyer subject to discipline for withdrawing from the representation? If so, why? If not, why not?

A. No, because Lawyer's ability to represent Client competently was compromised.

B. Yes, because Lawyer committed to represent Client up to and including any indictment, and to seek withdrawal at this time is contrary to the retainer's terms.

C. No, because there is no indication that such withdrawal will have a materially adverse effect on Client.

D. Yes, because Lawyer could not withdraw without its having a materially adverse effect on Client.

31. Lawyer is approached by Individual about a potential case Individual has against a local medical provider. Individual wants to retain Lawyer to represent Individual and shares information with Lawyer in order to explore whether Lawyer will agree to take on Individual's case. Individual claims to be the victim of medical malpractice. Because the case was the subject of some media attention when it occurred, Individual shares such publicly available information with Lawyer about the case. Lawyer believes Individual's case is quite strong. Without sharing any opinions with Individual about the relative strength of the case and without Individual sharing any confidential information about her claims, Lawyer informs Individual that Lawyer will not be able to take on the case. While Lawyer has the capacity to take on the case, Lawyer has begun to move away from medical malpractice cases and feels handling this case will bring him back into that area of practice.

Is Lawyer subject to discipline for declining to represent Individual? If so, why? If not, why not?

A. Yes, because once Lawyer agreed to hear about Individual's case, a reasonable expectation formed that Lawyer had agreed to represent Individual.

B. No, because Lawyer made no agreement, express or implied, to represent Individual.

C. Yes. Even though the information shared was publicly available, when Individual shared such information with Lawyer, Individual could reasonably assume that Lawyer had agreed to represent Individual.

D. No. Because Lawyer did not enter into a written retainer, no attorney-client relationship would have been formed between Lawyer and Individual under any circumstances.

32. As Client's case is nearing the end of discovery and getting ready for trial, the relationship between Client and Lawyer becomes tense. Client is a sophisticated businessperson who got caught up unwittingly in a social media campaign to "pump and dump" otherwise worthless stock. The pressure of preparing for the trial is starting to get to both Client and Lawyer because there are very high stakes involved in the litigation. Client faces the potential for a significant jail term should Client lose the case. Lawyer and Client often argue, sometimes heatedly, but they always seem to patch things up. They generally agree about strategy and tend to come to some fair resolution about tactics. At one key, strategic point in the representation, however, Lawyer and Client have a fundamental disagreement about a particular tactic to deploy. Lawyer believes it is malpractice to not deploy it in defense of Client, yet Client insists that Lawyer refrain from using that tactic. In the jurisdiction in which the case is being heard, permission from the tribunal is required to withdraw as counsel. Lawyer moves to withdraw before the tribunal hearing Client's case. The judge hearing the matter holds a hearing to inquire as to the reason for the request to withdraw and asks Client to express his wishes with respect to representation. Client says he would prefer that Lawyer continue to represent him, and the court denies the request to withdraw, ordering Lawyer to continue the representation.

Was it professional misconduct for Lawyer to seek to withdraw from the action? If so, why? If not, why not?

A. Yes. Because the court denied the motion to withdraw, Lawyer must have had no proper basis for seeking that withdrawal.

B. Yes, because Lawyer had no proper basis to seek to withdraw from the representation.

C. No, because Lawyer can seek to withdraw from representation for any reason.

D. No, Lawyer had a legitimate basis to seek to withdraw even if the court ultimately denied the motion to withdraw.

33. Lawyer represents Client, a stock trader who may be charged with making illegal stock trades involving the sale of A Corp. stock. Lawyer represents Client in the pre-litigation phase of the Securities and Exchange Commission's investigation of the matter. Lawyer has agreed to represent Client through that phase and through prosecution, should any occur. Client professes his innocence and Lawyer can make a good faith argument in the defense of Client with respect to the sale of A Corp. stock. During the course of the investigation, Client offers Lawyer an opportunity to get involved in a separate and unrelated stock trade. That trade would involve the purchase of B Corp. stock, and such a trade could yield a significant amount of financial gain for both Client and Lawyer, but Lawyer believes the transaction would be illegal. Lawyer declines participation in the transaction, counsels Client not to take the planned course of action with respect to the sale of the B Corp. stock, and says he will withdraw as counsel for Client unless Client agrees to not go ahead with the illegal transaction. Client reluctantly agrees to refrain from going through with that transaction.

Is Lawyer required to withdraw from representing Client in the underlying case involving the A Corp. stock trade?

A. Yes, because Client's behavior with respect to the proposed B Corp. stock indicates that Lawyer has actual knowledge the A Corp. transaction was also illegal.

B. Yes, because Client suggested Lawyer engage in illegal conduct.

C. No, because Lawyer successfully counseled Client to refrain from illegal conduct.

D. No, unless Lawyer affords Client an opportunity to consult outside counsel on Lawyer's desire to withdraw.

34. Lawyer represents Client in a bitter dispute regarding the dissolution of a partnership. Client and Lawyer have also had a difficult time dealing with the matter because Client is quite angry at her former partners and all sides to the dispute are taking every issue throughout the course of the litigation personally. Toward the close of the litigation, which is before a state trial court, Client insists that Lawyer take action that will needlessly delay the proceeding, and Client has no proper motive for wanting Lawyer to take the action. The procedural step Client wants to take is sound as a matter of law, but Lawyer does not believe it is appropriate to take the action because it will simply delay the proceeding, and she believes resolution of the proceeding is in Client's best interest. When Lawyer confronts Client and tells her that she cannot ethically take the procedural step Client wants her to take, Client insists that Lawyer must take it because Client asserts it is essential to obtaining the goals Client has for the representation. Lawyer believes, in good faith, that she must withdraw because Client is insisting she take actions that are unethical. She files a notice with the court adjudicating the partnership dispute that she is withdrawing from representing Client in the action. She sends Client all of her files and takes no further action in the proceeding.

Has Lawyer acted unethically?

A. No, because Client was insisting that Lawyer take an action which was itself a violation of her ethical obligations.

B. Yes, because Lawyer cannot withdraw without the permission of the tribunal, even if the action Client wanted to take was itself unethical.

C. No, because Lawyer had a good faith basis for withdrawing and believed a faster resolution of the matter was in Client's best interests.

D. Yes, because Client is entitled to representation to the conclusion of the matter.

35. Lawyer represents Plaintiff in an antitrust case on behalf of a technology company. Lawyer is working on a contingency basis and believes the award in the case will be substantial. She has already worked over 200 hours on the case in preparing the complaint, although no complaint has yet been filed. Lawyer anticipates she will work many more hours on the case before it has reached its conclusion. Plaintiff informs Lawyer that Lawyer is being discharged as counsel for the company and that it has identified new counsel to represent it. Lawyer knows the statute of limitations is about to expire on Plaintiff's case and, if the complaint is to be filed, prompt action must be taken to protect Plaintiff's interests. New Counsel for the firm reaches out to Lawyer to obtain Plaintiff's files in order for New Counsel to prepare the complaint in a timely fashion. Lawyer insists that she will cooperate with New Counsel only on the condition that she continue to serve as co-counsel in the case.

Is Lawyer subject to discipline for failing to cooperate with New Counsel?

A. No, because Lawyer is entitled to reasonable compensation for her work before she must relinquish her role as counsel.

B. No, because Lawyer was given no reason for her discharge.

C. Yes, because Lawyer must cooperate with New Counsel to mitigate any potential harmful consequences to Plaintiff.

D. Yes, unless Lawyer reasonably believes that her staying on as co-counsel is in the best interests of Plaintiff.

36. Lawyer has long represented Client, a company that sells specialized beer brewing tanks to beer breweries across the United States. For many years, Lawyer has provided legal assurances to the purchasers of these tanks that they satisfy all U.S. Food & Drug Administration (FDA) requirements for the use of such tanks. Recently, Client changed the metal alloys it uses in the tanks. Client has informed Lawyer that the new alloys all continue to satisfy the FDA's guidelines for the manufacturing of such tanks. Based on those assurances, Lawyer provides a written legal opinion that the new tanks comply with FDA regulations and that legal opinion is shared with prospective purchasers of these new tanks. Before the new tanks are sold to any purchasers, Lawyer learns that the alloys used by Client in the new tanks actually contain lead, a substance banned by the FDA in the manufacturing of these tanks. Lawyer confronts Client on this matter and Client admits the error, stating, in good faith, that it did not realize that lead was a prohibited substance, which is why it did not report it to Lawyer when it provided assurances to Lawyer that the new tanks complied with the FDA's requirements. None of the new tanks has been sold to any customers, and they are no longer being offered for sale. Client halts the manufacturing of these tanks and lets any potential purchasers know that they are no longer available. Client tells its customers to disregard the information about the new tanks and the legal opinion prepared by Lawyer because both were inaccurate.

Must Lawyer withdraw as counsel and/or send written notice to potential customers of Client to inform them that

Lawyer disavows the legal opinion about the tanks?

A. Lawyer must withdraw as counsel and disavow the legal opinion about the new tanks.

B. Lawyer is not required to withdraw and does not have to disavow the legal opinion because Client has already done so.

C. Lawyer is not required to withdraw but still must disavow the legal opinion.

D. Lawyer must withdraw but does not need to disavow the legal opinion.

37. Lawyer has been representing Client for several years in a range of matters involving Client's business, mostly handling litigation before the Court of International Trade regarding international business transactions. Lawyer and Client come to a dispute over a fee Lawyer wants to charge involving one of these matters. Client believes Lawyer did not put in as many hours on the case as Lawyer reported and claimed. Lawyer and Client submit the dispute over fees to an impartial arbitrator, which is the procedure set forth in Lawyer's retainer for fee disputes. Lawyer ultimately prevails in that arbitration and establishes that Lawyer did, in fact, put in the work described in the litigation that was the subject of the dispute. Client accepts the decision of the arbitrator and pays Lawyer in full for the services rendered. Lawyer is still representing Client in an additional matter pending before the Court of International Trade, a body that requires consent of the tribunal to withdraw. It is possible that Client will be inconvenienced and disadvantaged should Lawyer seek to withdraw from representing Client in that pending action. Lawyer believes, correctly, that the trust between Client and Lawyer has evaporated because of the dispute over the fees and that the ongoing representation of Client has now become objectively unreasonably difficult. Client is demanding daily reports on the progress of the case and asks for a daily breakdown of all work done and fees to be charged for each day's work. These are not demands Client had imposed on the representation before the fee dispute. Because of this change in the relationship, Lawyer will seek to withdraw from the pending matter before the Court of International Trade and will ask the tribunal's permission to do so.

Is it unethical for Lawyer to seek to withdraw from the pending action? If so, why? If not, why not?

A. No, because the representation has become unreasonably difficult.

B. No, because Lawyer is seeking permission from the tribunal to do so.

C. Yes, because Client will be adversely impacted by the withdrawal.

D. Yes, because the fee dispute has been resolved and Client is maintaining all of its obligations to Lawyer.

38. Prospective Client Cam was injured at the local hospital during a routine medical procedure to remove a bunion from his foot. The surgery was botched and the incision became infected, causing him severe discomfort that affected his ability to compete in tryouts for the U.S. Olympic skating team. He was considered a favorite to win an Olympic medal, and he stood to make millions of dollars in endorsements as a result. Just days before the statute of limitations is about to run on Cam's medical malpractice claim against the hospital that performed the surgery, Cam appears in lawyer Leslie's office for the first time to ask her to represent him. Leslie reviews Cam's case and says she does not have adequate time to research the matter in order to file a lawsuit on Cam's behalf before the statute of limitations expires. She declines the opportunity to represent Cam, reminding him that he needs to act quickly to try to find another lawyer if he wants to file an action, because once the statute of limitations expires, he will lose the right to pursue his claim.

Has Leslie engaged in professional misconduct by failing to take action on Cam's behalf before the statute of limitations expires?

A. No, because Leslie made an accurate assessment of the strength of Cam's claims and was under no obligation to file a frivolous case.

B. Yes, because Leslie acted incompetently by not researching Cam's claim.

C. Yes, because Leslie should have taken what action she could to preserve Cam's rights.

D. No, because Leslie declined the representation and gave him guidance on the statute of limitations issue.

39. Lawyer represents a mortgage bank (Bank) and has prepared a standard mortgage agreement that provides several express warranties that indicate Bank is in compliance with all applicable banking laws. Lawyer proceeds in good faith when she prepares this agreement, basing it on material supplied to her by Bank. Lawyer learns, after several of these agreements have been executed, that the information upon which she relied in drafting the provisions was false, and thus the warranties are fraudulent. Lawyer confronts members of Bank's leadership team, and they say they are aware of the problem but refuse to take action to correct the errors in the agreements. Lawyer withdraws as counsel for Bank. She learns that Bank is preparing to use the mortgage agreement she had drafted when she represented Bank in future transactions. She writes a letter to prospective borrowers who would be asked to accept these fraudulent terms to inform them that the documents contain flawed warranties.

Is Lawyer subject to discipline for disclosing to future customers of Bank the defects in the mortgage agreements that she prepared?

A. No, because Lawyer is disaffirming a prior document that she prepared.

B. No, because Lawyer no longer represents Bank.

C. Yes, because the information Lawyer revealed is confidential information.

D. Yes, because the duty of loyalty extends beyond the duration of the representation.

1.10 Formative Assessment Quiz

Use these questions to test what you have learned in this chapter.

40. Lawyer enters into a partnership with Computer Specialist, a former agent for local law enforcement. The two provide advice and counsel to local financial institutions on their data security obligations. Lawyer describes the functioning of the office as a "one-stop shop" for all of its clients' data security needs, from their legal compliance to their understanding of the technical requirements of maintaining appropriate data security. Lawyer and Computer Specialist often work together in serving the partnership's clients, providing comprehensive compliance and data security advice to those clients, including legal guidance and technical information regarding data security. Computer Specialist has a data security certification from the state's division of licensing services that permits him to practice in the area of data security and hold himself out as an expert in the field. Lawyer only provides advice regarding legal matters, and Computer Specialist cannot control Lawyer's exercise of her professional judgment.

Is Lawyer subject to discipline for entering into the relationship with Computer Specialist?

A. Yes, because Lawyer is not competent to provide data security advising to the partnership's clients.

B. Yes, because a lawyer may not enter into a partnership with a non-lawyer if one of the services provided by the partnership is the provision of legal services.

C. No, because Lawyer always has control over the exercise of her professional judgment on legal matters.

D. No, because a lawyer is permitted to partner with another professional provided the professional possesses professional certification in their field.

41. Lawyer is a fixture in a local courthouse, handling small claims and traffic matters for her clients. Lawyer, who appears to know her way around the courthouse (and does), is often approached by individual litigants who have court appearances and who ask Lawyer for guidance about where the clerk's office is, where particular courtrooms are, and even for the locations of the bathrooms in the building. Occasionally, a litigant will ask Lawyer a substantive question about their case. Lawyer generally gives broad advice like "You should talk to the clerk and let them know what your arguments are in your defense," or "You might want to talk to the attorney for the town about paying that fine you failed to pay because penalties might be accruing against you every day." One day, Litigant observes Lawyer handling cases that involve traffic stops that end in Lawyer's clients' paying relatively small fines for various moving violations, like speeding or driving through stop signs, so Litigant asks Lawyer for guidance about Litigant's legal rights. Litigant was pulled over and given a ticket for speeding. During the stop, Litigant alleges his car was ransacked by the police, ostensibly in a search of the vehicle for illicit drugs, which uncovered none. Litigant discovered later that several items of value that were in the car prior to the stop were missing, and Litigant fears the police might have taken them. Lawyer has heard this type of story before and usually does not believe such tales, but this story is more detailed than usual and Lawyer believes Litigant. Lawyer informs Litigant that Lawyer does not handle this sort of matter and suggests that Litigant might want to consult with an attorney who does. Lawyer recommends several attorneys who handle this sort of case and also warns Litigant that there is a time limitation on bringing such a case, and therefore Litigant should act quickly to contact some of the attorneys whose name Lawyer gave Litigant.

Has Lawyer created an attorney-client relationship with Litigant? If so, why? If not, why not?

A. No, because Lawyer dispensed no legal advice and it would be unreasonable for Litigant to think that an attorney-client relationship had been formed by the communication.

B. Yes, because Lawyer created an attorney-client relationship with Litigant by informing Litigant about the potential statute of limitations issue in Litigant's matter.

C. No, because no attorney-client relationship could be formed in any instance without a formal, written retainer agreement.

D. Yes, because Lawyer's advice was unsolicited and Litigant could reasonably rely on the advice given.

42. Lawyer has represented Client for many years, and Lawyer and Client have an excellent relationship. Lawyer's main role in representing Client consists of defending Client in cases in which Client's former employees sue Client over claims for unemployment compensation. Lawyer feels that he has developed an understanding, over time, of Client's position in most cases in terms of what Client will accept to settle such cases. Lawyer is rarely wrong about Client's approach to settlement. After handling many such cases, Lawyer begins to resolve matters without bothering Client to obtain final consent to the settlements. Client reviews the settlement terms of the cases after the fact and does not object to the terms contained in any of them.

Has Lawyer acted unethically in the manner in which he has begun to resolve cases on behalf of Client?

A. Yes, because Lawyer is obligated to have obtained Client's written consent to each settlement, either before the settlement or immediately thereafter.

B. No, because Client found no grounds for objecting after the fact to the settlements obtained.

C. Yes, because Lawyer should have obtained Client's consent to each settlement or secured advanced consent before entering into any settlement.

D. No, because Lawyer's long-standing relationship with Client means he has implied authorization to accept the settlements on Client's behalf.

43. Lawyer meets with Client to discuss whether to take on Client's case. Lawyer communicates to Client that she is "the best negotiator" and tells Client that she "never has to take a case to trial." After discussing the strength of Client's case, Lawyer agrees to represent Client in the matter and they shake hands. Client has a dispute with her former employer over back pay that she claims she is owed from before she resigned her position. Before Lawyer files a lawsuit on behalf of Client, Lawyer reaches out to try to negotiate the claim with the attorney for Client's former employer, whom Lawyer knows. The negotiations fail and Client has to decide whether to file a lawsuit to obtain her back pay. At this point, Lawyer informs Client that she will not represent the Client in any lawsuit because she is not a litigator.

Is Lawyer subject to discipline for her actions?

A. Yes, because Lawyer should not have agreed to take on Client's case if she is not a competent litigator.

B. No, because Lawyer made it clear to Client that she would not handle the case if it went to trial.

C. No. Because Client agreed to have Lawyer represent her given what Lawyer said about her practice, Client impliedly authorized Lawyer to act on her behalf in a limited capacity.

D. Yes, because Client should have been given the opportunity to consent to any limitation Lawyer might impose on the representation.

44. Lawyer provides representation to tenants in landlord-tenant proceedings in a jurisdiction in which Lawyer is admitted to practice law. In addition to representing individual tenants, Lawyer is also engaged in advocacy work in the community. As part of Lawyer's community work, Lawyer provides know-your-rights guidance to tenants, speaking at community forums and events at local schools. Lawyer offers only general information and does not provide individualized guidance to any specific tenant in light of a tenant's particular facts and circumstances. Lawyer also advises local community organizers who do not work for Lawyer's organization but who assist local tenants, tenant groups, and community associations. These community organizers sometimes go into court to assist tenants when he cannot do so. Lawyer gives the organizers strict instructions about the use of the information he provides to them. Lawyer makes it clear what kinds of actions they might take that would constitute the unauthorized practice of law to ensure that the organizers do not engage in such conduct. He directs the organizers to only provide generalized advice and not to give any information tailored to an individual tenant's personal situation. Lawyer knows that these tenants will not receive any legal assistance unless the organizers are equipped with information to provide guidance to them about their cases, but Lawyer does not wish to run afoul of unauthorized practice of law rules in the jurisdiction. Lawyer also believes in good faith that the organizers understand the scope of information and guidance they may give to the tenants so that they do not engage in the unauthorized practice of law. Despite these warnings and this guidance, the organizers routinely do provide particularized advice to tenants about their legal rights based on information they have gleaned from other sources about tenants' rights. They also assist those tenants by negotiating with the tenants' landlords to resolve the tenants' cases. Under the applicable statute of the jurisdiction, the organizers are clearly engaged in the unauthorized practice of law.

Is Lawyer subject to discipline for assisting the organizers who engage in the unauthorized practice of law? If so, why? If not, why not?

A. No. Because Lawyer is an attorney admitted to practice in the jurisdiction, Lawyer's efforts are permissible.

B. Yes, because Lawyer was directly engaged in the unauthorized practice of law.

C. No, because Lawyer does not appear to have assisted the organizers in the unauthorized practice of law.

D. Yes, because Lawyer is assisting others to engage in the unauthorized practice of law by advising the community organizers in their work.

45. A small social media company, GoBig, has created a platform on which small investors can harness their resources and their funds to take concerted action against institutional investors that have taken "short" positions on stocks. GoBig is really a pair of college students who have very little money themselves. GoBig has attracted the attention of regulators and institutional investors. The institutional investors have filed a multi-million-dollar civil action against GoBig, which would bankrupt the company if successful. The founders of GoBig have no money to pay for counsel. Hearing about the case and GoBig's need for legal representation through Lawyer's child who goes to school with the company's founders, Lawyer contacts them with the goal of taking on the representation of GoBig and offers to do so without charge, at least in terms of defending against any claims. Lawyer believes the action could generate fees due to a fee-shifting provision in antitrust laws and agrees to take on the matter with the understanding that GoBig will countersue under these antitrust statutes, hopefully prevail, and then win an award of attorney's fees as a result. GoBig agrees to the representation even though they are aware that Lawyer is not competent to handle the representation at the time the company retains the Lawyer. Lawyer has not handled this type of case before. Lawyer puts in extra hours on nights and weekends so that Lawyer is able to provide zealous representation to GoBig. Although the case involves complicated and cutting-edge issues of securities and antitrust law, in a matter of weeks, Lawyer is able to develop the competence necessary to represent GoBig according to the requisite standard of care in the jurisdiction. During the weeks Lawyer spent preparing to handle the matter competently, no action was required of GoBig or its Lawyer because the complaint had just been filed by the institutional investors suing GoBig, and the deadline had not yet passed by which Lawyer had to file the client's answer to the action.

Is Lawyer subject to discipline for agreeing to represent GoBig when Lawyer was not competent to handle the matter at the outset of the representation? If so, why? If not, why not?

A. Yes, because a lawyer may never agree to represent a client in a case the lawyer is not competent to handle.

B. No, because Lawyer was able to develop competence to handle the case in a timely manner.

C. Yes. Even though Lawyer was not charging GoBig unless it prevailed in the countersuit, Lawyer should not have agreed to take on the matter if Lawyer was not competent to handle it.

D. No, because GoBig was aware of Lawyer's lack of competence to handle the matter but agreed to have Lawyer represent it despite this lack of competence.

46. Supervising lawyer, Sally, is responsible for the supervision and training of junior lawyer, Justin. Justin is a recent graduate of law school. He took part in clinical training while in law school and has experience, as a student, taking depositions. Sally begins Justin's training by allowing him to sit in on several depositions that she takes. She always consults with him after the depositions to review her strategy in particular depositions and to see if he has any questions about the taking of depositions in general. She begins to allow Justin to be the primary lawyer conducting depositions in a case where significant interests are at stake. She always attends the depositions and provides guidance to him during the recesses of the depositions. Despite being trained on the proper way to conduct a cross-examination during a deposition, on one occasion during one of these depositions, Justin makes several mistakes as to the form of the question, failing to ask leading questions as he is allowed to do on cross-examination. This means the questioning takes somewhat longer than usual as it is harder to elicit the information Justin would like to obtain from the witness. During a recess, Sally corrects Justin's errors and provides guidance on how to conduct proper cross-examination of a deponent. Justin resumes the deposition and is able to ask more pointed and appropriately leading questions. As a result, he is able to elicit the information Sally and Justin had hoped they would obtain from the deponent.

Is Sally subject to discipline for the manner in which she supervised Justin in the taking of the deposition?

A. Yes, because Justin should not have been allowed to conduct a deposition for which he was not prepared.

B. Yes, because Sally is responsible for Justin's actions and his failure to conduct a proper cross-examination was malpractice.

C. No, because Sally took reasonable steps to ensure Justin provided competent services to the client.

D. No, because Justin is responsible for his own compliance with his ethical obligations.

47. Lawyer handles worker compensation cases on behalf of a local manufacturing plant (Plant), defending Plant when employees have worker compensation claims. Lawyer has represented Plant for ten years, operating under a retainer that says that Lawyer will charge $1,000 for each case, which is a reasonable sum for such representation in the jurisdiction. However, the original terms of the retainer have expired. The retainer stated that the agreement would be in place for three years, but that period has long since run its course. Neither party to the retainer has sought to extend the term of the retainer. Lawyer has continued to handle worker compensation cases on behalf of Plant whenever they arise and has represented Plant in roughly twenty cases since the expiration of the retainer. Lawyer decides he no longer wants to handle Plant's cases. A new case has been filed against Plant by an employee named of Dwight Schrute, and Lawyer is notified of the Schrute case by a secretary at Plant. However, Lawyer fails to defend Plant in the proceeding, and a default judgment is entered against Plant as a result. Lawyer is notified by Plant of the judgment in the Schrute case, and Lawyer states that by the terms of the retainer he no longer represents Plant and was not its counsel in the proceeding.

Is Lawyer subject to discipline for failing to take action with respect to the Schrute case?

A. Yes, because Plant reasonably believed Lawyer would represent it in the matter.

B. Yes, unless Lawyer had a reasonable belief that his failure to represent Plant would not affect Plant adversely.

C. No, because the express terms of the retainer had relieved Lawyer of the obligation to represent Plant.

D. No, because Plant had no reasonable expectation that Lawyer would represent it in the Schrute matter.

48. Lawyer has been retained by three companies, Company 1, Company 2, and Company 3, (Companies) which are separate companies all pursuing a joint action suing a large multinational cloud storage company, IronCloud. The companies' interests are all aligned, and it does not appear that there is a conflict of interest between the companies in the representation. IronCloud makes an offer to settle the case in which it will pay each company $100,000. Lawyer has been independently authorized by each company, in writing, to settle the case on its respective behalf for at least $80,000 for each company. During the course of the negotiations, IronCloud's lawyer informs Lawyer for Companies that the data breach involving one of the companies the Lawyer represents (Company 3) was far more extensive than the breaches of the other two companies. IronCloud's Lawyer details the extent of Company 3's data breach, which is far more damaging than Company 3's representative is presently aware. Lawyer believes that the advance consent to settle the case that she received from all three companies is sufficient to allow her to accept the settlement on behalf of Companies. Moreover, she believes that the settlement for Company 3 is fair and equitable even in light of this new information.

Is Lawyer subject to discipline for accepting the settlement on behalf of Company 3 consistent with the advance consent she received from that company?

A. No, because the advance consent authorized Lawyer to accept at least $80,000, even for Company 3.

B. Yes, because Lawyer should have consulted again with Company 3 in light of the new information, prior to accepting the $100,000 settlement.

C. No, because Lawyer believes in good faith that settling the case for $100,000, even for Company 3, was a fair settlement.

D. Yes, because Lawyer must get any settlement approved individually by each company prior to entering into any aggregate settlement of their respective claims.

49. Lawyer has a family friend and former neighbor, Applicant, who is completing law school and applying for membership to the bar of a state in which Lawyer does not practice. Lawyer is listed as a reference for Applicant as part of his application for bar membership. Before Lawyer was herself admitted to practice law, and before Applicant even went to law school, Lawyer learned of Applicant's run-ins with the law, including acts of larceny around the neighborhood, like stealing items of significant value from neighbors. These items were always found and returned. While Applicant was charged with misdemeanors for these actions when he was caught, the charges were always withdrawn, and he was never convicted of any crimes. Since Lawyer is listed as one of Applicant's references, she receives a questionnaire from the jurisdiction's bar admission committee which asks her whether she knows of any conduct on the part of Applicant that would reflect on his fitness to practice law. Lawyer is informed by the admission committee that Applicant has reported in his application that he has never been charged with any crimes.

Is Lawyer subject to discipline should she fail to correct the admission committee's impression that Applicant has never been charged with any crimes?

A. No, because Lawyer is under no obligation to respond to the committee's request for information because she is not admitted to practice law in the jurisdiction where Applicant has applied.

B. No, because the knowledge Lawyer possesses about Applicant's past is subject to the attorney-client privilege, and she is under no obligation to reveal it to the committee.

C. Yes, because a lawyer listed as a reference in a bar admission application must always reveal any information they have about the applicant, regardless of its source or the nature of the inquiry.

D. Yes, because Lawyer is obligated to correct the committee's misapprehension that Applicant has never been charged with any crimes.

50. Law Student works as an intern at a local non-profit legal aid office. Law Student has been trained to assist clients of the office with filing for unemployment benefits. Law Student is competent to provide such limited services and has Supervising Lawyer at the student's disposal should the Law Student run into situations related to unemployment benefits that the Law Student does not know how to handle. Supervising Lawyer runs the internship program at the organization and is responsible for the training and supervision of all law student interns. Law Student was never advised by Supervising Attorney or anyone else at the organization that students, like this Law Student, trained only in unemployment matters, are not to give information to callers about topics beyond the scope of unemployment insurance. One day, while Law Student is staffing a telephone hotline the office designates for calls related to unemployment benefits, Law Student receives a call related to benefits under a different type of program: worker compensation. Law Student has not been trained to provide assistance related to worker compensation but looks at the non-profit organization's public website for basic guidance on what appears to be a simple question related to worker compensation. Law Student did not ask many questions related to the caller's worker compensation claim, and based on the information Law Student provided to the caller, the caller lost out on certain types of benefits. Law Student had provided the wrong information to the caller because Law Student was not trained to seek critical information about the caller's case. A competent professional would have inquired about such information and steered the caller in the appropriate direction.

Is Supervising Attorney subject to discipline for Law Student's actions? If so, why? If not, why not?

A. Yes, because the supervision, training, and guidance should have prepared students for any calls that they might receive.

B. Yes, because the supervision, training, and guidance should have made clear that students should only assist clients with matters they are competent to handle.

C. No, because it was reasonable for Supervising Attorney to expect that Law Student would not offer assistance that she was not competent to provide.

D. No, because Supervising Attorney had no reason to know that Law Student was going to provide incompetent service to the caller.

51. Law firm utilizes a computer system that is connected to the internet. The network administrator at the firm learns of a new cybersecurity threat to which the firm's system is vulnerable. To protect against this vulnerability, the firm will have to purchase a new yet inexpensive software update. Supervisory lawyers in the firm are made aware of the threat to their computer system by the network administrator in a timely fashion. The system contains sensitive and confidential client matters, but the supervisory lawyers at the firm take no precautions to secure their network. They insist they have done all they are required to do because they updated the system's security measures three year ago. The firm's system is breached, and sensitive information is obtained by hackers and released on the internet for public consumption.

Are the supervisory lawyers subject to discipline for their inaction?

A. Yes, because the supervisory lawyers had to take all possible precautions to protect their clients' sensitive information.

B. No, because the supervisory lawyers were not required to constantly update the security system to respond to every threat.

C. No, because the supervisory lawyers could not subject their judgment to that of a non-lawyer.

D. Yes, because the supervisory lawyers were required to take reasonable precautions to protect against threats to their computer system.

52. Lawyer serves in a "Lawyer-for-the-Day" program and volunteers at the local housing court, helping tenants who are facing eviction. Lawyer enters into a limited retainer that provides that Lawyer will only attempt to negotiate settlement agreements on behalf of the tenants. Such retainers are common in this jurisdiction. If the case cannot settle, and the matter must go to trial, Lawyer states in the limited retainer that Lawyer is not able to represent the tenant in that situation. Any prospective client is made aware of the restrictions on Lawyer's ability to represent the tenant should the matter not settle. Such tenants who wish to proceed with the representation through such a limited-scope retainer provide informed consent, in writing, to the arrangement only if they do, in fact, consent to it. If the tenants do not consent to the arrangement, they understand they are declining Lawyer's assistance.

Is Lawyer subject to discipline for offering clients retainers with a limitation that states that Lawyer will not continue to represent a client if the matter cannot settle? If so, why? If not, why not?

A. No, because the limitation on the representation is reasonable and those clients who accept the arrangement all give informed consent to it.

B. No, because a lawyer is permitted to put any restrictions on a representation that are deemed appropriate by that lawyer.

C. Yes, because once a lawyer agrees to represent a client, that lawyer must do so zealously despite potential inconvenience to that lawyer and must see the representation in the matter through to its conclusion.

D. Yes, because the limitation on representation was unreasonable under the circumstances.

53. Lawyer serves as in-house counsel for a large corporation, handling all matters regarding compliance with state and federal securities laws applicable to the operation of the company. She is admitted to practice in the jurisdiction in which the corporation is based. Occasionally, she is asked to offer her opinion about state regulatory matters for a subsidiary of the company that is based in a jurisdiction in which Lawyer is not admitted. When a question arises as to the application of such a jurisdiction's laws, she always consults with counsel for the subsidiary who is admitted to practice in the jurisdiction before offering her opinion.

Is Lawyer subject to discipline for providing services to the subsidiary in this way?

A. Yes, because Lawyer is not admitted to practice in the jurisdiction in which the subsidiary is located.

B. No, because Lawyer consults with an attorney admitted to practice in the jurisdiction before she dispenses advice related to the laws of that jurisdiction.

C. Yes, because Lawyer has established a systematic and continuous presence in a jurisdiction in which she is not admitted to practice.

D. No, because Lawyer does not represent the subsidiary.

54. Lawyer represents Tony Tosca (Tony), a reputed mafia boss. Tony appears in Lawyer's office and asks for a "sit down." Lawyer and Tony go into a private portion of the office, and Tony asks Lawyer the following: "So, let's say, hypothetically, a person were to engage in some creative disposal of toxic waste into the local water supply, what are the steps that person might take to avoid detection of such conduct?" Lawyer begins to discuss the likely legal ramifications of such behavior, including the likelihood that such conduct would be illegal.

Is Lawyer subject to discipline for the counseling he has provided to Tony?

A. Yes, because the conduct likely will lead to reasonably certain death or substantial bodily harm.

B. Yes, because Lawyer is counseling Tony how to engage in conduct Lawyer knows is illegal.

C. No, because Lawyer is discussing the potential legal consequences of the conduct and the application of the law to the conduct.

D. No, because the communications were confidential and Lawyer is under no obligation to report such conduct, even if there is a substantial likelihood that the conduct will lead to reasonably certain death or substantial bodily harm.

55. Lawyer A is supervised by Supervising Lawyer. Lawyer A's Client, whom Lawyer A represents in a civil matter, has informed Lawyer A that she intends to proffer specific testimony at trial. While Lawyer A is not absolutely certain this testimony is false, Lawyer A concludes, correctly, that any reasonable person aware of the facts at Lawyer A's disposal would infer that the proffered testimony is false. At the same time, Lawyer A also believes that it is unlikely that Lawyer A's adversary will be able to obtain information that could impeach Client's testimony. No further facts surrounding the issue that Lawyer knows or might uncover would indicate—or even help shed light on—whether the statement will constitute perjury. Lawyer A consults with Supervising Lawyer on the right course of action. Lawyer A tells Supervisory Lawyer that he believes he will have to disclose the perjury to the court if Client proffers it. Supervisory Lawyer asks whether, if Client proffers the testimony, the information Lawyer A possesses about the testimony is confidential. Lawyer A confirms that the information in his possession that leads him to believe the testimony is false is, in fact, confidential client information. Supervising Lawyer directs Lawyer A to present the testimony because, Supervisory Lawyer says, the information that leads Lawyer A to believe Client's testimony will be false is itself confidential, meaning that Lawyer A cannot reveal such information or disclose the perjury.

May Lawyer A proceed in accordance with Supervisory Lawyer's direction without being subject to discipline? If yes, why? If not, why not?

A. Yes, because Supervisory Lawyer is the supervisory lawyer, and Lawyer A, as the subordinate attorney, must always follow the supervisor's direction.

B. Yes, because Supervisory Lawyer's resolution of the matter was reasonable in light of the relevant professional duty.

C. No, because all lawyers are subject to discipline for their actions in every situation, whether they are acting under the guidance of a supervisory lawyer or not.

D. No, because Supervisory Lawyer's resolution of the matter is unreasonable in light of the clear professional duty in this instance.

56. Lawyer has been admitted to practice law for forty-five years and takes pride in her self-described "old-school practice." Lawyer does not generally know how to use a computer for such basic tasks as word processing and conflict checking. In the midst of a global pandemic, Lawyer is forced to make court appearances via video conference. Lawyer has a great deal of difficulty logging in to such appearances and keeping track of her cases now that the courts have moved all of their functions to web-based calendaring of cases, and Lawyer misses several court appearances as a result. In one case, the court enters a default judgment against Lawyer's client, which will take a considerable amount of time and effort for Lawyer to vacate. Lawyer is overwhelmed by the new demands on Lawyer's time that stem from her having to learn new processes for shifting work to a remote format. Lawyer does not understand the relevant court's e-filing processes, even though the court website has several simple tutorials that explain the process to litigants and lawyers with easy-to-understand instructions. Lawyer fails to file a motion to vacate the default judgment in a timely fashion as a result. Because of this failure, Lawyer's client, who suffered the default, is responsible for paying the opposing party over $1 million in damages.

Does Lawyer's conduct constitute misconduct in any way?

A. Lawyer is guilty of misconduct for failing to understand the technology necessary to represent her client competently but not for failing to file a timely motion to vacate the default judgment.

B. Lawyer is not guilty of misconduct regarding the reason for the default judgment but is guilty of misconduct for failing to file a timely motion to vacate the default judgment.

C. Lawyer is guilty of misconduct both for failing to understand the technology necessary to represent her client competently and failing to file a timely motion to vacate the default judgment.

D. Lawyer is not guilty of misconduct because of the actions that led to the default judgment but is guilty of misconduct for failing to file a timely motion to vacate the default judgment.

57. As Dan's case is nearing the end of discovery and getting ready for trial, the relationship between Dan and Lawyer who represents Dan becomes tense. Dan is a sophisticated businessperson caught up in a social media campaign to "pump and dump" otherwise worthless stock. The pressure of preparing for the trial is starting to get to both Dan and Lawyer because there are very high stakes involved in the litigation. Dan faces a significant jail term should Dan lose the case. Lawyer and Dan often argue, sometimes heatedly, but they always seem to patch things up. They generally agree about strategy, and tend to come to some fair resolution about tactics. Nevertheless, Dan worries that Lawyer is not being a zealous advocate for him, despite Lawyer's protests that Lawyer is working as hard as humanly possible to protect Dan's interests. Dan decides to terminate the attorney-client relationship with Lawyer and retain another lawyer. The substitution of new counsel is approved by the tribunal. This decision will set Dan's defense back a bit, however, and could possibly materially and adversely impact the new lawyer's ability to represent Dan since the trial is just a few weeks away.

Is Lawyer subject to discipline if Lawyer permits the new lawyer to take over Dan's case? If so, why? If not, why not?

A. Yes, because the substitution of counsel will likely have a materially adverse effect on the representation of Dan.

B. Yes, because there are no suitable grounds for Lawyer to withdraw as Dan's counsel.

C. No, because the relationship between Lawyer and Dan had become contentious.

D. No, because Dan, as the client, is in control of the representation and can generally change attorneys as Dan wishes, even if it is to Dan's material disadvantage to do so.

58. A relatively inexperienced law firm associate (Associate) is handling a real estate closing for a firm client. In reviewing the case with the senior lawyer at the firm who is Associate's immediate supervisor, they discover two pieces of information related to the sale of the property. First, that the client (Seller), the owner of the property, has not paid real estate taxes for some time on the property, and second, that there is asbestos on the property which Seller has not revealed to Buyer. Associate has reviewed the correspondence in the file and noticed that the attorney for Buyer has sent a standard questionnaire typically used in a sale of real estate in the community. The questionnaire includes the following:

Question 2: Is Seller current on all real estate taxes on the date on which this statement is signed?

Question 7: Is there any asbestos on the property on the date on which this statement is signed?

Under applicable state law, a seller who fails to answer these questions truthfully can be subject to a damages action on behalf of a buyer after the sale if the buyer experiences any harm as a result of the misrepresentations on the form. The time limit under law to respond to the questionnaire will expire in five business days. There are also statutory penalties for submitting untrue statements on these forms, and a misrepresentation could lead to perjury charges because the statements are to be notarized and affirmed as true.

Associate discusses the matter with the senior lawyer, who suggests the following course of action. First, Seller should promise Associate that he will pay all outstanding real estate taxes and fees within three months. The senior lawyer says that the sale of the property will not take place for at least four months; if Buyer agrees to buy Seller's house, which is still not certain to happen, Seller can simply make sure he pays all of the taxes before the sale takes place. The senior lawyer says that if Seller simply promises Associate that he will pay the outstanding real estate taxes before the property transaction is completed, Question 2 can be answered in the affirmative. The senior lawyer explains this is because no one will know whether the taxes were actually paid when the questionnaire was signed since Buyer's attorney will only do a final search of the property records on the eve of the closing—nearly four months away at the earliest. Second, Seller should be instructed to remove all asbestos from the premises prior to the date on which the statement is to be signed so that Seller can answer Question 7 in the negative.

Is Associate subject to discipline for following either, both, or neither of these courses of action on behalf of Seller?

A. Associate is subject to discipline for following the planned course of action with respect to both questions.

B. Associate is subject to discipline for following the planned course of action with respect to the taxes but not the asbestos.

C. Associate is subject to discipline for following the planned course of action for the asbestos but not the taxes.

D. Associate will not be subject to discipline for following either course of action.

59. Lawyer is concerned that Client is engaging in money laundering activities as part of what appears to be an otherwise legitimate business operation. Client's business is the type of business that has been known recently to likely to take part in illegal money laundering. Lawyer counsels Client on the risks inherent in Client's business, the scrutiny such business operations are likely to come under, the poor reputation of some of the foreign companies with which Client is doing business, the fact that law enforcement officials tend to scrutinize domestic individuals and entities that might conduct business with those foreign companies, and the punishment associated with money laundering under U.S. law.

Is Lawyer subject to discipline for counseling Client in this manner?

A. Yes, because Lawyer is aiding in the commission of criminal conduct by advising Client on the risks associated with Client's actions.

B. Yes, because Lawyer is cooperating in perpetrating a crime.

C. No, because Lawyer cannot be subject to discipline for advice communicated to Client that is protected by the attorney-client privilege.

D. No, because Lawyer is merely giving Client advice regarding the potential legal consequences of Client's actions.

Chapter 2

Conflicts of Interest

Paragraph 9 to the Preamble to the Model Rules provides as follows: "In the nature of law practice, however, conflicting responsibilities are encountered. Virtually all difficult ethical problems arise from conflict between a lawyer's responsibilities to clients, to the legal system and to the lawyer's own interest in remaining an ethical person while earning a satisfactory living." This chapter explores the many ways in which lawyers can encounter conflicts in their representation of clients.

2.1 Client Conflicts Generally

This section introduces issues surrounding conflicts of interests generally. Use it to begin to build your knowledge and familiarity with the issues that can create conflicts for lawyers that impact their ability to represent their clients competently.

1. Lawyer represents a landlord in an eviction proceeding against a tenant. The tenant is appearing in the matter without representation. The landlord and tenant have a relatively amicable relationship, even though they are in court in litigation. The landlord reports that the reason he brought the tenant to court is that there is a charity that will pay the tenant's back rent, but only if the tenant has an eviction case filed against her. Once the case is commenced, the parties convene out of court with Lawyer present, in an effort to resolve the matter. They are able to reach a draft settlement agreement through which the tenant agrees to pay the back rent that is owed. Though the settlement agreement has not yet been finalized with the court, the tenant contacts the charity for assistance in paying the back rent due under the agreement. The charity says it can only help tenants who are represented by an attorney. The tenant approaches Lawyer and asks if Lawyer will represent her in court when the case is next scheduled to be heard, solely for the purposes of filing the settlement agreement, so that the tenant can seek the back rent payment from the charity. Lawyer obtains the informed consent of both the landlord and the tenant to appear as counsel in the eviction proceeding for both parties.

Is Lawyer subject to discipline for appearing as counsel on behalf of both the landlord and the tenant in the same proceeding?

A. Yes, because the proceeding involves the assertion of a claim by one client against the other.

B. Yes, unless the court approves the representation.

C. No, because there are no longer any issues in dispute between the parties, and the lawyer was acting more as a mediator than an advocate.

D. No, because both parties gave informed consent, confirmed in writing.

2. Lawyer represents Able, Baker, and Charlie (Defendants) in a criminal case in which they are accused of engaging in a conspiracy to distribute pirated DVDs of newly released Hollywood films. Defendants are all indigent, and Lawyer has been assigned as counsel to represent all three. At the trial court level, during pre-trial conferences in the case and throughout the trial, no one raises the issue of potential conflicts of interest among Defendants that might arise due to the joint representation. The case proceeds, and all three are convicted and receive lengthy sentences. During the trial, Defendants presented a united legal front, and Lawyer represented them to the best of her ample abilities, raising novel and creative defenses, objecting at appropriate times, and serving them zealously. As is common in trials like this, none of Defendants testified on his or her own behalf, although Lawyer called several witnesses in defense of Defendants. Defendants' defense was not impacted adversely by the joint representation. Although the jury deliberated for several days, it ultimately found against Defendants. Seeking to overturn their convictions, Defendants now raise the issue, for the first time on appeal, that the representation was constitutionally ineffective.

What is the likely outcome of the request to overturn the convictions based on ineffective assistance of counsel?

A. The convictions will be overturned because the court failed to inquire into the possibility of a conflict of interest prior to holding the trial.

B. The convictions will be overturned because one can assume that the joint representation constituted a conflict of interest and that such conflict of interest must have had an actual impact on Lawyer's representation of Defendants.

C. The convictions will be upheld because Lawyer provided competent, conflict-free representation to Defendants that was not adversely affected by the joint representation.

D. The convictions will be upheld because Defendants failed to raise the conflicts issue at the trial court level.

3. Lawyer represents two employees in a suit alleging employment discrimination at a law firm. One of the employees, Arliss, is a junior associate at the law firm, and the other employee, Bernie, is a senior associate at the same law firm. The two employees claim they were denied promotions and bonuses on grounds covered by relevant discrimination laws. The two have a joint representation agreement and have consented that any confidential information shared with Lawyer by either employee can be shared with the other employee. When Lawyer for Arliss and Bernie interviews Bernie as part of investigating the employees' claims, Bernie reveals to Lawyer that Bernie was privy to communications with law firm superiors that prove Arliss was the subject of discrimination; however, Bernie does not want Arliss to know about these communications because Bernie could be implicated in the discrimination and could be liable to Arliss for such discrimination. Bernie insists that Lawyer maintain this information as confidential.

What is Lawyer's correct course of action?

A. Lawyer must preserve the confidences of Bernie but may continue the representation of both Arliss and Bernie.

B. Lawyer must preserve the confidences of Bernie but must withdraw from representing both Arliss and Bernie.

C. Lawyer must preserve the confidences of Bernie and may continue to represent Bernie, but must withdraw from representing Arliss.

D. Lawyer may not preserve the confidences of Bernie but may continue to represent both Arliss and Bernie.

4. Lawyer works at a firm that has several offices. Lawyer represents a large company, Xen, handling all of its litigation and business transactions, although he does not formally serve as counsel to any of Xen's subsidiaries because they all have separate counsel. One of Xen's subsidiaries, YO, is being sued by another company, Acme, in an antitrust action in which tens of millions of dollars are at stake. Acme is being represented by an attorney in Lawyer's firm, but out of a firm office in another city. Xen is a long-standing client of the firm. Acme has just retained the firm as counsel for this lawsuit. YO is not represented by Lawyer or by anyone in Lawyer's firm. The two firm offices (i.e., the one representing Xen and the one representing Acme) share no confidential information about any cases on which they work, do not have access to each other's files, and do not share strategy on cases on which they work. If Acme wins in court against YO, however, Xen will be responsible to pay the substantial damages award against Acme because YO is a wholly owned subsidiary of Xen, and Xen has agreed to assume all liabilities of YO in the event its liabilities exceed its assets, which is what would happen should Acme win a large damage award against YO.

Is Lawyer's firm subject to disqualification in the representation of Acme?

A. No, provided the attorneys representing Acme are screened from Lawyer.

B. No, because Lawyer is not representing YO but is only representing Xen.

C. Yes, because there is a significant threat that Xen will incur significant liabilities in the case brought against YO by Acme.

D. Yes, because Lawyer may have had access to confidential information related to YO.

5. Lawyer routinely represents mortgage banks in real estate transactions and is one of the most highly respected real estate attorneys in her community. Lawyer learns that her sister plans to take out a mortgage from one of Lawyer's clients, AMCO Bank (AMCO), to secure funds to purchase a new home. Lawyer's sister asks her to handle the closing as her attorney even though Lawyer will represent AMCO on the transaction. At first, Lawyer expresses her willingness to represent her sister and says she will not charge for her services. She reflects on the matter for several days, however, and is concerned that she cannot adequately represent AMCO and her sister because there are some provisions in the mortgage agreement AMCO typically uses that are unfavorable to borrowers. Lawyer consults with AMCO, and AMCO refuses to change those terms. Moreover, AMCO prohibits Lawyer from discussing these unfavorable aspects of the agreement with Lawyer's sister. Bank representatives say they are starting to question Lawyer's loyalty, and, if she insists on reporting this information to her sister, they may have to take the bank's business elsewhere. There is no statutory bar in the jurisdiction to a lawyer's representing a borrower and a lender in the same transaction. Lawyer believes, however, that this representation is conflicted, and she cannot provide competent services to her sister should she represent both her sister and AMCO because she cannot advise her sister of the less favorable terms contained in the standard AMCO mortgage which AMCO insists her sister must accept. Lawyer is pressured by her sister to make a decision about whether Lawyer will represent her. Without revealing the unfavorable terms of the mortgage agreement to her sister, Lawyer talks to both parties and they both consent, in writing, that Lawyer can represent both the sister and AMCO in the transaction.

May Lawyer represent both parties in the transaction?

A. Yes, because the representation is not prohibited by law in the jurisdiction.

B. No, because the lawyer does not reasonably believe she can provide competent representation to both parties in the transaction.

C. Yes, because both parties consent, in writing, to the joint representation.

D. No, because Lawyer cannot represent a party against a close family member without advising that family member of the potential unfavorable components of the transaction.

6. Lawyer represents two pharmaceutical companies (Clients) that are challenging a regulatory ruling of the U.S. Food and Drug Administration (FDA) that makes it more difficult for them to bring certain of their drugs to market. During the course of the representation, Lawyer will need access to the confidential trade secrets of each company related to the drugs affected by this ruling. In advance of Lawyer's undertaking the representation, in a written agreement in which Clients are each represented by independent and separate counsel, Clients consent that such trade secrets should not be shared between representatives of the companies but that each company can privately share such trade secrets with Lawyer. By virtue of this agreement, Lawyer will be prohibited from sharing the secret formulas of one company with the other and will continue to represent these companies in the dispute with the FDA.

Is the agreement that will prevent the sharing of information between the jointly represented Clients proper, or will Lawyer need to withdraw from representing each client in this matter once exposed to this confidential information?

A. Because jointly represented clients can limit the extent to which Lawyer can share confidential trade secrets as between the parties, sharing such information was proper, and Lawyer will not be required to withdraw from the representation of either party.

B. Because clients can waive confidentially when they enter into joint representation agreements it was proper to share such information but Lawyer will need to withdraw from representing both parties once Lawyer learns these trade secrets.

C. Because the clients may waive confidentiality with respect to trade secrets, sharing such information was proper, but the fact that Lawyer possesses these trade secrets of these potentially adverse parties means Lawyer will now have to withdraw from representing both of them.

D. It was improper for jointly represented clients to limit the extent to which Lawyer can share confidential trade secrets as between the clients, but, once they do so, Lawyer's ability to represent both clients will not be affected and the Lawyer will not have to withdraw from representing either party.

7. Lawyer represents several neighbors (Clients) who are suing over the negligent release of sewage waste by the town that flooded the street and seeped into each of the neighbor's homes. Clients all agreed to joint representation and stated that they understood that information shared with Lawyer could not be maintained as confidential among the Clients. Neighbor Aaron approaches Lawyer and admits to her that, on the night of the sewage release, he intentionally diverted some of the waste to neighbor Beatrice's property, meaning Beatrice likely has a cross-claim against Aaron if Beatrice were to find out about it. Such conflict was unforeseeable at the outset of the representation. Aaron asks Lawyer to maintain this information as confidential. Lawyer agrees to continue the representation of both clients and not share Aaron's confidential information with Beatrice.

Is Lawyer subject to discipline for continuing the representation of Aaron and Beatrice?

A. Yes, because there is an irreconcilable conflict that impacts Lawyer's ability to proceed as a zealous advocate for both clients.

B. Yes, because Lawyer never should have agreed to the joint representation in this context.

C. No, because Lawyer must preserve Aaron's confidences.

D. No, because the clients consented to the joint representation.

2.2 Specific Conflicts Issues

While the previous section dealt with conflicts issues more generally, this section deals with the specific conflicts rules contained mostly in MR 1.8.

8. Lawyer has been approached to represent Client in a workplace discrimination case in which Lawyer will be paid on a contingency-fee basis. Client is a wealthy and prominent actor who has been involved in lawsuits before and has become frustrated with not only the delays often associated with the litigation but also the high cost of litigation. Lawyer drafts a retainer for Client to sign which states that Lawyer will cover any court costs and litigation expenses during the course of the litigation and Client will only be responsible for repaying them should Client win her case. Relieved by this approach to the expenses, Client signs the retainer.

Is Lawyer subject to discipline for entering into the retainer with Client in this fashion?

A. Yes, because Client was not given a reasonable amount of time to consult with independent counsel prior to signing the retainer.

B. No, because Lawyer may advance court costs and litigation expenses, with their repayment contingent on the outcome of the case.

C. No, because Client would be denied access to the courts and to Client's attorney of choice if Lawyer did not advance the court costs and expenses.

D. Yes, because a lawyer cannot pay a client's court costs and expenses unless the client is indigent.

9. Lawyer represents Client for several years, on several different matters, until Client is ultimately acquitted in a criminal trial. Lawyer obtained a verdict of not guilty in a highly contested and high-profile criminal action in which Client was accused of raising prices on pharmaceutical products his company sells in alleged violation of criminal antitrust laws. The retainer between the parties stipulates that Lawyer's service to Client ends at the conclusion of the trial, and that service has now ended with respect to all matters on which Lawyer had represented Client. The prosecutor is not appealing the verdict. Lawyer wants to move on from not only his representation of Client but also his law practice generally, because he feels he has accomplished much in his career and wants to start writing non-fiction legal thrillers. Client is incensed about the unfair treatment he received in the media and is looking to sell the literary rights to his life story. Client says Lawyer did such a good job of representing him that he believes Lawyer is in a great position to tell his story in a positive light. Lawyer and Client begin negotiations for the literary rights to Client's life story. The negotiations run smoothly. Lawyer provides Client with a written statement regarding the essential terms of the agreement, and it clearly states that Lawyer is not representing Client in the transaction. Client signs the statement, giving his informed consent to the transaction and the arrangement.

Is Lawyer subject to discipline for Lawyer's conduct in purchasing the literary rights from Client?

A. Yes, because Lawyer cannot obtain literary rights in Client's life story.

B. No. Because Lawyer's representation of Client had ended, there were no restrictions on Lawyer's purchase of Client's literary rights.

C. Yes, because Client should have been given an opportunity to seek separate counsel in the transaction transferring Client's literary rights.

D. No, because the manner in which Lawyer reached this agreement with Client was consistent with the Lawyer's ethical obligations.

10. Lawyer was orphaned as a teenager and developed a close relationship with Neighbor, who effectively raised her after the death of her parents. Lawyer is now an adult but has continued to maintain a close, familial relationship with Neighbor. Neighbor writes Lawyer and asks her to prepare a will for him. Neighbor is childless and his spouse died several years ago. He wants to leave all of his property, which is valued at over $1 million, to Lawyer in the will. "You've always been like a daughter to me, and I want to make sure you are taken care of," says Neighbor in his written request to have Lawyer prepare the will.

Is Lawyer subject to discipline if she prepares the will for Neighbor and honors his wishes regarding the distribution of his property to her?

A. No, because the relationship between Lawyer and Neighbor is a close and familial one.

B. No, because Neighbor made the request to Lawyer to prepare the will in writing.

C. Yes, because the relationship between Lawyer and Neighbor is not a traditional familial relationship.

D. Yes, because a lawyer may not prepare a will in which the lawyer receives a substantial gift.

11. Lawyer runs a small private practice in an immigrant community. He cannot possibly handle all of the prospective clients that come to him for assistance. He does what he can, however. Since many of his clients are low-wage workers, he offers low-fee services at a sliding scale. He also does a fair amount of pro bono work and works for people he does not expect will ever pay him for the services he renders. He knows that's how it works, and he doesn't mind. He is building goodwill in the community and hopes that some of the clients may come to him for paying work in the future or will refer their friends who can afford to pay him. Because many of his clients work in dangerous occupations, occasionally he gets a personal injury case for which he pursues fees based on a contingency-fee arrangement.

One day, a former client of his (Client), appears at his office with just that kind of case. Client works in a bakery, and she was recently badly injured by a truck delivering baking supplies to the bakery. Because the truck was not owned by her employer, she can sue the owner outside the worker compensation system, meaning the damages can be significant for the substantial injuries she sustained. One of the problems with the case is that Client is indigent and now cannot work. The worker compensation payments she can receive are not enough to pay her rent and utilities while the case is pending. Her status in the United States is legal, but, if she cannot pay her rent and utilities, she will have to move back to her native country, France. Lawyer knows that if she has to move back to France, she will not pursue her case, which is very strong. Lawyer is confident that Client will win a considerable amount in damages. The defendant's counsel has already offered Client $250,000 to settle the case. Lawyer knows Client could accept it tomorrow if she wants or wait for the case to go to trial, where she will probably win a lot more. Because Lawyer knows the strength of Client's case, he is willing to give Client an advance of funds based on Lawyer's near certain belief that Client will ultimately win, even if she does not accept the pending settlement offer. He understands her situation and does not want her to have to worry about not being able to pay her rent while the case is pending or to have to accept the settlement if she wants to hold out and take the case to trial.

If Lawyer provides financial support to Client under these circumstances, would such conduct subject him to discipline? If so, why? If not, why not?

A. Yes, because Lawyer may not give client financial support to help the client pay her living expenses.

B. No, because Lawyer may pay the reasonable living expenses of the client in order to ensure that she can have access to justice.

C. Yes, because, if Lawyer provides Client an advance to pay her living expenses, repayment may only be conditioned on whether she is ultimately victorious.

D. No, because Lawyer has a near-certain belief that Client would prevail in her lawsuit.

12. Lawyer enters into an agreement to represent Client. Client agrees, orally, to pay Lawyer's going rate of $500 an hour to represent her in securing a patent for her invention. This is consistent with what a lawyer of similar skill and ability would charge for this service in the community, based on Lawyer's assessment of the complexity of the case at the time she agreed to handle the matter. Lawyer begins to represent Client in the matter. Lawyer puts in roughly ten hours per week on Client's application and does so for about four months. After this four-month period, Lawyer begins to realize several things about the case. First, the patent application is far more complicated than she believed it was when she agreed to take on the case. Second, the commercial value of Client's invention, should she be able to secure a patent for Client, is extraordinary. Lawyer feels the company could be the next Silicon Valley darling. Indeed, she thinks it could be a "unicorn" in the parlance of the business, a company worth more than $1 billion. Because of this conclusion, she thinks the amount she is charging is far less than what Client can and should pay. She contacts Client and tells Client that she is going to send over a written retainer agreement that doubles Lawyer's hourly fee. She says, correctly, that this higher fee is consistent with what a client would typically pay in the community for work involving a potentially high-value invention like the one at issue in Lawyer's representation of Client. Client is excited that Lawyer assesses the invention as being potentially very lucrative and agrees on the spot to increase the hourly rate, signs the agreement, and faxes it back to Lawyer.

If Lawyer is found to be subject to discipline for her actions, what would be the most likely reason?

A. Lawyer's fee was unreasonable.

B. Lawyer cannot change the fee structure once the representation has commenced.

C. Lawyer failed to treat the revision of the fee structure as entering into a business transaction with the client and affording the client all of the protections required in doing so.

D. Lawyer's original fee arrangement was not in writing.

13. Lawyer represents two Clients, Client A and Client B, who have sued a former employer, a state legislator, for claims of sexual harassment. Lawyer has entered into a joint retainer with Clients, and Lawyer's adversary has made an aggregate settlement offer to Lawyer's Clients. Lawyer has been transparent with Clients about the negotiations with the adversary and shares with them the full details of the aggregate settlement offer. The settlement offer contains an unequal division of a lump sum of money: $200,000 of the settlement will go to Client A and $100,000 will go to Client B. From the outset of the representation, Clients were made aware of and consented to the likelihood that Client A would receive a larger amount as an award or settlement from the case because Client A served the legislator for more years and was subject to more egregious abuse. When advising Clients on whether they should consider the settlement, Lawyer shares with Clients the full nature of all of the claims asserted by both Clients and the terms of the settlement agreement. Lawyer first engages in this discussion with Clients together so they are aware of all of the terms of the settlement. Lawyer then counsels each Client privately and separately and has each Client sign a separate written agreement with Lawyer stating that each understands the terms of the agreement and consents to accept its terms. Clients then each give informed consent to the settlement itself, and Lawyer forwards a signed copy of the settlement agreement to their adversary.

Is Lawyer subject to discipline for actions related to the aggregate settlement? If so, why? If not, why not?

A. Yes, because there was an inherent conflict of interest between the clients that could not be waived.

B. Yes, because Lawyer was required to alert the clients to the advisability of obtaining separate counsel prior to entering into the settlement agreement and to provide each client a meaningful opportunity to secure such separate counsel.

C. No, because the settlement agreement was in the best interests of the clients.

D. No, because each client gave informed consent to the terms of the settlement and was aware of the participation of each other in reaching the agreement.

14. Lawyer is approached by Client to handle a case asserting novel civil rights claims. Lawyer is concerned that these claims are untested, and she is not sure of the strength of the claims, particularly in light of recent jurisprudential trends suggesting the courts are presently hostile to such claims. At the same time, Lawyer believes she has a good faith basis for asserting these claims on behalf of Client. Lawyer wants to limit the potential exposure she may have for malpractice should she bring the case, and thus she drafts a retainer for Client through which Client will waive any malpractice claim she may have against Lawyer should Lawyer file the case on behalf of Client. The agreement is objectively reasonable and fair, and it only limits a claim for malpractice if Lawyer otherwise performs in a competent, zealous fashion. Lawyer consults with Client about the positive and negative aspects of the agreement and affords Client time to consider whether to sign it. Client ultimately gives her informed consent to the representation and signs the retainer with the waiver of malpractice claims.

Is Lawyer subject to discipline for securing the advanced waiver of malpractice from Client?

A. No, because the client gave informed consent after a period of time to consider whether to sign the retainer.

B. No, because the terms of the agreement were objectively reasonable.

C. Yes, because a client cannot offer an advanced consent to waive a malpractice claim.

D. Yes, because the client was not represented by separate, independent legal counsel when she entered into the agreement.

15. Lawyer runs a small private practice in an immigrant community. He cannot possibly handle all of the prospective clients that come to him for assistance. He does what he can, however. Since many of his clients are low-wage workers, he offers low-fee services at a sliding scale. He also does a fair amount of pro bono work and works for people he does not expect will ever pay him for the services he renders. He knows that's how it works, and he doesn't mind. He is building goodwill in the community and hopes that some of the clients may come to him for paying work in the future or will refer their friends who can afford to pay him. Because many of his clients work in dangerous occupations, occasionally he gets a personal injury case.

One day, a former client of his (Client), appears at his office with just that kind of case. Client works in a bakery, and she was recently badly injured by a truck delivering baking supplies to the bakery. Because the truck was not owned by her employer, she can sue the owner outside the worker compensation system, meaning the damages can be significant for the substantial injuries she sustained. One of the problems with the case is that Client is indigent and now cannot work. The worker compensation payments she can receive are not enough to pay her rent and utilities while the case is pending. Her status in the United States is legal, but, if she cannot pay her rent and utilities, she will have to move back to her native country, Trinidad. Lawyer knows that if she has to move back to Trinidad, she will not pursue her case, which is very strong. Because Lawyer knows the strength of the case, he is willing to pay for the court costs associated with the litigation, which

Client could never pay. He tells her that she does not have to pay him back. He understands her situation and does not want her to have to worry about paying the court costs while her case is pending. She has many other things to worry about, he says. Moreover, he knows the potential payout on the case could be large, and he is willing to keep the case going so that he can obtain his contingency fee in the litigation.

Was Lawyer's conduct ethical? Is Lawyer subject to discipline for paying Client's court costs? If so, why? If not, why not?

A. No, because Lawyer may not pay Client's court costs. Client has a responsibility to pay these fees, and if Lawyer were to do this, it would permit her to maintain the case, which would be an improper influence of Lawyer on the legal system.

B. Yes, because Lawyer may pay the reasonable living expenses of the client, including court costs, in order to ensure that she can have access to justice.

C. No. While a lawyer is allowed to provide an indigent client with funds to offset reasonable living expenses during the course of representation, he or she cannot pay the costs associated with litigation, such as court costs.

D. Yes, because Lawyer may pay an indigent client's court costs.

16. During the course of representing Client, Lawyer develops a close relationship with Client. Client is a very sophisticated businessperson who has brought a great deal of business to Lawyer's firm. The current matter on which Lawyer is working involves a multi-million-dollar antitrust action against Client's company brought by the U.S. Department of Justice. Client is very strong willed, as is Lawyer, and both are very careful not to allow their personal relationship to impact the professional relationship. Indeed, they are successful at insulating the personal relationship from the representation. After some time passes, they begin to date and have sexual relations during the course of the litigation. Client and Lawyer are open about their relationship and the leadership of the firm is aware of it. The firm reassigns Lawyer once the sexual relationship begins. A partner senior to Lawyer takes over the case and the relationship has no inappropriate impact on the representation. The new lawyer is successful in defending the antitrust action, and the DOJ agrees to not prosecute any appeal. Given the successful outcome in the case, there is no evidence that the personal/sexual relationship had any impact on the firm's representation of Client.

Is Lawyer subject to discipline based on these facts? If so, why? If not, why not?

A. Yes, because the relationship was unethical even if it had no impact on the representation.

B. No, because assigning the senior partner to oversee the matter was an appropriate and a reasonable step to ensure (and one which ultimately did ensure) that the relationship did not impact the attorney-client relationship.

C. No, because there was no evidence that Lawyer took advantage of the attorney-client relationship to commence a sexual relationship with the client.

D. Yes, because the client should have been given an opportunity to seek separate counsel and to give informed consent to the continued representation.

17. Lawyer represents a company that sells luxury linens. Lawyer is always treated well when he visits with Client to discuss matters pertaining to the legal aspects of the operation of the business. Lawyer always stops to look at the merchandise in Client's showroom prior to his meetings with Client. Client has fallen on hard times, however. Client must offer many of her products at a discount and may have to ultimately liquidate the business and file for bankruptcy. One day, when Lawyer is visiting with Client to discuss Client's business affairs, Lawyer sees a beautiful tablecloth imported from Italy that he would like to purchase for his home. He notices that the advertised price of the tablecloth has been reduced, and he knows the reason is that Client is trying to sell as much merchandise as possible to raise desperately needed funds to maintain the business and avoid bankruptcy. Lawyer goes to the store counter and pays a store clerk the advertised price for the tablecloth. He then enters the business office to meet with Client to discuss legal matters.

Is Lawyer subject to discipline for the manner in which he purchased the tablecloth from Client?

A. Yes, because Lawyer did not ensure Client had independent counsel in the transaction.

B. Yes, because Lawyer used his knowledge of the economic state of Client to the disadvantage of Client by purchasing the tablecloth at a bargain price.

C. No, because Lawyer did not use his position as counsel to Client to the disadvantage of Client.

D. No, because Lawyer paid the price that would have been charged to any patron of Client.

18. Lawyer failed miserably in his representation of Client in a medical malpractice case. During the course of the representation, Lawyer missed a critical filing deadline. Lawyer feels terribly about this and wants to settle the case with Client, who is now a former client because Lawyer was terminated by her soon after he informed her that the case had been dismissed, essentially as a result of Lawyer's malpractice. Lawyer does not dispute that he was guilty of malpractice in handling Client's case. Lawyer speaks with his insurance company and advocates that Client should be paid essentially whatever Lawyer had originally assessed as the value of Client's medical malpractice claim. Lawyer for the insurance company reviews the claim and approves it. Lawyer sends a letter to Client, informing her that he is offering her payment through his insurance company that will compensate her for the full amount of the alleged medical malpractice claim. He includes in the correspondence a check for the entire amount of what Lawyer believes Client is owed. In the communication, Lawyer asks Client, to accept the payment and to sign a written release which accompanies the communication admitting liability. Lawyer informs Client that she should take her time and reflect on the matter, suggesting that she take at least thirty days before making her decision. Client waits the thirty days as suggested, signs the release, cashes the check, and returns the release form.

Is Lawyer subject to discipline for the manner in which he attempted to resolve Client's potential malpractice claim against him?

A. No, because Lawyer agreed to compensate her for the full amount of her original damage claim.

B. No, because Lawyer no longer represented the client and no special duty was owed a former client in this situation.

C. Yes, because Lawyer did not advise Client on the wisdom of securing independent counsel and did not afford her an opportunity to secure such counsel.

D. Yes, because Lawyer entered into an agreement to settle a claim of malpractice without ensuring the client had independent counsel to advise her in the resolution of the claim.

2.3 Conflicts of Interest with Former Clients

One of the more challenging topics in professional responsibility deals with the conflicts that can arise between lawyers and former clients, including situations where lawyers "migrate" to a new firm and bring their conflicts with them. This section explores these complex topics.

19. Lawyer has just left her firm, Able Baker (AB), in order to work at a new firm, Chisholm Dean (CD). When working at AB, Lawyer represented a consortium of owners of sports teams in their advocacy before the U.S. Congress to preserve their antitrust exemption. Lawyer did not formally represent any individual sports team that made up the consortium but was given access to confidential financial information about each team. Lawyer's new firm, CD, represents Client, a star basketball player who claims she was discriminated against by her former team (Team), which is a team included in the consortium Lawyer represented when she was at AB. Client is seeking punitive damages, and the financial information Lawyer received related to Team during the prior representation of the consortium is relevant to Client's punitive damages claim against Team.

Would Lawyer's representing Client in the discrimination action against Team constitute a conflict of interest warranting Lawyer's disqualification?

A. Yes, because the representation of Client is substantially related to the prior legal matter involving Team.

B. Yes, because Lawyer is precluded from representing a client adverse to any member of the consortium by virtue of her representation of the consortium.

C. No, because Lawyer did not represent Team, only the consortium.

D. No, because the representation of the consortium and the representation of Client are not substantially related.

20. Lawyer used to represent Company, a company that develops wind farms. Lawyer assisted Company in seeking permits from the State of New York to operate wind turbines within the state and create wind farms there. That representation has concluded, and Lawyer no longer represents Company in any capacity. Lawyer has moved to Massachusetts, where Lawyer is also admitted to practice. Lawyer has been retained by a group of landowners on Martha's Vineyard who want to challenge the siting of a wind farm that Company seeks approval to construct off the coast of that island. The permitting process in Massachusetts is very different from that which Lawyer navigated for Company in New York, and Lawyer possesses no confidential information about Company that would be relevant in any litigation involving Company's application for a permit in Massachusetts. The landowners want to sue Company to prevent Company from obtaining final permission to construct the wind farm off the coast of Martha's Vineyard, and Lawyer handles that litigation. Company seeks to disqualify Lawyer from representing the landowners.

Is Lawyer disqualified from representing the landowners in the Massachusetts action against Company? If so, why? If not, why not?

A. Yes, because the matters are substantially related.

B. Yes, because Company is a former client of Lawyer.

C. No, because the two matters are not substantially related.

D. No, because the representation of Company occurred in New York State and the new action is taking place in Massachusetts.

21. Lawyer represented Bank in connection with a mortgage transaction with Buyer, but Lawyer's representation of Bank has concluded, and Lawyer no longer represents Bank in any capacity. Several years later, after Buyer has refinanced that original mortgage transaction through a separate bank, Buyer approaches Lawyer in relation to a new transaction with Bank through which Buyer will take out a business loan for the operation of Buyer's business. There is no risk that confidential information related to Bank that Lawyer possesses will be relevant to Buyer's new transaction with Bank. At the same time, there are issues related to Buyer's financial situation that Bank might want to know prior to entering into the transaction with Buyer. Buyer reveals all of the information that Bank seeks in considering Buyer for the business loan, but Buyer does not reveal information that a borrower is not required to reveal for the transaction. Still, Bank probably would have wanted to know this information prior to entering into the new transaction. Lawyer feels a duty of loyalty to Bank and reveals this information to Bank, even though Buyer did not consent to its release.

Is Lawyer subject to discipline for revealing this information to Bank? If so, why? If not, why not?

A. No, because Lawyer had a duty of loyalty to the former client and was required to reveal this information to it.

B. No, because Buyer was engaged in fraudulent conduct with respect to Bank, a former client of Lawyer.

C. Yes, because the matters are not substantially related.

D. Yes, because the information was Buyer's confidential information and Lawyer owed no duty to Bank to reveal this information to it.

22. A prospective client approaches Lawyer, seeking representation in a proceeding in which the local government seeks to seize her property by eminent domain. Lawyer used to represent the city government as outside counsel in similar proceedings, but Lawyer has no knowledge of any confidential information related to the prospective client's property or of the city's present tactics and strategies in such cases by virtue of his prior role as outside counsel for the local government. Lawyer's firm has terminated its representation of the local government in these sorts of proceedings and any other matters. Lawyer wants to represent prospective client and defend her in the eminent domain proceeding.

Is Lawyer subject to discipline for representing the prospective client in the eminent domain proceeding against the local government?

A. Yes, because Lawyer likely has confidential government information related to the local government's tactics in these sorts of proceedings.

B. Yes, because the prospective client's case is substantially related to matters which Lawyer handled for the local government.

C. No, because the prospective client's case is not substantially related to matters which Lawyer handled for the local government.

D. No, because Lawyer was outside counsel for the local government.

2.4 Conflicts and Government Lawyers

Some special rules apply to conflicts of interest as they relate to current and former government lawyers. This section explores these rules in detail.

23. Lawyer works for the prosecutor's office as a supervising attorney of the office's commercial fraud unit. The unit mostly prosecutes cases of identity theft. Lawyer is not involved with the work of the financial fraud unit, which tends to prosecute financial institutions. The two units do not share information about their respective cases, and Lawyer does not take part in strategy sessions with lawyers from the financial fraud unit. The financial fraud unit has filed a case against Taconic Bank & Trust (Bank). That suit is resolved through a large settlement in which Bank agrees to create a fund for all of the victims of its fraudulent acts. The firm representing Bank subsequently hires Lawyer to work at the firm and represent Bank as the administrator of the fund Bank created as part of the settlement of the case brought by the prosecutor's office where Lawyer used to work. The firm could not screen Lawyer from knowledge about the case because Lawyer would be fully integrated into all aspects of the litigation by virtue of the fact that Lawyer would be administering the settlement fund. The court before which the case was heard will retain jurisdiction over the matter to ensure proper administration of the fund.

Is it unethical for Lawyer to now represent Bank in the matter brought by the prosecutor's office in which Lawyer formerly worked?

A. Yes, because Lawyer would be switching sides and the firm will not screen him from confidential information about the proceeding that led to the creation of the settlement fund.

B. Yes, because the prosecutor's office for which Lawyer worked is now adverse to Bank in ensuring the settlement fund is administered properly.

C. No, because Lawyer was not involved personally and substantially in the Bank litigation while he was employed at the prosecutor's office.

D. No. Because Lawyer was engaged in public service while employed at the prosecutor's office, there is a rebuttable presumption that he may serve in this capacity in the firm that represents Bank.

24. Lawyer works in the legal department of the local city government. As a part of his duties, he routinely reviews confidential reports from public health officials about drinking water quality in the city. These reports are based on confidential disclosures made to the local government from several industrial actors in the community. Lawyer learns from one of these reports that in one area of the city, the drinking water has become contaminated with a chemical that likely comes from a local factory that produces the chemical. The chemical is mildly toxic and can cause intestinal distress if ingested in large quantities. Lawyer decides he wants to leave his role in city government to join a plaintiff-side firm that specializes in environmental litigation. Once he joins the firm, he informs his partners that they could file a lawsuit against the factory that produced the chemical because the factory has likely contaminated the water supply, though he cannot take part in the action, should be screened from it within the firm, and cannot share in any fees from such an action.

Is Lawyer subject to discipline for his actions?

A. Yes, because Lawyer is required to get informed consent from his former employer before sharing confidential information with his partners.

B. No, because Lawyer had no attorney-client relationship with the factory and thus was under no obligation to keep confidential the information about the water contamination.

C. Yes, because Lawyer had an obligation to keep confidential the information about the water contamination.

D. No, because the firm was planning on taking appropriate precautions, once it commenced the action, to screen Lawyer from the firm's activities related to the information.

25. Lawyer formerly worked at the Federal Securities and Exchange Commission (SEC). While a section chief in that office, Lawyer oversaw much of the work of the section, including an investigation that was conducted of BioCar, a publicly traded company that is designing electronic autonomous vehicles. Through the investigation, overseen by Lawyer in her supervisory capacity but carried out by more junior lawyers in the division, the SEC obtains confidential trade secrets about BioCar's research, and Lawyer reviews the files containing such materials as she supervises the junior lawyers on the matter. This research was germane to the investigation because BioCar's SEC filings trumpeted the great success BioCar was having in the field, and the SEC needed to ensure those claims were not misleading. The investigation is concluded, but no charges are filed against BioCar as the company is cleared of all wrongdoing. Lawyer finds that she enjoyed learning about BioCar's work and leaves the SEC to join the law firm representing Hessla, a BioCar competitor. Soon after Lawyer joins the firm representing Hessla, Hessla sues BioCar for theft of intellectual property. When working at the SEC, Lawyer was exposed to BioCar's trade secrets which are now at the center this Hessla-BioCar dispute. BioCar moves to disqualify Lawyer so that she cannot work on the Hessla-BioCar litigation.

Will Lawyer be precluded from working on the Hessla-BioCar litigation?

A. Yes, because Lawyer cannot be screened from the matter once she moves to the law firm representing Hessla.

B. Yes, because Lawyer was personally and substantially involved in the matter while working at the SEC.

C. No, because Lawyer was not personally and substantially involved in the matter while working at the SEC.

D. No, because Lawyer never had an attorney-client relationship with BioCar.

26. Lawyer was formerly employed as an attorney working in the law department of a local government. During the course of her service to the city administration, Lawyer was responsible for prosecuting housing code violations. As part of this work, Lawyer had knowledge of the confidential financial information of landlords whom the city was investigating. After leaving this local government role, Lawyer moves to a firm that represents landlords in the types of housing code violation cases she used to handle for the local government. In addition, Lawyer's new firm intends to represent one of those landlords, Able, in negotiations to purchase some commercial property that is currently owned by a second landlord, Baker. During Lawyer's tenure as a lawyer with the local government, Lawyer was exposed to confidential government information about Baker's economic situation that could be beneficial in Able's negotiations to purchase Baker's property. Lawyer's firm intends to screen Lawyer from the Able-Baker negotiations and apportion no fee to her from that representation.

What additional steps, if any, must Lawyer's current firm take to permit the firm's representation of Able in the negotiations with Baker?

A. The firm need not take any additional steps to enable it to represent Able in the negotiations with Baker.

B. The firm must obtain the consent of Baker to carry out the Able-Baker negotiations on behalf of Able.

C. The firm must obtain the consent of the city administration to ensure that it can represent Able in the Able-Baker negotiations.

D. Lawyer's firm must give notice to the city administration of the procedures the firm is putting in place to screen Lawyer from the Able-Baker negotiations.

27. Lawyer works for a government agency that has been investigating Company for potential antitrust infractions. The government agency concludes its investigation, in which Lawyer was involved personally and substantially. The government agency chooses to bring no enforcement action against Company, but the head of the agency testifies in a public hearing before the U.S. Congress and lays out its findings. The presentation is recorded on C-Span, and the agency head's testimony is published in written form on the agency's website. Lawyer leaves public service and joins a plaintiff-side law firm that wishes to bring a lawsuit against Company. Lawyer will take the lead in the case, and Lawyer will rely on the information contained in the agency head's written and oral testimony in preparing a case against Company. Lawyer was exposed to no other confidential information about Company that might be relevant to the affirmative litigation brought by private parties against Company.

Is Lawyer disqualified from personal involvement in the lawsuit that Lawyer's new firm will file against Company? If so, why? If not, why not?

A. No, because Company was never Lawyer's client and thus there is no conflict of interest.

B. No, because any information to which Lawyer was exposed that is relevant to the subsequent representation is part of the public record.

C. Yes, because Lawyer is in possession of confidential government information about the Company that will now be used against the Company.

D. Yes, because Lawyer participated in the matter personally and substantially as a government attorney.

28. Lawyer formerly represented Town as town attorney. During the course of the representation, Lawyer handled a range of land use planning and personnel issues on behalf of Town. He proceeds to enter private practice and has several matters that might involve bringing litigation or the handling of legal matters against Town. He reviews the work of the firm he has joined to assess which matters he could ethically handle, and there are three such matters he will need to review. First, a group of residents is bringing a challenge to the siting of a waste treatment facility in Town. The decision to take this action occurred after Lawyer left the employment of Town. Lawyer is familiar with the regulations followed in reaching the decision, although such regulations were adopted prior to Lawyer's representation of Town. Second, another group of residents wishes to challenge a decision of the zoning board issued after Lawyer left Town's employment; however, Lawyer had prepared pre-decisional and confidential memoranda on which the board relied in reaching its decisions. Third, a former sanitation worker employed by Town seeks to challenge her termination, which occurred after Lawyer left the employment of Town. The worker is bringing a constitutional challenge to the procedures followed by Town in terminating her, and Lawyer drafted those procedures when Lawyer was employed by Town.

Which of the following matters, if any, may Lawyer handle in private practice?

A. A challenge to the siting of a new waste treatment plant.

B. The challenge to the zoning board decision.

C. The decision to terminate the employment of the sanitation worker.

D. The lawyer may handle none of these matters.

2.5 Formative Assessment Quiz

Use these questions to test what you have learned in this chapter.

29. Lawyer is asked by a prospective client (Client) to handle a matter involving negotiations on behalf of an employee with Client's employer, Huli. Huli's CEO is married to one of the junior associates at Lawyer's firm. The firm does not presently represent Huli in any matter. The junior associate at the firm who is married to the Huli CEO will not participate in any way in the representation of Client. That junior associate will be screened from having any access to confidential information and will share no portion of the fee related to the representation. At the same time, the firm does hope that, at some point, it will be able to represent Huli. With that goal in mind, some of the named partners at the firm tell Lawyer to "go easy" on Huli in the negotiations. Lawyer is a senior associate at the firm and mindful that the partners will soon determine Lawyer's career path within the firm, including voting on whether Lawyer will make partner. Those named partners say the following to Lawyer: "Don't do anything to harm Client, of course, but don't hurt Huli either." Lawyer believes in good faith that Lawyer can still be a zealous advocate for Client despite these instructions. Lawyer advises Client of the fact that a junior associate of the firm is married to the CEO of Huli and that junior associate will not be involved in the case in any way. Lawyer does not disclose that the firm may want to one day represent Huli in the future, even if the firm does not represent Huli now, and does not disclose the guidance Lawyer received from the named partners at the firm. Client consents to the representation with knowledge of the relationship between the junior associate and the CEO of Huli only.

Has Lawyer taken the steps necessary to permit the firm to represent Client in this matter? If so, why? If not, why not?

A. Yes, because the relationship between the associate and the Huli CEO creates only a personal conflict that is not imputed to the firm and does not have to be disclosed to the Client.

B. Yes, because Lawyer believes in good faith that Lawyer can still serve as a zealous advocate for Client and nothing more is required to permit the representation to go forward.

C. No, because there is a potential conflict with respect to Lawyer's representation of the Client in negotiations with Huli, and Client must give informed consent to the representation in light of this potential conflict.

D. No, because the relationship between the associate at the firm and the Huli CEO disqualifies the entire firm if Client consents to the relationship without first securing independent representation to review the arrangement.

30. Lawyer agrees to handle a personal injury action on behalf of Client. Client is a diplomat who wants to sue his former employer, the federal government, for failing to provide adequate protection to its employees, like Client, who were potentially exposed to harmful toxic material that might have been placed near the embassy where Client worked. Lawyer, a prominent attorney who used to serve in the U.S. State Department over a decade ago, now primarily represents government whistleblowers. Client and Lawyer both want to expose the fact that the government failed to protect members of the diplomatic corps, like Client. Lawyer was not exposed to any confidential information while in her government service relevant to Client's case. While investigating Client's claims, Lawyer learns that some of her former colleagues at the State Department, with whom Lawyer maintains cordial relations, may have been involved in a cover-up with respect to the alleged injuries to Client. Lawyer fears that her efforts in representing Client might embarrass her former colleagues, who are now her friends, and that some will be named defendants in the action. Despite this fear, Lawyer believes that she can still provide competent, even zealous, service to Client. Lawyer discusses the situation with Client, and Client consents in writing to Lawyer's continuing to serve as Client's lawyer. Lawyer does not provide notice to, nor does Lawyer seek or obtain consent to the representation of Client from, the defendants in the action, who are all State Department officials.

Is Lawyer disqualified from representing Client in this matter? If so, why? If not, why not?

A. Yes. Lawyer, as a former government lawyer, was obligated to give advance notice to and obtain the consent of the Defendants regarding the representation.

B. Yes. Lawyer's relationship with some Defendants and Lawyer's concern for their well-being created a non-waivable conflict of interest.

C. No. Lawyer never represented the State Department officials, and thus no conflict of interest existed.

D. No. Lawyer can provide zealous representation to Client, Lawyer disclosed the potential conflict to Client, and Client consented to it.

31. Lawyer and Andy are in an intimate relationship. Andy is a successful songwriter who gets into a dispute with his record label. Lawyer is one of the nation's leading entertainment lawyers, and the firm has been itching to get Andy as a client. The managing partner at the firm is concerned, however, about taking on Andy as a client given that Lawyer is an attorney with the firm. The partner brings Lawyer into her office and says that the firm would love to have Andy as a client, and Lawyer would be the obvious attorney at the firm to handle Andy's case. Both the partner and Lawyer agree that Lawyer should handle Andy's case if the firm does represent Andy.

Is the firm subject to discipline if Lawyer represents Andy?

A. Yes, because such relations are unethical even if they have no impact on the representation.

B. Yes, unless another lawyer is assigned to the matter instead of Lawyer.

C. No, because the intimate relationship pre-dates any agreement to represent Andy.

D. No, provided Andy is given an opportunity to seek separate counsel and to give informed consent to the representation.

32. Lawyer is a successful private lawyer who handles criminal defense matters. A wealthy prospective client (Client), comes to Lawyer's office seeking assistance. Client is charged with taking part in a vast embezzlement scheme that cost wealthy residents of the community millions of dollars. Lawyer is very uncomfortable handling the matter given the nature of the charges. She does not think she can be a zealous advocate on behalf of Client. There are several defendants involved in the case, but Lawyer has not been asked by any other defendants in the action to represent them. Work on behalf of Client would not be in conflict with any other work Lawyer is currently performing or plans to perform in the future. At the same time, Lawyer fears other potential clients will not want to be associated with her for defending someone charged with embezzling money from wealthy members of the community, the very individuals she tends to represent. She shares her misgivings about handling such a case with Client, and Client says that he knows Lawyer is the best in the community and will consent to the representation even if Lawyer is uncomfortable taking on the case. Client states he knows Lawyer will be a great advocate for him because he believes in her professionalism and her desire to win above all else. Lawyer is grateful for the confidence, but she is certain she cannot be a zealous advocate given the charges against Client and the likely impact that taking on this representation might have on her future business.

Is it unethical for Lawyer to represent Client?

A. No, because Client has given informed consent to the representation even though Client knows of Lawyer's misgivings about taking on the case.

B. Yes, because Lawyer does not believe she can be a zealous advocate for Client.

C. Yes, if the representation is likely to damage Lawyer's prospective business interests.

D. No, because there are no conflicts of interest that would preclude Lawyer from taking on the case.

33. Lawyer represents a group of homeowners in an action against a local government that wants to change the local zoning ordinance. Of the five homeowners, four express their concerns that the change to the zoning ordinance will devalue their property. The fifth states that he wants to fight the zoning ordinance because he fears that low-income people will move into the neighborhood. Lawyer is strongly opposed to that idea's animating the work she is doing on behalf of the group and knows she cannot be a zealous advocate for the fifth client given his beliefs. Nevertheless, Lawyer believes she can pursue the legitimate claims of the four clients whose motives she can support and will therefore represent all five clients despite her misgivings about representing the fifth client. That fifth client, in pursuit of his own interests, wants Lawyer to raise several claims that would further his interests, but Lawyer refuses, even though these claims would strongly limit the extent to which low-income people could reside in the neighborhood. Despite these issues, all five clients consent to Lawyer's representation of them.

Can Lawyer proceed with the representation of all five clients in this litigation?

A. No, because the conflict Lawyer has revealed is not one to which the fifth client can consent.

B. Yes. As long as all clients consent to the conflict, the representation is proper.

C. No, because Lawyer has a legitimate concern that the sentiments of the fifth client could be ascribed to Lawyer.

D. Yes. Even if the issues present a conflict for Lawyer, the client can consent to representation, provided the consent is informed.

34. Lawyer has agreed to represent Client in selling properties that are part of a residential condominium development. Lawyer tours the building in which the condominium apartments are located and decides she wants to purchase one of the units for her personal use. Lawyer corresponds with Client about her intention to purchase the property. Lawyer agrees to pay whatever the current listing price for the property is, which is consistent with the price for which similar units are being sold. Lawyer explains to Client, in writing, the terms of agreement for sale, which, again, are similar to those in the sale of other, similar units, and such terms are generally fair. Lawyer advises Client, also in writing, on the desirability of obtaining outside counsel in the transaction and offers Client a reasonable opportunity to obtain such counsel. Lawyer also communicates to Client, in writing, that she will not represent Client in the transaction transferring ownership of the unit to her. Client consents, in writing, to the terms of the sale and that he understands Lawyer is not representing him in the transaction. Client, a sophisticated housing developer, agrees to proceed with the transaction without obtaining his own counsel.

Is Lawyer subject to discipline should she go ahead with the transaction, regardless of whether Client proceeds with separate counsel?

A. No. By advising the client of the desirability of having separate counsel and affording him an opportunity to retain such counsel, Lawyer went beyond what was required of her provided the terms of the agreement were fair.

B. Yes, because Lawyer cannot enter into a business transaction with a client unless the client has separate counsel.

C. Yes, because Lawyer should have provided separate counsel to Client at her own expense if she wanted to pursue this sort of transaction with the Client.

D. No. Lawyer may proceed with the transaction regardless of whether Client ultimately decides to retain separate counsel.

35. Lawyer at a private firm is handling a matter on a pro bono basis for an indigent client, Client. Client seeks to establish an important constitutional right regarding Client's civil rights. Filing the case requires Client to pay the typical court filing fees and will involve the reasonable costs for items like depositions and the acquisition of trial transcripts. Client is incapable of paying these costs and so the case will not be filed unless Lawyer pays them on behalf of Client. Lawyer agrees to do so out of her own salary. Lawyer does not ask Client to be responsible for these costs even if Client should prevail in the action.

Is it professional misconduct for Lawyer to pay Client's court costs and litigation expenses?

A. Yes, because paying these costs and expenses constitutes providing financial assistance to a client, which is unethical unless the repayment of those costs and expenses is expressly conditioned on the client's succeeding in the action.

B. No, because the costs and expenses were not uncommon and were reasonable under the circumstances.

C. Yes, because Lawyer worked for a private firm and only attorneys working at non-profit organizations are permitted to provide financial assistance to their clients.

D. No, because Lawyer is permitted to pay court costs and litigation expenses on behalf of an indigent client.

36. Lawyer has just left her firm of Able Baker (AB) in order to work at a new firm, Chisholm Dean (CD). When working at AB, Lawyer represented a local sports team (Team), in matters related to the construction of a new stadium downtown, handling all land use matters on behalf of Team. Lawyer's new firm, CD, represents Client, a star basketball player who claims she was discriminated against by Team. Client is seeking punitive damages against Team, and any information Lawyer received during the course of representing Team is irrelevant to Client's claims against Team.

Would Lawyer's representing Client in the discrimination action against Team constitute a conflict of interest warranting Lawyer's disqualification from that representation?

A. Yes, because Team is a former client of Lawyer.

B. No, because the representation of Team and the representation of Client are not substantially related.

C. Yes, because the representation of Client is substantially related to the prior legal matter involving Team.

D. No, because the nature of the legal action brought against Team and filed on behalf of Client is different from the nature of the legal representation Lawyer handled when she represented Team.

37. Lawyer represents Client Archer and Client Baker (Clients). Clients are plaintiffs in a case involving employment discrimination. Archer is likely to have a much stronger claim than Baker because Archer worked for more years under a system that failed to promote Clients under their employer's employment policy scheme which, Clients allege, was discriminatory. Clients both understand that, should the jury render a verdict in favor of Clients, Archer will likely receive more in both compensatory and punitive damages from the defendant company. Both Clients, who are fully apprised of the potential for conflict arising between them by virtue of the fact that Archer might receive a larger award than Baker, provide their informed consent to the joint representation arrangement, in writing. They also agree that Lawyer's fee will consist of twenty-five percent of any award or settlement, which is consistent with what lawyers charge in the community for this type of case. At the outset of the representation, despite a general awareness that Archer's claims are probably more valuable than Baker's, Lawyer does not discuss in advance the potential division of a settlement award as between Clients, should one arise. As the case proceeds and a trial appears imminent, the defendant makes a generous offer to Clients and Lawyer communicates the substance of that offer to Clients simultaneously, over a video conference. Lawyer explains to Clients that the defendant has made a "lump sum" offer of settlement and that the defendant does not care how Clients divide up the proceeds of the settlement. Both Clients ask Lawyer what Lawyer thinks would be a fair division of the proceeds of the settlement. Lawyer conducts a thorough assessment of the relative strengths and weaknesses of the two clients' claims and the seriousness of each client's claims in relation to those of the other. As a result of this assessment, Lawyer recommends a sixty-forty split of the net proceeds: Archer will receive sixty percent of the award and Baker the remaining forty percent, after Lawyer's fees are deducted from the settlement amount. Clients both agree to this arrangement in writing after Lawyer explains it to them, and Lawyer divides up the proceeds in accordance with this formula, after subtracting Lawyer's fees from the award.

Is Lawyer guilty of professional misconduct for any of Lawyer's actions with respect to Clients? If so, why? If not, why not?

A. Yes, because Lawyer should have fully explained the manner in which the proceeds of any settlement might be divided between Clients prior to the representation.

B. No, because Lawyer explained the elements of the aggregate settlement to Clients and Clients agreed to those elements in writing.

C. Yes, because Lawyer should not agree to settle a case in the aggregate when attorney's fees are involved.

D. No, because Lawyer fully informed Clients of the manner in which Lawyer was recommending that Clients divide the proceeds of the settlement.

38. Lawyer represents Association, a trade group of clean energy producers. The purpose of Association is to lobby for subsidies for renewable energy. There are thirty separate companies based throughout the country that are official members of Association. Lawyer does not have a separate attorney-client relationship with any of the individual entities that make up Association. While an individual entity may share publicly available information about each group, none shares confidential information about itself with the group. Individual companies within Association are under investigation for alleged tax-evasion schemes. Association attempts to distance itself from the individual corporate members that are the subject of the investigation, and those entities withdraw from Association. Association receives a subpoena from the Internal Revenue Service, the entity conducting the investigation of the companies that have now left Association. Lawyer is asked by Association to commence a lawsuit to challenge the subpoena. The companies that are the target of the investigation, and which are now no longer members of Association, believe it will help their case if the government is able to subpoena records of Association because those records will show that all members of Association believed that the way in which these companies obtained favorable tax treatment for their actions was consistent with how every member of Association operated. Communications around this issue were not confidential, however, and Association's position on this matter is posted on Association's publicly available website. Those former members of Association now seek to disqualify Lawyer from representing Association in the effort to quash the subpoena, claiming Lawyer has a conflict of interest with those companies.

Is Lawyer subject to a conflict of interest in Lawyer's representation of Association in efforts to quash the government subpoena? If so, why? If not, why not?

A. No, because the matters are not substantially related.

B. Yes, because the matters are substantially related.

C. Yes, because Lawyer may not appear on the opposite side of any matter against a former client.

D. No, because Lawyer never formally represented any individual company that made up the association.

39. Prospective Client seeks to retain Lawyer to represent him in a lawsuit that will raise creative claims under the First Amendment to the U.S. Constitution. Lawyer is nervous that such claims are so creative that they might be frivolous. She is also afraid that if she loses the case, Prospective Client, who is clearly litigious, may sue her for malpractice. Lawyer agrees to take on Prospective Client's case only if he agrees to enter into an agreement prospectively limiting any malpractice claim against her. Prospective Client agrees, and Lawyer drafts a retainer containing a prospective limit on malpractice claims. Lawyer suggests, in writing, that Prospective Client have independent counsel review the agreement and gives him an opportunity to seek such outside review, but Prospective Client declines to do so and signs the agreement.

Is Lawyer subject to discipline for entering into this agreement prospectively limiting malpractice claims in this manner?

A. Yes, because the client in this situation must have independent counsel in order to enter into such an agreement.

B. Yes, because a lawyer cannot enter into an agreement prospectively limiting malpractice claims.

C. No, because Prospective Client was given an opportunity to seek outside counsel and declined to do so.

D. No, because a lawyer may condition representation on a prospective waiver of malpractice, especially in cases in which the client is potentially litigious.

40. Lawyer is hired by Firm, a boutique law firm that handles government ethics matters, including criminal proceedings brought against former state workers. Lawyer used to work in the state attorney general's office which prosecutes workers in these situations. Firm is approached by Baker, a former state worker charged with embezzlement. Lawyer was involved in the investigatory stage of the Baker case while she was employed by the state.

Which of the following is NOT relevant to Firm's potential representation of Baker?

A. Whether Lawyer worked personally and substantially on the Baker case when she was employed by the state.

B. Whether Lawyer can be effectively screened from the representation of Baker given the size of the firm.

C. Whether Baker consents to the representation.

D. Whether the state consents to the representation.

41. Lawyer represents Able, Baker, and Charlie (Defendants) in a criminal case in which they are accused of engaging in a conspiracy to distribute pirated DVDs of newly released Hollywood films. Defendants are all indigent, and Lawyer has been assigned as counsel to represent all three. At the trial court level, during pre-trial conferences in the case and throughout the trial, no one raises the issue of potential conflicts of interest among Defendants that might arise due to the joint representation. The case proceeds, and all three are convicted and receive lengthy sentences. During the trial, Defendants presented a united legal front. To ensure that Defendants presented a united front, Lawyer decided to keep all three off the stand. One defendant in particular, Charlie, could have testified and implicated the other two defendants as more important players in the conspiracy; had Charlie testified in this manner, he would have received a lighter sentence. However, Lawyer was concerned that if Charlie were to testify, the other two defendants would get more serious sentences. Although the jury deliberated for several days, it ultimately found all three defendants guilty. In the end, Able and Baker received the same sentence as Charlie. Charlie's sentence was lengthier than the one he would have received had he testified on his own behalf, but Able and Baker's sentences were shorter than the ones they would have received had Charlie testified. Seeking to overturn his conviction, Charlie now raises, for the first time on appeal, that his representation by Lawyer was constitutionally ineffective.

What is the likely outcome of the request to overturn Charlie's conviction based on ineffective assistance of counsel?

A. Charlie's conviction will be overturned because the court failed to inquire into the possibility of a conflict of interest prior to holding the trial.

B. Charlie's conviction will be upheld because Lawyer provided competent representation to all defendants that was not adversely affected by the joint representation.

C. Charlie's conviction will be upheld because he failed to raise the conflicts issue at the trial court level.

D. Charlie's conviction will be overturned because the joint representation resulted in an actual conflict of interest that had an adverse impact on Lawyer's representation of Charlie.

42. In representing Client, Lawyer failed to file a complaint on behalf of Client in a timely fashion. Client's claims become time barred as a result of the expiration of the statute of limitations on those claims. Lawyer has a justifiable reason for failing to file the complaint within the statute of limitations: Client failed to provide information critical to Lawyer's making a determination as to the statute of limitations' expiration date. Nevertheless, Client plans to bring a malpractice action against Lawyer for failing to file the complaint in a timely fashion. Because Lawyer believes he did nothing wrong, he offers Client a modest sum to settle the claim, which is nowhere near the potential value of Client's claim had it not been time barred. Lawyer feels bad about missing the statute of limitations even though he does not feel it was his fault and wants to give Client something to resolve the malpractice claim. He proposes an agreement that will settle the claim but does not admit to any wrongdoing as part of the settlement. Client accepts the settlement, stating that it was likely all a misunderstanding anyway.

Was it unethical for Lawyer to settle the malpractice claim in the manner in which he did?

A. Yes, because Client was required to have separate counsel in negotiating the settlement of the malpractice claim.

B. Yes, because Client should have been advised about the desirability of having outside counsel and have been given an opportunity to obtain it with respect to the agreement.

C. No, because Lawyer and Client essentially agreed that the Lawyer did nothing wrong.

D. No, because Lawyer did not admit to any wrongdoing and yet compensated Client nonetheless.

43. Lawyer is a staunch advocate for animal rights. Her firm is approached by Company, which produces pharmaceuticals and engages in what it believes is humane testing of its products on animal subjects. Lawyer learns of the possibility that the firm will represent Company and asks that the firm not assign her to the case because she cannot be a zealous advocate on behalf of Company. The firm intends to take on Company as a client and does not assign Lawyer to Company's case. It does not impose any restrictions on Lawyer's access to confidential information, but it bars Lawyer from sharing in the fees obtained from Company and obtains Company's consent to the firm's representation of Company. Other lawyers at the firm assigned to the case are fully capable of providing competent, zealous services to Company and do so without incident.

Is Lawyer's firm disqualified from the representation of Company because of the conflict Lawyer has with the representation?

A. Yes, because Lawyer's conflict is imputed to all lawyers in the firm.

B. Yes, because the firm failed to impose effective screens that would shield Lawyer from confidential information related to the representation of Company.

C. No, because the lawyer's conflict is not imputed to all lawyers in the firm.

D. No, provided Client consents to the conflict.

44. Lawyer works as an attorney in the consumer frauds unit of the State Attorney General's Office. During the course of her work at that office, Lawyer conducted a confidential investigation of Company for a potential fraud claim involving a product. The Attorney General's Office had reason to believe that Company had defrauded its customers by selling a product that Company knew was not an effective disinfectant, yet it sold the product anyway. Many customers of Company purchased the product. It is likely that those customers relied on the advertised qualities of the product to their detriment. The Attorney General lost a bid for re-election, partly because the opponent was well-funded by a Political Action Committee created by Company. After the new Attorney General is sworn in, the investigation against Company is terminated. Lawyer leaves the employment of the Attorney General's Office, partly because she is upset that the investigation was dropped. Lawyer goes to work at a firm that is putting together a class action lawsuit against Company for false advertising involving the disinfectant. Lawyer never represented Company in any way. In fact, Lawyer was leading the investigation of Company on behalf of the State Attorney General's Office. Lawyer was exposed to confidential information about Company by virtue of Company's being the subject of the Attorney General's investigation. Such information would be relevant to any subsequent suit by private parties against Company related to the sale of the disinfectant. Lawyer intends to work on just such a civil action against Company while at Lawyer's new firm.

Is Lawyer subject to disqualification in an action brought by Lawyer's new firm

against Company that involves the disinfectant? If so, why? If not, why not?

A. Yes, because Lawyer worked personally and substantially on the fraud investigation involving Company's disinfectant while employed at the State Attorney General's Office.

B. No, because Lawyer never represented Company during the Attorney General's investigation, and thus Company is not a former client of Lawyer.

C. Yes, because Lawyer was exposed to confidential information about Company during the course of the investigation she conducted at the Attorney General's Office that would be relevant to the current litigation against Company relating to its sale of the disinfectant.

D. No, because the Attorney General never brought a formal case against Company; thus, the matters are not substantially related.

Chapter 3

Confidentiality

A critical duty the lawyer owes the client is to maintain the client's confidences. This chapter explores this critical obligation. It largely covers the different components of MR 1.6. Essential to understanding the duty of confidentiality is grasping what information is considered confidential and what information might also be considered communications covered by the attorney-client privilege. Once it is determined that the lawyer owes a duty to preserve information as privileged and/or confidential, the questions become when can the lawyer release such information and when is the lawyer prohibited from doing so. This chapter explores these issues and more.

3.1 Understanding Confidentiality

This first section covers material that will help you understand some of the basic issues surrounding the duty of confidentiality.

1. Client consults with Lawyer and hires her to provide representation in a matter involving a property line dispute with a neighbor. Client asserts that the property line is five feet into what is generally considered to be the neighbor's property, giving Client nearly 2,000 square feet of additional acreage. During the course of the representation, Lawyer obtains the following records:

   1. Several property documents in Client's possession containing evidence that the property line is inconsistent with Client's position.
   2. Some property records contained in the town hall supporting Client's position and some not supporting it.

   Lawyer knows that there is unfavorable evidence against Client's position but can make a good faith argument as to why Client should prevail in obtaining the entire disputed strip of property between Client and his neighbor. In discussing the case with Client, Client informs Lawyer that he would accept a deal through which the property line is moved by two feet into neighbor's current property. Knowing that some of the records Lawyer has obtained might preclude such a settlement, Client asks Lawyer not to share those damning records unless he is ordered to do so by the court.

   Lawyer believes in good faith that Client can settle the matter to obtain at least the settlement that Client has informed Lawyer he is willing to accept. In an effort to obtain such a settlement, but without consulting further with Client, Lawyer sits down with the neighbor's attorney and shares all of the documentary evidence he has in his possession. He believes doing so will help him appear trustworthy, which might facilitate the settlement Client is willing to accept. Despite Lawyer's best efforts, the settlement negotiations fail. Opposing counsel subsequently files a summary judgment motion in the lawsuit, using the evidence that was shared during the negotiations, and Lawyer does not object to its introduction in support of the motion. Although the motion is denied because there are genuine disputes as to several material facts, the judge indicates that she is disinclined to rule in Client's favor at the bench trial, which would follow the denial of the motion for summary judgment. The neighbor's attorney, who might have been willing to consider settlement before hearing the judge's views on the evidence that was presented in the summary judgment motion, now is no longer willing to discuss settlement further and begins to prepare for a trial.

Is Lawyer subject to discipline for revealing the documentary information to the neighbor's attorney?

A. Yes. The information was covered by the attorney-client privilege and to reveal it meant the privilege was waived.

B. Yes. Lawyer should have consulted with Client and obtained Client's consent prior to releasing the information in the settlement negotiations.

C. No. None of the information was protected by the attorney-client privilege.

D. No. Lawyer's belief that disclosure would help facilitate settlement meant that Lawyer could infer Client had impliedly consented to disclosure of the records to opposing counsel when Client discussed his settlement position with Lawyer.

2. During the course of representing a client on a tax matter, Lawyer learns that Client, a chemical manufacturer, inadvertently released toxins into the local water supply. The greatest threat from the toxins is to children under the age of two years old. Ingestion of the toxin threatens reasonably certain death in such children. Client has taken instant remedial measures to halt the release.

Is Lawyer subject to discipline if she does not reveal this information in such a way that would warn the public of the risk of ingesting the polluted water?

A. No. Lawyer is under no obligation to report the release of the toxins.

B. No. The risk of ingesting the toxins is not serious enough to justify such a warning.

C. Yes. The risk of ingesting the toxins is serious enough that Lawyer is obligated to report it.

D. Yes. Any harm to the community will likely result in liability to Client, and thus Lawyer must take such steps as are necessary to mitigate the harm.

3. Lawyer is handling a criminal matter on behalf of Client, who has been charged with attempting to defraud investors. Client is very difficult to deal with generally, and Lawyer and Client sometimes get involved in heated exchanges in which they disagree about all manner of trial tactics and strategy. In one of these exchanges, Client insists that Lawyer make a particular argument, but Lawyer is very uncomfortable doing so. Lawyer states that the strategy Client wants to utilize certainly has the potential to succeed, but it is risky and could have a negative domino effect: it could lead to the jury's ruling against Client on not just this argument but several others as well. It is over this issue that Lawyer and Client have one of their most heated exchanges, and Client threatens to discharge Lawyer if Lawyer will not advance the argument Client wants Lawyer to make. Lawyer informs Client that Lawyer needs time to consider the issue. Lawyer is under a great deal of stress as a result of handling this case and turns to a friend, another attorney who is Lawyer's consultant on issues of legal ethics. Lawyer commiserates with this consultant about the situation, sharing confidential information about Client's case in an effort to "blow off steam," as Lawyer says.

Is Lawyer subject to discipline for sharing confidential information with the consultant? If so, why? If not, why not?

A. No, because Lawyer was free to share confidential information with a third party in an effort to understand Lawyer's ethical obligations.

B. No, because Lawyer was permitted to share confidential information to resolve a potential conflict with Client.

C. Yes, because Lawyer may not share confidential information about Client, even to obtain a better understanding of Lawyer's ethical obligations.

D. Yes, because Lawyer does not appear to have shared this information in an effort to understand Lawyer's ethical obligations to Client.

4. Lawyer works in a firm that practices plaintiff-side employment law. Lawyer has built a practice on bringing very successful claims involving employees of Silicon Valley companies and challenging the noncompete clauses these companies utilize routinely with their employees. Lawyer conducts a brainstorming session for all attorneys who are members of the firm's employment group so that they can learn more about his practice in the event they face similar challenges. He also shares with them some challenges he is facing in his practice so that he can gain their advice on strategies he could use. Lawyer shares confidential information with the members of the firm, even information that is otherwise maintained behind password-protected firewalls within the firm's data management system. Lawyer also shares with the other members of the firm confidential communications he has had with some clients. As a consequence, should any attorney who has been briefed on the Lawyer's work seek to change firms, that attorney would be conflicted out of representing any party with a claim adverse to one of the firm's current clients.

Is Lawyer subject to discipline for creating potential future conflicts of interest with other attorneys in the firm by virtue of the fact that he shared confidential information with them?

A. No, because Lawyer is free to share confidential information within the firm.

B. Yes, because Lawyer was reckless with client confidences.

C. No, because the Lawyer's purpose in sharing the information with the other attorneys in the firm was to educate them and gain their advice on how to litigate his cases.

D. Yes, because Lawyer should not intentionally impede another attorney's potential career advancement by needlessly exposing that attorney to confidential information that would disqualify the attorney from future opportunities.

5. Lawyers work at a firm that is located in a commercial building with a coffee shop on the ground floor and several businesses located on different floors of the building. The managing lawyers at the firm learn from their technology consultant that the computer system they utilize within the office is vulnerable to hackers and is close enough to the coffee shop that someone in the coffee shop could easily breach the security of the computer system and gain access to their files. Lawyers work with the consultant to deploy state-of-the-art security measures to secure their computer system. Despite these efforts, a particularly crafty hacker is able to get into their system and access confidential client files.

Are Lawyers of the firm subject to discipline for this security breach and the hacker's gaining access to confidential files?

A. Yes, because Lawyers are responsible for any breach of their clients' confidences.

B. Yes, because Lawyers should not have utilized a computer system that could be breached.

C. No, because Lawyers could not anticipate that the computer system was vulnerable to being hacked.

D. No, because Lawyers took reasonable efforts to prevent unauthorized access to their clients' confidential material.

6. Lawyer, an experienced criminal defense attorney, represented Client, an individual accused of a criminal offense, at trial. Lawyer was very forthcoming and transparent with Client throughout the trial, reviewing trial strategy, discussing the evidence and arguments that would be presented, and going over the strategy for the closing arguments. During the course of the trial, the prosecution offered evidence of Client's whereabouts on the evening of the incident, providing the EZ Pass records that tracked Client's movement in her car on that night. After discussing with Client the effort to introduce such evidence, Client and Lawyer agreed not to object to the evidence's introduction because Lawyer was unaware of any basis upon which to challenge it and because Client essentially admitted that the information was accurate. Ultimately, the trial did not go well for Client; she was convicted on all counts, with the EZ Pass records proving central to the prosecution's case. After conviction, Client obtains separate counsel and brings a malpractice action against Lawyer. Client's new attorney articulates a non-frivolous argument for why the EZ Pass evidence might have been excluded. It is a novel argument that has not been tested before in a context like Client's case. Lawyer does not want to contest the malpractice case because it would require Lawyer to reveal communications protected by the attorney-client privilege related to the decision not to challenge the EZ Pass evidence.

Is Lawyer subject to discipline for not divulging communications related to the decision not to challenge the EZ Pass evidence? If so, why? If not, why not?

A. Yes. Lawyer is required to divulge this information in self-defense; otherwise, Client will be able to make a false accusation against Lawyer.

B. Yes. Lawyer is required to divulge this information because the charge of malpractice, if proven, would raise a substantial question as to Lawyer's fitness to practice law.

C. No. Lawyer is under no duty to disclose this information, even in self-defense.

D. No. Lawyer is obligated to preserve this information as confidential and there is no potential exception to that duty in this circumstance.

7. Lawyer has been asked by Client to help secure the lease on a prominent property in the Warehouse District of the local city where Client plans to open a high-end restaurant. Lawyer has been given Client's statement of net worth, which, Lawyer believes, in good faith, was prepared by an accounting firm in a foreign country. According to this statement, Client claims to own several large real estate assets and to possess a large trust fund. Lawyer is representing Client in an effort to assist Client in securing financing to lease the building and build it out according to Client's vision. Lawyer shares the statement of net worth with an investment bank that is doing its due diligence while considering making a loan to Client. Lawyer subsequently learns that the statement of net worth contains significant factual errors, not the least of which is that no foreign accounting firm exists, the statement was fabricated by Client, and the statement of net worth wildly exaggerates Client's actual net worth; however, Lawyer does not inform the investment bank of this knowledge. The investment bank approves a loan of $10 million and Client absconds with the proceeds of the loan, fleeing the country. The local district attorney who is pursuing Client for fraud clears Lawyer of any personal criminal liability and decides not to press charges against Lawyer for his participation in Client's scheme. Nevertheless, the investment bank files an ethics complaint against Lawyer for not divulging information about the fraudulent financial statement to the bank while it was conducting its review.

Is Lawyer subject to discipline for not revealing that the statement of net worth was fraudulent prior to the bank's mak-

ing its decision on the loan to Client? If so, why? If not, why not?

A. Yes, because Lawyer's advocacy on behalf of Client was not protected by the attorney-client privilege because it was in furtherance of a fraud, even if Lawyer was not prosecuted for it.

B. No, because Lawyer was under no obligation to reveal the information about the fraudulent statement of net worth even though Lawyer's services contributed to the injury to the investment bank.

C. Yes, because Lawyer's services were used to further a fraud that resulted in substantial injury to the financial interests of the investment bank.

D. No, because Lawyer did not know that the information was fraudulent at the time he shared it with the investment bank.

8. Lawyer formerly represented a Client, a wealthy business tycoon who recently died. During the course of Lawyer's representation of Client, he learned a great deal of personal information about her, including some of her aggressive and secret actions taken during several high-profile business acquisitions Client was able to secure. If this information comes out, it will likely be very damaging to Client's legacy. Lawyer learns that a famous biographer is considering writing a tell-all biography about Client and has been given a great deal of inside information about Client's business practices from one of Client's children. Client, when she was alive, shared this information with this child out of a belief that such conversations would still remain confidential. Client had a close relationship with this child and shared all of her business secrets with him. Client and this child had become estranged in the final years of Client's life, however. The conversations between Client and her child were always considered confidential by Client and occurred out of the presence of Lawyer. The child has not divulged this information to anyone other than the biographer and the biographer has not made public any of her findings drawn from these conversations, at least not yet. The biographer has called Lawyer to confirm some of the details provided by Client's child to the biographer.

Is it unethical for Lawyer to communicate with the biographer to confirm information the biographer has learned about the late Client's business practices from Client's child?

A. No, because Client is deceased, and the attorney-client privilege does not extend beyond Client's death.

B. No, because the information is not protected by the attorney-client privilege because it was shared with the child prior to Client's death.

C. Yes, because the information is still confidential and not presently known by the general public.

D. Yes, because the biographer is prohibited from probing the attorney-client communications through correspondence with Client's child, and Lawyer cannot be a party to such actions.

3.2 Attorney-Client Privilege

Within the body of information protected as confidential, which is covered generally by rules of ethics, information subject to attorney-client privilege is protected by rules of evidence, and those rules offer more protection in some respects than the rules of ethics do, as the material in this section shows.

9. Lawyer has been retained by a foreign business entity (Company) that wants Lawyer to assist it in navigating through export/import controls and U.S. customs laws. The CEO of Company does not speak English, and neither does Company's general counsel, who is an employee of Company. Lawyer does not speak any language those company representatives speak. Lawyer, CEO, and general counsel of Company conduct a video conference call to discuss Company's plans. Participating in the video conference session is an interpreter provided by Company, who is employed by neither Company nor Lawyer's firm. The interpreter translates the communications between the CEO, general counsel, and Lawyer. During the course of the conversation, the CEO and general counsel inform Lawyer that Company wants to misrepresent the nature of the products it is importing to the United States to mask those products' potential use for military purposes, which would violate U.S. export/import laws. Violation of these laws can result in criminal as well as civil penalties. Company representatives want Lawyer to advise them on how to get away with violating these laws without getting caught.

Are the communications between Lawyer, CEO, and general counsel of Company protected by the attorney-client privilege? If so, why? If not, why not?

A. Yes, despite the fact that an interpreter participated in the call.

B. Yes, because the communications were for the purpose of obtaining legal advice and client Company wanted them to remain confidential.

C. No, because the communications were in furtherance of a crime or fraud.

D. No, because there was a third party present for the call.

10. Client consults with Lawyer and hires her to provide representation in a matter involving a property line dispute with a neighbor. Client asserts that the property line is five feet into what is generally considered to be the neighbor's property, giving Client nearly 2,000 square feet of additional acreage. During the course of the representation, Lawyer learns the following:

1. Property documents in Client's possession contain evidence that the property line is consistent with Client's position.
2. Client communications with Lawyer indicate that Client is willing to accept a settlement of the action that moves the property line only two feet into the neighbor's yard.
3. Lawyer's research into the property records contained in the town hall reveal that some records support Client's position and some do not.

Lawyer knows that there is unfavorable evidence against Client's position but can make a good faith argument as to why Client should prevail in obtaining the entire disputed strip of property between Client and his neighbor. During the discovery phase of the litigation, Lawyer for the opposing party seeks the following from Client: "All information, in whatever form, relating to Client's claims on the disputed strip of property, including Client's position regarding his willingness to settle the dispute."

What information, if any, is protected from disclosure by the attorney-client privilege?

A. None of the information is protected by the attorney-client privilege.

B. Only the property records in Client's possession are protected by the attorney-client privilege.

C. Only the property records contained in town records are protected by the attorney-client privilege because they are harmful to Client's position.

D. Only the Client's settlement position is covered by the attorney-client privilege.

11. During the course of representing Client, Lawyer must visit Client at Client's place of work to secure his signature on several documents. Client works in an office facility run by Company, which markets itself as co-working space. Company markets to its customers the availability of what it describes as sound-proof "pods" throughout the office, where customers can have what Company represents as "confidential communications." Lawyer asks Client if he can reserve one of these pods, and Client is able to do so. Lawyer and Client utilize one of these pods, and after the documents are signed, they enter into a conversation about trial strategy that involves the sharing of information protected by the attorney-client privilege. Lawyer learns later that Company, as part of its effort to improve service to its customers, has been secretly recording conversations in the pods, including in the one Lawyer and Client used. Company says it needs to understand the types of communications its customers want to preserve as confidential so it can better cater to its customers' needs. Lawyer's adversary learns of Company's practice of recording these communications and makes a discovery demand for the recorded conversations between Lawyer and Client in the pod. Lawyer objects to the demand for discovery. Lawyer's adversary asserts that because a third party was able to overhear the conversations, those communications are not protected by the attorney-client privilege.

Were the Lawyer-Client communications carried out within the Company pod protected by the attorney-client privilege? If so, why? If not, why not?

A. Yes, because Lawyer and Client had a reasonable expectation that their communications were confidential.

B. No, because a third party that was not present to facilitate the communication overheard the conversation.

C. No, because Lawyer failed to act competently to preserve Client's confidences.

D. Yes, because Company's actions were fraudulent.

3.3 Grounds Permitting Disclosure

The previous sections explored some of the parameters of the rules of confidentiality and attorney-client privilege generally. This section explores potential grounds for disclosure in greater depth.

12. Lawyer has learned that her client (Company) has been releasing toxic chemicals into a local water supply. Lawyer believes this release of toxins could result in substantial bodily harm and even death in the community. Lawyer has learned this fact only through confidential communications with the CEO of Company, the individual designated by Company as its constituent duly authorized by its board of directors to act on its behalf. Lawyer is considering whether to reveal the information to local authorities so that such authorities can warn the community of the health risk posed by Company's actions. Before divulging such confidential information, however, Lawyer consults with the outside ethics expert that works with Lawyer's firm. This outside expert is also a lawyer but is not a member of Lawyer's firm, and Lawyer does not have Client's consent to speak with the outside expert. Lawyer shares Client confidences with the expert in an effort to secure legal advice about the Lawyer's proper course of action moving forward. Only information needed to secure such advice is shared with the outside expert. The outside expert says Lawyer is certainly within her rights to divulge information regarding the potential release of toxic chemicals should Lawyer choose to do so. Lawyer does not share the information with the authorities. A young child dies after ingesting the chemicals released into the water supply by Company. Had Lawyer revealed information about the water supply to the authorities in a timely manner, the child's death would have been avoided.

Is Lawyer subject to discipline for any of the described action or inaction?

A. Lawyer is subject to discipline for sharing the confidential information with the outside ethics expert but not for the failure to reveal the information to the authorities.

B. Lawyer is subject to discipline for the failure to follow the expert's advice and reveal the information to the authorities in a time frame that would have saved the child's life.

C. Lawyer is subject to discipline for both sharing the confidential information with the outside expert and for failing to make the disclosure in a timely fashion.

D. Lawyer is not subject to discipline for disclosing the information to the ethics expert and is not subject to discipline for failing to disclose it to the authorities in a timely fashion.

13. Client, a famous architect, is represented by Lawyer in a personal injury action. On the eve of trial, the defendants in the case make an offer of settlement that would award Client less than what she feels she can obtain by taking the case to trial. Lawyer disagrees and feels that the jury will either return a verdict against Client or award her less than what the defendants are offering. Lawyer and Client discuss the settlement offer, and Client wants to reject it despite Lawyer's advice. The case goes to trial. At trial, Lawyer performs competently, even admirably, but the Client is awarded far less than she wanted, and certainly less than the amount defendants had offered to settle the matter. Client commences a malpractice action against Lawyer, alleging that Lawyer's advice to her regarding the settlement offer was negligent and constituted malpractice. Angered by Client's action against her, Lawyer plans on introducing information related to Client's business practices, which Lawyer learned during the course of representing Client, that could subject Client to embarrassment and the loss of her own clients.

Is Lawyer subject to discipline for revealing the information she plans on introducing at trial against Client?

A. No, because Lawyer may reveal all of this information as a means of self-defense.

B. Yes, but only because the information Lawyer wants to reveal is not related to preventing reasonably certain death or substantial bodily harm.

C. Yes, because Lawyer may introduce only the information necessary to defend herself in the malpractice action.

D. No, because the information Lawyer wants to reveal will uncover fraud on the part of Client, and such fraud is not covered by the attorney-client privilege.

14. Lawyer represents Client, who is charged with creating a pyramid scheme that resulted in the loss of hundreds of millions of dollars in investments, mostly from small investors. Lawyer helped Client create the company but always believed, in good faith, like all of these investors, that Client was on a trajectory to create the next big medical technology breakthrough to revolutionize the delivery of health care throughout the United States and possibly the world. Lawyer personally oversaw the filing of test results with the U.S. Food & Drug Administration (FDA) that permitted Client to obtain the licenses needed to bring Client's products to market. Lawyer also helped to facilitate the sale of pre-public offering equity and investments in the company and then handled the initial public offering for Client. Client asked Lawyer to create offshore bank accounts where the proceeds from these investments would be deposited while Client's company was ramping up production of its products overseas. Client alleged that the purpose of doing so was to bring such funds closer to the entities providing the raw materials for Client's products so that purchasing such products would be quicker and easier. Lawyer initially did not think there was anything wrong with such an arrangement but began to get a little suspicious upon realizing that all of the countries in which Client wanted the accounts set up happened to be tax havens, and none really had any of the raw materials Client needed for production of the company's products. Client also began to ask Lawyer to convert much of the company's assets into cryptocurrency, which really raised Lawyer's concerns. Not long thereafter, Client was arrested and sued by the federal government for both criminal and civil fraud violations. Lawyer learns then that the tests Lawyer certified to the FDA were completely fabricated. Lawyer has all of the information about the offshore accounts and the "digital keys" to the cryptocurrency Client had Lawyer purchase. Concerned about the substantial financial harm Client's investors have suffered as a result of what Lawyer now correctly concludes was a giant pyramid scheme, Lawyer turns information over to the government to allow the government to seize those offshore accounts and get control over Client's substantial cryptocurrency holdings so that Client's assets could be used to compensate the victims of Client's scheme.

Is Lawyer subject to discipline for revealing information about Client's bank accounts and turning over information that would enable the government to access Client's cryptocurrency holdings? If so, why? If not, why not?

A. No. Lawyer was required to turn over this information due to the fact that it was in furtherance of a crime or fraud.

B. Yes. Lawyer was prohibited from turning over this information to the government because it was protected by the duty of confidentiality.

C. No. Lawyer is permitted to turn over this information because Client's conduct resulted in substantial financial harm and Lawyer's services were utilized in causing that harm.

D. Yes. Lawyer may not release this information unless subjected to a lawful demand for it, and there is no indication that the government has sought this information.

15. Lawyer represents Client, the landlord of a commercial development. Lawyer is authorized by Client to enter into negotiations related to the rental of commercial units within this development. Client is a sophisticated developer and has long handled negotiations on his own, without representation, but has since delegated this responsibility to Lawyer. Lawyer and Client both know that the longstanding, standard practice in the industry within the community in which Client operates is to share with prospective tenants, during the course of negotiations related to commercial tenancies, information related to the costs associated with renting commercial units in the community. Such costs include the typical charges tenants in a particular development pay for utilities. Lawyer is aware of the estimates of the costs associated with renting units in Client's development and shares such information with prospective tenants when they ask for it. Since the cost of utilities in Client's development tends to be higher than average compared to other developments in the community, prospective tenants sometimes balk at these charges and end up not entering into lease arrangements with Client.

Is Lawyer subject to discipline for sharing information about average utility charges that prospective tenants might have to pay should they enter into commercial leases with Client? If so, why? If not, why not?

A. No, because Lawyer had implied authorization to share such information since doing so was standard in the industry and community.

B. Yes, because Lawyer did not have express consent to share such information with prospective tenants.

C. No, because Lawyer had a duty to reveal this information to prospective tenants since such disclosure was standard in the industry.

D. Yes, because revealing such information was clearly not in Client's interest since it resulted in potential tenants' declining to rent properties from Client.

16. Lawyer is concerned that Client is engaging in money laundering activities. Lawyer counsels Client on the risks inherent in Client's business, the poor reputation of some of the foreign companies with which Client is doing business, the fact that law enforcement officials tend to scrutinize domestic individuals and entities that might conduct business with those foreign companies, and the punishment associated with money laundering under U.S. law. Lawyer consults with a legal ethics expert, a lawyer who does not work within her firm, to determine whether her actions in providing assistance to Client are unethical. Lawyer provides the outside expert with only enough information to help the expert determine Lawyer's rights and obligations under the law; however, some of the information Lawyer provides involves confidences pertaining to the representation of Client.

Is Lawyer subject to discipline for sharing confidential client information with the legal ethics expert?

A. Yes, because Lawyer was obligated to preserve all client confidences.

B. No, because Lawyer was permitted to share confidences as necessary to secure guidance on her ethical obligations.

C. No, because the information shared was not confidential because it was in furtherance of a crime or fraud.

D. Yes, because Lawyer should have conducted her own research and did not need to share client confidences to obtain guidance on her actions.

17. Lawyer represents Client in a case involving the dissolution of a partnership that provided accounting services to high-wealth investors. Client reveals to Lawyer some reasons for the dissolution of the partnership, which involved personality clashes and differences of opinion about the direction of the company. Client admits that one of the reasons for the dissolution was Client's desire to change the partnership's billing practices to increase the overhead charges it could pass on to its customers. Client had even prepared a slide deck to pitch this idea to the other partners. Although Client never presented this information to the other members of the partnership, those members knew that Client had prepared the slide deck and was planning to present it to them. The information contained in the deck was not protected by the attorney-client privilege, nor did it reveal any potential criminal conduct on the part of Client or anyone else. At the same time, the information in the deck would be embarrassing to Client if it were revealed to customers of the partnership. Client, who is now trying to persuade as many of the partnership's customers to stick with Client as their accountant moving forward, would likely lose many of these potential customers if Client's plan to change the partnership's billing practices were to become publicly known. Several of the other partners involved in the partnership dissolution proceedings have joined forces in this litigation and served a lawful demand during the course of discovery in the matter. As part of that discovery demand, these adversaries have sought a copy of the deck that Client had prepared to share with the other partners, which details Client's strategy for increasing the costs that the partnership

charges its customers. Lawyer asserts all non-frivolous defenses to prevent the court adjudicating the dispute from requiring that Lawyer divulge this information. The court rejects such defenses and orders Lawyer to turn over the information sought. Lawyer concludes, correctly, that there are no non-frivolous grounds upon which to seek to appeal the court's decision through an interlocutory appeal.

Which statement most accurately reflects Lawyer's ethical obligations regarding the information related to Client's proposal to increase the expenses the partnership can charge to its customers?

A. Lawyer is not permitted to turn over such information because it is confidential client information.

B. Lawyer may turn over such information now that the court has ordered it be released to Lawyer's adversary.

C. Lawyer is not permitted to divulge such information because it is subject to the attorney-client privilege.

D. Lawyer had no obligation to withhold such information in the first place because it was merely embarrassing and not subject to any protections.

3.4 Competence, Supervision, Confidentiality

Lawyers have an obligation to act competently to preserve their clients' confidences, and supervisory lawyers have an obligation to ensure that those working under their supervision do the same. *See* MR 1.6(c), Comment 18 to MR 1.6, MR 5.1, and MR 5.3.

18. Lawyer is the managing attorney at a firm that practices entertainment law and represents some of the most sought-after movie stars in the country. Lawyer is responsible for the practices of the firm in maintaining as confidential any material relating to its clients. The firm provides a wide range of legal services for its clients, including the handling of highly sensitive matters which could damage the clients'

reputations and harm their employment prospects if any information about the matters were to leak out. Much of the information about the representation of its clients is stored electronically on the firm's computer server; however, the firm has decided that the cost of storing this information in-house has become too high and that such storage is becoming too technologically complex for the firm to continue to handle it safely on its own. Under Lawyer's direction, the firm contracts with a remote storage company to retain much of its information remotely and on the cloud. Lawyer works with a cyber security expert to review the practices of several cloud service companies to determine which can provide the best security for the firm's data. The firm, acting through Lawyer, chooses IronCloud to provide this service. IronCloud is generally considered to have the best security system in the industry. Indeed, many law firms in the area have begun to use IronCloud because it is considered a safer option than attempting to maintain a high level of data security without assistance. Soon after transferring the firm's data to the cloud service company, IronCloud's servers are breached, and a great deal of confidential client information is exposed to hackers as a result. Much of this information is then released into the public domain, causing many of the firm's clients embarrassment and some to lose lucrative contracts.

Is Lawyer subject to discipline for utilizing the services of the cloud services company to store the firm's confidential information?

A. No, because Lawyer took reasonable measures to ensure IronCloud provided adequate protection for confidential information of the firm's clients.

B. No, because IronCloud, not Lawyer, was responsible for the data breach, and so Lawyer cannot be held vicariously liable.

C. Yes, because Lawyer's efforts were unreasonable given the fact that IronCloud ultimately provided inadequate protection for the confidential information of the firm's clients.

D. Yes, because Lawyer was under an ethical obligation to maintain the confidentiality of the firm's client information, and any breach of that confidence will subject Lawyer to discipline.

19. Lawyer is the managing attorney at a small law firm (Firm) and is responsible for overseeing all of the activities of its subordinate lawyers and non-legal staff. Lawyer is also in charge of ensuring that Firm's systems, which are all operating on the cloud in light of social distancing protocols, are protected from cyber security breaches. Firm has long contracted with a company, IT Solutions (ITS), to provide information technology support to Firm, including cyber security assistance. Lawyer feels loyalty to ITS because it helped Firm install its first computer mainframe back in the 1980s. It is also a company that specializes in serving law firms. Lawyer has learned from some of the subordinate attorneys in the office that there is a new and particularly insidious security threat that is menacing some of Firm's competitors, particularly those with the same internet security system utilized by Firm and monitored by ITS. A recent and relatively inexpensive update to the security system is available from the company that offers the security software, but Lawyer is resistant to purchasing it, saying that the security system was upgraded just eighteen months ago.

Is Lawyer subject to discipline for failing to upgrade the security system at Firm in light of the new threat? If so, why? If not, why not?

A. Yes, because Lawyer failed to act competently in light of the new security threat.

B. Yes, because Lawyer is strictly liable for not protecting Firm against any possible threats to its system.

C. No, because Lawyer acted competently by upgrading the system eighteen months ago and was under no obligation to upgrade the system so soon thereafter.

D. No, because Lawyer is not a technology specialist and does not have a special duty to know about internet security threats to Firm.

3.5 Specific Issues Related to Organizational Clients (MR 1.13)

Rule 1.13 provides special rules for serving organizational clients. While all provisions of MR 1.6 still apply in such situations, there are some unique circumstances that warrant special treatment, as this section explores.

20. Lawyer is an in-house counsel representing Media Company (Company), which has been the target of terrorist threats because of its reporting from a war-torn part of the world where a particularly vicious terrorist organization operates. Recently, one of Company's reporters was abducted by this terrorist organization. The terrorist organization intends to kill the reporter if its demand for a ransom is not met. The bureau chief who supervises the reporter instructs Lawyer to pay the terrorist organization what they want: the equivalent of $1 million in cryptocurrency. Lawyer is concerned that paying this ransom will require Company to violate federal law and could result in substantial legal liability for Company. Lawyer reports this information to the Company board, the highest authority within Company authorized to act on its behalf. The board disregards Lawyer's advice and goes forward with the editor's plan to pay the terrorist organization for the reporter's release, despite its clear illegality. Lawyer intends to inform the legal authorities of Company's plan to pay the ransom.

Is it professional misconduct for Lawyer to inform the legal authorities of Company's intent to pay the ransom? If so, why? If not, why not?

A. Yes, because the information will be embarrassing to Company if revealed, and thus Lawyer is not permitted to disclose it.

B. No, because payment of the ransom will likely result in injury to Company.

C. Yes, because payment of the ransom is likely to help prevent substantial bodily injury or death to the reporter.

D. No, because the financial injury that will come to Company did not involve the use of Lawyer's services.

21. Lawyer represents Company, which is under investigation for improperly dumping toxic chemicals into a local water supply. During the course of the investigation of the illegal release, Lawyer interviews several low-level employees who admit that they participated in the illegal scheme to dump the chemicals. There is potential civil liability for Company and possible criminal liability for the individual employees who participated in such illegal conduct. Lawyer's strategy on behalf of Company will be to argue that the employees were not working at the direction of Company leadership, and thus there should be no civil liability for Company itself. The information Lawyer receives from these individuals will be used to assist the local prosecutor in considering whether to charge those employees for having engaged in criminal acts. In dealing with the employees, Lawyer neither discloses that she represents only the corporation, nor does she claim to represent the employees. Further, during the course of her communications with the low-level employees, she does not dispense any legal advice to them.

Is Lawyer subject to discipline for communicating with the individual employees in the manner in which she did?

A. No, because Lawyer did not dispense legal advice to the employees during the course of her communications with them.

B. No, because Lawyer was representing Company zealously.

C. Yes, because Lawyer was not permitted to speak to these employees once a conflict of interest arose between Company and these employees.

D. Yes, because Lawyer should have indicated that she was only representing Company when the interests of Company and the employees became adverse.

22. Lawyer is a junior lawyer in a firm that has a robust white collar criminal defense practice. Lawyer is supervised by Sam, an experienced criminal defense attorney. Lawyer is hired to assist Sam in conducting an investigation on behalf of a company (Client) to determine whether any of Client's employees engaged in violations of criminal laws governing bank fraud, as is charged by federal prosecutors. During the course of the representation, Lawyer discovers that Client did engage in bank fraud, as is alleged by the prosecutors attempting to conduct their own outside investigation of Client as Lawyer and Sam conduct the internal company investigation. The violation, if discovered by those prosecutors, is likely to result in significant financial penalties for Client. Lawyer informs Sam of what she has uncovered and says she believes Client will likely suffer significant financial penalties as a result of this conduct. She also tells Sam her research indicates that financial institutions which self-report such violations receive much less serious penalties from federal authorities than those that do not self-report. Sam tells her that they should report these facts to Client. Lawyer provides her advice to Client's leadership on what action it should take. When the highest authority within Client company takes no action as a result of Lawyer's advice, however, Sam says Client is under no obligation to report the conduct to the authorities.

Is Lawyer required to report this misconduct on the part of Client despite Sam's supervisory guidance?

A. No, because Sam is her supervisor and she is required to follow his directive.

B. No, because there is no obligation to report this conduct, and Sam's guidance is reasonable under the circumstances.

C. Yes, because the potential harm to Client is significant if it takes no action, and therefore Sam's guidance is unreasonable.

D. Yes, because although Sam's guidance is reasonable, the professional obligation to report the conduct is clear.

23. Lawyer represents Bell Oil (Company), a large, multinational corporation that is based in Texas. Company is being charged with illegal hazardous waste disposal for failing to properly dispose of the by-product of some of its deep-water oil rigs located in the Gulf of Mexico within the territorial waters of the United States. The leadership of Company assigns Lawyer, outside counsel, to conduct an investigation into the matter. Lawyer learns that Company's low-level employees have been illegally dumping oil-production waste into the Gulf of Mexico, adversely affecting the migratory habits of one small species of shrimp that lives in the area but otherwise causing no other noteworthy harm. Nevertheless, the actions are illegal. If this information about Company's illegal activities were to be released to the authorities, Company would likely be harmed as a result, in the form of having to pay environmental penalties. Lawyer reports this information to Company's board of directors. The board takes no action and orders Lawyer not to reveal the information to the authorities. Lawyer feels compelled to report the information about the illegal waste disposal to the proper authorities because it constitutes a violation of the law.

If Lawyer reports the information to the proper authorities, will Lawyer be subject to discipline? If so, why? If not, why not?

A. Yes, because Lawyer has been tasked with investigating the matter on behalf of Company and may not reveal information that is the subject of the investigation to the authorities in these circumstances.

B. No. Because of the risk of injury to the environment, Lawyer is permitted to reveal the information to the authorities.

C. No. Because of the risk of injury to the environment, Lawyer is required to reveal the information to the authorities.

D. Yes, because Lawyer may not disobey a direct order of Company with respect to confidential information.

24. Lawyer represents the Acme Corporation (Corporation), which manufactures durable medical equipment. Corporation is under investigation for insurance fraud, and Lawyer conducts an investigation to determine whether lower-level employees were responsible for engaging in a fraudulent scheme to provide medical products to seniors who did not require such products. Lawyer interviews Employee, one of the employees implicated in the scheme. At the commencement of the interview, Lawyer explains to Employee that she represents Corporation as part of the investigation and that any information Employee shares with Lawyer will be given to the leadership of Corporation so that company officials can make decisions about how to defend Corporation against the fraud charges. Employee asks Lawyer if Lawyer represents him or just Corporation. Lawyer says that she represents Corporation but adds the following: "Depending on what you tell me, we could talk about whether I could represent you as well." Lawyer asks Employee if he wants to proceed with the interview, and Employee agrees to do so. Employee admits to his role in the fraud scheme and gives Lawyer the names of the other employees involved in the scheme. At the conclusion of the interview, Employee states, "It was really great to talk about this. I realize now how much it was weighing on my conscience. I'm really glad you're in my corner." At that point, Lawyer states that, based on what Employee has told her, she cannot represent him. Lawyer then informs Employee that she intends to share the information Employee gave to her with Corporation officials as part of her investigation. Employee protests, saying that Lawyer told him she would represent him and he considers her his attorney. Furthermore, he will not consent to her sharing those communications with Corporation officials because, he asserts, they were confidential. Lawyer shares the information with Corporation officials nevertheless.

Is Lawyer subject to discipline for sharing Employee's interview responses with Corporation officials?

A. Yes, because Lawyer obtained the information using false pretenses.

B. No. Although Lawyer may have obtained the information under false pretenses, she was under no obligation to maintain the information Employee shared with her as confidential.

C. No, because Employee's belief that Lawyer was representing him and that the communications would be kept confidential as a result were unreasonable under the circumstances.

D. Yes, because Employee was operating under the reasonable understanding that he was Lawyer's client, and thus the information he shared with her was confidential.

3.6 Duties to Prospective Clients (MR 1.18)

The duties concerning confidentiality only attach to clients the lawyer actually represents. However, there are certain obligations that arise even with respect to what the rules refer to as a "prospective client," that is, someone who has sought out the lawyer's services. *See* MR 1.18. This section addresses issues related to such individuals and entities.

25. Lawyer is on "intake" one day at the private law firm where she works. The office employs ten attorneys and handles matrimonial matters, among other issues. Lawyer does not handle matrimonial cases but does handle intake screening for all cases. Lawyer interviews a prospective client (Client) at intake, who shares only his identity and the identity of his spouse, against whom he has filed for divorce. Lawyer learns nothing substantive, damaging, or confidential during the interview. Lawyer informs Client that she will conduct a conflicts check immediately and will contact him in the event the firm has already agreed to represent his spouse (Spouse). Upon conducting the conflicts check, Lawyer learns the firm is, in fact, representing Spouse, and Lawyer informs Client that the firm will not be able to represent him. Client is upset and says that he refuses to consent to Lawyer's firm representing Spouse.

May Lawyer's office continue to represent Spouse in the divorce proceeding against Client?

A. No, because Lawyer failed to take reasonable measures to protect against the disclosure of confidential information.

B. No, because there is a conflict of interest if the office represents Spouse.

C. Yes, because Lawyer did not obtain information about Client during the course of the intake interview that would disqualify the firm from continuing to represent Spouse.

D. Yes, but only if Lawyer is effectively screened from the representation of Spouse.

26. Law Firm maintains a website that invites prospective clients to submit inquiries regarding whether the firm will represent them. The firm's website clearly indicates that any inquiries submitted through the website will go through a two-stage process. First, the inquiring party will provide information about the parties involved in the case. Then, after the case is cleared for conflicts of interest, additional information will be sought from the inquiring party. The firm employs an experienced lawyer to screen the inquiries that come through the website. One day, the lawyer reviews the initial information submitted from a prospective client. Based on the information provided, it does not appear that there is a conflict with the prospective client's case. Unbeknownst to the lawyer, the prospective client (Client A), had given her spouse's married name (Client B) through the website, not her maiden name. Client B is already a client of the firm and has been retained to represent Client B in the divorce proceeding with Client A, but Client B's name is listed in the firm's conflict-checking software under her maiden name, not her married name. (In other words, Client A has given a different name to the lawyer than that which is in the firm's conflict-checking database.) The lawyer clears the case for representation even though a conflict exists because the firm already represents Client B in the divorce proceeding. Client A then shares some initial confidential information pertaining to the divorce with the firm over the web portal and the lawyer reviews it. Only after reviewing this first submission of confidential information does the lawyer realize that the firm is conflicted out of representing Client A because it already represents her spouse, Client B, in the divorce proceeding between them. Immediately thereafter, lawyer contacts Client A and asks that she submit no additional information through the website. The lawyer is also immediately and effectively screened from the representation of Client B and receives no fee from the representation. Client A is informed that the firm cannot handle her case and receives prompt written notice from the firm of the conflict and the intent of the firm to continue to represent Client B.

Is the firm now disqualified from representing Client B in the divorce proceeding against Client A?

A. Yes, because the firm has obtained confidential information related to Client A and the entire firm's knowledge of such information is now inferred.

B. No, because the firm took appropriate measures after the disclosure of confidential information to prevent disqualification of the firm.

C. No, because the sharing of such information was unilateral, and the unilateral acts of a prospective client cannot result in disqualification of the firm.

D. Yes, because the firm is supposed to have reasonable measures in place to avoid the receipt of confidential information from parties that are adverse to those it already represents.

3.7 Formative Assessment Quiz

Use these questions to test what you have learned in this chapter.

27. Lawyer represents Client, a private entity that constructs water filtration plants for local municipalities. Lawyer is tasked by the board of directors of the company with undertaking an environmental review of one of its plants before it commences operations and begins supplying water to a community. In Lawyer's investigation, Lawyer discovers that the water filtration plant fails to filter out certain extremely harmful toxins. Because of this, the water filtered by the plant, if it is actually released into the water supply, is likely to cause serious bodily injury or even death to residents of the community. Lawyer reports this information to the highest authority in Client company, which takes no action. Lawyer wants to reveal this information to the authorities because Client's water filtration plant is about to begin operations, which will result in the release of toxins into the water supply.

Which statement most accurately reflects Lawyer's ethical obligations in this situation?

A. Lawyer may reveal this information in order to prevent loss of life or substantial bodily harm.

B. Lawyer must reveal this information if it is reasonably certain to prevent loss of life or substantial bodily harm.

C. Lawyer is not permitted to reveal this information because it is confidential and was acquired during the course of conducting an investigation on behalf of Client.

D. Lawyer is not permitted to reveal this information because Lawyer's services were not used in furtherance of the activities causing the potential harm.

28. Lawyer represents Client, who is charged with creating a pyramid scheme that resulted in hundreds of small, middle-class investors being defrauded out of millions of dollars in the aggregate. Client is under investigation by the State Attorney General's Office for carrying out this scheme, but Lawyer is not representing Client on that matter and Lawyer's services were not used in furtherance of the scheme. Lawyer believes that he should aid the Attorney General's investigation by turning over to the Attorney General Lawyer's privileged communications with Client. He believes he should do this because of the serious financial injury Client caused these small investors and because there is the possibility that such information might lead the Attorney General's Office to the location of offshore assets unrelated to the matter. The seizure of such assets could help to create a fund to ameliorate some of the financial harms Client caused the victims of the scheme.

What is the most appropriate description of Lawyer's duty with respect to sharing privileged communications between Lawyer and Client with the State Attorney General's Office?

A. Lawyer is required to turn over these communications to the Attorney General's Office.

B. Lawyer is prohibited from turning over these communications to the Attorney General's Office.

C. Lawyer is permitted, but not required, to turn over these communications to the Attorney General's Office.

D. Lawyer is permitted, but not required, to withhold these communications from the Attorney General's Office.

29. Lawyer A and Lawyer B practice together in the same firm. Lawyer A has been representing Client, who is charged with allegedly fraudulently manipulating stock prices. Lawyer A and Lawyer B speak frequently about Client, including discussing Client's engagement in a wide range of other transactions that have not yet come to the attention of the authorities but which, once discovered, could subject Client to civil actions brought by the financial victims of Client's activities. Those victims are typically institutional investors, and the damages such investors might have suffered as a result of Client's activities are hardly noticeable because of the high value of their overall holdings. Nevertheless, if those institutional investors were to learn of these illegal activities of Client which have not yet come to public attention, they would likely seek to bring civil lawsuits against Client for restitution and to deter others from engaging in similar illegal transactions. Lawyer A only provides representation to Client on the criminal investigations and did not represent Client when such transactions took place. Moreover, Lawyer A never provided services to Client related to the matters that might result in separate civil liability. In conversations with Client, Client makes it clear that any information Client reveals to Lawyer A about Client's activities is strictly confidential. Lawyer A, and Lawyer B, because of their conversations regarding Client's case, are both aware of the full scope of Client's activities. Lawyer B, who does not represent Client directly, shares information related to those other activities with some institutional investors who likely have civil claims against Client. Upon receiving such information, those inves-

tors hire separate counsel and bring civil actions against Client.

Is Lawyer A subject to discipline for Lawyer B's actions with respect to Client's confidential information? If so, why? If not, why not?

A. Yes, because Lawyer B should never have received confidential information about Client.

B. Yes, because the restrictions on Lawyer A that prohibit the release of confidential information about Client extend to all lawyers who practice with Lawyer A in the same firm.

C. No, because Lawyer B did not represent Client and the prohibitions on revealing confidential information about Client do not extend to Lawyer B.

D. No. Client's information was not subject to the protection of the attorney-client privilege because it was used in furtherance of a crime or fraud.

30. Lawyer learns that Company has been releasing toxic chemicals into a local water supply. Lawyer works at a private firm and is not in-house counsel at Company. Lawyer has been asked by the CEO of Company to investigate the matter for Company's internal purposes. As Lawyer learns more about the release during this investigation, Lawyer believes this release of toxins could result in substantial bodily harm and even death in the community. Lawyer has learned this fact only through confidential communications with the CEO of Company pursuant to this investigation. Lawyer is considering whether to reveal the information to local authorities so that the authorities can warn the community of the risk to health caused by Company's actions. Before divulging such confidential information, however, Lawyer consults with the outside ethics expert that works with Lawyer's firm. This outside expert is another lawyer but not someone who is a member of Lawyer's firm. Lawyer shares client confidences with that expert in an effort to secure legal advice about Lawyer's proper course of action moving forward. Only such information needed to secure such advice is shared with the outside expert.

Is Lawyer subject to discipline for sharing confidential information with a legal ethics expert who is not a member of Lawyer's firm so that Lawyer may secure advice about Lawyer's own professional obligations? If so, why? If not, why not?

A. Yes, because it is an ethical violation for the firm to not have adequate methods internally for conforming to the rules of the profession.

B. Yes, because Client did not consent to Lawyer's sharing such confidential information outside the firm, and the information was only learned by virtue of the investigation conducted at the behest of the company.

C. No, because Lawyer sought assistance to understand Lawyer's own ethical obligations and only shared such information to the extent necessary to achieve such understanding.

D. No, because Lawyer was permitted to reveal this confidential information to prevent reasonably certain death or substantial bodily harm.

31. Lawyer is sued for malpractice by a former client (Client). Client claims Lawyer failed to file legal action within the required statute of limitations. In Lawyer's own defense, Lawyer reveals that Client admitted that the claims she wanted to pursue were frivolous and that she had no case to file. Lawyer produces documentation of this fact and reveals to the court in the malpractice action that Lawyer informed Client that Lawyer would not file the case because it was frivolous. Lawyer also reveals evidence to show that Client was involved in several fraudulent schemes unrelated to the lawsuit.

Is Lawyer subject to discipline for revealing all or part of the information he revealed in his self-defense?

A. No, because Lawyer is permitted to reveal the information showing why he did not file the case and why he could not continue to represent Client.

B. Yes, because Lawyer was required to maintain Client confidences even after the termination of the lawyer-client relationship.

C. No, because Lawyer could not allow his services to be used as part of a fraudulent scheme, and thus there was no attorney-client privilege for such communications.

D. Yes, because the information related to Client's alleged fraudulent schemes was not related to Lawyer's efforts to defend himself from the malpractice claim.

32. Lawyer is approached by Prospective Client, who would like Lawyer's firm to represent her. Lawyer asks for certain identifying information of Prospective Client and learns right away that Prospective Client's adversary is already a current client of the Lawyer's firm. The firm takes immediate steps to screen Lawyer from the representation of Current Client, Lawyer will receive no fee from the representation, and Prospective Client is notified immediately that the firm will not be able to take her case. The firm does not obtain consent from Prospective Client or Current Client for the continued representation of Current Client.

Is the firm disqualified from the representation of Current Client? If so, why? If not, why not?

A. No, because Lawyer only learned identifying information from Prospective Client and took appropriate steps to protect both Prospective Client and Current Client.

B. Yes, because neither Current Client nor Prospective Client has given consent to the continued representation.

C. No, because receiving information about a prospective client cannot result in the disqualification of a firm from representing a current client.

D. Yes, because the firm received disqualifying information from Prospective Client that rendered the representation of Current Client subject to a disqualifying conflict of interest.

33. Lawyer is an entertainment lawyer who represents Client, a social media influencer. During the course of Lawyer's representation of Client, Lawyer learns that Client has started to enter into an arrangement with a supplier of dietary supplements that, it turns out, are just sugar pills with no medicinal value. These sugar pills are fraudulently marketed as memory boosters. Client is aware that the marketing scheme is a fraud. Most of the unwitting customers who purchase the sugar pills are elderly people on fixed incomes who are afraid their memories are beginning to fail them. Despite having no medicinal value, the pills will not cause any physical injury to those who ingest them. Lawyer informs Client that she will not provide assistance to Client with respect to this new business venture. Lawyer wants to report Client to law enforcement authorities for this behavior.

Is Lawyer subject to discipline should she report Client to the authorities for the scheme to market and sell fake dietary supplements?

A. No, because Client is engaging in illegal and fraudulent behavior, and thus the information shared is not protected by the attorney-client privilege.

B. No, because Lawyer is not representing Client in the dietary supplement scheme.

C. Yes. Although Lawyer did not obtain the information during the course of representing Client, the release of this information would be embarrassing to Client.

D. Yes, because Lawyer learned about the fraudulent scheme during the course of representing Client and no exception to the duty of confidentiality applies.

34. Lawyer represents Corporation, a real estate developer that is engaged in transactions involving the sale of homes in a residential development. Lawyer is aware that Corporation has used substandard products in the construction of the septic system serving the development and has misrepresented in its contracts with homeowners the nature of the materials used. Given these substandard products, it is reasonably certain that the septic system will fail within the next five years. The homeowners, although they are not likely to suffer any physical injuries, are almost certain to suffer significant financial harm as a result of the failure of the septic system. Lawyer knows Corporation is prepared to dissolve as a corporation soon after the last home is sold so that the homeowners will have no recourse against the corporation when the septic system fails. Lawyer prepared all of the contracts of sale of the homes, which included the false representations regarding the materials used in constructing the septic system; negotiated the contract for the construction of the septic system; and is preparing the documents to dissolve the corporation. If not for the contracts' false representations about the septic system's construction, the homeowners would have been unlikely to purchase homes in the development. Lawyer is considering whether to alert the homeowners to the false representations about the septic system that are contained in the contracts of sale.

Is Lawyer subject to discipline if he reveals the state of the septic system to the homeowners?

A. Yes. The information related to the septic system is confidential information, and therefore Lawyer cannot reveal it to an adverse party.

B. Yes. There is no evidence that revealing the information will help to avoid imminent death or substantial bodily harm.

C. No. Lawyer must reveal this information because of the nature of the harm the failure of the septic system will cause.

D. No. Lawyer may reveal this information because his services were used in carrying out Corporation's actions.

35. Lawyer is counsel to Company, a multinational corporation with branch offices throughout the world. The management of Company is concerned that some of its employees have been engaged in corrupt practices in foreign countries in violation of federal law. Lawyer is assigned to investigate the matter. During the course of the investigation, Lawyer learns that one of the branches has engaged in illegal environmental practices. Lawyer consults with her supervisor within the general counsel's office and they determine a course of action that will both mitigate the harms from these practices and resolve any potential legal liability Company may face for such infractions. Because of the liability rules in the foreign country, the fact that the highest authority in Company was not aware of these environmental infractions is actually a defense to further liability. Lawyer and her supervisor are confident the matter has been satisfactorily resolved and Company will face no further consequences from these actions.

Are Lawyer and her supervisor obligated to inform the highest authority in Company about the environmental infractions and the actions Lawyer and supervisor took to rectify them?

A. Yes, because Lawyer and the supervisor are obligated to report such information to the highest authority in Company because it is in the best interests of Company for them to do so.

B. No, because Lawyer and the supervisor are not obligated to report such information to the highest authority if it is not in the best interest of Company for them to do so.

C. Yes, because the highest authority must learn of this information in order to take necessary corrective action.

D. No, because the information related to the environmental violations and the actions taken to rectify them are confidential and protected by the attorney-client privilege.

36. Lawyer has been retained by Client to handle a matter involving litigation over a title dispute regarding a parcel of land. The matter is still in the early stages of litigation in state court. While researching the matter, Lawyer learns that Client has no viable claim to the property and confronts Client. During the course of advising Client to withdraw the claim, Client admits that she has no non-frivolous claim to the property. While the claim is not viable, asserting it would not constitute fraud or a crime in the jurisdiction; it would simply be frivolous. Client states that she wants Lawyer to press Client's case in court nonetheless. Lawyer informs Client that he will not assist her in presenting her claim to the court, and he insists that Client either agree to not present frivolous claims or find substitute counsel. Client agrees to retain different counsel. Substitute counsel who agrees to take on the matter is found, and that new counsel files a motion seeking approval of the court to the substitution of counsel. The court approves the request. Client files an ethics complaint with the local authorities responsible for overseeing attorney misconduct, claiming that Lawyer refused to act competently in the representation of Client. Lawyer wants to introduce the substance of the conversations between Lawyer and Client in which Client admitted to having no viable claim. Client objects to Lawyer's seeking to use evidence of such communications in the attorney-discipline proceeding. Client argues that this information is covered by the attorney-client privilege and thus cannot be introduced in the disciplinary action.

In the disciplinary proceeding filed against Lawyer by Client, is Lawyer prohibited from introducing the substance of the communications between Lawyer and Client regarding Lawyer's advice about Client's claim to the property? If so, why? If not, why not?

A. Yes, because the information is protected by the attorney-client privilege.

B. No, because the information is not protected by the attorney-client privilege.

C. Yes, because the information is confidential.

D. No, because Lawyer is using this information to defend himself against claims of misconduct.

37. Lawyer has long represented Client, a political figure who is now charged with obstruction of justice as part of a criminal probe. Lawyer is concerned that Client may also be responsible for potential corruption charges as part of a larger conspiracy, but Lawyer is uncertain whether the prosecutor's office is aware of these other potential criminal charges that could be filed against Client. Lawyer learns that some of the assistance she gave Client over the years regarding the application of campaign finance laws to Client's fundraising activities may have inadvertently given Client the guidance he needed to commit violations of those laws. Lawyer communicates with her own ethics counsel, another lawyer who works in a separate firm, about whether she is under any obligation to report Client's potential violations of the law, especially because it is possible Client used Lawyer's services to violate the law. Lawyer shares confidential information about her predicament with the ethics counsel. She shares only information that is necessary for the ethics counsel to provide ethical guidance to Lawyer. The ethics counsel is able to discern the identity of Client because of the high-profile nature of this matter.

Is it professional misconduct for Lawyer to have shared confidential information about Client with the ethics counsel?

A. No, because Lawyer's services were utilized in carrying out violations of the law, and thus she is free to share this information.

B. Yes, because Lawyer should have preserved the identity of Client as confidential.

C. No, because Lawyer was permitted to share confidential information in an effort to secure guidance on her own compliance with her professional obligations.

D. Yes, because Lawyer's services may have been used to further a crime or fraud.

38. Lawyer is handling an investigation for Company, a corporate client of Lawyer, for alleged violations of federal securities laws. If Lawyer finds violations of the laws, it is likely that the firm will have to report these violations on upcoming securities filing statements. Lawyer interviews all individuals who were involved in the conduct that has raised questions about whether Company has engaged in securities violations. Through the investigation, Lawyer learns that several employees did, in fact, engage in the sharing of insider information leading up to Company's largely successful initial public offering. Lawyer informs the leadership of Company about what she has found. Company agrees that it will accurately report this information as required in upcoming securities filings. Lawyer does not believe that such disclosure is enough for Company to satisfy its obligations under the law, however. Lawyer believes she may reveal that Company personnel have violated the securities law because failing to do so could result in substantial financial injury to Company.

May Lawyer reveal to the appropriate authorities that employees at Company engaged in insider trading?

A. Yes, because revealing such information could prevent Company from suffering substantial injury.

B. No, because the information Lawyer obtained about the conduct was the product of an investigation to determine Company's compliance with the law.

C. No, because the injury is only financial and Lawyer's services were not used in furtherance of the crime or fraud.

D. Yes, because the injury is the result of illegal conduct and Lawyer's services were used to cover up the activities.

39. Lawyer represents Client in an employment discrimination case. Client claims she was discriminated against because of her ethnicity, having been passed over for promotion and ultimately terminated from her job as a vice president at a regional bank (Bank). Client tells Lawyer, in confidence, that she also has a disability which she does not believe played any part in the discrimination she experienced. Client believes that the disability did not impact her performance and that Bank was not even aware of it. Client asks Lawyer not to raise the issue of Client's disability in the case. Lawyer believes Client's case would be made stronger if discrimination based on disability could also be alleged. Lawyer communicates with counsel for Bank in an effort to settle Client's claim before bringing an action on behalf of Client. Bank's attorney is eager to try to settle the case to avoid the filing of a potentially embarrassing lawsuit against it. Lawyer informs Bank's attorney that Client was discriminated against because of both Client's ethnicity and disability. Lawyer intends to use the information regarding Client's disability only for the purposes of negotiating a potential settlement with Bank. Lawyer has no plans to assert that Client was discriminated against based on her disability should the negotiations fail and Lawyer ends up filing a discrimination case on Client's behalf.

Strictly as a matter of legal ethics, and without regard to whether the disclosure violated laws related to health matters, is Lawyer subject to discipline for informing Bank's attorney that Client has a disability? If so, why? If not, why not?

A. No, because Lawyer believed in good faith that it would advance Client's case to reveal the information, and such information was shared only to achieve a settlement and in contemplation of litigation.

B. No, because Lawyer had implied consent to share this information because it would make Client's claims stronger, and releasing this information was a tactic designed to achieve Client's goal.

C. Yes, because Lawyer could not reveal any confidential client information of any nature without the express consent of Client.

D. Yes, because Lawyer did not have consent, express or implied, to share this confidential information with Bank's attorney, even in negotiations.

40. Lawyer is sued by a former client who claims Lawyer overcharged him. Lawyer represented the client in a range of matters in the client's personal capacity, including with respect to the client's involvement in several business ventures. Lawyer plans to defend against this action, and in doing so, intends to provide testimony related to the nature and value of the services rendered to the client, including reporting on a confidential investigation that the client had asked Lawyer to conduct into one of the client's business partners. The client is concerned that if information regarding the investigation of the business partner were to come out, it would be damaging personally and professionally to the client and would likely mean the dissolution of the partnership. Lawyer informs the client that the fees Lawyer is seeking include the work performed in conducting that investigation. The former client states that he will concede to pay Lawyer for the work involved in conducting this investigation and will not challenge those fees, but he will continue to challenge the fees related to other aspects of the representation.

May Lawyer reveal information about the work performed in conducting the investigation into the client's business partner to justify the overall fee charged to the client? If so, why? If not, why not?

A. No, because the fact of the investigation is confidential, the client objects to its release, and no exception exists to permit Lawyer to reveal the information related to the investigation.

B. No, because a lawyer is never permitted to reveal confidential information without a client's consent, express or implied.

C. Yes, because the client was involved in fraudulent acts that utilized the services of Lawyer.

D. Yes, because Lawyer is permitted to reveal this information in self-defense and to justify the overall fee charged.

41. Lawyer speaks to a potential witness in preparing her defense of Client in a civil case brought by victims of what is alleged to have been a fraudulent scheme operated by Client to defraud seniors out of the proceeds of their pensions. Lawyer receives documentary evidence in the form of emails between Client and the witness in which Client often described the investors in his scheme as "useful idiots" and "doddering old fools" who are "easily parted from their money." Lawyer knows this information would be embarrassing were it to come out in the discovery phase of the litigation. Opposing counsel serves Lawyer with a lawful subpoena seeking all email communications between the witness and Client. Lawyer does not want to turn over the email evidence because it will be embarrassing to Client.

Is Lawyer subject to discipline if she does not turn over the emails that are sought through discovery?

A. Yes, because they are confidential but not privileged.

B. No, because they are privileged but not confidential.

C. Yes, because they are neither privileged nor confidential.

D. No, because they are both privileged and confidential.

42. Firm has been approached by Iron Bank (Bank) to represent it in litigation against Lannister LLC (Lannister), a family-owned company known for "always paying its debts." This time at least, Bank claims Lannister has not made payments on a mortgage Bank holds on the property known as Casterly Rock. While considering whether to represent Bank, leadership at Firm have a discussion with a junior associate at Firm, Arya Stark (Stark), who used to work at the firm that represents Lannister. Stark is asked by the leadership of Firm whether Stark thinks Firm should represent Bank in a foreclosure action against Lannister related to Casterly Rock. Stark warns the leadership of Firm that Lannister can be a vicious adversary, but by virtue of Stark's prior representation of Lannister, Stark knows that Lannister is under some financial pressure and is facing a potential hostile takeover by WinterFell Properties, a minority shareholder in the Lannister corporation. This is not public knowledge. Stark informs the leadership of Firm that, based on Stark's knowledge of this information, she believes Lannister will probably surrender Casterly Rock without much of a fight because it is more interested in addressing the potential hostile takeover bid. Firm agrees to represent Bank and proceeds immediately to screen Stark from the representation of Iron Bank. After commencing a foreclosure action against Lannister on Casterly Rock, Lannister's attorneys quickly agree to turn over the subject property to Bank without even submitting an answer in the foreclosure action, just as Stark predicted would happen. Stark is apportioned no part of the fee Bank pays Firm, and Stark did not participate in any strategy sessions after Firm agreed to represent Bank.

Was it professional misconduct for Firm to communicate with Stark in the manner in which it did in advance of agreeing to represent Bank? If so, why? If not, why not?

A. No, because Firm was permitted to communicate with Stark prior to agreeing to represent Bank.

B. No, because the representation of Bank was not substantially related to Stark's former representation of Lannister.

C. Yes, because Firm should have instituted screens as soon as practicable once it learned of the potential conflict, even before Firm agreed to represent Bank.

D. Yes, because once Firm realized Stark had a conflict with the potential representation of Bank, it should have cut off all communications with Bank and declined the representation.

43. Lawyer is on "intake" one day at the private law firm where she works. The office employs ten attorneys and handles matrimonial matters, among other issues. The lawyer does not handle matrimonial cases but does handle intake screening for all cases. Lawyer interviews a prospective client, Paul, at intake, who shares confidential information with Lawyer about his case, providing a wide range of information about every aspect of the ongoing dispute with his estranged spouse, against whom he has filed for divorce. Lawyer learns a great deal about Paul's claims against his estranged spouse, particularly secret financial information about his personal investment holdings, which he has tried to shield from the estranged spouse so that they do not become a part of the division of assets in the case. Toward the end of the interview, Paul gives Lawyer the name of his spouse—Sarah. Lawyer then informs Paul that the office will run a conflicts check to determine if there are any conflicts issues and that someone will get back to him shortly after that. Lawyer runs a check with the office's conflict-checking software and determines that the office has already agreed to represent Sarah in the divorce action against Paul. Lawyer contacts Paul and informs him that the office cannot represent him but intends to continue to represent Sarah.

May Lawyer's office continue to represent Sarah, Paul's spouse, in the divorce proceeding against Paul?

A. Yes, if both Paul and Sarah give informed consent to the representation, confirmed in writing.

B. No, because Lawyer failed to take reasonable measures to protect against the disclosure of confidential information.

C. No, because there is a conflict of interest if the office represents Sarah.

D. Yes, provided Lawyer is effectively screened from the representation of Sarah.

Chapter 4

Attorney's Fees

Most attorney-client relationships involve the payment of fees by the client to the lawyer for the lawyer's services. Fee arrangements present potential risks for the lawyer, and this chapter explores those risks and provides guidance regarding the issues of professional responsibility that surround attorney's fees.

4.1 Understanding Attorney's Fees

This section provides a basic introduction to the issue of attorney's fees, which is mostly addressed in MR 1.5. At the same time, because fees can sometimes address issues of conflicts, or what happens to a lawyer's fee after they are discharged, other rules and principles sometimes come into play, as this section shows.

1. Lawyer agrees to represent Client in a personal injury action. Lawyer and Client enter into a formal, oral retainer agreement that Lawyer will take thirty percent of any award, which is consistent with the practice in the community for this type of proceeding. Lawyer understands she will not charge a fee if she does not prevail in the case on behalf of Client. Lawyer explains that she will pursue punitive damages in the case as part of the action, which could increase the amount Client is able to obtain through the litigation, and Client is excited about the prospect of a large award. Through exceptionally creative and zealous advocacy, Lawyer is able to secure a large damage award, which includes a large sum that the jury assigns as punitive damages. Lawyer receives the payment from the defendant and places the payment in her escrow account. She then provides an itemized bill regarding the portion of the award she wishes to retain from the escrow account as her fee, and the balance she will forward to the Client. Client refuses to authorize the release of the funds to Lawyer that Lawyer alleges represents the fees she is owed.

Were Lawyer's actions regarding the fee arrangement proper?

A. Yes, because the fee was not unreasonable and was accepted by the client at the outset of the representation.

B. Yes, because Lawyer was exceptionally zealous in her advocacy and secured a large judgment for her client, and she was thus entitled to a premium for her services.

C. No, because the agreement regarding fees was not made in writing.

D. No, because the fee was excessive given the large punitive damages award.

2. Lawyer is approached by a client who alleges that she was physically abused while in police custody after being arrested for an act of alleged larceny. Lawyer agrees to represent Client in the criminal case but also plans to file a civil action for the damages Client allegedly sustained as a result of the abuse while in custody. Lawyer agrees in writing to represent client on contingency in both cases, saying that she believes she can get the larceny charges dismissed, particularly if Client will reduce the amount at which she will agree to settle the civil case. Lawyer offers to take twenty-five percent of any award in the civil case, an amount less than what is typically charged in the community for such matters. With respect to the criminal case, Lawyer says that she will not ask Client to pay Lawyer if Client is convicted of the larceny. If she is acquitted or accepts a plea at a lesser amount than the initial charge, she will only seek from Client the equivalent of $250 an hour for the criminal case representation, a rate far less than that which is typically charged in the community.

Is Lawyer subject to discipline for either or both of these fee arrangements?

A. Lawyer is subject to discipline for both fee arrangements.

B. Lawyer is subject to discipline for the fee arrangement in the civil case but not the criminal case.

C. Lawyer is not subject to discipline for either of these fee arrangements.

D. Lawyer is subject to discipline for the fee arrangement in the criminal case but not the civil case.

3. Lawyer represents financial institutions in mortgage foreclosure actions. Lawyer has handled such cases for a local bank, Lannister, over the years. She has not handled cases for Lannister for several years, however. When representing Lannister, she entered into a new retainer for each foreclosure action she handled for the bank. Since she last represented Lannister, her fee structure has changed. Lawyer now charges $2,000 to handle a mortgage foreclosure action, which is over fifty percent greater than what she used to charge Lannister when she represented it. This is still commensurate with what other lawyers in the community charge for similar matters. A representative of Lannister reaches out to Lawyer to ask her to represent it in several upcoming mortgage foreclosure actions. Lawyer forwards a new, written retainer to Lannister that includes her new fee structure. The Lannister representative signs the retainer and accepts the new fee structure.

Is it professional misconduct for Lawyer to have changed the fee structure with Lannister in this manner?

A. Yes, because Lawyer's new fee represents an unreasonable increase in the total amount charged for each representation.

B. No, because Lawyer's new fee was reasonable and it was appropriate for Lawyer to charge Lannister this new fee.

C. Yes, because Lawyer was required to advise Lannister of the desirability of obtaining outside counsel with respect to the retainer and should have given the bank an opportunity to secure such outside counsel.

D. No, because Lawyer properly communicated the change in the fee structure to Lannister.

4. Parent reaches out to and secures the representation of Lawyer to defend her adult son who is accused of identity theft. Parent is of high income and pays for Lawyer's services. Parent tells Lawyer that she wants a "regular report" of how the representation is going. Lawyer and Parent enter into an agreement solely between the two of them indicating that Lawyer should update Parent on a monthly basis about the progress of the case. Son consents to this arrangement in writing, and he is fully informed of the potential ramifications of such consent. Lawyer begins an investigation and learns that Son has been a prolific hacker, having hacked even Parent's credit cards. Lawyer discovers further that Son has stolen roughly $1,000 from Parent, but that theft was not a subject of the criminal charges faced by Son and which Lawyer is handling on behalf of Son. Son directs Lawyer not to tell Parent of the theft. As far as Lawyer can tell, this conduct is well in the past, long before Lawyer agreed to represent Son, and Son has agreed he will never do it again. As part of Lawyer's monthly report to Parent, Lawyer informs Parent of the credit card theft by Son of Parent.

Is Lawyer subject to discipline for any of these actions?

A. No, because Son gave informed consent to the Lawyer to confer with Parent on the subject matter of the representation.

B. No, because Lawyer could exercise her professional judgment in revealing confidences from Son to mitigate the financial harm Parent has suffered at the hands of Lawyer's client.

C. Yes, because Son revoked the consent to share the confidential information with the Parent.

D. Yes, because Lawyer should never have sought the consent of Son to reveal the confidential information to the Parent in the first place.

5. Lawyer enters into an agreement to represent Client in litigation regarding a complex business transaction that failed. The case could take years to litigate, and Lawyer fears that he may lose other clients in the future should the case go to trial because he will be so preoccupied with representing Client during the trial in this matter. Lawyer's retainer, which is in writing, states that lawyer will receive $250 an hour for her services, which is reasonable in light of the fees a lawyer of similar experience charges in the community. The retainer states that the $2,500 initial deposit is non-refundable if the client terminates the agreement within one week of the retainer's being signed by the parties. Lawyer works four hours on client's case, which mostly involves trying to reach a settlement between the parties. Much to everyone's surprise, the case settles immediately, with Lawyer only having to work for those four hours on the case. Client terminates the agreement between Lawyer and Client, and yet Lawyer does not return any portion of his retainer. Given the successful outcome, the amount the Lawyer ultimately earned, roughly $625 per hour, was not objectively unreasonable in light of community standards.

Is Lawyer subject to discipline for keeping the entire retainer amount at the conclusion of the representation?

A. Yes, because Lawyer did not earn the entire retainer amount based upon the hourly rate the parties agreed Lawyer would charge.

B. Yes, because the hourly rate Lawyer would ultimately earn exceeded that which an attorney would generally charge in the community.

C. No, because Client obtained a favorable settlement.

D. No, because Client entered into the agreement knowing that Lawyer might lose other clients for taking on the matter.

6. Lawyer has been representing a client in a complex antitrust case that is likely to result in a multi-million-dollar damage award in favor of the client. Lawyer has been working for several years on the matter. It is one of the most significant cases Lawyer has ever handled. Although Lawyer was a relatively junior lawyer when the case was first commenced, she has since developed into a seasoned attorney and is well-positioned to handle the trial competently and with zeal. Nevertheless, Lawyer's client begins to worry about the possible outcome of the trial and wants to retain a new lawyer with a higher profile and more name recognition, out of a belief that such a new lawyer, with a better reputation, might impress the jury. Client discharges Lawyer and hires the higher-profile attorney. Lawyer was to be paid on a contingency fee basis and will have to await the outcome of the trial to determine whether and to what extent she will be compensated for her years of work. Lawyer has many boxes of records and exhibits that she was preparing for trial, and she is uncomfortable sharing all of this work product with the new counsel. She believes this work product constitutes the fruit of her labor and that she should not have to share it with the new counsel without being paid in some way for that work. Any delay in sharing this information with Client's new counsel could have an adverse impact on that new lawyer's ability to represent Client.

Is it unethical for Lawyer to withhold the trial preparation materials from the new counsel until she is compensated for her work?

A. Yes, because Lawyer had entered into a contingency fee arrangement, and until that contingency occurs, she must cooperate with the new counsel.

B. No, because Lawyer was improperly discharged and is entitled to be compensated for her work.

C. Yes, because despite the manner in which Lawyer was terminated, she is obligated to see the representation through to completion and must cooperate with the new counsel.

D. No, because Lawyer is under no obligation to cooperate with the new counsel in this way.

7. Lawyer has represented Client in defense of worker compensation claims made against Client, an employer in the community. Lawyer has historically charged this client and some other employers he represents $1,000 for each case, which tend to involve fairly routine matters. Lawyer's retainer with his clients generally and with this client in particular indicates that this amount is the standard flat rate that will be charged for such cases. One case he handles for Client becomes extremely protracted, however, and Lawyer feels that, given his experience, expertise, and the stakes involved, he should be paid on an hourly basis for this work. Because he has a long-standing relationship with Client, Lawyer bills Client at half the normal hourly rate he charges clients that are not billed at the flat rate. The $120 per hour rate he charges Client in this case is lower than what most lawyers in the community would charge. The bill for this case, based upon an hourly rate, comes to a total of $4,000, which is a reasonable total for a protracted worker compensation case in the community.

May Lawyer charge the Client $4,000 for this protracted worker compensation case?

A. No. The $4,000 charge is unethical because it does not correspond to what the Lawyer typically charges in worker compensation cases.

B. No. Lawyer's decision to change the fee structure for this case should have been communicated to the client in advance of that change.

C. Yes. Lawyer's hourly rate is reasonable because it is below what he would generally charge and because it is in line with what other lawyers in the community charge for such cases.

D. Yes. Lawyer's fee is reasonable in terms of the total amount charged for a protracted worker compensation case.

4.2 Assessing Reasonable Attorney's Fees

The general requirement regarding attorney's fees, as set forth in MR 1.5, is that a lawyer's fee must be reasonable. This section provides guidance on what makes a reasonable—and unreasonable—fee.

8. Lawyer is a prominent personal injury lawyer in the community. Because of her prominence and reputation, she is often able to secure settlements that exceed what a lawyer might typically be able to secure for clients. Lawyer generally proceeds in her representation on a contingency basis with her clients, taking roughly twenty-five percent of her client's earnings, which is consistent with what is typically charged in the community. She is retained by a new client who wants the Lawyer to press some novel claims. Because of the novelty of the claims and the risks involved in taking on the case, Lawyer offers to represent the client but would like to claim a forty-percent share in any settlement or judgment. She communicates this fee, in writing, to this client. The client, represented by separate counsel in negotiating the retainer and fee arrangement, accepts the terms of the representation. This fee arrangement represents a somewhat higher percentage than what is typically charged in the community for such a case, although not for one that raises novel claims as this one does. Lawyer begins the representation and is able to secure a significant settlement for the client, which results in a large attorney's fee award.

Is Lawyer charging an unethical fee?

A. Yes, because the contingency fee arrangement is higher than what is typically charged in the community for similar work.

B. No, because Lawyer communicated the fee to the client in writing and the client agreed to it while represented by outside counsel in the fee negotiations.

C. No, because the nature of the claims and the risks associated with the representation mean the fee is not unethical.

D. Yes, because Lawyer was required to clarify that she was not representing the client in the negotiations over the retainer.

9. Lawyer provided excellent service to a group of plaintiffs who brought a personal injury action alleging that a large company had polluted a local aquifer. Lawyer was working for a contingency fee, one in which he stood to claim one-third of the plaintiffs' recovery if the case were successful. Plaintiffs sought $10 million in actual damages and an additional $90 million in punitive damages. The jury returned a verdict for the plaintiffs, and they were awarded the full $100 million they sought in the action. The attorney's fee award was thus $33 million, bringing Lawyer's rate to roughly $1,000 an hour.

Which of the following is the *least* important factor in determining whether Lawyer's fee is ethical?

A. The relationship between the damages awarded in this case compared to those issued in other similar cases.

B. Whether Lawyer had to turn down other work to accept the case.

C. The fee customarily charged in the jurisdiction for a similar case.

D. The experience, reputation, and ability of Lawyer.

10. Lawyer worked for many months to pursue a case for a Client and ultimately secured a significant settlement for Client. Client is a company that claimed it had been defamed by a cable news host. The original claims sought by Client exceeded $1 billion. Those claims were novel and quite creative. Because of the nature of the claims, it was a highly risky case for Lawyer to take on; there was a high probability that Client would lose, with no damages being awarded, meaning Lawyer would not receive any payment for services. Lawyer had to forego many other clients to take on this emergency case, and it was also likely that Lawyer might face public criticism for taking on such a politically charged lawsuit. Indeed, many other lawyers had declined the representation for just these reasons. Following months of negotiations, which occurred after the filing of the initial complaint but before any significant discovery or other litigation got underway, the case settled, with the news anchor's agreeing to pay Client $100 million. As a result of the written retainer agreement between Lawyer and Client, Lawyer is entitled to $30 million as a contingency award, with the contingency being securing damages from the defendant either through trial or settlement. Thus, Lawyer's effective hourly rate, based on the amount of work Lawyer performed in this case, amounted to roughly $10,000 per hour. This hourly rate is somewhat higher, on average, than the fees an attorney with similar experience might be able to charge for services in a standard defamation case.

Is Lawyer subject to discipline for seeking to collect the fees described above? If so, why? If not, why not?

A. No, provided Lawyer acted competently in handling Client's case.

B. No, because of the significant risks associated with the representation and because Lawyer had to forego assisting other clients to handle Client's case.

C. Yes, because the fee charged is larger than that which a lawyer with similar experience might charge in the community.

D. Yes, because Lawyer is not permitted to seek a contingency fee in a defamation suit because to do so is likely to create a conflict of interest with the client.

11. Lawyer represents a corporation (Client) that is engaged in transactions regarding the sale of homes in a residential development. Client is low on funds because it is using all of its resources to ensure that the development is built as soon as possible, due to a belief that Amazonia, a Silicon Valley company, may be planning to build a new headquarters in the area, which will likely boost the value of the homes. It is generally understood in the community that the possibility of this happening is low because many other cities are competing to lure Amazonia. Lawyer is offered a chance to take a percentage of the sale price of each of the homes as they are sold, rather than being paid a set amount prior to the sale. Lawyer and Client, acting through its Chief Executive Officer (CEO), agree that Lawyer shall take one percent of the sale of each home regardless of the price. The CEO has her in-house counsel within the client company review and approve the fee arrangement. Both sides agree that the value of the homes could go up if the new Amazonia headquarters is built nearby but that they could go down considerably if Amazonia decides to build elsewhere. Prior to any announcement of Amazonia's new headquarters, the first few homes are sold and Lawyer makes a modest amount on each sale, far less than she would have earned in a typical home closing. But once Amazonia announces it is going to build its headquarters near the housing development, the home values in the development increase dramatically. Client begins to receive orders on homes that have not even been constructed yet. Because of the increase in property values, Lawyer's fee doubles, which is now roughly twenty-five percent more than

what is typically charged in a home closing in the area.

Is Lawyer subject to discipline for the fee arrangement and/or the fee ultimately charged for the home closings that occur after the value of the homes increase?

A. Yes. The fee charged was unreasonable because it far exceeded the amount typically charged in the community for such services.

B. Yes, because Lawyer is not permitted to take what was, in effect, a contingency fee in a real estate transaction.

C. No. The fact that there was a fair degree of risk involved in the representation permitted the fee ultimately charged.

D. No, because Client was represented by separate counsel in the execution of the fee agreement.

4.3 Formative Assessment Quiz

Use these questions to test what you have learned in this chapter.

12. Lawyer worked for many months to pursue a case for a Client and ultimately secured a significant settlement for Client. Client is a company that claimed it had been defamed by a cable news host. The original claims sought by the Client exceeded $1 billion. Those claims were novel and quite creative. Because of the nature of the claims, it was a highly risky case for Lawyer to take on; there was a high probability that Client would lose, with no damages being awarded, meaning Lawyer would not receive any payment for services. Lawyer had to forego many other clients to take on this emergency case, and it was also likely that Lawyer might face public criticism for taking on such a very high profile and politically charged matter. Indeed, many other lawyers had declined the representation for just these reasons. Following months of negotiations, occurring after the initial complaint was filed but before any significant discovery or other litigation got underway, the case settled, with the news anchor's agreeing to pay Client $100 million. As a result of the terms of the written retainer agreement between Lawyer and Client, to which Client gave its informed consented, Lawyer is entitled to $30 million as a contingency award. Thus, Lawyer's effective hourly rate, based on the

amount of work Lawyer performed in this case, amounted to roughly $10,000 per hour. This hourly rate is significantly higher, on average, than the fees an attorney with similar experience might be able to charge for services in a standard defamation case.

Is Lawyer subject to discipline for seeking to collect the fees described above? If so, why? If not, why not?

A. No, because Client consented to the terms of the retainer.

B. Yes, because the fee charged is larger than that which lawyers with similar experience might charge in the community for a standard defamation case.

C. No, because of the significant risks associated with the representation and because Lawyer had to forego assisting other clients to handle Client's case.

D. Yes, because Lawyer is not permitted to seek a contingency fee in a defamation suit because to do so is likely to create a conflict of interest with Client.

13. Lawyer has a bustling personal injury practice and generally has opportunities for more work that her small firm can handle. She routinely has to turn down many cases just because her practice does not have the personnel to handle them. She regularly accepts cases on contingency, earning compensation only when her clients prevail. One day, a potential client comes to her office with a case that could be extremely lucrative and is likely to be a sure victory. Indeed, in this personal injury action, the facts are so compelling that Lawyer believes the defendant will likely settle for a large amount, and fairly quickly. Moreover, the case is not that complicated factually, procedurally, or legally, and does not require any special expertise. However, one problem is that the statute of limitations in the case is set to expire in just a few months, so Lawyer would have to forego much of her other work and turn down promising cases in the interim were she to take it on. Furthermore, if the case goes to trial, Lawyer will definitely have to devote all of the firm's resources to the case and turn down many other cases. Lawyer is also concerned that the case could turn out to be rather lengthy, demanding significant resources should the defendant not settle quickly. Lawyer explains all of these factors to the prospective client. Lawyer then proposes, in writing, a compensation plan under a retainer with two potential outcomes. The first outcome would be triggered if the case is settled quickly; in that event, Lawyer will receive twenty percent of any award. The second outcome would be triggered if the case goes to trial; in that event, Lawyer will receive forty percent of any award. The first contingency fee percentage is lower than most contin-

gency fee arrangements in the community. The second is significantly higher than most contingency fee arrangements in the community, though not out of line with those arrangements falling at the higher end.

Is this retainer agreement unethical?

A. No, because the arrangement was communicated to Client in writing.

B. Yes. The work for Client is not complicated and does not require any special expertise, and thus the fee is unreasonable.

C. No, because the retainer agreement is consistent with other fee arrangements in the community despite being on the higher end, and because it takes into account Lawyer's possibly having to forego other work to take on the client's case.

D. Yes, because Lawyer has no justification for charging a fee that is at the higher end of what lawyers in the community would charge.

14. Lawyer Lisa and Lawyer Kate are in separate firms but have agreed, in writing and with the consent of the Client, to handle a matter that is likely to go to litigation. Both lawyers agree to accept joint responsibility for the case. Lisa has agreed to handle the discovery phase of the case and Kate has agreed to handle the trial. The written agreement between the two lawyers and Client states that the lawyers will split any attorney award equally and that the contingency fee shall be twenty-five percent of any recovery. The agreement is silent as to expenses, however. Lisa puts in about fifty hours in the case during the discovery phase. Kate puts in about three hours preparing for trial, but on the eve of trial, the case settles for $400,000. The contingency fee award comes to $100,000. Lisa informs the client that she had $100,000 in reasonable expenses associated with the discovery and states that she will deduct that from the client's portion of the settlement agreement, but only after the attorneys' respective fees are calculated and deducted from the award. This approach is consistent with lawyer practice in the community. Client says the $100,000 should be deducted from the overall settlement amount before calculating the attorney's fee; this method reduces the fee to $75,000.

May the lawyers deduct the expenses from the overall award in such a way as to maximize their own contingency fee?

A. Yes, because it is reasonable to deduct expenses related to the work performed.

B. Yes, because the client is ultimately responsible for the expenses associated with the litigation, and to do otherwise would constitute unethical financial assistance to a client in litigation.

C. No, because deducting the expenses from only Client's portion of the settlement amount is unreasonable despite being consistent with community practice.

D. No, because the method of deducting expenses should have been communicated to Client in writing in advance of the representation through the retainer.

15. Lawyer agrees to handle a personal injury action on behalf of Client, a sophisticated diplomat who wants to sue her former employer, the federal government, for failing to provide adequate protection to its employees, like Client, who were potentially exposed to harmful toxic material that might have been placed near the embassy where Client worked. Lawyer, a prominent attorney who primarily represents government whistleblowers, discusses with Client the nature of the representation and the Lawyer's conditions for representation. Lawyer agrees to handle Client's case on a contingency fee basis, with Lawyer's receiving twenty percent of any recovery in the action. Both Lawyer and Client understand that Client is unlikely to recover any damages from the government through the lawsuit, however, and that, as a result, the case is unlikely to generate any fees. Client and Lawyer both want to expose the government's failure to protect members of the diplomatic corps, like Client. Expressing that she fully understands the risks involved in the representation and the terms of the retainer, including the arrangement concerning fees, Client gives informed consent to the representation orally.

Is Lawyer subject to discipline for entering into an oral retainer of this nature with the Client? If so, why? If not, why not?

A. Yes, because an agreement containing a contingency fee is required to be in writing and signed by the client.

B. Yes. Given the novel nature of the claims, Lawyer should have insisted that the retainer be in writing.

C. No. Because Lawyer knew that the case was unlikely to generate fees, the retainer did not need to be in writing.

D. No, because Client gave informed consent to the representation.

16. Lawyer represents Company, a meatpacking plant, and handles most of its worker compensation cases involving Company employees. Lawyer maintains an account on behalf of Company and consisting of Company funds, from which Lawyer is permitted to reimburse himself when Company asks Lawyer to handle worker compensation cases on its behalf. Given the dangerous nature of the work at the plant, Lawyer has a steady stream of cases involving Company employees, roughly four cases each month. Lawyer charges Company a flat fee of $1,000 for every case he handles on behalf of Company, a fee which is reasonable and consistent with what other lawyers charge in the community for similar work. Lawyer bills Company monthly based on the number of new cases referred to Lawyer by Company and withdraws the billed amount from the account Lawyer maintains on Company's behalf. As a courtesy, Lawyer is sometimes notified by the worker compensation board that new cases have been filed against Company. On occasion, however, Company chooses not to challenge a worker's application for worker compensation benefits and therefore does not refer that case to Lawyer. Because Company does not refer every case filed against it to Lawyer, there is sometimes a mismatch between the cases the worker compensation board reports to Lawyer as being filed against Company and the cases actually referred to Lawyer by Company. Because of this mismatch, sometimes Lawyer reimburses himself from the Company account for cases that Company ultimately chooses not to send to Lawyer for representation. When Lawyer realizes any such error, he substitutes new cases that he actually handles

on behalf of Company for those that were incorrectly reported to Company as cases Lawyer handled. At the end of each calendar year, Lawyer always ensures that he has not charged Company for any cases he did not actually handle.

Is the manner in which Lawyer managed Client's account improper? If so, why? If not, why not?

A. Yes, because Lawyer was charging an unreasonable fee for the cases he did handle.

B. No, because Lawyer always corrected the billing errors after learning of them.

C. Yes, because Lawyer charged Client for cases Lawyer did not actually handle, even if Lawyer corrected these errors after the fact.

D. No, because Lawyer's errors were unintentional.

17. Lawyer represents Client, an individual who engages in high-frequency trading. Client faces a potential criminal indictment for her alleged participation in a massive fraud scheme. Client faces the prospect of twenty years in prison for the offenses law enforcement has uncovered in its investigation. Client is obviously very concerned about what will happen should she be convicted, in part because Client could be subject to a bar that will prevent her from trading stocks in the future, even if she enters into an agreement settling any potential charges with the prosecutor without the matter's coming before a tribunal. Client retains Lawyer because Lawyer has proven very successful in securing "restitution-only plea deals," that is, deals without jail time and the loss of a client's securities license. In the retainer between Lawyer and Client, Lawyer agrees to represent Client up to and including any presentation of the matter to the grand jury, but the retainer is limited and leaves open only the possibility that Lawyer will represent Client after that point if Client is indicted. The retainer also says that Client will only pay Lawyer under two scenarios: (1) Client is not indicted, or (2) Client enters into a plea agreement in which Client is not required to serve jail time, pays less than $10 million in restitution, and does not lose her trading license. Client is aware of both aspects of the retainer: the limit on the scope of the representation and the fee arrangement. The Client is represented by her personal attorney throughout the retainer negotiations. Client provides her informed consent to both aspects of the retainer, in writing.

Is Lawyer subject to discipline for any aspect of the retainer with Client?

A. Lawyer is subject to discipline because the retainer's limitation on the scope of representation is unreasonable under the circumstances.

B. Lawyer is not subject to discipline for any aspect of the retainer because Client was independently represented by counsel in the negotiation of the retainer.

C. Lawyer is subject to discipline for both aspects of the retainer: the limitation on the scope of the representation and the fee arrangement.

D. Lawyer is subject to discipline only for the fee arrangement.

18. Lawyer represents Client, a defendant in a criminal case who is charged with driving under the influence of alcohol. Client is a young adult, and his parents, Paul and Paula, are paying his legal fees. Client is offered a plea deal that will result in his incarceration in county jail for thirty days. Client has consented to Lawyer's communicating with Paul and Paula about the substance of the representation. Paul and Paula feel that thirty days in the county jail might help Client because, they say, it will "teach him a lesson." Client does not want to accept the plea deal and insists on taking the case to trial. Lawyer reasonably believes that Client has several good faith defenses to the action but also has a reasonable belief, which he shares with Client, that there is a good chance Client will lose at trial and will face a sentence of up to six months in the county jail, with a minimum sentence of three months. Lawyer believes in good faith that Client should take the plea deal and counsels Client accordingly. Client is emphatic that he wants to take the case to trial. Despite the urging of Paul and Paula, Lawyer communicates to the prosecutor on the case that Client will reject the plea deal.

Is Lawyer subject to discipline for refusing to abide by the express wishes of Paul and Paula with respect to the plea deal?

A. Yes, because Client controls the decision whether to accept a plea deal in a criminal proceeding, and Paul and Paula were, for all intents and purposes, Lawyer's clients.

B. No, unless Lawyer did not believe it was in Client's best interests to reject the plea deal.

C. No, because Client must control the representation, despite the fact that other parties are paying Lawyer's fee.

D. Yes, because Client gave consent to Lawyer to confer with Paul and Paula about the representation.

Chapter 5

Ethics in Advocacy

This chapter covers issues that arise in advocacy. Most of these issues relate to litigation, but some relate to other matters, such as, for example, how lawyers may deal with third parties, the safekeeping of client property, or the sale of a law practice. The chapter is thus relevant not only to the work litigators do but to the work all lawyers do.

It is often said that a lawyer's duty is to be a zealous advocate within the bounds of the law. Use this chapter to understand the concept of zealous advocacy as well as where the bounds of the law lie.

5.1 Meritorious Claims and Contentions

Fundamental to the lawyer's obligation to act within the bounds of the law is the notion that a lawyer should only raise meritorious claims and factual assertions where there exists a good faith basis for making them. This section explores the contours of these issues.

1. Lawyer represents Client in a criminal proceeding that could result in the client's incarceration if found guilty. Client admits to Lawyer in a confidential communication that Client was present at the scene of the crime, an armed robbery, but Client denies playing any part in the crime. The only eyewitness to the robbery, the bank teller, testifies both that he has a photographic memory and that Client was present at the scene of the crime. The witness claims he saw Client inside the bank when he opened it in the morning. Client's presence at the scene of the robbery, which would indicate that he was trespassing at the bank, is an element of the criminal charge in the proceeding. Lawyer wants to cross-examine the witness to see if she can undermine the witness's account that he saw Client at the scene of the crime.

Is Lawyer subject to discipline if she challenges the eyewitness's testimony that he saw Client present at the scene of the crime?

A. Yes, because the witness has a photographic memory.

B. No, because Lawyer can defend the proceeding to ensure that the prosecution establishes every element of the criminal charge.

C. Yes, because Lawyer knows Client was present at the scene of the crime.

D. No, because Client's statement to Lawyer that Client was present at the scene of the crime is protected by the attorney-client privilege.

2. Lawyer has been approached by a natural gas company to challenge a new law passed by the state legislature regarding the prohibition of hydraulic fracturing, a practice more commonly known as "fracking." Lawyer is a prominent civil rights lawyer in the state and is unsure of why the company is seeking to retain her. She discusses the matter with the company's general counsel, who informs her that the company believes its civil rights are being violated by the legislation because the law infringes on its freedom to contract, a right that, the general counsel argues, is enshrined in U.S. Supreme Court jurisprudence. Lawyer agrees that such a right has existed in the past, but she also states that such a right has long been undermined by subsequent Supreme Court precedent. Even so, Lawyer agrees to consider the matter. She conducts some initial research into the claims, including a review of the backgrounds and prior rulings of recent appointments to the Supreme Court. As a result of her research and this information, she believes it is possible that she could revive the freedom of contract doctrine. She believes she has some credible arguments that might persuade a majority of the Supreme Court to rule in the company's favor. She does not believe, however, that the lower courts would be in a position to ignore decades of Supreme Court precedent. Nevertheless, she agrees to represent the company and challenges the legislation. She loses in the trial court. The appellate court, one step below the Supreme Court, agrees with the district court and also rules against her. She then pursues a review of the appellate court's decision from all judges of the appellate court (i.e., an "en banc" ruling) but does not win a single judge to her position. She files an application to the Supreme Court for review of the lower courts' rulings. The petition for review is denied. She learns that two Justices would have granted the petition for review, but two votes is not enough for her to obtain review by the Supreme Court. Moreover, the basis for their voting to grant review is not known; it is possible that they voted to accept the case so that the Court could rule definitively against Lawyer's position.

Is Lawyer subject to discipline for her actions in filing the case on behalf of the client-company?

A. Yes, because she lost at all levels of the federal court, including at the Supreme Court, when it ultimately denied review.

B. No, because she was able to persuade two Justices that her case should be heard by the Supreme Court.

C. Yes, because she did not have a good faith basis for bringing the action.

D. No, because she had a good faith basis for bringing the action.

3. Lawyer represents a corporate client (Client) that is charged with unlawful discrimination in the termination of an employee. Client asserts that the employee who was terminated had consistently performed poorly in his job responsibilities. Lawyer is reviewing the records and learns that there really is no evidence that Client had ever given the employee a poor review of his job performance. Lawyer consults with Client's director of human resources (Director) and informs him that the argument that the employee had performed poorly in his job responsibilities is not strong, given the lack of a record of poor job performance evaluations. Director says that he is certain there are poor job performance evaluations in the employee's files. Lawyer informs Director that he has conducted a full and careful analysis of all records supplied to Lawyer and could find no evidence of such poor evaluations. Director informs Lawyer that there must be some mistake. Director asks for some time to review the records himself. After a few days, Director shares three poor job performance evaluations for the employee which, it is claimed, were prepared prior to the employee's termination. After Lawyer reviews the evaluations, Lawyer has a reasonable belief that they were generated after the fact, are false, and were fabricated. Lawyer does not know for certain that is the case, however. At trial, Client wants Lawyer to introduce the three poor job performance evaluations Director had produced. Lawyer chooses not to do so.

Is it unethical for Lawyer to have refused to submit the poor job evaluations as evidence?

A. No, because he had a reasonable belief that they were false and fabricated.

B. Yes, because he did not know for certain that they were false and fabricated.

C. Yes, because his knowledge that they were false and fabricated can be inferred from the facts.

D. No, because a lawyer has control over the means of the representation, including the introduction of evidence.

5.2 The Duty of Candor to the Tribunal

Lawyers can sometimes find themselves in situations where they fear that a client or witness may have committed perjury. The lawyer's duty to serve as a zealous advocate for their clients might suggest that a lawyer should ignore perjury when it occurs and take no remedial action. But a lawyer is also an officer of the court and should not assist another in engaging in such acts. When a lawyer must take action in light of a client's or witness's presenting perjured testimony is explored in this section.

4. Lawyer represents a tenant in an eviction proceeding. Lawyer has stated on the record at the trial that the tenant notified his landlord that the kitchen sink in the tenant's apartment was defective. Lawyer had a reasonable belief that this statement was true when she made it. Notice to the landlord of such a condition was an element of the tenant's warranty of habitability defense. During a recess in the trial, in a private conversation between Lawyer and Client, Client informs Lawyer that Client never gave the landlord notice about the defective sink. Lawyer did not know at the time she made her statement in open court that it was false.

Is Lawyer subject to discipline if she does not alert the tribunal to the falsity of her statement about Client's having given notice of the defective sink?

A. Yes, because Lawyer must correct a false statement previously made to the tribunal by Lawyer.

B. No, because the communication alerting Lawyer to the falsity of her statement was protected by the attorney-client privilege.

C. Yes, unless Lawyer had a reasonable belief that the statement was true at the time she made it.

D. No, because Lawyer did not know the statement was false at the time she made it.

5. Lawyer is serving as trial counsel for a plaintiff in an antitrust lawsuit against a large technology company. Lawyer represents an app developer who alleges it was forced to accept the onerous terms of the technology company's app platform. Lawyer calls a witness, a former employee of the technology company, to testify about that company's business practices with respect to app developers. During the preliminary and introductory stages of the testimony, the witness makes several misrepresentations of her credentials and talks in grand terms about her role in the company prior to her departure from the technology company. Although this testimony is not material to the case, Lawyer knows that the self-aggrandizing statements about the witness's background and role in the company are false and will likely serve as grounds Lawyer's adversary will be able to exploit in cross-examination of the witness. Lawyer now has a reasonable belief that the material parts of the testimony the witness is planning to give will also be fabricated and exaggerated. Lawyer ends the examination of the witness abruptly. This witness's substantive testimony, which Lawyer will not now present, could have bolstered plaintiff's case. Without it, there is a good chance the plaintiff will lose the case. Lawyer takes no further steps to correct the record with respect to the infor-

mation the witness did provide on direct examination regarding her credentials and role in the company.

Is Lawyer subject to discipline for his conduct with respect to this witness? If so, why? If not, why not?

A. No. Because the witness is a former employee of the defendant and not a client of Lawyer, Lawyer had no obligation to correct the material misrepresentations found in the witness's testimony.

B. No, because the witness's testimony was not material to the case, Lawyer ended the witness's testimony, and Lawyer asked no further questions upon his reasonable suspicion that the witness was providing false testimony.

C. Yes, because Lawyer had an obligation to take reasonable remedial measures with respect to the witness's perjury.

D. Yes, because Lawyer had a duty to present the witness's testimony in order to advance his client's case, even if doing so would expose the witness to cross-examination based on the material falsehoods in her testimony.

6. During the course of extended litigation, Lawyer has been citing a decision from a trial court in the controlling jurisdiction that is favorable to his client's legal position. Lawyer recently learned that, in an unreported decision from an intermediate appellate court that is also from the controlling jurisdiction, the trial court's decision was vacated. Lawyer knows that the intermediate appellate decision is being appealed, and Lawyer has a reasonable belief that this decision will be overturned from the jurisdiction's highest court within a reasonable amount of time. The appellate court decision was not reported, however, and it is unlikely that Lawyer's adversary or the court hearing the case will learn of the decision.

Is Lawyer subject to discipline if he does not disclose the adverse legal authority to the tribunal?

A. Yes, because the lawyer has a duty to disclose adverse legal authority from the controlling jurisdiction.

B. No, because it is an unreported decision, and his adversary and the court are unlikely to discover it.

C. Yes, because he has a duty to disclose any material authority that is relevant to the proceeding.

D. No, because the decision is likely to be overturned.

7. Client is an Olympic downhill skier whose longer-than-expected recovery from surgery means that she will probably miss this year's Winter Games. In a privileged communication between Lawyer and Client during preparation for trial, Client informs Lawyer that she did not always follow the post-operative instructions related to her physical therapy and, instead, engaged in extensive training exercises contrary to her doctor's express directions. Both Lawyer and Client understand that this likely helped contribute to the delay in Client's recovery. When Client is cross-examined by the attorney for the doctor who performed the surgery, Client testifies that she followed the post-operative instructions to the letter.

Which answer best describes Lawyer's proper course of action in this situation?

A. Lawyer may reveal that the client committed perjury in her testimony.

B. Lawyer must take reasonable measures to mitigate the introduction of false testimony, including, if necessary, disclosure to the tribunal.

C. Lawyer is under no obligation to reveal the confidential information because she personally did not offer the false testimony; rather, the testimony regarding the Client's post-operative behavior was elicited in cross-examination by opposing counsel.

D. Lawyer must not reveal the fact that Client testified falsely because Lawyer only knows this fact by virtue of privileged communications between Lawyer and Client.

8. In order to prepare for the trial of Alvin, a client who is alleged to have been a part of a drug conspiracy, Lawyer attends the trial of Bertrand, another defendant in the same conspiracy. Lawyer has no advocacy role in Bertrand's case and watches the trial from the public gallery in the court room. After Bertrand testifies but before the conclusion of Bertrand's trial, Lawyer reviews publicly available documents that lead Lawyer to believe Bertrand likely committed perjury when he testified in his own defense. For some reason, however, the prosecutors handling Bertrand's prosecution do not seem to be aware of the existence of those documents, despite their public availability.

Is Lawyer required to reveal to the prosecutors that Bertrand likely committed perjury?

A. No, because the documents are publicly available.

B. Yes, because Lawyer is an officer of the court and must reveal the likelihood that Bertrand committed perjury.

C. No, because Lawyer is not involved in a representational capacity in Bertrand's trial.

D. Yes, because the information related to Bertrand's perjury is not confidential.

9. Lawyer is preparing a client to testify at trial. One of the issues Client would like to testify about is tangential to the core of Client's case, but Client wants to testify about it nonetheless. After discussing the matter with Client, Lawyer knows that some of the testimony with respect to this tangential matter is false, and so Lawyer does not want to probe this line of inquiry. Since the issue is tangential to the case, Lawyer does not believe the absence of testimony pertaining to it will affect Client's overall position or likelihood of success, nor does Lawyer believe it is critical that Client give this testimony. Client agrees with Lawyer's assessment and consents to dropping the tangential matter. Client insists she will testify however she wants, even falsely, if the tangential issue comes up on cross-examination. Lawyer proceeds to allow Client to testify despite knowing this. Client's testimony concludes without her committing perjury because the issue about which she was prepared to testify falsely does not arise during her direct or cross-examination.

Is Lawyer subject to discipline for allowing Client to testify on any matter, knowing that Client would testify falsely on the tangential matter were it to arise in the proceeding?

A. Yes, because once Lawyer knew there was a possibility that Client would testify falsely, she was prohibited from allowing Client to testify in any way and on any subject.

B. No, because Lawyer did not know whether Client's testimony would contain perjury, even if the tangential matter was introduced through cross-examination.

C. Yes, because Lawyer should not have allowed a client with such a callous disregard for the truth to testify.

D. No, because Lawyer is permitted to offer a portion of Client's testimony that does not constitute perjury.

10. Lawyer and Client have been involved in a six-week trial, and the jury has just returned a verdict in favor of the Client. As they are walking out of the courthouse, and before any deadline has passed for the losing party to appeal the judgment in the case, Lawyer praises Client for his testimony, saying he made an excellent witness and withstood some pretty tough cross-examination conducted by the adversary's lawyer. Client smiles and says, "Well, you know, much of what I said was pure fiction." Lawyer, rendered somewhat speechless by this statement at first, asks Client what he meant by that statement. Client then smiles again and says, "Better that you don't know so you won't have to tell anyone." Lawyer reflects on the matter briefly and decides in good faith that, even if Client did commit perjury, correct answers to the questioning would not have changed the outcome of the case.

Is Lawyer subject to discipline if she does not take steps that ultimately correct the record in the proceeding?

A. Yes, because Lawyer must report any statements of fact which she reasonably believes were not true.

B. No, because the duty of candor with respect to Client's testimony terminated once the jury reached its verdict.

C. Yes, because Lawyer's knowledge of the perjury can be inferred from the circumstances and the duty of candor has not yet terminated.

D. No, because Lawyer believes in good faith that revealing the Client's perjury would not change the outcome of the case.

11. Lawyer learns that her client is about to be evicted from her home by the local government authority. The city government believes, from a visual inspection of the building's façade, that the client's home is in imminent danger of collapse and poses an immediate threat to the client and anyone who might be walking past the building. Lawyer knows the reasons for the city government's belief that the building is in imminent danger of collapse, but Lawyer believes in good faith that the client has taken sufficient precautionary measures inside the building to prevent a collapse. Client has received an emergency vacate notice from the city, which empowers the city to remove Client from the building without legal process. Lawyer rushes to court to commence an action to halt Client's imminent eviction without legal process. Once Lawyer's case is filed on behalf of Client, Lawyer seeks an ex parte order from the court to halt the planned eviction, claiming it is illegal. Lawyer explains to the court that the city is planning on taking emergency action against Client without commencing a proceeding in court, which would normally violate state law. That city officials believe there are dangerous conditions in the building allows the city to take the emergency action it plans on taking—in other words, the existence of such a good faith belief on their part means the planned eviction without legal process would not be illegal. Lawyer believes in good faith, however, that the building structure is sound, and Lawyer does not inform the court that city officials believe the building is unsafe.

Is Lawyer subject to discipline for failing to raise the issue of the city officials' reasonable belief about the safety of the

building in the ex parte communication with the judge?

A Yes, because Lawyer is under an obligation to reveal any material facts known to the lawyer to assist the court in making an informed decision.

B. Yes, because in an ex parte proceeding, a lawyer is obligated to reveal any adverse facts held in good faith by the opposing side.

C. No, because Lawyer believes in good faith that the city's position is incorrect.

D. No, because Lawyer is under no obligation to reveal the position of an adversary if there is no controlling legal authority to support the city's position.

12. Lawyer represents Defendant in a criminal action. Defendant is charged with participating in a criminal conspiracy to distribute drugs. He was caught at the airport with a large amount of powder cocaine in his luggage. Defendant alleges that he is a salesman for a company that manufactures laundry detergent, and he routinely travels with large amounts of sample products his company makes. He claims that he was unaware that powder cocaine had been substituted for the samples he usually carries. During the course of preparing for Defendant's trial, Lawyer begins to suspect that Defendant is not telling the truth, and so he confronts Defendant. Defendant admits that he knew he was carrying drugs, but that it was just one time; he had never done it before. Defendant does not want to admit that he knew what he was carrying was an illegal substance. Defendant insists that he wants to take the stand and testify because he believes he can come across as trustworthy. He believes he can convince the jury that, contrary to fact, he was unaware that what he was transporting was cocaine. Lawyer threatens to ask the court to permit him to withdraw as Defendant's counsel if Defendant insists on lying on the stand. Defendant wants Lawyer to continue to represent him and agrees to tell the truth in his testimony. The trial progresses, Defendant testifies truthfully, and Defendant is convicted. As is customary in the jurisdiction, Lawyer is permitted to talk to the jury after the trial. The members of the jury all agree that Defendant appeared very trustworthy and that had he testified that he did not know the product he was carrying was cocaine, they would have believed him and acquitted him. For the first time on appeal, Defendant brings

an ineffective assistance of counsel claim against Lawyer for his actions, seeking to overturn his conviction.

Will Defendant succeed in his effort to overturn his conviction based on ineffective assistance of counsel?

A. Yes. Lawyer should not have threatened to withdraw as Defendant's counsel because he knew that he would need permission from the court to do so.

B. No. Defendant had failed to raise the issue of ineffective assistance of counsel prior to his conviction.

C. No. It is not ineffective assistance of counsel to counsel someone to testify truthfully, even if that means threatening to withdraw as counsel.

D. Yes. The outcome of the trial would have been different but for Lawyer's actions.

5.3 Preserving Potential Evidence

In addition to finding themselves in situations where a client or witness presents perjured testimony, lawyers may also find themselves in situations where they believe a client possesses documents or other materials that could have evidentiary value if the client is being sued or is under threat of a lawsuit. This section discusses the duties associated with such evidence or potential evidence.

13. Lawyer represents an accounting firm that has served a local businessperson for years. Lawyer learns from a friend at the local prosecutor's office that the accounting firm, although not a target of an investigation, is likely to receive a subpoena as part of the office's investigation of the businessperson. No charges have yet been filed against the businessperson, but such charges are imminent. The records in the accounting firm's possession are likely to be the final pieces of information the prosecutor's office needs to bring an indictment against the businessperson. Lawyer communicates to the accounting firm the likelihood of its being served with a subpoena. The firm reports that it has no records for the businessperson that have been generated in the last six months and that the firm's normal records retention practices include destroying records after six months. Nonetheless, the firm

wants to assess whether it has records older than six months related to the businessperson and, if it finds any, wants to know whether it can destroy any such records as part of its routine practice of destroying such older records.

Can Lawyer advise the firm to destroy any records related to the businessperson as part of its routine records destruction practice?

A. Yes, because Lawyer will not be personally destroying the records and the accounting firm is not a party to any proceeding.

B. No, because the records have potential evidentiary value in a proceeding that is reasonably foreseeable.

C. Yes, because no proceeding has yet been filed against the businessperson and no subpoena has yet been filed on the accounting firm.

D. No, because a records destruction practice that destroys any records of the firm after six months is unreasonable.

14. Lawyer is outside counsel to a local hospital. An individual working in the hospital's risk management department informs Lawyer that the hospital has learned that a procedure performed on a patient, Peter, five months ago likely involved medical malpractice. Peter was just informed that the procedure may have involved error on the part of the hospital. The hospital is taking medically appropriate steps to remedy the harm Peter suffered as a result. The hospital administrator informs Lawyer that Peter still appears quite trusting of his doctor, despite his having received the news that the procedure went awry. The administrator believes Peter will commence an action once he learns the extent of the malpractice, which should occur at Peter's next appointment with his treating physician. Although an appointment with his physician is not currently scheduled, Peter will need a follow-up visit in the coming weeks. Applicable law in the jurisdiction makes it unlawful to destroy evidence having potential evidentiary value in a pending proceeding or in one that is reasonably foreseeable. The hospital's standard records retention policy allows it to destroy all electronic records after six months unless there is some reason to preserve them. The hospital administrator wants to keep things quiet with Peter and destroy the records once six months has elapsed from the date of the procedure.

Is Lawyer subject to discipline if she does not instruct the hospital to preserve the records related to Peter's procedure?

A. Yes, unless the records retention policy permits the hospital to destroy the records.

B. Yes, because a proceeding against the hospital is reasonably foreseeable, even if not has not yet been filed.

C. No, because Peter is unlikely to file an action against the hospital.

D. No, not if the hospital waits six months before destroying the records, in accordance with the hospital's records retention policy.

15. Lawyer is representing an employer who is accused by a former employee of permitting a hostile work environment to exist for that former employee. The former employee is represented by counsel who has attempted to resolve the matter without resort to litigation, but who has also threatened that litigation is imminent if the matter cannot be resolved amicably and in a satisfactory fashion. In preparing a response to an informal request for information from the former employee's attorney, Lawyer discovers that sexually explicit emails were routinely circulated within the department to all members of the department, including to the employee who claims to have been harassed. Lawyer believes this could have potential evidentiary value should the former employee commence a lawsuit against the employer, but Lawyer believes in good faith that the matter is going to be resolved without resort to litigation. Accordingly, Lawyer instructs the company's information systems manager that she may destroy the emails.

Is Lawyer subject to discipline for directing the destruction of the emails?

A. No, because Lawyer believed in good faith that the matter would be resolved without litigation.

B. No, because litigation had not yet been commenced at the time Lawyer directed that the emails may be destroyed.

C. Yes, because Lawyer was under an obligation to preserve any items having potential evidentiary value in relation to the plaintiff's claims.

D. Yes, because Lawyer was under an obligation to preserve any item that might lead to admissible evidence.

5.4 Lawyer as Potential Witness

There are times when a lawyer might have to give testimony on behalf of a client. In such situations, the lawyer may be disqualified from serving as an advocate on behalf of the client in that case. There are exceptions to that general rule, however. This section covers both the instances in which a lawyer will face disqualification and also the exceptions to that general rule. *See generally* MR 3.7.

16. Lawyer, a solo practitioner, represents Client in litigation in which one of the central issues is the effect of a particular loan instrument. Lawyer claims to have witnessed Client sign the instrument. Lawyer plans to testify to having witnessed Client's signature in order to properly authenticate the document for admission into evidence. Lawyer's testimony will not be contested, but the court deems it necessary for Lawyer to testify to ensure that this critical document is properly admitted into evidence. Because Lawyer will serve as a witness in the case and testify in front of the jury hearing the matter, the attorney representing Client's adversary objects to Lawyer's continuing representation of Client. If Lawyer is disqualified, substitute counsel from a firm with which Lawyer often collaborates is available to take over the matter so that Client will not be disadvantaged as a result of the disqualification.

Will Lawyer be disqualified as a result of testifying in the case on behalf of Client? If so, why? If not, why not?

A. Yes, because a lawyer cannot be an advocate in a case in which that lawyer must provide witness testimony necessary to the case.

B. No, because Lawyer is a solo practitioner and because no substitute lawyer can truly handle the case in Lawyer's stead, which creates a hardship for Client.

C. Yes, because Lawyer may have to cross-examine himself with respect to his testimony, which creates a conflict of interest.

D. No, because Lawyer is testifying about an uncontested matter in the dispute.

17. Lawyer represents Employer in a case alleging that Employer created a hostile work environment for its employees. Employer's defense is that Lawyer provided critical training to all employees that should have helped to prevent the hostile work environment. Employer alleges that despite these best efforts, several rogue employees were responsible for the hostile work environment and Employer should not be held liable for those employees' actions. Lawyer will likely be asked to serve as a witness as to the training she provided to the employees in question. The content of the training about which Lawyer will testify will be a contested issue at the trial. Employer indicates that it wants Lawyer to handle the matter because she is so knowledgeable about the facts. Employer is a large, multinational corporation and has no shortage of other attorneys at Lawyer's firm it can call on to handle the case, several of whom have a similar factual knowledge of the case and are fully competent to handle the matter.

Will Lawyer be disqualified from handling the matter?

A. Yes, because Lawyer cannot handle the matter if she has a conflict of interest.

B. No, because the disqualification of Lawyer will work a substantial hardship on Employer.

C. No, because Lawyer is in the best position to provide zealous representation for Employer due to Lawyer's knowledge of the subject matter of the representation.

D. Yes, because the disqualification of Lawyer will not work a substantial hardship on Employer.

18. Lawyer A is employed by the XYZ firm. Lawyer A is a potential witness in a case involving a client the XYZ firm represents. Lawyer A will not be involved in the representation of this client in any way. Lawyer B, another lawyer at XYZ firm, will handle the case on behalf of the client. Lawyer A's testimony is going to be relatively straightforward and is not likely to face much cross-examination. It is possible, however, that one aspect of Lawyer A's testimony may not be favorable to XYZ's client, and Lawyer B may need to seek to undermine Lawyer A's credibility with respect to that portion of the testimony. Lawyer B is aware that Lawyer A had been charged with filing false allegations as an advocate in a case from several years ago and received a private reprimand from the court for doing so. Lawyer B only has that knowledge because of confidential communications that occurred within the firm. Such information is not publicly available. Lawyer B considers whether to use such information in the event Lawyer A's testimony is damaging to Lawyer B's client. If it is, Lawyer B will want to undermine Lawyer A's credibility because Lawyer B feels a duty of loyalty to the client to do so. At the same time, Lawyer B does not want to embarrass Lawyer A by disclosing this private reprimand, which could also have an adverse financial impact on the XYZ firm.

Is Lawyer B disqualified from representing the XYZ firm's client in the case in which Lawyer A is a witness? If so, why? If not, why not?

A. Yes, because Lawyer A's conflict with respect to giving testimony in this case is attributable to the entire firm.

B. Yes, because Lawyer B has a potential conflict that would prevent Lawyer B from engaging in effective examination of Lawyer A.

C. No, because Lawyer A's conflict with respect to giving testimony in this case is not attributable to the entire firm.

D. No, because Lawyer B does not have a conflict that would prevent Lawyer B from engaging in effective examination of Lawyer A because doing so is in the Client's best interest.

19. Client is a successful businessperson. Lawyer handles Client's criminal cases. One of Client's favorite activities is to golf, which she does several times a week. Lawyer is often invited to golf with Client, which Lawyer does as part of her "client relations" activities. She generally does not bill Client for the time spent with Client on the golf course. She always advises Client that, since other parties are present during these excursions, no confidential communications should be shared on the golf course. On one such golf outing, Client invites a business competitor with whom Client is friendly to join the outing. Client and the business competitor are discussing a hot-shot job applicant both want to hire. Each agrees to offer the applicant the same low salary so that they are not competing with each other over the applicant's compensation. As a result of this golf course collusion, the applicant is offered the same compensation from the companies owned by Client and Client's competitor. The applicant sues both Client and the competitor in a civil suit alleging anti-competitive behavior. Client retains Lawyer's firm to handle the civil action, but Lawyer will not take part in the representation. Lawyer is subpoenaed to act as a witness by the plaintiff-applicant in the action.

Is Lawyer subject to discipline for testifying about what she overheard on the golf course?

A. Yes, because the communications were confidential.

B. Yes, because a lawyer cannot testify against a client.

C. No, because the lawyer is not also acting as an advocate in the proceeding.

D. No, because the lawyer was subpoenaed to testify.

5.5 Special Responsibilities of a Prosecutor

While all lawyers have the duty of presenting only good faith legal claims and factual contentions, the rules impose special burdens on prosecutors. This section explores those rules. *See generally* MR 3.8.

20. Prosecutor prosecuting a public corruption case believes that a low-level official, Daenerys, likely has information relevant to the investigation that relates to the illegal actions of some of her superiors. In order to convince Daenerys to cooperate with the larger investigation, for which there is already more than enough evidence to charge a number of high-level defendants, Prosecutor files criminal charges against Daenerys. Although Prosecutor does not believe he has probable cause to bring the charges, he nevertheless hopes the filing of these charges is enough to secure Daenerys's cooperation with the larger corruption conspiracy case to make it "airtight," as Prosecutor describes it. Prosecutor plans to ultimately withdraw the charges against Daenerys, regardless of whether she agrees to testify against her superiors in the larger investigation.

Is it professional misconduct for Prosecutor to proceed against Daenerys in this way?

A. Yes, because Prosecutor knows he does not have probable cause to bring the charges.

B. No, because Prosecutor intends to withdraw the charges.

C. Yes, because Prosecutor should not press charges against a defendant to pressure that defendant into offering testimony against another possible defendant.

D. No, because Prosecutor is free to use tactics designed to assist in the prosecution of legitimate claims.

21. Prosecutor is alerted by local law enforcement officials that they have apprehended an individual whom they believe is responsible for a string of automobile thefts that have occurred in a residential area of the city in which the prosecutor works. Prosecutor comes down to the police station immediately and sees that the individual the police have apprehended is fairly young in age. Prosecutor believes the individual is a minor, based on her appearance and demeanor. An individual who is a minor cannot be questioned without the permission of the individual's parents or a guardian, and any consent that individual may give to be questioned by the police without a lawyer present is invalid. Law enforcement officials state that they do not believe the individual is a minor, but they also say that she did not have identification; that they have not asked her for any personal information, including her age; and that they have not asked her if she wants a lawyer present during her interrogation, as required by law. Prosecutor asks for an opportunity to interrogate the accused and begins to do so.

Was it professional misconduct for the prosecutor to interrogate the accused in this fashion?

A. Yes. Prosecutor could have allowed the law enforcement officials to continue to interrogate the accused but should not have personally taken part in the interrogation.

B. Yes. Prosecutor should have taken reasonable measures to ensure the protection of the rights of the accused.

C. No. Prosecutor did not know whether the accused was a minor.

D. No. Prosecutor was under no obligation to ensure the accused was not a minor.

22. After obtaining a conviction against David for money laundering, the prosecutor on the case learns from newly discovered evidence that it is reasonably likely that David was unaware of the illegality of the transactions for which he was convicted. Under applicable law in the jurisdiction, the prosecution must establish the knowing intent to engage in money laundering.

What must the prosecutor do, if anything, with respect to this newly found information?

A. Prosecutor need not take any action because the evidence regarding David's potential innocence is not clear and convincing.

B. Prosecutor need not take any action because he does not know that David is innocent.

C. Prosecutor must disclose the newly discovered evidence to David and commence an investigation to determine his potential innocence.

D. Prosecutor must seek to remedy the conviction, including, if necessary, applying to void it.

5.6 The No-Contact Rule

Lawyers, skilled in the art of persuasion, would have an unfair advantage in adversarial matters if they were able to speak to the clients of their adversaries outside the presence of, and without the permission of, those adversaries. Rule 4.2, generally referred to as the "no-contact" rule, prohibits lawyers from speaking to the clients of an adversary without the adversary's consent. There are limitations on the rule's application, however. This section covers the rule itself and when it does not apply.

23. Lawyer handles divorce proceedings, and one she is presently working on is particularly contentious. Lawyer feels that the contentiousness of the case is likely the result of the bad relationship she has with opposing counsel and that it has nothing to do with the state of the relationship between her client and her

client's spouse, which is otherwise cordial, civil, and cooperative. What is worse, the contentiousness of the case is also increasing the attorney's fees for both sides. Lawyer receives a call from Harry, the client of the adversary, saying that he would like to discuss settlement of the matter. Lawyer informs Harry that she cannot speak to him without the consent of her client, Sally. She places Harry on a brief hold so that she can contact Sally. Sally gives Lawyer consent to speak to Harry. Lawyer then returns to the call with Harry, and they begin to negotiate the matter, bringing it to a successful resolution that is beneficial for all parties involved and that also brings down the cost of legal representation, since the parties will no longer have to litigate the matter.

Is Lawyer subject to discipline for her actions?

A. Yes. She should have made sure she obtained written consent from Harry before discussing the matter with him outside the presence of Harry's lawyer.

B. No. It was in the best interest of her client to negotiate directly with Harry, and she obtained a beneficial settlement on her client's behalf.

C. No. She had the consent of her client prior to discussing the matter with Harry.

D. Yes. She should have obtained the consent of Harry's lawyer before discussing the matter with Harry.

24. Lawyer is handling a personal injury action on behalf of a pedestrian struck by the truck of a local utility company. The incident happened at a busy intersection, and several utility company employees were present at the time of the incident. Client was struck by a vehicle operated by Aaron, who was at that time a new employee of the utility company. Aaron was being supervised and trained in vehicle operation by Baker, who had been employed by the utility company at the time of the incident but who has since retired from the company. Charlie, an employee of the utility company who had no role in the operation of the vehicle that injured Client, was also present during the incident. Charlie witnessed the incident from twenty yards away while on his lunch break. Lawyer wishes to interview Aaron, Baker, and Charlie about the incident, without giving notice to the utility company's lawyers and without seeking a court order that would allow the lawyer to do so.

Is it unethical for Lawyer to communicate with Aaron, Baker, and/or Charlie without first obtaining the permission of the utility company's lawyers?

A. Lawyer may not speak to any of the three outside the presence and without the permission of the utility company's lawyers.

B. Lawyer may not speak to Aaron but may speak to Baker and Charlie without the permission of the utility company's lawyers.

C. Lawyer may only speak to Charlie without obtaining the permission of the utility company's lawyers.

D. Lawyer may speak to all three individuals without obtaining the permission of the utility company's lawyers beforehand, but Lawyer must give the company's lawyers notice of such communications after the fact.

25. Lawyer is handling a medical malpractice case on behalf of a patient injured in a medical procedure at the local hospital. Lawyer brings an action against the hospital and Doctor Jones, who performed the procedure. In all of the two dozen cases that Lawyer has handled against the hospital, the same lawyer has represented both the hospital and the medical professional involved, and so Lawyer expects the same lawyer to represent both in this matter as well; however, he has not yet received the answer to the complaint he has filed in the case. That answer would generally make it clear whether the same lawyer is representing both defendants. Lawyer's outgoing message on his voicemail, which all callers receive, instructs such callers not to leave any confidential information in their messages and states that any callers who might be represented by a lawyer in the matter about which they are calling should not communicate with Lawyer directly about the substance of the matter. Despite hearing this outgoing message when she contacts Lawyer, Doctor Jones leaves a detailed message on Lawyer's voicemail. Doctor Jones identifies herself and says that although she is represented by counsel, she wants to try to settle the case on her own. She then proceeds to communicate the terms upon which she would settle the case filed against her on behalf of Lawyer's client. Lawyer retrieves the message and listens to it in its entirety.

Is Lawyer subject to discipline for listening to the message from Doctor Jones?

A. No, because Lawyer took reasonable precautions to ensure he did not receive communications from a represented party.

B. Yes, because Lawyer has a reasonable belief Doctor Jones will be represented by counsel in the proceeding.

C. No, because Lawyer does not know that Doctor Jones is represented by counsel in the proceeding.

D. Yes, because Lawyer knows that Doctor Jones is represented by counsel in the proceeding.

26. Lawyer represents the City of Albany in code enforcement actions against residential landlords who are not maintaining their buildings in accordance with the local housing code. Many of these landlords rent to students from the many universities and colleges in the region and tend to neglect those properties, knowing that the tenants are mostly transient in nature and likely will not complain to the city about the poor quality of the housing stock they are renting from those landlords. Under pressure from the heads of the local institutions of higher education to rein in this behavior, because, they say, the poor housing stock is making it hard for these institutions to attract students, the mayor announces a concerted campaign to go after landlords who rent to students to make sure those landlords are maintaining their properties according to code. After extensive outreach to student-tenants to encourage them to come forward and report housing code violations, Lawyer, who has been tapped to coordinate this new campaign, focuses in on a few landlords who seem to be the biggest perpetrators of these bad practices. Lawyer starts preparing legal filings that will be used in cases against the landlords who are the biggest offenders. Lawyer knows these landlords well, having brought code enforcement actions against all of them previously, so Lawyer knows that in such actions, these specific landlords are always represented by a single law firm, one that is known for handling almost all code enforcement defense work in the city. Working with investigators from the city's buildings department who are not themselves lawyers, Lawyer has those investigators conduct inspections of a select number of buildings owned by the tar-

geted landlords. During the inspections, the investigators typically interview the maintenance personnel charged by the respective landlords for each building with maintaining the properties and keeping them in compliance with local housing ordinances. Lawyer uses the information gleaned through those interviews to establish the factual and legal basis for actions against the targeted landlords.

Was it improper for city investigators to have spoken to the maintenance personnel working for the landlords targeted in Lawyer's investigation? If so, why? If not, why not?

A. No, because Lawyer did not interview the maintenance personnel personally, and those individuals were mere witnesses to the conditions of the properties.

B. No, because legal actions had not been commenced, and thus Lawyer did not know the landlords were represented by counsel.

C. Yes, because Lawyer was not permitted to instruct the investigators to have conversations with the maintenance personnel until an action was commenced.

D. Yes, because the maintenance personnel's statements about the landlords' practices could legally bind the landlords and be used against them in subsequence actions.

27. Lawyer is representing Jane, a welder who is injured while working on a new bridge spanning the Hudson River. Jane is employed by Arc, which is protected by the worker compensation system. Jane's injury occurs when a crane operated by Steel, Inc. (Steel), the provider of steel beams to the site, drops a steel beam on Jane's foot. One of the allegations in the proceeding is that the crane operator who caused the accident did not have adequate training to operate the crane.

Which of the following individuals, all current employees of Steel, may Lawyer interview without the permission of counsel for Steel?

A. Steel's crane operator whose conduct led to the accident with the beam.

B. Steel's foreperson who was directing the operations of the crane operator.

C. Steel's crane operator who was on a break from her shift when she observed the operations of the crane that injured the plaintiff.

D. The Steel employee who trained the crane operator.

28. Lawyer is representing Client, a former employee of a local car dealership, in an employment discrimination case against her former employer. During discovery, Lawyer visits the car dealership to survey the physical layout of the location so that she can picture in her mind some of the events that led to Client's employment termination. During the visit, Lawyer sees on the car dealer's lot a late model Dodge Charger for sale, like the one she had as a college student. She approaches the owner of the car dealership, who is named personally as a defendant in the lawsuit and whom Lawyer knows is represented by counsel in the proceeding, and indicates that she is willing to pay the listed purchase price for the Charger. Lawyer pays the car dealer the purchase price for the Charger in cash.

Is Lawyer subject to discipline for her actions in dealing with the owner of the car dealership in any way?

A. Yes, because Lawyer did not give the owner of the car dealership an opportunity to consult outside counsel before entering into the transaction.

B. Yes, because the owner of the car dealership was represented by counsel in the employment discrimination suit.

C. No, not unless Lawyer knew the owner of the car dealership was represented by counsel and did not obtain that lawyer's consent to speak to the owner of the car dealership.

D. No, provided Lawyer only communicated about matters outside the subject of the representation.

29. Lawyer represents a former prisoner in a case involving alleged mistreatment while the prisoner was in custody at a prison run by the state government in the state in which the lawyer practices. The action is filed against, the State Department of Corrections (SDOC), the warden of the facility, a correctional officer commander who was responsible for supervising the correctional officers accused of taking part in the mistreatment of the prisoner, and correctional officers immediately charged with the abuse of the prisoner, among others. Lawyer knows that several individuals witnessed the incident, and Lawyer wants to communicate with them outside the presence of the lawyer representing the defendants. There are three potential witnesses Lawyer wants to interview, none of whom are named parties to the action, but all of whom are either current or former employees of SDOC. The first potential witness, Officer 1, was present during the incident, was on duty, and, according to the rules governing the operation of the facility, had a responsibility to intervene to try to de-escalate the situation but took no action to do so. The second potential witness, a food service worker, was on duty in the cafeteria where the incident occurred and witnessed it but, as a food service worker, had no duty to intervene in such an altercation. The third potential witness, Officer 2, was a line supervisor at the time of the incident who was responsible for overseeing a small group of officers, including those who are defendants in the action. Officer 2, who is embarrassed by the publicity the incident involving the plaintiff has received, has since retired from service and is no longer an employee of SDOC. Officer 2 witnessed the incident, was on duty

at the time it occurred, and, like Officer 1, had a duty to intervene to de-escalate the incident but took no action to do so. A lawyer from the State Attorney General's Office for the state in which the prison is located is representing all defendants and will not consent to plaintiff's lawyer's having direct contact with any of these witnesses without being present.

Which of the following individuals, if any, may Lawyer interview without the consent of the lawyer for those defendants?

A. The food service worker only.

B. Officer 1 and Officer 2 only.

C. Officer 2 and the food service worker only.

D. None of the individuals.

5.7 Dealing with Third Parties

Although a lawyer does not come up against the no-contact rule explored in the last section when dealing with unrepresented parties, there are, nevertheless, in accordance with MR 4.3, limitations on how lawyers should engage with unrepresented parties to ensure that they do not take advantage of them. This section covers the application of that rule.

30. Lawyer is representing Lannister Bank (Lannister) in a mortgage foreclosure action against Able. While in court representing Lannister, Lawyer is approached by Baker, a homeowner being sued in foreclosure by Stark Bank (Stark). Lawyer used to represent Stark in mortgage transactions, but never in foreclosures, and she no longer represents it in any capacity. Lawyer also did not handle the original Baker mortgage transaction, which occurred prior to Lawyer's representing Stark, and Lawyer did not have access to any confidential information about Baker when Lawyer represented Stark. Baker begins to discuss his foreclosure case with Lawyer, who does not indicate that she used to represent Stark. Lawyer provides Baker with basic information about how mortgage foreclosure actions proceed because Lawyer feels bad about Baker's situation.

Has Lawyer acted unethically in the manner in which Lawyer communicated with Baker?

A. No, because Lawyer did not have an interest in Baker's case and the advice provided helped Baker engage in self-representation.

B. No, because Lawyer was free to provide any advice to Baker, even though Lawyer had an interest in Baker's case.

C. Yes, because Lawyer cannot state or imply that Lawyer had no interest in the case.

D. Yes, because Lawyer had a relationship with Stark Bank and thus could only advise Baker to seek independent counsel.

31. Lawyer opens up her email one morning and realizes her opposing counsel inadvertently hit "reply all" to a recent email. His email contained confidential information related to his client's settlement position.

What is Lawyer's correct course of action?

A. She may not read the email and must alert her opposing counsel to his error.

B. She may read the email and is under no obligation to alert her opposing counsel to his error.

C. She may read the email and must alert her opposing counsel to his error.

D. She may not read the email but is under no obligation to alert her opposing counsel to his error.

32. Lawyer is representing Landlord in an eviction proceeding. Tenant in the matter is representing himself pro se. Lawyer prepares a settlement agreement, favorable to Landlord, that will result in Tenant's surrendering his apartment. Landlord's claims against Tenant are supported by the law, but Tenant, if he were to present his case to the judge, might obtain more time to surrender his apartment than the time given by the settlement agreement. Lawyer knows this but hands the settlement agreement to Tenant for Tenant's signature. Tenant, who knows Lawyer represents Landlord, asks Lawyer nonetheless if the settlement is a "good deal" for Tenant, and Lawyer responds that she cannot give Tenant legal advice. Lawyer states that this is the offer her client is willing to make and adds that if Tenant wants legal advice, he should try to retain his own counsel.

Is Lawyer subject to discipline for the action described?

A. Yes, because the terms of the agreement are not as favorable to the unrepresented party as they might have been under applicable law.

B. Yes, because Lawyer should not have prepared the settlement agreement without Tenant's being represented by counsel.

C. No, because Lawyer should have informed Tenant that he could obtain better terms if he asked the judge for assistance in resolving the matter.

D. No, because Lawyer merely presented the terms on which her client would settle the matter and suggested that Tenant should seek his own attorney.

33. Lawyer works at a non-profit legal organization that provides legal assistance to low-income tenants. Part of the job entails engaging in "community education," that is, providing basic advice to low-income tenants who will appear pro se in housing court. The topics of the trainings include the functioning and processes of housing court. Lawyer does not give individualized, tailored legal assistance to any particular tenant; rather, Lawyer simply gives information detailing court procedures and how tenants can act to protect their rights and interests when they represent themselves.

Is Lawyer subject to discipline for assisting these tenants in this way?

A. Yes. It is misconduct for Lawyer to assist tenants in representing themselves, which necessarily entails engaging in the unauthorized practice of law.

B. Yes. Lawyer should not give legal advice to anyone with whom he does not have an attorney-client relationship.

C. No. Lawyer can give advice to individuals that is related to their efforts to represent themselves without counsel.

D. No. Lawyer has not formed an attorney-client relationship with these individuals and is therefore not bound by any ethical constraints in his dealings with them.

34. Lawyer Able is negotiating the sale of a luxury yacht to the client of Lawyer Baker. Able and Baker agree, as part of the negotiation process, to obtain an independent appraiser's assessment of the value of the yacht. Able obtains the report from the appraiser because she paid for it and learns that the appraiser has valued the yacht at $2 million. Able reports to Baker that the appraiser has valued the yacht at $2.5 million. She also says that her client's "bottom line" is that she will accept no less than $2 million for the yacht. In reality, Able's client will accept $1.7 million for the yacht because she is eager to sell it.

Is Able subject to discipline for either or both of her statements during the course of the negotiations surrounding the sale of the yacht?

A. Able is subject to discipline for both statements.

B. Able is subject to discipline for the statement regarding the value of the yacht but not for the statement regarding the client's bottom line.

C. Able is subject to discipline for neither statement.

D. Able is subject to discipline for the statement regarding the client's bottom line but not for the statement regarding the value of the yacht.

5.8 Clients with Diminished Capacity

Lawyers may face situations where a client is unable to provide the guidance necessary for the lawyer to protect and defend the client's interests. Rule 1.14 covers situations where a client has what the rule refers to as "diminished capacity." The rule provides guidance to practitioners to enable them to advance and protect such client's interests. This section examines the application and provisions of this rule.

35. Lawyer represents Client, an individual with a serious psychiatric disability. Client is a beneficiary of a large trust fund, created by his parents, from which he is supposed to pay his ongoing living expenses. Client has begun to take weekend trips to Atlantic City, where he loses tens of thousands of dollars in a given weekend. These actions are beginning to diminish significantly the total amount in Client's trust fund. Without obtaining Client's consent to do so, Lawyer contacts Client's psychiatrist to determine the appropriate course of action to take on Client's behalf. During this conversation, Lawyer reveals confidential information about Client with the goal of determining what actions are necessary to protect his interests.

Is Lawyer subject to discipline for revealing confidential information to the psychiatrist?

A. Yes, but only if he did not have Client's explicit consent to speak to the psychiatrist.

B. Yes, because he revealed confidential information to the psychiatrist.

C. No, because he was impliedly authorized to reveal the confidential information.

D. No, but only if Lawyer has Client's explicit, written consent to speak to the psychiatrist.

36. Lawyer represents Client, an individual who suffers from partial dementia. On several occasions, Client has shown up at Lawyer's office without an appointment but cannot recall why she is there. Lawyer is handling the donation to a local museum of several very expensive and rare pieces of art from Client's extensive collection. Client's children are very upset about this transaction because the art is extremely valuable and they were hoping to receive such art through Client's will upon her death. Lawyer has represented Client for a long time, and Client has long professed a desire to donate these pieces of art to the museum. Client had set the process in motion to do so years before the dementia set in. Client's children insist that Lawyer must seek a mental examination of Client and file for a legal guardian to be appointed to manage Client's affairs.

Is Lawyer subject to discipline for failing to seek either a mental examination of Client or the appointment of a legal guardian?

A. No, provided Lawyer reasonably believes that Client can adequately act in Client's own interest.

B. No, because Lawyer must always maintain a normal client-lawyer relationship and should not act contrary to Client's wishes.

C. Yes, because Lawyer should know that Client is operating under a diminished capacity.

D. Yes, because Lawyer may not assist in carrying out Client's wishes if Client's capacity is questioned by her next-of-kin.

37. Lawyer is asked to represent Client, the elderly parent of two adult children who have agreed to pay Client's legal fees. Client is in the early stages of dementia and recently was charged with reckless driving, which could result in Client's facing jail time because the incident resulted in physical injuries to several bystanders. Client has not come to grips with her worsening medical condition and insists that she is not at fault for the accident, claiming instead that she was driven off the road by a large truck. No witnesses can confirm Client's account. In fact, the opposite is true. All witnesses state that Client was simply driving recklessly, and that there were no other cars or trucks in the vicinity of the incident. The prosecutor on the case, who is sympathetic to both Client's and Lawyer's predicament, is offering to plea the charges down to a relatively minor infraction if Client agrees to attend remedial driving lessons and to submit to a mental examination to assess her fitness to drive. Client is adamant about her innocence and her competence to drive. Client insists on taking the case to trial where she is confident she will prevail. Lawyer has a reasonable belief that taking the case to trial is not in Client's best interests because she will most certainly face considerable jail time if convicted. Lawyer believes in good faith that Client's conviction at trial is the most likely outcome of any adjudication of the charges against her. Lawyer also has a reasonable belief that Client could decompensate and see her condition worsen if she does not receive adequate care for her condition while incarcerated. Finally, Lawyer possesses a reasonable belief that Client's irrational behavior with respect to the generous offer the prosecution has made is a product of her mental condition. Client gives Lawyer explicit direction to reject the plea deal, but Lawyer refuses to do so and asks the prosecutor for more time to provide Client's response. Prosecutor grants Lawyer that extension of time to respond to the plea deal. Despite not having permission to speak to Client's adult children about the case, Lawyer reaches out to them to explain the situation and enlist their help in convincing Client to accept the plea arrangement. In this communication with the children, Lawyer divulges only that confidential information which is related to the plea deal.

Is Lawyer subject to discipline for sharing confidential information with Client's adult children? If so, why? If not, why not?

A. Yes, because Lawyer shared confidential information with the adult children without Client's consent.

B. No, because Lawyer had implied consent to share confidential information with Client's adult children.

C. Yes, because the harm that could befall Client was merely speculative.

D. No, because Lawyer could share confidential information with the adult children because they were paying Lawyer's fees.

5.9 Safekeeping Client Property

Lawyers are often asked or required to keep client property safe. Rule 1.15 provides guidance to the lawyer with respect to the manner in which such property must be maintained, and this section covers issues related to that rule.

38. Lawyer handles real estate transactions for his clients. When a client sells property with the assistance of Lawyer, the proceeds of the sale are deposited in an escrow account set up specifically for each client. Lawyer's retainer with each client sets forth that Lawyer has a lien on the proceeds of any sale of property until a final accounting is completed for the funds related to each sale. Upon such accounting, Lawyer compensates himself for any reasonable fees and expenses related to the sale, in accordance with the terms of the retainer agreement; shifts to his own account the amount of funds that reflect his fee for work actually performed and related expenses; removes the lien; and releases the remaining balance to the client. Lawyer sends to his clients an individualized, automated, confidential email on a weekly basis that contains up-to-date accountings of all transactions related to their respective escrow accounts.

Is Lawyer subject to discipline for the manner in which he maintains client escrow accounts on behalf of clients? If so, why? If not, why not?

A. No. It is appropriate for Lawyer to maintain a lien over the proceeds of the sale of property until Lawyer is compensated for his services.

B. No, because Lawyer must provide a weekly accounting to each client for all activity related to these escrow accounts, which Lawyer provides.

C. Yes, because Lawyer is not permitted to maintain an interest in the subject matter of the representation.

D. Yes, because Lawyer is required to release all proceeds of the sale and permit the client to return any payment reflecting the fees earned and expenses incurred.

39. Lawyer maintains a client escrow account for a wealthy client (Client) through which she routinely pays out the proceeds of settlements she secures for Client. Lawyer is also supposed to use this account to pay herself for services she provides to Client. Client runs a business that operates a high-volume cement manufacturing plant in a rural area. Client's employees who drive cement trucks tend to drive in an unsafe fashion, and local residents who travel on the same roads as these cement trucks often suffer injuries as a result. Lawyer generally enters into confidential agreements with the company's victims and pays them out of proceeds in the escrow account. Lawyer is enriched by her representation of Client and tends to lead a bit of an extravagant lifestyle. Occasionally, and without Client's consent or knowledge, Lawyer will withdraw funds from the escrow account to pay her own personal expenses prior to earning her fees for her work for Client. Lawyer always ultimately earns the money she withdraws and even gives Client a discount to serve as interest on these advance payments.

Is Lawyer subject to discipline for the manner in which she manages the client's escrow account?

A. Yes, because Lawyer should give the client a full accounting of her management of the funds after engaging in these transactions.

B. Yes, because Lawyer is withdrawing funds that represent her fees before they are earned.

C. No, because Lawyer always earns the money she withdraws and offers her services at a discount.

D. No, because the client is not harmed in any way by Lawyer's actions.

40. Lawyer represents a plaintiff class in a class action and has secured a large settlement which has been put into a fund to be distributed to members of the class. The fund is placed in an escrow account under the lawyer's supervision and management. According to the lawyer's original retainer agreement with the class representatives, if the case were to be settled and a fund established, Lawyer would charge $500 per hour for his time on this phase of the action and would submit monthly time sheets accounting for his activities. The hourly rate is reasonable according to standards in the community for this type of activity. The lawyer is also permitted to withdraw his fees from the settlement fund as he earns them. After several months go by, with Lawyer submitting his time sheets and withdrawing the fees he claims he is owed, some of the beneficiaries of the fund begin to question the amount Lawyer is taking as his fee, believing he may be misreporting the hours worked. Lawyer submits his bill for the month of January 2020, and the beneficiaries communicate to the court that still retains jurisdiction over the matter that they dispute the amount of hours Lawyer claims to have worked on their case in January 2020. They state that the lawyer should not withdraw any funds from the account until the question of the propriety of the January 2020 report is resolved. Lawyer has a good faith basis for the time sheets he has submitted and withdraws the amount he claims he is owed for the month of January 2020, agreeing to pay back any unearned or excessive amount should the court determine his fees were inappropriate in any way.

Is Lawyer subject to discipline for his actions?

A. No, because Lawyer submitted his bills in good faith and agreed to pay back any funds he withdrew in the event the court found them excessive.

B. No, because the parties agreed to Lawyer's hourly rate, which was not unreasonable.

C. Yes, because Lawyer should not have withdrawn any disputed fees.

D. Yes, because Lawyer was charging an unreasonable fee due to his not working all of the hours he claimed he worked.

41. Lawyer represented several plaintiffs in a personal injury action involving an accident that occurred on a public bus. The action was settled, and the bus company deposited a sum of money with Lawyer to be deposited in Lawyer's trust account that would be distributed to each victim using a formula based on the extent of that victim's injuries. A dispute arises between Lawyer's clients as to how much each client should receive under the settlement. Each is entitled to $40,000 out of the settlement fund, but they dispute how the remaining $20,000 in the fund should be distributed. The settlement agreement provides that the judge who oversaw the litigation and ultimately approved the settlement will resolve any disputes between the plaintiffs over the disbursement of funds under the agreement. Lawyer says she cannot distribute any of the funds until the dispute is resolved. She makes a motion asking the judge who presided over and approved the settlement to resolve the dispute.

Is Lawyer subject to discipline for the manner in which she is planning on resolving the dispute between the plaintiffs?

A. No, because the parties cannot reach an agreement on a proper distribution of the proceeds of the settlement.

B. Yes, because Lawyer should release any undisputed amount to the clients and maintain only those funds that are in dispute in Lawyer's trust account until the court can resolve the dispute.

C. Yes, because Lawyer should not commingle the clients' funds in the same account.

D. No, because Lawyer is following the procedure for resolving a dispute between the parties over the distribution of the settlement funds in accordance with the terms of the settlement.

5.10 Sale of a Law Practice

There are instances where a lawyer or law firm may sell all or part of their practice to another lawyer or law firm. Rule 1.17 covers the sale of a law practice and provides procedures to ensure that the clients affected by such a sale have their interests and rights protected during and after such a sale. This section addresses those procedures.

42. Lawyer is nearing her desired retirement age and wants to slow down a bit in her practice. She currently represents individuals in both real estate transactions and in personal injury litigation defense work, mostly for her real estate clients. She wishes to sell only her litigation work to an eager young lawyer in the community. Lawyer sends written notice to the clients for whom she provides litigation services of her intent to sell that practice area to the local attorney. Although she represents some clients in both practice areas—transactions and litigation—she will sell only the litigation practice with respect to those clients and will continue to represent them in their transactional work. All litigation matters will be sold in the sale of the lawyer's litigation practice. All clients affected by this sale are informed there will be no charge for the transfer of their litigation matters; they can select other counsel and obtain their case files should they so choose; the fees for the services they receive will not increase; and their consent to the transfer of their litigation matters will be presumed if they do not object within ninety days of receipt of the notice.

Is Lawyer subject to discipline for the manner in which she is selling her litigation practice?

A. Yes. Lawyer may not sell just a portion of her practice if it involves clients she represents in other matters.

B. Yes. Lawyer should not force clients who do not object to the sale of the practice to have their matters referred to the new lawyer.

C. No. Lawyer is entitled to wind down her practice as she sees fit and has good cause for doing so.

D. No. Lawyer may sell an entire practice area from her practice and has followed the procedural requirements for doing so.

43. Lawyer intends to retire and sell her entire law practice. Written notice is given to her current clients relating the fact that she is proposing to sell her practice. Such notice reaches all of her clients. Clients are advised that they can seek different counsel and can retain their files. Clients are advised that the new law firm purchasing the practice from the retiring Lawyer will not raise its fees with respect to these clients. Most clients consent to the transfer, but several clients do not respond to the notice. The new law firm continues to represent all of the clients, even those who have not responded to the notice. The firm presumes that even those clients who have not responded to the notice have consented to the sale and transfer. The firm fails to obtain a court order confirming the firm's ability to represent the clients who have not formally and explicitly consented to the transfer.

Was it misconduct for the new law firm to fail to obtain a court order with respect to those clients who did not consent to the transfer?

A. Yes, because a court order was required for the new law firm to represent the clients who did not consent to the transfer.

B. No, because a court order was not required for the new law firm to represent the clients who did not consent to the transfer.

C. Yes, because the new law firm should have ensured the clients who did not consent were advised of the advisability of obtaining separate counsel and given an opportunity to do so.

D. No, because the new law firm properly purchased the entirety of the lawyer's practice.

44. The Smith Firm is a successful law firm that has several practice areas, including a lucrative practice in employee-side labor law. Lougle is a large company that has just purchased a smaller company located in the community in which the Smith Firm operates, and the smaller company will become a subsidiary of Lougle. Lougle has announced it will move its new headquarters into the area, creating 10,000 new jobs in the region. Having previously been the victim of bad press due to some of its employment practices, Lougle approaches the Smith Firm in the hope that enlisting a plaintiff-side firm will help strengthen its reputation for being "pro employee." Lougle seeks to secure the Smith Firm's representation in labor and employment law matters, even though the firm generally handles plaintiff-side representation in this practice area. The Smith Firm has several cases in which it represents former employees suing the newly purchased Lougle subsidiary. The Smith Firm fears these cases will create a conflict of interest in its representation of the company because the subsidiary is the alter ego of Lougle, meaning that any damages awards against the subsidiary will have a significant financial impact on Lougle. The Smith Firm decides to transfer those cases against the subsidiary to another firm by selling them to that other firm, even though the Smith Firm plans on maintaining its employment and labor practice generally. The Smith Firm charges a reasonable fee for the transfer of those cases, and the clients are given notice of the transfer, an opportunity to switch attorneys, and the ability to obtain their files should they wish.

Is the Smith Firm subject to discipline for selling the cases against Lougle's subsidiary to another firm?

A. No, because there likely would have been a conflict of interest had the Smith Firm continued to represent the clients in those cases after taking on Lougle as a client.

B. Yes, because the Smith Firm did not sell the entire employment practice area.

C. No, because the Smith Firm charged a reasonable fee to sell those cases and the clients were given the requisite notice that would enable the Smith Firm to do so.

D. Yes, because the Smith Firm failed to obtain the clients' informed consent to the sale of their cases.

5.11 Formative Assessment Quiz

Use these questions to test what you have learned in this chapter.

45. Lawyer is representing Jane, a welder who is injured while working on a new bridge spanning the Hudson River. Jane is employed by Arc, which is protected by the worker compensation system. Jane's injury occurs when a crane operated by Steel, Inc. (Steel), the provider of steel beams to the site, drops a steel beam on Jane's foot. Lawyer sues Steel on Jane's behalf, and Lawyer is made aware that Steel has counsel in the proceeding. One of the allegations in the proceeding is that the crane operator who caused the accident did not have adequate training to operate the crane.

Which of the following individuals may Lawyer interview without the permission of counsel for Steel?

A. Steel's foreperson who was directing the operations of the crane operator.

B. Steel's site manager who was responsible for all actions taken by Steel employees at the site of the incident.

C. Steel's crane operator who was directly responsible for the accident but is no longer employed by Steel.

D. The Steel employee who trained the crane operator and who witnessed the incident in which Jane was injured.

46. Lawyer is a prominent intellectual property lawyer who represents Lougle, a large internet company, in an action claiming that it stole the intellectual property of a competitor. Lawyer is informed by employees at Lougle that a professor at a local university had first published material setting forth the theory of the search engine Lougle and its competitor use long before the competitor filed its patent, meaning the patent should never have been issued by the U.S. Patent and Trade Office. Lawyer is shown evidence of this publication, has no reason to doubt its veracity, and represents this fact before the court in oral argument on a motion for summary judgment made by Lougle's competitor. Based on this fact, the court denies the motion. Lawyer later learns that the paper was fabricated and posted by Lougle on its own, and that Lougle had changed the digital history of the paper to suggest that it was published before the issuance of the patent. Lawyer learns this information soon after receiving the court's decision on the motion, and before the case proceeds to trial. The case ends up proceeding to trial on other points related to Lougle's actions. The issue of the patent is never revisited by Lawyer, the competitor's lawyers, or the court.

Is Lawyer subject to discipline for his actions?

A. Yes, because Lawyer should never have made the false statement in the first place.

B. No, because Lawyer reasonably believed the statement was true at the time Lawyer made it.

C. No, because Lawyer was never asked to restate the fact after learning it was not true.

D. Yes, because Lawyer failed correct a false statement previously made to the tribunal.

47. Lawyer Paula, representing the plaintiff, and Lawyer Danny, representing the defendant, are engaged in settlement negotiations over a personal injury action. Danny asks Paula for her client's "bottom line," that is, the lowest amount the plaintiff will accept. Paula says, "There is no way my client will accept less than $100,000." Although Paula knows that her client will accept $80,000, she does not admit that. Danny says, "Well, my client has only authorized me to offer $75,000. I believe I have a little wiggle room but nowhere nearly enough to get us to $100,000, so I guess these negotiations are over." Paula, knowing that defense counsel often use these sorts of ploys to get adversaries to lower their demands, and not feeling any particular pressure to settle, responds, "I guess so. See you in court." Several weeks go by, and Danny spends roughly eighty hours preparing a motion to dismiss the action. Danny's client is nervous that the motion Danny is preparing will be denied, and the case will then end up going to trial where he could face a large damage award. Accordingly, Danny's client asks Danny to go back to Paula and "sweeten the pot a little." Danny contacts Paula and says, "I am authorized to offer $80,000." Paula, having been authorized to accept a settlement at this amount, and knowing her client would prefer not to risk taking the case to trial, states that her client can accept this offer. Danny is incensed that Paula did not accurately state her client's bottom line earlier, before he spent eighty hours preparing his motion to dismiss. Moreover, Danny believes Paula's representation of her client's $100,000 bottom line was a knowing factual misrepresentation of her client's settlement position. For these reasons, Danny wants to file disciplinary charges against Paula.

Does Paula's failure to accurately state her client's bottom line subject her to discipline?

A. Yes, because Paula knowingly failed to correct a misapprehension of opposing counsel.

B. No, because under normal conventions of the profession, a lawyer is not obligated to reveal confidential settlement positions during negotiations.

C. No, but only if Paula truly believed she was speaking honestly to Danny about her client's settlement position.

D. Yes, because Paula made a materially false statement to a third party.

48. Lawyer is victorious in pursuing claims on behalf of two employees who faced discrimination in the workplace. A lump sum of $450,000 in damages is transmitted to Lawyer's escrow account on behalf of these clients. A dispute arises as to how the judgment proceeds should be distributed. Lawyer believes in good faith that one client, Able, should be awarded $250,000, and the second client, Baker, should receive $200,000 from the proceeds of the judgment. Prior to commencing the representation, the clients agreed in writing that any disputes concerning the distribution of any judgment should be referred to arbitration. Baker believes the funds should be divided evenly, so that each client receives $225,000.

What is Lawyer's proper course of action?

A. Lawyer should distribute none of the proceeds of the judgment until the matter can be resolved through arbitration.

B. Lawyer should distribute $225,000 to each client but still submit the dispute to arbitration.

C. Lawyer should distribute $250,000 to Able and $200,000 to Baker because that is what Lawyer in good faith believes the proper distribution of the funds should be, but Lawyer should still submit the dispute to arbitration.

D. Lawyer should distribute $200,000 to each client and retain the remainder of the proceeds of the judgment in Lawyer's escrow account until the disagreement over the disputed amount can be resolved through arbitration.

49. Lawyer represents a client who is suing a marina for its failure to properly protect boats docked there from the consequences of a tropical storm that hit the harbor where the marina is located. The marina is a closely held corporation that is owned by an individual, Marita, who holds all of the shares in the marina. Lawyer also docks her own sailboat in the marina, but her boat was not damaged. Lawyer routinely discusses maintenance of her sailboat with marina personnel and regularly has conversations with the owner of the marina regarding issues related to her boat's care and maintenance. Lawyer knows that the marina, as a corporate entity, is represented by counsel, but she does not seek or obtain the permission of the marina's lawyer to communicate with the marina's employees or its owner. Lawyer believes that she can zealously serve her client in litigation against the marina's owner and will not feel conflicted by the representation.

Is Lawyer subject to discipline for communicating with the employees or the marina owner in the manner described without first obtaining permission of the marina's counsel?

A. Yes. A lawyer must always seek permission of counsel prior to talking to any representatives of a corporate client, especially the owner of all of the stock in a closely held corporation.

B. Yes. Given the subject matter of the conversations, Lawyer was required to obtain prior consent of counsel before having such communications.

C. No. Given the subject matter of the conversations, Lawyer was not required to obtain prior consent of counsel before having such communications.

D. No, because Lawyer did not seek to gain an unfair advantage in communicating with the marina employees or its owner and did not exact any concessions or harmful information through such communications.

50. Lawyer is asked to take on a case involving a novel claim regarding discrimination in the workplace which will be filed under the jurisdiction's state constitution. Lawyer seeks and obtains a written waiver of prospective malpractice from Client. Client is represented by separate counsel in executing that waiver. Although Lawyer has a good faith basis for filing the claim, she does not believe the claim will prevail in court at present, given what she believes are the positions of the justices on the state's highest court in light of their previous rulings on similar claims.

Is it professional misconduct for Lawyer to file the claim?

A. Yes, because she does not believe the claim will prevail.

B. No, because she has a good faith basis for filing the claim.

C. No, because the client has properly waived any claim of malpractice prospectively.

D. Yes, because it is her professional assessment that the justices of the state's highest court will not rule in her client's favor.

51. Lawyer is a solo practitioner in a rural community where she is contracted to serve as a public defender for indigent individuals charged with crimes. Lawyer is walking outside the courthouse one day when she witnesses one of her former clients, Carol, involved in a fistfight. Carol and the other individual with whom she was fighting are both charged with assault, battery, and disturbing the peace. What Lawyer witnessed would seem to her to indicate that Carol was only acting in self-defense, but the prosecution will contest this account. Lawyer is assigned as counsel for Carol, even though she will likely be needed as a fact witness to testify in Carol's defense. There are no due to conflicts of interest related to representing her. The matter cannot be referred to another jurisdiction without causing Carol undue hardship.

Is Lawyer barred from testifying on behalf of Carol and serving as an advocate in her criminal trial?

A. No, because disqualifying Lawyer would work a substantial hardship on the client.

B. No. Because Lawyer will not testify adversely against the client, there is no conflict of interest.

C. Yes, because Lawyer cannot serve as a witness in a matter in which she is also the advocate representing Carol.

D. Yes, because the testimony does not relate to an uncontested matter.

52. Lawyer appears as counsel on behalf of his client, a landlord, in housing court, to prosecute an eviction case on behalf of the client. Many of the tenants who appear as defendants in these proceedings are unrepresented. While waiting outside the courtroom for this case to be called by the judge hearing it, the tenant whom Lawyer is suing on behalf of the landlord sits down next to Lawyer. The tenant, who has never met Lawyer before and does not know that Lawyer represents the tenant's landlord, begins to ask Lawyer for advice about the tenant's case. Lawyer does his best to give objectively accurate advice to the tenant about the tenant's claims and defenses.

Is Lawyer subject to discipline for his conduct?

A. Yes. Lawyer should never give legal advice to an unrepresented person.

B. No. Lawyer did not initiate the conversation.

C. No. Lawyer gave objective advice to the tenant.

D. Yes. Lawyer did not identify himself as having an interest in the tenant's case.

53. Lawyer represents Client in a civil trial concerning breach of contract. After the final day's testimony, Client reveals to Lawyer that Client lied during his testimony. Lawyer is concerned that she has a duty to reveal this perjury to the court if Client is not willing to recant the testimony and correct the record. Minutes after she learns that Client committed perjury, Lawyer is alerted that the jury has reached its verdict and Client is victorious in the proceeding. Lawyer's adversary indicates that she intends to file a notice of appeal with respect to the jury verdict and does so immediately, preserving her client's right to appeal.

What action, if any, must Lawyer take to mitigate the client's perjury?

A. Lawyer is under no obligation to take any action because the jury reached its verdict.

B. Lawyer is obligated to withdraw as counsel from representing Client in the appeal.

C. Lawyer is obligated to take reasonable remedial measures at this time, including, if necessary, disclosure to the tribunal to mitigate Client's perjury.

D. Lawyer must counsel Client to submit an affidavit correcting the record on appeal, but if Client refuses, Lawyer is under no obligation to take further action.

54. Lawyer is handling litigation before a judge who has appeared hostile to Lawyer and Lawyer's client throughout the proceeding. During the discovery phase, the judge made several very damaging rulings against Lawyer's client, including requiring the client to sit for a deposition for several days, which is much longer than is generally permitted under applicable rules; putting strict limits on what Lawyer can obtain through discovery from the opposing party; and requiring Lawyer's client to submit to mental and physical examinations even though the client is not pursuing any claims related to the client's physical or mental health. The case is a simple contract dispute, and the client's mental and physical condition is not even arguably relevant to the case, nor is it likely to lead to admissible evidence. Lawyer correctly believes that the order directing the client to submit to mental and physical examinations is patently improper. In a private communication protected by the attorney-client privilege, Lawyer directs the client to ignore the judge's order without seeking reconsideration of the order or an interlocutory appeal of it.

Are the Lawyer's actions consistent with Lawyer's ethical obligations in this situation? If so, why? If not, why not?

A. No, because the proper course of action would have been to follow the judge's instructions but then seek to disqualify the judge.

B. No, because the Lawyer's direction to the client to refuse to comply with the judge's direction was not done in an open fashion.

C. Yes, because the Lawyer may knowingly disobey a judge's ruling of this nature when there is no legitimate basis for that ruling.

D. Yes, because the communication regarding the disobedience of the judge's order was protected by the attorney-client privilege.

55. Lawyer is representing Defendant in a high-profile criminal trial in which Defendant is accused of participating in a bank robbery. One of the witnesses testifies that she was with Defendant the night of the robbery. If the witness is correct about Defendant's alibi, Defendant could not physically have been at the bank at the time of the robbery. Lawyer learns that the witness's testimony is false based upon information he learned from discussing the matter with Defendant. Defendant orally gave Lawyer a timeline of her activities that evening, backed up by credit card receipts, which the prosecution has not subpoenaed. Lawyer has no intention of attempting to have the witness correct the record because the source of Lawyer's knowledge about the witness's perjury is protected by the attorney-client privilege and Lawyer learned the information while conducting an investigation of Defendant's guilt or innocence as part of his representation of her. Lawyer also knows that any effort to undermine the alibi testimony will likely lead to Defendant's conviction.

Is Lawyer subject to discipline for failing to take steps to correct the record with respect to the witness's alibi testimony?

A. Yes, because Lawyer can only assert the attorney-client privilege to protect a client, not a mere witness.

B. No, because the knowledge that the witness had committed perjury was learned by Lawyer in a communication protected by the attorney-client privilege.

C. Yes, because Lawyer had an affirmative obligation to correct the record regardless of the source of the information undermining the witness's testimony.

D. No, because Lawyer is entitled to press the prosecution to prove every element of its case against Defendant, even if doing so includes presenting an alibi defense Lawyer now knows was false.

56. Lawyer represents Client, an individual charged with embezzlement in a criminal action. Lawyer knows Client has a range of offshore bank accounts that he says are trusts created from money he inherited decades ago. Client claims to have neither deposited any money in such accounts for several years nor to have withdrawn any money from those accounts. Client claims that although he is the only individual who has the ability to add funds to these accounts, the accounts are nevertheless in a blind trust, and so he does not know how the funds are invested. Lawyer sees some records from these accounts suggesting that they have grown considerably in recent years, increasing forty times over. More specifically, if there were, in fact, no deposits made to the accounts, it would mean that the accounts had garnered a clear return on the investment of over four-thousand percent in just the last year. Lawyer confronts Client with the facts about the growth in the accounts because Lawyer knows such returns are impossible, and therefore someone must be adding funds to the accounts. Client repeats that he has not added anything to the accounts. At Client's trial, Lawyer conducts direct examination of Client. In response to Lawyer's questions, Client testifies that the accounts were set up decades ago, that they are in a blind trust, that no funds have been added to the accounts, and that the source of the funds are Client's inheritance.

Is Lawyer subject to discipline if he takes no remedial measures with respect to Client's testimony about the accounts?

A. Yes, because Lawyer's knowledge that Client has committed perjury can be inferred from the circumstances.

B. No, because Lawyer did not know Client committed perjury.

C. Yes, because Lawyer had a reasonable belief Client committed perjury.

D. No, because Lawyer did not have a reasonable belief Client committed perjury.

57. Prosecutor wants to bring charges against an individual for potential violations of the state criminal code for several actions involving the unsafe operation of a vehicle. The vehicle in question, a truck, veered into a pedestrian lane, striking three pedestrians. The driver of the truck, who was also its owner, had failed to get the truck inspected within the last year as required by law. Prosecutor believes it is necessary to press the most serious charges in order to pressure the driver to accept a plea deal on lesser charges. The charges Prosecutor intends to bring include the following: Charge 1, operation of a vehicle with the intent to injure; Charge 2, the intentional operation of a vehicle in a pedestrian area; and Charge 3, the operation of a vehicle that had not been inspected in accordance with law. Prosecutor does not believe he has probable cause to bring Charge 1, but he does believe in good faith that it is necessary to bring that charge to get the defendant to accept a plea deal on Charges 2 and 3. Prosecutor has probable cause to bring both Charges 2 and 3 but believes, correctly, that it will be difficult to obtain a conviction on Charge 2. If the defendant will not accept a plea and the matter has to go to trial, Prosecutor intends to withdraw Charge 1.

Is Prosecutor subject to discipline for bringing any or all of the charges against the defendant?

A. Prosecutor is subject to discipline for bringing Charges 1 and 2.

B. Prosecutor is subject to discipline for bringing Charge 1 only.

C. Prosecutor is subject to discipline for bringing all charges.

D. Prosecutor is not subject to discipline for bringing any of the charges.

58. Lawyer represented Client, a local elected official who was term-limited, and whose term was set to expire at the end of the calendar year 2020. A lawsuit was filed against Client for civil rights violations as a result of acts carried out in Client's official capacity. Lawyer was aware that the case had been assigned to a local federal court judge with a reputation for moving her case docket along quickly, particularly for civil rights cases such as the one filed against Client. Lawyer also knew that the case would be dismissed as moot once Client was no longer in office. The case was filed in 2018, with plenty of time for it to come to trial while Client was still in office, especially given the judge's tendency to move cases along quickly. Lawyer used a number of non-frivolous tactics that resulted in a delay of the proceeding, including seeking to have the judge recuse herself from the action on claims that she might be biased against Client. Lawyer did not really believe that the judge would be biased against Client, but the allegations Lawyer asserted arguably raised questions about the potential appearance of impropriety of the judge's adjudicating Client's case. This and other tactics had no substantial purpose other than to delay the proceeding, an outcome that was in the best interests of Client. The judge declined to grant the request for recusal, but Lawyer succeeded in delaying the matter past the end of Client's term nonetheless, and the case was dismissed against Client.

Has Lawyer acted improperly in any way in the representation of Client? If so, why? If not, why not?

A. Yes, because despite its being filed in good faith, the recusal motion was likely to cast aspersions on the judge and prejudice the administration of justice.

B. Yes, because the tactics used had no substantial basis other than to delay the proceeding.

C. No, because none of Lawyer's actions were frivolous.

D. No, because Lawyer was simply zealously advocating for Client's interests.

59. Lawyer has been asked to represent Landlord, who wants to evict a tenant. Landlord is alleging that the tenant is creating a nuisance. Landlord presents Lawyer with a witness, an individual who works as a superintendent in the same building as the tenant Landlord is trying to evict. Landlord claims this witness can testify about the nature of the tenant's conduct in violation of the lease between the tenant in question and Landlord. After some basic questioning by Lawyer, Lawyer is certain, based upon confidential information provided by Landlord to Lawyer, that the witness is lying. Lawyer decides not to call the witness. Landlord loses the case and brings a malpractice action against Lawyer. If the witness had given the false testimony, it is likely that Landlord would have won the case.

Is Lawyer subject to discipline for failing to call the witness? If so, why? If not, why not?

A. Yes, because Lawyer only knew that the witness was lying because of confidential information the Lawyer possessed.

B. Yes, because Lawyer's failure to call the witness resulted in Landlord's losing the case.

C. No, because Lawyer was permitted to refuse to call the witness.

D. No, because Lawyer was merely acting competently to preserve client confidences by not calling the witness.

60. Lawyer represents URX, a company that is moving crude oil on trains through a residential area in a local community. Lawyer is also a homeowner in that community. The local legislative body holds hearings on whether it should attempt to take action to try to ensure that the trains moving through the community do so in as safe a manner as possible. There is also a movement afoot to try to get the locality to ban the movement of crude through the community for safety reasons. At URX's request, Lawyer provides testimony in public hearings the local legislative body holds on the matter. Lawyer states, correctly, that she is an attorney admitted to practice in the state and that she is also a homeowner in the affected community. Lawyer states that she is there to provide testimony as a private citizen only. Lawyer fails to disclose that she has appeared at the request of URX to give this testimony. Lawyer goes on to offer a description of the legal issues related to the movement of crude oil through the community and states, accurately, that local governments have little power to prevent this from occurring.

Is Lawyer subject to discipline for any of her public statements or omissions? If so, why? If not, why not?

A. No, because the substance of Lawyer's testimony was accurate even if Lawyer did not divulge that she was appearing on behalf of a client.

B. Yes, because Lawyer failed to indicate that she was testifying at the request of a client.

C. No, because Lawyer indicated that she was testifying in her personal capacity as a homeowner in the affected community only.

D. Yes, because Lawyer's conduct can be subject to discipline even when she is not appearing in a representational capacity.

61. Lawyer is representing a tenant in an eviction proceeding. While waiting in court for the case to be called, Lawyer is approached by an individual who asks her whether she represents the tenant. Lawyer says that she does, and the individual begins to discuss the case. Lawyer is aware that the landlord in the action is represented by counsel, but she does not recognize this individual as a lawyer. She asks the individual's identity, and he says he "represents the landlord." Lawyer is surprised because she thinks the individual seems a little young to be a lawyer but nonetheless proceeds to communicate with him. After some discussion of the facts of the case, Lawyer realizes that the individual is not a lawyer, and the individual admits that he is not. Lawyer then says that she cannot discuss the matter with him. The individual goes on to identify himself as a representative of the company that manages the tenant's building and which brought the action against Lawyer's client. He states that he has authority to discuss the matter with Lawyer because of his position in the company. Moreover, the individual says that he gives consent to the Lawyer to discuss the matter, and Lawyer continues with the conversation. She and the individual discuss the contours of a potential settlement of the dispute.

Is Lawyer subject to discipline for continuing the conversation with the landlord's representative after he admitted he was not the landlord's lawyer?

A. Yes, because a lawyer must always be truthful in dealings with interested persons.

B. No, because the landlord's representative gave consent to the communication.

C. Yes, because the landlord's representative could not give consent to the communication.

D. No, because the landlord's representative was a sophisticated individual, and Lawyer did not improperly take advantage of him in any way.

62. Lawyer works in the local civil court and handles debt collection cases for a local bank. Lawyer's practice mostly entails dealing with unrepresented defendants in the actions she brings on behalf of her client. Most of Lawyer's cases settle, and when dealing with unrepresented parties, she identifies her role as representing the plaintiff in the case against the unrepresented defendant. She typically prepares the agreement settling the case and presents it to the unrepresented party, indicating that these are the terms upon which her client is willing to settle the case. The defendants usually ask her whether the settlement is a "good deal." Lawyer responds that she cannot provide the defendant with legal advice other than to consult an attorney, although she does not generally pause the negotiations to afford the defendant an opportunity to seek independent representation. If the defendant declines to accept the agreement, Lawyer indicates that she understands that is the defendant's position, and she and the party typically conference the case before a judge, though occasionally the matter is resolved at trial.

Is Lawyer subject to discipline for the manner in which she deals with unrepresented parties in these proceedings?

A. No, because Lawyer does not state or imply that she is disinterested in the proceeding and does not give the unrepresented party any legal advice other than the advice to consult an attorney.

B. Yes, because Lawyer fails to provide the defendants a reasonable opportunity to consult counsel even though she properly identifies herself as having an interest in the cases.

C. No, because once Lawyer properly identifies herself as having an interest in the matter, she is not limited in the advice she may give to an opposing party, even one that is not represented by counsel.

D. Yes, because Lawyer should not negotiate with an unrepresented party outside the presence of court personnel to ensure those unrepresented parties' rights are overseen by an impartial individual.

63. Lawyer Lin is an employee-side employment lawyer handling workplace discrimination claims. Lin is given the names of former employees of Client's employer because Lin wants to investigate whether there was a hostile work environment at Client's place of employment, which is the basis of Client's claim. Lin identifies a supervisor who is no longer employed by the employer but who used to be responsible for overseeing Client's work site, which included monitoring improper behavior of employees at the site. Lin wants to interview the supervisor about the work environment at the site and what she did or did not do to combat any workplace harassment. During the course of the conversation with the supervisor, Lin learns that the employer's lawyer had also conducted an investigation of the issue of workplace harassment at Client's work site, which included interviewing the supervisor while she was still employed by the employer. Lin asks the supervisor about the outcome of that investigation, probing what the supervisor was asked by the employer's lawyer and what she told that lawyer. Lin did not seek, nor did she obtain, the consent of the employer's lawyer to speak to the supervisor.

Was it unethical for Lawyer Lin to speak to the supervisor in the manner in which she did while conducting her investigation of Client's claims?

A. No. Because the supervisor was a former employer, consent of the employer's lawyer was not required for Lin to speak to the supervisor.

B. Yes, because a lawyer conducting an investigation is not permitted to reveal confidential information related to that investigation.

C. Yes, because Lin should not have inquired as to information likely covered by the employer's attorney-client privilege.

D. No, because the supervisor was being asked about matters outside the scope of her employment, and thus her acts or omissions would not bind the corporation.

Chapter 6

Addressing Misconduct

The previous chapters explored various issues related to lawyer professional responsibility. This chapter explores issues related to formal lawyer misconduct, the punishment that can attach to it, and the lawyer's duty to report others for such misconduct.

6.1 Identifying Misconduct

Attorney misconduct cannot be addressed if it cannot be identified. Use this introductory section to develop an understanding of when an attorney is or is not engaged in misconduct.

1. Lawyer A supervises Lawyer B. Lawyer A represents a client, and Lawyer B is not involved in that representation. Lawyer A directs Lawyer B to contact a party that is adverse to the client to see if the adverse party would agree to settle a matter pending before a tribunal between the adverse party and Lawyer A's client. Lawyer A knows that the adverse party is represented by counsel, but Lawyer A never informs Lawyer B of this fact. Lawyer A cannot personally make this contact because Lawyer A is formally representing the client involved in the case. Lawyer B does not seek consent from the adverse party's lawyer because Lawyer B has no actual knowledge that the adverse party is represented by counsel. Lawyer B does what Lawyer A asks Lawyer B to do.

Is Lawyer A subject to discipline for her actions? If so, why? If not, why not?

A. Yes. Although Lawyer A's resolution of the matter was reasonable, the duty was clear.

B. Yes, because Lawyer A could not act through another to avoid Lawyer A's own ethical obligations.

C. No, because the prohibition on contacting represented parties only applies to the lawyer who is actually handling the matter, not to the entire firm.

D. No, because Lawyer A's resolution of the matter constituted a reasonable resolution of what was at most an arguable question of professional duty.

2. Lawyer is a prominent legal practitioner in the City of Saratoga Springs. As a hobby, though a lucrative one, she also runs a horse farm where she breeds thoroughbred horses. Her hobby has no relationship to her practice of law. Recently, it has come to light that she fabricates the pedigrees of the horses she breeds so that she can enter them into, and charge a higher price for them at, the annual thoroughbred auction in Saratoga Springs, where each horse is sold for at least $1 million. If she did not fabricate their pedigrees, then she would not be able to enter these horses into the auction, and in turn she would not be able to sell them for more than $10,000 each.

Do Lawyer's actions related to misrepresenting the pedigrees of the horses she sells at auction constitute professional misconduct?

A. No, because her horse breeding business is not related to her practice of law.

B. Yes, because this conduct involves dishonesty, fraud, deceit, and misrepresentation.

C. No, because her actions with respect to her horse breeding do not reflect adversely on her practice of law.

D. Yes, because any improper conduct on the part of a lawyer can subject the lawyer to discipline.

6.2 Reporting Misconduct

According to MR 8.3, a lawyer who "knows that another lawyer has committed a violation of the Rules of Professional Conduct that raises a substantial question as to that lawyer's honesty, trustworthiness or fitness as a lawyer in other respects, shall inform the appropriate professional authority." This duty is mandatory, and a lawyer who finds out about but does not report such inappropriate conduct on the part of another lawyer may be in violation of the rule. The question then becomes whether that other lawyer's actions raise a "substantial question" as to that lawyer's fitness to practice law. This section explores this and other issues related to the reporting requirement of MR 8.3.

3. Lawyer is representing a homeowner in a mortgage transaction. Lawyer's adversary, Allie, represents the mortgage bank in the transaction. Lawyer learns that Allie has been misrepresenting to the bank the nature of the interest the bank will assume when it executes the mortgage. Homeowner already has a mortgage on her home, and this new mortgage is for a second mortgage so that she can help pay for her child's college tuition. The value of the home has increased considerably over the last ten years, there is a substantial amount of equity in the home, and the second mortgage is not for a significant amount. In the event the homeowner defaults on either of the mortgages, the original mortgage or the second mortgage, the home could easily be foreclosed upon, and there would be enough proceeds in the sale of the home to satisfy the two mortgages. The bank has agreed to make the loan only as a first mortgage. In other words, the bank would have to have its interest satisfied first in the event of default. Allie, the lawyer for the bank, leads the bank to incorrectly believe that its mortgage takes precedence over the existing mortgage on the property. Lawyer asks Allie why she is doing that, and Allie says that she really likes Lawyer's client and wants to make sure she can get the second mortgage. Allie is confident that the homeowner will not default on any mortgage and will quickly pay off the second mortgage. Allie also tells Lawyer that she "does this all the time and no one ever gets hurt. It's my client who is being ridiculous. What they don't know can't hurt them." Allie insists, correctly, that it is almost impossible that Allie's client will be harmed by having a second mortgage and not the priority mortgage. Lawyer discusses the matter with her client, who does not wish to enter into a mortgage agreement under false pretenses and tells Lawyer to terminate the negotiations. Lawyer also receives the client's consent to divulge the information to the proper disciplinary authorities should Lawyer choose to report Allie to them.

Is Lawyer subject to discipline if she does not report Allie for misrepresenting the nature of the interest Allie's client has in the mortgage?

A. Yes, because Allie's conduct constitutes a clear violation of the rules of ethics.

B. No, because the transaction was terminated before Lawyer's client could consummate the deal.

C. Yes, because Allie's conduct raises a substantial question as to her fitness to practice law.

D. No, because Allie's conduct did not represent a clear violation of the rules of ethics.

4. Lawyer Linda represents Saul, an attorney who is charged with a disciplinary violation before the local committee on character and fitness (the committee). During the course of Linda's representation of Saul, Saul admits to her that he commingled his own funds with those of his clients, many of whom are alleged drug kingpins. In a lawful request for information from the committee, Linda is asked by the committee if she is aware of any reason why Saul's fitness to practice law should reasonably be questioned.

Must Linda divulge the information she knows about Saul's financial practices to the committee?

A. Yes, because his financial practices raise a substantial question about Saul's fitness to practice law.

B. Yes, because Linda must provide truthful information to the committee with respect to Saul's disciplinary proceeding.

C. No, because Linda does not have actual knowledge that Saul engaged in unethical behavior.

D. No, because Saul's communications regarding the commingling of funds are protected by the attorney-client privilege.

5. Lawyer is engaged in protracted settlement negotiations with Opposing Counsel over the proceeds of a trust fund set up for three sisters. Lawyer represents one sister, and Opposing Counsel represents the second. The third sister was unrepresented but dies during the course of the dispute. In that sister's will, which is not contested, she turned over her interest, in equal shares, to the existing trust, indicating that her surviving sisters should divide her share equally. During the negotiations, Lawyer learns that Opposing Counsel has been using trust funds to pay himself the fee he anticipates he will earn from representing his client in the fee dispute. There is no doubt that both surviving sisters will earn $1 million each from the trust. What is in dispute is the interest that has accumulated and how the parties should apportion it. Opposing Counsel's fee for the services he is rendering is reasonable, and he has an agreement in place to receive ten percent of whatever trust proceeds he is able to secure for his client once those funds are released to his client. While reviewing the records for the trust, Lawyer learns that Opposing Counsel has withdrawn a total of $5,000 from the trust over time, in increments of $500, and has always replaced whatever he withdraws shortly after doing so. This is far less than the $100,000 he is, at a minimum, expected to earn once the trust dispute is resolved. In fact, Lawyer and Opposing Counsel are close to reaching an agreement to release the $2 million from the trust, divided equally, to the sisters while the issue of the trust proceeds (i.e., the interest that has accrued) can be resolved.

Is Lawyer obligated to report Opposing Counsel for misconduct for his actions? If so, why? If not, why not?

A. Yes. Lawyer has a duty to report the conduct because the clients of the two lawyers were unaware this was happening and neither gave informed consent.

B. Yes. The nature of the conduct triggers an obligation on the part of Lawyer to report the misconduct.

C. No. Opposing Counsel always replaced the funds he withdrew, and no one was harmed.

D. No. The funds Opposing Counsel withdrew were a small fraction of the funds he was entitled to withdraw as payment for his services and there was little doubt that he would ultimately earn them.

6. Lawyer has been retained by another lawyer, Tyrion, to represent him in his upcoming disciplinary hearing before state authorities who are considering whether to discipline him for alleged misappropriation of client funds. Lawyer believes she can disprove the charges against Tyrion, which would absolve him of any outstanding charges against him. While conducting her investigation into the misappropriation charges, Lawyer discovers that Tyrion has knowingly sold confidential client information to adversaries for his own personal gain. What Lawyer discovers is that Tyrion would routinely share his clients' confidential settlement positions with opposing counsel, thereby weakening his clients' ability to obtain better settlements.

Is Lawyer obligated to report Tyrion for professional misconduct related to sharing his clients' confidential information?

A. Yes, because the misconduct raises a substantial question as to Tyrion's fitness to practice law.

B. No, because Lawyer obtained this information during the course of representing Tyrion for professional misconduct.

C. No, because the misconduct does not raise a substantial question as to Tyrion's fitness to practice law.

D. Yes, because the misconduct was not related to Lawyer's representation of Tyrion.

7. Lawyer is standing on line at the local coffee truck outside the courthouse one morning. Unbeknownst to a judge who is also standing on line at the same coffee truck, Lawyer can hear the conversation the judge is having with another person on the line. Lawyer recognizes that person as a star witness in a case presently before the judge, but not the case in which Lawyer is serving in a representational capacity. The judge and witness are engaged in an animated conversation, which strikes Lawyer as odd to begin with. Then Lawyer hears some of what they are discussing, and it is clear that the judge and witness are having a substantive conversation about the case in which the witness is involved before the judge.

Is Lawyer required to report the judge's conduct to the appropriate authority overseeing judicial behavior in the jurisdiction?

A. Yes, because the behavior raises a substantial question as to the judge's fitness to serve in a judicial capacity.

B. Yes, unless the communications were confidential.

C. No, because Lawyer is not serving in a representational capacity in the case discussed by the judge and witness.

D. No, because Lawyer may, but is not required to, report such conduct.

6.3 Misconduct Related to Diversity and Inclusion

Lawyers can also engage in misconduct by discriminating against certain protected classes. Although some states vary in the exact language of their corresponding rule, MR 8.4(g) makes it misconduct to "engage in conduct that the lawyer knows or reasonably should know is harassment or discrimination on the basis of race, sex, religion, national origin, ethnicity, disability, age, sexual orientation, gender identity, marital status or socioeconomic status in conduct related to the practice of law." At the same time, this subsection "does not limit the ability of a lawyer to accept, decline or withdraw from a representation in accordance with [MR] 1.16," nor does it "preclude legitimate advice or advocacy consistent with these Rules." Use the questions in this section to understand the relationship between diversity, equity, and inclusion and professional responsibility.

8. Lawyer proudly claims that he "pulled himself up by his bootstraps," was raised by a single parent, and built his career without having the financial support of family or friends. He has made a successful career for himself and does not understand why others cannot do the same. He volunteers at a local legal services office and counsels former military veterans on obtaining military benefits post-discharge. Whenever individuals come to him for assistance, he finds out if they have children and then, if so, asks if they are married. If they say they are not married, he responds that he cannot, in good conscience, represent them because he does not believe in what he calls "illegitimate" parenting. He works diligently to find those individuals other counsel who can represent them.

Is Lawyer subject to discipline for his actions?

A. No, because a motive for his behavior is not financial.

B. No, because he cannot be a zealous advocate for clients with whom he has a fundamental disagreement and works diligently to find them other counsel.

C. Yes, because he is discriminating against these prospective clients on the basis of their marital status.

D. Yes, because these prospective clients are entitled to representation to the conclusion of the matter for which they have sought assistance.

9. Lawyer forms a new legal organization that advocates for the rights of incarcerated women by bringing class action lawsuits and engaging in legislative reform work. One of these suits concerns the failure on the part of the prison where several of Lawyer's clients are housed to provide adequate health care to its female inmates on account of their gender, in violation of various equal protection principles. The prison long housed only men but over the last decade has begun to house women as well. Lawyer believes the health care provided to the women in the facility does not adequately meet their needs and that this inadequacy is a result of gender-based discrimination. Lawyer is contacted by a male inmate who is also housed at the same facility as Lawyer's clients. The male inmate states that he is receiving inadequate health care, which is not inaccurate, although though the inadequacy is not the result of gender-based discrimination. This male inmate asks for permission to participate in the class action lawsuit Lawyer has filed on behalf of the female inmates at the prison. Lawyer refuses to grant such permission, informing him that the class action only encompasses the claims of female inmates receiving inadequate health care on account of their gender, and provides a referral to another organization that might assist him.

Is Lawyer subject to discipline for refusing to represent the male prisoner on account of his gender?

A. Yes, because Lawyer may not discriminate based on gender in conduct related to the practice of law.

B. Yes, because Lawyer has no legitimate, non-discriminatory reason for declining to represent the male prisoner.

C. No, because the main purpose of Lawyer's work was not for personal pecuniary gain.

D. No, because Lawyer is engaged in legitimate advocacy on behalf of female clients and is permitted to decline the representation of the male prisoner as a result.

6.4 Formative Assessment Quiz

Use these questions to test what you have learned in this chapter.

10. Two lawyers, Able and Baker, are engaged in litigation in which they represent different plaintiffs in separate actions against the plaintiffs' employer, a large, multinational corporation. During the course of the representation, the lawyers for the multinational corporation make a settlement offer that would result in a sizable award for each of the plaintiffs. This award is less than the plaintiffs might receive should their individual cases go to trial and win, but there is certainly no guarantee that either plaintiff will win. And even if plaintiffs did win, there is no guarantee that they would necessarily receive a higher award that what the defendant is offering. Able wants to inform her client about the settlement offer, while Baker does not want to inform his. Baker knows that if Able's client hears about the settlement offer, so will Baker's, because the two clients communicate all the time about their respective cases. Baker honestly believes that accepting the settlement offer is not in the best interests of either client. Baker, without first seeking the permission of the clients or of Able, contacts the lawyers for the corporation and informs them that both clients are rejecting the settlement offer.

Is Able under an obligation to report Baker to the appropriate disciplinary authorities for Baker's behavior? If so, why? If not, why not?

A. Yes, because Baker's behavior was highly questionable and constituted malpractice.

B. Yes, because Baker's behavior raises a substantial question regarding Baker's fitness to practice law.

C. No, because Baker was acting with the clients' interests in mind.

D No, because a lawyer always has the authority to reject a settlement offer because that represents a decision related to the means and not the ends of the representation.

11. Lawyer A and Lawyer B are negotiating over the settlement of a hostile work environment case involving a group of employees in a large media company. Lawyer A represents the plaintiffs, and Lawyer B represents the defendant company. The case has received a lot of media attention from other news outlets, which view their intense coverage of the case as a means of harming a competitor by driving away both advertising dollars and viewers from its television channel, newspapers, and radio stations. Defendant company has seen a reduction in viewership and a significant drop in its stock price as a result of the negative and relentless coverage of the case. Lawyer B has been instructed to try to settle the case with Lawyer A. Lawyer B asks Lawyer A for the plaintiffs' "bottom line." Lawyer A and Lawyer A's clients know that they have a lot of leverage at this point in the negotiations because of all of the negative publicity the company is receiving, and so without conferring with the clients, Lawyer A reports that the clients' bottom line is a settlement of $1 billion. Shocked by this demand, Lawyer B says that he is not authorized to make a settlement offer even close to that amount and breaks off the negotiations. The case proceeds through the discovery phase, and the defendant company continues to suffer financially because of the negative publicity, which only gets worse as more and more stories come out describing the company's toxic work environment. On the eve of trial, Lawyer B makes one last-ditch effort to settle the case and offers plaintiffs $100 million. Lawyer A confers with the clients who now agree that their leverage is at its peak, but they do not know where things will stand once the

case goes to trial. They inform Lawyer A that they want to accept the offer. Lawyer A informs Lawyer B of this news and lets Lawyer B know that had the defendant simply made this sort of offer earlier, a lot of the negative impact on the defendant could have been avoided.

Is Lawyer B under an obligation to report Lawyer A for misconduct as a result of the misstatement of the clients' bottom line in the negotiations?

A. Yes, because Lawyer A's misstatement of the clients' bottom line raises a substantial question as to Lawyer A's fitness to practice law.

B. Yes, because Lawyer A caused significant financial injury to the defendant due to Lawyer A's unethical conduct.

C. No, because Lawyer A was free to make material misrepresentations about anything related to negotiations.

D. No, because Lawyer A's conduct does not raise a substantial question as to Lawyer A's fitness to practice law.

12. Lawyer Linda represents Lawyer Danny in a disciplinary proceeding in which Danny is accused of failing to file a complaint within an applicable statute of limitations. Danny admits that he did not comply with the statute of limitations as charged, but what the committee does not know is that the reason for the failure was that he had financial dealings with the party that would have been the defendant in the case. He had not revealed this fact to his client prior to taking on the case, and his reason for not filing the complaint was that he was afraid doing so would harm his personal investment in the company that was to be the defendant in the case and the subject of the complaint. The disciplinary committee has not asked Danny to explain his reasons for failing to file the complaint in a timely fashion but has proposed a settlement in the case to resolve it before holding a hearing on the matter. Danny does not want the case to go to a hearing for fear he will have to perjure himself or disclose the reason for the malpractice. He instructs Linda to accept whatever restitution the disciplinary committee suggests he make to the client he was representing when he failed to file the complaint.

Is Linda subject to discipline should she fail to disclose the reason for Danny's failing to file the complaint in a timely fashion?

A. No, because Danny's behavior does not raise a substantial question as to his fitness to practice law.

B. No, because the communications are protected by the attorney-client privilege.

C. Yes, because Danny's behavior raises a substantial question as to his fitness to practice law.
D. Yes, because the communications regarding Danny's reasons for his actions are not confidential.

13. Lawyer Able is representing a client in a matter involving a dispute over the creation of a trust. Lawyer reviews the work of the client's former lawyer, Baker. Baker prepared the client's trust document that is the subject of the probate matter. Able discovers that Baker made some fairly basic errors in the preparation of the trust documents that will likely result in significant tax penalties for the client. During the course of the representation of the client, Able communicates with the local bank that maintains the trust and is told by the branch manager that Baker has done this sort of thing before, and other bank clients have had similar tax penalties imposed on them based on Baker's shoddy work. Able learns that Baker prepared these trust documents soon after graduating law school and was operating as a solo practitioner at the time. It is also clear to Able that Baker had no prior training or guidance in setting up these trust documents. Able does some further research and comes across a basic trust form available on a website, and it is clear to Able that Baker used this form when setting up the client's trust. That template was for a different jurisdiction and a different type of trust. It is apparent to Able that Baker downloaded this template, simply inserted some basic information (names, addresses, etc.) into it, and tried to pass off those documents as legitimate trust documents in the jurisdiction, which they are not. That template and the document Baker ultimately created failed to include key provisions required by the jurisdiction in which the trust was created. Any practitioner with the level of skill of a general practitioner in the jurisdiction would have realized that this template was not appropriate to

use in this jurisdiction or for the purpose Baker used it.

Is Able required to report Baker to the disciplinary authorities for Baker's actions in creating these trusts? If so, why? If not, why not?

A. Yes, because Baker committed malpractice in creating these trusts.

B. No, because Able learned of Baker's alleged misconduct during the course of an investigation for a client.

C. Yes, because Baker's conduct raises a substantial question as to Baker's fitness to practice law.

D. No, because Baker's conduct does not raise a substantial question as to Baker's fitness to practice law.

14. Lawyer represents a plaintiff in a personal injury action against a department store where the plaintiff was injured when an elevator malfunctioned. Lawyer has retained the services of a private investigator to determine the cause of the malfunction. Lawyer instructs the investigator to visit the department store and try to communicate with the individual who services the elevator, to determine what went wrong on the day of the accident in which the plaintiff was injured. Lawyer knows the department store is represented by counsel in the lawsuit filed by the plaintiff. The private investigator, unaware the department store is represented by counsel, visits the scene of the incident and, without identifying his interest in the dispute, discusses the incident with one of the service staff of the department store, the individual responsible for servicing the elevator.

Is Lawyer subject to discipline for the investigator's actions in discussing the matter with the employee of the department store?

A. Yes, because the investigator attempted to gain information about the incident without identifying himself as having an interest in the matter.

B. Yes, because Lawyer attempted to evade Lawyer's obligations under the rules through the acts of another.

C. No, because Lawyer had no direct communication with a represented party.

D. No, because the investigator was not aware that the department store was represented by counsel.

15. Lawyer is engaged in protracted settlement negotiations with Opposing Counsel over the proceeds of a trust fund set up for three sisters. Lawyer represents one sister, and Opposing Counsel represents the second. The third sister was unrepresented but dies during the course of the dispute. In that third sister's will, which is not contested, she turned over her interest, in equal shares, to the existing trust, indicating that her surviving sisters should divide her share equally. There is no doubt that both surviving sisters will earn $1 million each from the trust. What is now in dispute is the interest that has accumulated and how the parties should apportion it. Opposing Counsel's fee for the services he is rendering is reasonable, and he has an agreement in place to receive ten percent of the funds he is able to secure for his client. The agreement says he can collect his fee once any funds are released to his client. Lawyer and Opposing Counsel reach an agreement to release the $2 million from the trust, divided equally, to the sisters while the issue of the trust proceeds (i.e., the interest that has accrued) can be resolved. The undisputed amount is released from the trust to each sister, through the two attorneys. Opposing Counsel distributes the undisputed funds to his client less the fee of $100,000 he earned to date for his efforts.

Is Lawyer obligated to report Opposing Counsel for having engaged in any misconduct for his actions? If so, why? If not, why not?

A. Yes. Lawyer has a duty to report the conduct because Opposing Counsel should not have taken any share of the proceeds until all disputes related to the trust were resolved.

B. Yes. The nature of the conduct triggers an obligation on the part of Lawyer to report the misconduct.

C. No. Opposing Counsel's conduct does not raise a substantial question as to his fitness to practice law.

D. No. Opposing Counsel's conduct does not raise a compelling question as to his fitness to practice law.

16. Lawyer is a prominent trusts and estates lawyer in the community who is looking to hire a new junior associate at her firm. One day she begins to interview a candidate who has a stellar academic record and strong recommendations. During the course of the interview, Lawyer learns that, although assigned the male gender at birth, the candidate identifies as a woman and is soon going to have gender reassignment surgery. Upon learning this information, Lawyer concludes the interview and informs the candidate that Lawyer cannot hire the candidate to join her firm because of what Lawyer callously describes as the candidate's "life choices." The local jurisdiction does not make discrimination on the basis of gender identity illegal.

Is Lawyer subject to discipline for refusing to consider the candidate for the position at the firm on the grounds of the candidate's gender identity?

A. No, because the conduct of screening candidates for employment is not related to the practice of law.

B. No, because the candidate has no property right in future employment with Lawyer.

C. Yes, because a lawyer cannot engage in discrimination based on gender identity in conduct related to the practice of law.

D. Yes, but only if the substantive law of the jurisdiction prohibits discrimination based on gender identity.

17. Lawyer is engaged in protracted settlement negotiations with Opposing Counsel over the proceeds of a trust fund set up for two sisters. It becomes apparent that the relationship between Opposing Counsel and his client has turned acrimonious. Lawyer and Opposing Counsel commiserate about the difficulty he is having dealing with his client, but Opposing Counsel expresses his honest belief that he can continue to represent his client in a zealous fashion and never reveals any confidential information to Lawyer. Although Opposing Counsel asserts all legitimate claims on behalf of his client, Lawyer gets a sense that Opposing Counsel cannot wait to conclude the negotiations due to the deterioration in the relationship with his client. However, Lawyer does not feel he has gained an advantage in the negotiations given the state of the relationship between Opposing Counsel and his client. The matter is ultimately settled and both parties express their satisfaction with the agreement.

Is Lawyer obligated to report Opposing Counsel for having engaged in any misconduct by his actions?

A. No, because Opposing Counsel's conduct does not raise a substantial question as to his fitness to practice law.

B. Yes, because Lawyer knows that the relationship between Opposing Counsel and his client was such that Opposing Counsel's continued representation was unethical.

C. Yes, because Opposing Counsel's behavior raised a substantial question as to his fitness to practice law.

D. No, because Opposing Counsel's conduct did not raise a compelling question as to his fitness to practice law.

Chapter 7

Attorney Free Speech Rights

American lawyers have free speech rights like any other citizen. But they are also officers of the court and are trained in the art of persuasion, which, courts have said, means that states have some degree of latitude in curtailing lawyer commercial speech to a certain degree. In addition, lawyers, through their advocacy, also engage in political speech, which courts have held is entitled to even greater latitude than commercial speech. This chapter explores questions about the extent of lawyer free speech rights.

7.1 Attorney Advertising

For roughly the first two centuries of the American legal profession's history, lawyers were largely prohibited from engaging in formal advertising. They had to find their clients through word of mouth, personal connections, and "hanging out a shingle" and hoping clients showed up. In *Bates v. State Bar of Arizona*, 433 U.S. 350 (1977), the Supreme Court held that blanket bans on attorney advertising violated the First Amendment to the U.S. Constitution. Since then, lawyer advertising has become ubiquitous, but states are still permitted to impose restraints on it, particularly with respect to in-person solicitation of clients. This section explores the issue of attorney advertising.

1. Lawyer is a young solo practitioner trying to make his professional name in the community. He is asked by a lawyer in a large firm handling a massive security breach case against EquiFacts, a company that handles online payments for millions of customers, to represent a small co-defendant in the matter that has little stake in the outcome. As a favor to Lawyer's father, who is one of the firm lawyer's former partners in the firm, the firm lawyer asks Lawyer to serve as a conflicts counsel. Lawyer serves as a caretaker of the co-defendant's interests but does little in the case. Lawyer has little experience with such matters but represents the client in a competent fashion. The matter is settled with the law firm's client agreeing to create a $50 million fund to compensate victims of the EquiFacts breach, and Lawyer's client is dismissed from the action with no liability. After the case is resolved, Lawyer believes he has found an exciting and interesting area in which to practice and begins to advertise through local media that he is now handling "security breach cases" for plaintiffs who are victims of such breaches. He also states that he "helped secure $50 million for the victims in the EquiFacts data breach case." The advertisement includes his name and contact information.

Is Lawyer subject to discipline for making either or both of the statements about his services?

A. Both statements would subject him to discipline.

B. The statement about his area of practice would subject him to discipline but not the statement about his involvement in the EquiFacts case.

C. The statement about his involvement in the EquiFacts case would subject him to discipline but not his statement about his area of practice.

D. Neither statement would subject him to discipline.

2. Lawyer advertises on his website that he conducts "private counseling services via telephone." The advertisement also says that he charges $50 for the first hour of the counseling. What the lawyer does not indicate in the advertisement is that if the session goes longer than one hour, he charges $100 for each tenth of an hour, for a rate of $1,000 an hour, which is a reasonable rate for a lawyer of his skill and experience. When clients sign up for the services, they are asked to submit a credit card before the services are provided, and the total charge appears on their credit card at the conclusion of the session.

Is Lawyer subject to discipline for the manner in which he advertises his services and the fee structure applied thereto?

A. Yes, because the advertising is materially misleading.

B. Yes, because Lawyer is charging an unreasonable rate for his services.

C. No, because Lawyer is charging a reasonable rate for his services.

D. No, because Lawyer has not engaged in false or misleading communication regarding his services.

3. Lawyer handles bankruptcy matters in a private firm. Lawyer learns that Cersei, one of Lawyer's neighbors, but one with whom Lawyer does not have a personal relationship, is contemplating filing for bankruptcy for one of her companies. Lawyer knows that Cersei is an experienced businesswoman who has in many previous instances used legal services to file for bankruptcy for a large percentage of her companies. She often makes strategic use of bankruptcy to improve her bargaining position with the labor unions whose members work for her companies. If she can exact concessions from the unions, it makes her companies more attractive investment targets for investment funds that want to invest in her business activities. Lawyer knows Cersei would be a lucrative client for his firm and approaches her in person at a cocktail party hosted by one of their mutual neighbors. He informs her that he would like to serve as her counsel in the planned bankruptcy that appears imminent with one of her businesses. He offers to do so at a discount for the first case, hoping that he can convince her that she should take all of her business to Lawyer's firm. Cersei says she will consider having him serve as her counsel, but she wants to think about it first before giving him an answer.

Was it improper for Lawyer to approach Cersei in this manner to solicit her as a client?

A. No, because Cersei did not respond right away, asked for a period of time to contemplate Lawyer's offer, and Lawyer offered Cersei a discount on his services.

B. No, because Cersei is someone who routinely seeks this type of legal service.

C. Yes, any in-person solicitation of potential clients is improper because it is difficult to regulate and fraught with the potential for overreach on the part of the lawyer.

D. Yes, because Lawyer utilized a social gathering to make a professional solicitation.

4. Lawyer has created a podcast, "Law Through History," in which Lawyer interviews legal historians about the origins of different laws and the stories behind some of American history's most iconic litigators and most important court cases. Lawyer also answers listener questions about legal history which are emailed to an email address dedicated to the podcast. Lawyer is careful never to give direct and particularized legal advice to individuals who send in questions. Lawyer also always stays clear of dispensing formal legal advice that might create an attorney-client relationship between Lawyer and any particular listener. At the beginning of the podcast, Lawyer reads a disclaimer stating that the content of the podcast is not intended as legal advice and that anyone in need of legal representation should always consult an attorney. Lawyer profits personally from the advertising on the podcast, which includes advertising from Lawyer's firm as well as other law firms. Lawyer always fully discloses who is supporting the podcast and indicates further that the mere fact that the firms are advertising on the podcast does not create an attorney-client relationship with any listener. The podcast is very popular, and Lawyer has developed an extremely loyal following. Partly as a result of the popularity of the podcast, Lawyer's firm has seen a significant increase in prospective clients contacting the firm to inquire about representation. The payments for the advertising are modest and also consistent with payments typically made by advertisers on other podcasts of similar popularity. All firms, including the lawyer's firm, that advertise through the podcast also include their name and contact information.

Is Lawyer or any firms that advertise on the podcast subject to discipline for any of their actions? If so, why? If not, why not?

A. Yes, because the payments for the podcast advertisements by the other firms constitute an inappropriate distribution of legal fees among lawyers.

B. Yes, because the use of podcast media by Lawyer's firm is a deceptive practice designed to drive potential clients to the firm.

C. No, because there is nothing inappropriate about paying for or receiving reasonable payment for the advertisements and the source of the funds was always disclosed.

D. No, because the advertisements are appropriate as long as the podcast contains a disclaimer indicating that neither the advertisements nor anything else on the podcast creates an attorney-client relationship.

5. Lawyer exclusively represents victims of discrimination in higher education. Most of these cases involve violations of civil rights laws ensuring that athletic programs at colleges and universities do not discriminate in their programming based on the gender of the athletes. Lawyer has provided such representation and handled such matters exclusively for over twenty years. On her firm's website, she is described as a "certified specialist in discrimination in athletics in higher education." Any advertisement that contains such information includes her name and contact information.

Is Lawyer subject to discipline for the contents of her advertisement?

A. Yes. It is unfair and deceptive for Lawyer to advertise that she specializes in an area of law because lawyers are held to the standard of a general practitioner.

B. Yes, because the advertisement fails to identify the authority that has certified her as a specialist.

C. No, because a lawyer may list a specialty area of practice and it does not appear that this advertisement is false or misleading in any way.

D. No, but only because Lawyer always included her name and contact information on any advertisement.

6. Lawyer practices personal injury law. He is a solo practitioner working on a for-profit basis. He describes himself as an "ambulance chaser, but an ethical ambulance chaser." He never actually chases ambulances, but instead sends very respectful letters to accident victims when he reads about accidents in the newspaper. The letters are limited in the information they include, stating simply that if the victim wants legal representation, he or she should consider contacting the lawyer at that individual's convenience. On the outside of the envelope appears Lawyer's name, return address, and the term "Advertising Material" printed in large-font type. He learns of a new rule that the state has imposed requiring that a lawyer wait thirty days from the date of an accident before contacting any victim, even if the contact is made in writing in the manner described here. Lawyer believes his free speech rights are being infringed and challenges the thirty-day waiting period.

Is the thirty-day ban on lawyer contact with accident victims unconstitutional? If so, why? If not, why not?

A. Yes. A state cannot impose a ban on any written contact with persons known to be in need of legal representation.

B. No. Such a state ban does not improperly infringe on lawyers' free speech rights.

C. Yes. A state cannot impose a ban on written communication with persons known to be in need of legal representation if that communication is not fraudulent or deceptive.

D. No. Because Lawyer's purposes in reaching out to prospective clients are pecuniary in nature, the state only must show a legitimate state interest in regulating such speech in this manner.

7. Lawyer handles personal injury cases representing plaintiffs. The primary way in which Lawyer obtains his clients is through a pre-paid legal services plan. Through this plan, operated by a local union, union members receive, as a benefit for paying their union dues, free referrals to legal services providers when they need them. This lawyer referral service is approved by the local disciplinary authority. Lawyer does not control the functioning of the plan in any way. Representatives of the plan routinely contact members of the union by telephone to inquire whether they need legal services. Whenever anyone indicates that he or she might have a personal injury claim, they are given Lawyer's contact information.

Is Lawyer subject to discipline for the manner in which he obtains clients through the union's plan?

A. Yes, because the union members are contacted directly through live telephone communications.

B. No, because Lawyer is participating in an approved, pre-paid legal services plan.

C. No, because Lawyer is not personally engaged in the live telephonic outreach to the members of the union.

D. Yes, because the clients are in a vulnerable position and susceptible to personal contact from the union.

8. Lawyer works at a non-profit legal services organization that provides free representation to low-income clients facing eviction in housing court. Part of her practice involves providing to tenants advice over the telephone about navigating housing court procedures should the tenants have to represent themselves, as many in this jurisdiction do. She only provides information to low-income tenants and does not give advice to the small number of landlords who are unrepresented and contact her for assistance. Lawyer draws a salary for her work but does not charge for her services. One of the main goals of the organization for which she works is to ensure that low-income tenants have information to help them represent themselves if the organization is not able to represent them. A group of landlords is upset that Lawyer provides these free services to tenants and not to landlords. They successfully lobby the state courts to issue a rule that anyone who provides legal information to pro se litigants must do so regardless of the characteristics of the individual seeking advice, including his or her party status. The state court says the harm it is aiming to prevent is that of having pro se assistance available to only one type of litigant.

If Lawyer challenges this court rule, by what standard will it be assessed to determine whether it complies with restrictions on free speech?

A. Whether the state interest is compelling and the means of regulating lawyer speech are closely drawn to avoid unnecessary abridgment of associational freedoms.

B. Whether it is a reasonable time, place, and manner restriction.

C. Whether it advances a substantial governmental interest and does so only through means that directly advance that interest.

D. Whether it advances a legitimate public interest and was issued with due process of law.

9. Lawyer works for a large private firm and supports her local non-profit legal services organization by making monthly visits to a senior center in the community where she provides free estate planning counseling to the individuals who utilize the center. She generally makes a brief presentation over lunch at the center on a topic that is likely to be of interest to the guests in attendance, and then she engages in one-on-one counseling with those guests who want to speak to her privately. Lawyer does not charge for her services and sees this as her public service. Once every few months, an individual at the center who can afford her services will approach her and ask Lawyer to represent him or her. Lawyer is happy to provide free advice to these individuals, but they routinely insist on paying Lawyer for her services. In such instances, Lawyer gives the prospective clients her business card and asks them to make an appointment with the secretary at her office.

Is Lawyer subject to discipline for her conduct?

A. Yes, because Lawyer is engaged in improper in-person solicitation of clients.

B. Yes, because these clients are in a particularly vulnerable situation.

C. No, because Lawyer does not initiate the contact with the prospective clients.

D. No, because a significant motive for Lawyer's actions is not her own financial gain.

10. Lawyer handles trusts and estates matters. Lawyer's sister-in-law, Cersei, with whom Lawyer has a close relationship, is very wealthy, and Lawyer has long hoped to obtain her as a client. At a family gathering, Lawyer approaches Cersei to ask if he can represent her in preparing her will and generally ordering her affairs. Cersei tells Lawyer that she has her own counsel, does not need any assistance, and prefers that they keep their relationship "familial rather than professional." Undeterred, at the next family gathering, Lawyer again approaches Cersei, respectfully, telling her that he can be her counsel, can give her "a good deal" on his fees, and would charge her less than her current lawyer is charging her. Cersei again declines his assistance.

Was it professional misconduct for Lawyer to approach Cersei in any of these instances to solicit her business?

A. No. Both attempts to solicit Cersei's business are appropriate because they are close relatives.

B. Yes. Lawyer should have refrained from communicating with Cersei about representing her once she indicated she did not desire his assistance.

C. Yes. Any in-person solicitation of potential clients is improper because it is difficult to regulate and fraught with the potential for overreach on the part of the lawyer.

D. No. Because Lawyer was offering Cersei an opportunity to lower her legal fees, it was in her interests for Lawyer to solicit her business.

11. Lawyer is a real estate attorney in the Capital Region of New York State. She enters into a non-exclusive mutual referral arrangement with a local real estate broker through which Lawyer agrees to refer potential real estate clients to the broker and the broker agrees to refer his real estate clients who might need legal services to Lawyer. Lawyer is licensed in New York State to practice law but does not have a real estate broker's license. The real estate broker is licensed as a real estate broker but not as a lawyer. Lawyer and the broker are very careful not to mix their responsibilities or their fees, and the broker cannot direct Lawyer in the provision of legal services. Lawyer is completely in charge of the legal work, and the broker is completely in charge of delivering real estate broker services. The mutual arrangement turns out to be quite lucrative because it is convenient for the clients, but Lawyer and the broker never pay the other a finder's fee for referring any clients to the other. Each client is given notice of the arrangement and the fact that it is not exclusive. Lawyer and the broker are free to refer potential clients to other lawyers or brokers as appropriate, but they both find that this arrangement is working quite well for them, so they continue to send clients to each other while giving notice to clients of additional options.

Has Lawyer acted unethically in this arrangement with the real estate broker?

A. Yes, because the broker is not licensed to practice law, and therefore the provision of services through the arrangement is unethical and constitutes the unauthorized practice of law.

B. Yes, because a lawyer cannot enter into an agreement with a non-lawyer if any of the activities rendered through the agreement are the provision of legal services.

C. No, because the two professionals control their own work, no fee is imposed or collected, the arrangement is non-exclusive, and the clients are given notice of the arrangement.

D. No, because Lawyer and the broker do not share fees for the separate services they offer and each is responsible for delivering separate professional services consistent with their respective professional licenses.

7.2 Attorney Communications with the Media

Just as soliciting clients is a critical element of what lawyers do, so is engaging in advocacy in the court of public opinion through the press, thanks in part to today's twenty-four-hour news cycle. Model Rule 3.6 largely governs what a lawyer can and cannot say, and the limitations and permissions contained in that rule and the accompanying commentary are covered in this section.

12. Lawyer formerly represented an elected official in that official's successful efforts to defend his initial victory in a special election for the U.S. Congress. The representative loses his bid for re-election in the following general election, however. After the representative leaves office, it comes to light that he may have engaged in financial fraud and insider trading while in office by sharing information he received from official and confidential briefings to make stock trades. Lawyer, who is not a criminal defense lawyer, declines to represent the former elected official in this criminal trial. On the night before the jury is supposed to be selected in the ex-representative's criminal trial, Lawyer is contacted by a local radio station and gives a live interview about Lawyer's experiences representing the elected official. This interview is widely disseminated by the popular radio station and its several local affiliates. During the interview, Lawyer claims to be shocked by allegations, having always believed the ex-representative to be of the highest moral character. Lawyer also says that she got to know the elected official quite well during the time in which they worked together. Lawyer simply does not believe the allegations. "I was with my client and friend five hours a day for long stretches at a time," Lawyer says, "and I never saw any conduct like this and cannot believe the accused is capable of engaging in the alleged conduct that the prosecutor is saying serves as the basis of the charges." Lawyer states that she believes the allegations are politically motivated and hopes the jury acquits the former representative. When the prospective jury pool is empaneled the next day, a majority of the prospective jurors state that they heard the Lawyer's radio interview.

Is Lawyer subject to discipline for the statements to the press on the eve of trial? If so, why? If not, why not?

A. No, because Lawyer did not knowingly intend to influence the outcome of the trial.

B. No, because Lawyer was not involved in the representation of the former client in the criminal trial.

C. Yes, because Lawyer's comments were prejudicial to the administration of justice.

D. Yes, because Lawyer should have known there was a substantial likelihood that her statements, made on the eve of jury selection, could impact the trial.

13. Lawyer represents Client, who is accused of robbing a bank. The prosecutor on the case, Harvey Dent, is trying to make a name for himself as the new chief prosecutor in Gotham City. Dent holds a press conference where he lays out the case against Client in vivid detail, even posting pictures of several individuals killed in the bank robbery. Dent asserts that the bank is a local community bank and the funds stolen are from law-abiding members of the community, some of whom have now been deprived of their life savings. Dent also claims that Client is responsible for these deaths and was the mastermind behind the robbery—he alleges that Client not only pulled off the robbery but also systematically killed all of Client's accomplices, one-by-one, as they were carrying out the robbery, leaving Client with all of the proceeds of the robbery. The press conference takes place two days before jury selection for Client's trial is set to begin. Because of the high-profile nature of the robbery, all of the local press outlets and numerous online sources carry the press conference. The very next day, on the eve of jury selection, Lawyer holds a hastily arranged but well-covered press conference where Lawyer states that Client has confessed to the robbery itself but denies having killed anyone in the course of the robbery. Lawyer states that the bank was actually a front for an organized crime syndicate and Client has every intention of turning the stolen funds over to the authorities.

Is Lawyer subject to discipline for the statements made in the press conference held on the eve of jury selection in Client's trial? If so, why? If not, why not?

A. Yes, because the statement regarding the contents of a confession is the type of statement that is likely to taint the proceeding.

B. Yes, because the press conference occurred so close in time to jury selection.

C. No, because Lawyer was responding to the adverse publicity that resulted from Dent's press conference and only revealed that which was necessary to respond to such publicity.

D. No, because a defense lawyer has greater leeway to speak to the press to ensure the protection of the rights of the accused.

14. Lawyer is defense counsel in a high-profile prosecution of the former chief of staff of the sitting governor of Lawyer's state. The prosecutor in the case has political ambitions of his own and has been a frequent guest of cable news shows in which he talks generally about his efforts to root out corruption in every branch of the state government, without mentioning Lawyer's client in these statements. Lawyer wants to hold a press conference one week before the start of her client's trial to show that the indictment against her client is a political witch hunt. She wants to provide evidence to the press, which she will also present at trial, that the prosecution's star witness has himself been found guilty of perjury in the past.

Is Lawyer subject to discipline if she gives statements to the press regarding the credibility of the prosecution's witness?

A. Yes, because Lawyer should know that the information presented at the press conference has a substantial likelihood of materially prejudicing the proceeding.

B. No, because a lawyer may make statements to the press to counteract negative publicity about a client initiated by others.

C. No, because Lawyer is merely providing evidence that she will present at trial.

D. Yes, because a lawyer may not speak to the press on any subject this close to the commencement date of the trial.

15. Lawyer is a prosecutor in a high-profile criminal case in which it is alleged that a local business leader was engaged in a fraudulent scheme. The lawyer defending the business leader holds a press conference in which he alleges that one of the key witnesses for the prosecution was recently charged with embezzlement, but the charges against him were ultimately withdrawn. The prosecutor, who works at the office that would have brought such charges against the witness, knows the defense attorney's claim is false. The prosecutor holds her own press conference to correct the record regarding the witness. During this press conference, she highlights the fact that the witness was never a suspect in a criminal investigation; that no such charges were contemplated; and that the witness passed a polygraph test, proving that the witness is being truthful in his testimony generally against the defendant.

Which, if any, of the prosecutor's press conference statements are more likely than not to have a material prejudicial effect on the proceeding?

A. All aspects of the press conference were inappropriate because the prosecutor is held to a higher standard than the typical lawyer with respect to speaking to the press.

B. No aspects of the press conference were inappropriate because the prosecutor was merely responding to adverse publicity, and her statements were designed to correct the record.

C. The statements regarding the polygraph test.

D. The statements regarding whether the witness was or had been the subject of a criminal investigation.

16. Lawyer represents a criminal defendant in a pending proceeding. Lawyer learns that the local police chief has held a press conference in which she reported truthfully on the progress of the investigation in the case, without mentioning the name of Lawyer's client or casting Lawyer's client in a negative light in any way. The trial is just days away, however. Lawyer holds his own subsequent press conference to refute what Lawyer reasonably believes was a factually incorrect statement regarding the time of the next court hearing in the proceeding.

Is Lawyer subject to discipline for making this statement to the press?

A. Yes, because Lawyer was presenting this information in his role as advocate in the case.

B. No, because it does not appear that the statement Lawyer made has a substantial likelihood of materially prejudicing the proceeding.

C. Yes, because Lawyer is not responding to adverse publicity regarding his client.

D. No, because Lawyer is merely responding to adverse publicity regarding the trial.

17. Lawyer is a prominent and frequent guest on the nightly cable news shows and is highly sought after because she is known for saying fairly controversial things and speaking her mind. She has essentially stopped handling cases because her notoriety as a commentator has translated into an income. She now makes significant earnings on the speaker circuit and as a paid legal analyst on television. Her latest appearance involved commenting on the charges filed against a local elected official. On the eve of jury selection in the case, Lawyer appears on a local television show with a widely disseminated public broadcast. She is interviewed on a range of matters and is asked to comment on the credibility of the prosecution's witnesses. Lawyer gladly opines on the subject, casting aspersions on the prosecution's witnesses, calling them a "nest of vipers and scoundrels" and saying, "I wouldn't trust them as far as I can throw them, which is not very far." Lawyer is a partner in the firm that is representing the defendant in the action but is screened effectively from the matter and afforded no fees from the representation.

Is Lawyer subject to discipline for these statements?

A. No, because she is not serving in a representational capacity with respect to the prosecution of the elected official.

B. No, because the general public would know this is mere commentary and should not be taken seriously.

C. Yes, because the statements were likely to adversely affect the administration of justice.

D. Yes, because the statements had a substantial likelihood of materially prejudicing the proceeding.

7.3 Formative Assessment Quiz

Use these questions to test what you have learned in this chapter.

18. Lawyer is a regular contributor to her local newspaper, the *Town Bee*, writing what is called a "Dear Attorney" column. Lawyer responds to basic legal inquiries sent in from subscribers of the paper. In this column, Lawyer is careful to never give direct and particularized legal advice to individuals who write in to the paper for guidance. Lawyer also always stays clear of dispensing formal legal advice that might create an attorney-client relationship between her and any particular reader. The column bears a disclaimer at the end of it declaring that the column is not intended as legal advice and that anyone in need of legal representation should always consult an attorney. Lawyer is not paid for generating this column. Lawyer admits that she publishes this column in the hope that she might attract clients to her firm. Lawyer also pays to advertise in the newspaper, typically taking out a half-page ad with a line toward the bottom of it that reads: "Check out my column in the *Town Bee*, which appears on page nine every week." The advertisement also includes Lawyer's name and contact information.

Is Lawyer subject to discipline for any of her actions? If so, why? If not, why not?

A. Yes. While writing for the advice column is appropriate, Lawyer may not give anything of value to another for advertising, which includes advertising in the newspaper.

B. No. Lawyer does not dispense particularized legal advice through the column and there is nothing inappropriate about paying for the advertisement.

C. Yes. The advertisement is appropriate, but the advice column is clearly an inappropriate effort to solicit clients.

D. No. The advertisement is appropriate, and as long as the advice column has a disclaimer, the lawyer is free to use the advice column as a means of attracting clients, regardless of what information is communicated through the column.

19. Lawyer attends cocktail receptions designed to provide opportunities for local entrepreneurs to "pitch" their ideas to local investors (without seeking actual investments for fear of violating securities laws). Lawyer feels these events are a good way to get a sense of the "pulse" of the business community. Lawyer usually mingles with the crowd and talks to as many people as she can. If she learns that an entrepreneur in the room might be in need of legal services, she writes a letter inviting the entrepreneur to set up an appointment to discuss the possibility of Lawyer's representing the prospective client. Lawyer always includes her name and contact information on any communication.

Are Lawyer's efforts to recruit clients unethical in any way?

A. Yes. Lawyer should not attend the events and communicate with prospective clients in person because these actions constitute improper in-person solicitation.

B. Yes. Lawyer should not communicate in writing with prospective clients whom she knows are in need of representation.

C. No. Lawyer's actions do not constitute improper in-person solicitation, and her communications with the attendees during and after the receptions are not improper.

D. No. Lawyer fails to properly identify herself as having an interest in securing clients when she communicates with individuals at the cocktail receptions, and thus her actions are false and deceptive.

20. Lawyer learns that a video shot from a closed-circuit television camera appears to show her client engaged in the robbery of a convenience store. The prosecutor in the case displays the video during a press conference, arguing that it shows that Lawyer's client is guilty of the crime for which he is charged. Lawyer has strong reason to believe that the video does not portray her client but rather is a "deep fake," that is, a digitally altered video. She hires a forensic investigator to review the video, and the investigator confirms Lawyer's suspicion. Lawyer holds her own press conference, stating only that she believes the evidence will show that the video has been tampered with and will thus be inadmissible.

Is Lawyer subject to discipline for her statements at the press conference?

A. Yes, because she addressed the inadmissibility of evidence.

B. Yes, because she addressed the results of the forensic review of the video evidence.

C. No, because she was merely speaking honestly about her assessment of the credibility of the evidence against her client.

D. No, because she was responding to adverse publicity initiated by the prosecutor.

21. Lawyer works in a busy port town at a firm that handles cases in admiralty law. She has practiced in the field for over twenty years and holds an advanced degree, an LLM, on the subject. The state has not authorized any organization in the state to certify that any lawyer in the state specializes in admiralty law. Nevertheless, Lawyer wants to advertise in local print media, particularly in a trade publication for the local shipping industry titled *The Shipping News*, that she is a "specialist in admiralty law."

Is Lawyer subject to discipline for describing herself as a "specialist in admiralty law"? If so, why? If not, why not?

A. Yes, because Lawyer is not permitted to state or imply that she is a specialist in any particular field of law.

B. Yes, because there is no state-authorized organization available to certify Lawyer as a specialist in this field of law, and thus she cannot claim to be one.

C. No, because Lawyer is advertising her legal specialty in order to promote greater access to justice.

D. No, because Lawyer's description of herself as a specialist in admiralty law is permissible as long as it is not fraudulent or deceptive.

22. Lawyer works for a non-profit organization that advocates homeowner rights and typically brings litigation to attack what the group describes as eminent domain abuse by state and local governments. The organization tracks state court filings from around the country, and when it appears that condemnation proceedings have been instituted (the action a government typically undertakes to seize a property by eminent domain), Lawyer sends out a solicitation by mail to encourage the owner whose property is the subject of the lawsuit to contact the organization for free representation. Sometimes, if Lawyer does not get a response from a property owner, Lawyer will direct a staff member at the organization to visit the property to offer the organization's services to the property owner in person. Lawyer receives a salary for the work Lawyer performs for the organization. When Lawyer is retained to represent a property owner in a condemnation proceeding, Lawyer does not charge that property owner. However, because the cases typically involve the assertion of claims under statutes or constitutional provisions that allow a lawyer to pursue attorney's fees if victorious, the retainer with the property owner provides that the property owner will cooperate with the lawyer to seek fees from defendants in the case, should the property owner prevail.

Is Lawyer subject to discipline for any of these actions? If so, why? If not, why not?

A. No, because the in-person solicitation was performed by a staff member and not by Lawyer directly.

B. No, because Lawyer and the non-profit organization are engaged in protected political speech.

C. Yes, because Lawyer used another to engage in in-person solicitation that Lawyer is not permitted to conduct personally.

D. Yes, because Lawyer's efforts are not strictly for non-pecuniary purposes.

Chapter 8

Judicial Ethics

Members of the legal profession must also be aware of the duties that cover members of the judiciary and the ways in which those duties intersect with and affect practicing lawyers. In addition, the Multistate Professional Responsibility Examination typically asks at least a few questions under the Model Code of Judicial Conduct (MCJC). Unlike the Model Rules of Professional Conduct, which contains rules and comments, the MCJC preserves the old three-part "Code" structure of previous versions of legal ethics rules, containing general canons, rules, and comments. This chapter explores some key issues that arise at the intersection of judicial and attorney conduct and misconduct.

8.1 Judicial Misconduct

This first section provides an overview of the types of behavior that can be considered judicial misconduct under the MCJC.

1. Judge presides in a courthouse in which several different types of courts can be found, for example, family court, housing court, and civil court. While most parties in Judge's courtroom are represented, in these other courts, many litigants appear pro se. When Judge's courtroom is not in session, she routinely walks the halls of the courthouse just to observe what is transpiring there. During these walks, on five separate occasions, Judge witnesses a particular lawyer who has never appeared before her berating pro se litigants and demeaning them using racially charged language.

Is Judge required to report the attorney's conduct to the appropriate disciplinary authority?

A. Yes, because Judge has actual knowledge that the lawyer has engaged in unethical behavior.

B. No, because Judge did not observe the attorney's behavior while operating in her official judicial capacity.

C. Yes, because such conduct raises a substantial question as to the attorney's fitness to practice law.

D. No, because the attorney does not appear before Judge.

2. A judge handling the discovery phase of a litigated dispute in state court has agreed to supervise a deposition of a state elected official in the matter. The judge learns from court personnel that the lawyer representing the plaintiff in the dispute was recently taken to the hospital while in the midst of handling another matter in the same courthouse where Judge presides. Believing it will not give either party an advantage, Judge contacts plaintiff's lawyer's firm to ask about the health of the lawyer as well as to determine whether the deposition needs to be rescheduled. The firm responds that the lawyer was in fact hospitalized for observation, that the illness was not serious, and that another lawyer in the firm will handle the deposition at the time it was originally scheduled for. The judge promptly gives opposing counsel notice of this communication and affords it an opportunity to respond. The opposing counsel's firm confirms it received the information about the health of the other lawyer and that it understands the deposition is still scheduled to go ahead as planned.

Is the judge subject to discipline for these communications?

A. No, because the judge was discussing scheduling matters and promptly gave opposing counsel notice of the communication and an opportunity to respond.

B. No, because nothing of substance was discussed in the communications.

C. Yes, because the judge should not have had either of these communications without the participation of both sides.

D. Yes, because the judge should have given advance notice to both counsel of the judge's intent to have an ex parte communication with either of them.

3. Judge Jane Crummy, who currently holds an elected position as a trial court judge in her home state, is a candidate to be nominated by the U.S. President to serve as Director of the Federal Bureau of Investigation (FBI), a nonelected, appointive office. She plans to resign her judicial position once she is nominated, and certainly if she is confirmed by the U.S. Senate. She is concerned, however, that she needs to resign the position even while she is simply a candidate for the position. She is currently presiding over an exclusively civil docket, and no matters before her are currently being handled by the FBI. She does not plan to lobby the President or any members of the Senate to support her candidacy and is seeking no endorsements from any independent entities, partisan or non-partisan.

Does Judge Crummy need to resign her position as a state judge because she is a candidate to be nominated to serve as Director of the Federal Bureau of Investigation?

A. Yes, because once she is a candidate, she is tainted by the potential association with the President, who is a partisan official.

B. No, because it is an appointed, nonjudicial position, and resignation is not required while she is still just a candidate for the position.

C. No, because the FBI position is a federal position and the judge holds a state judicial appointment at present.

D. Yes, because it raises the appearance of impropriety.

4. A judge has been a distinguished member of the federal bench for nearly twenty years. The judge has been a leader and trailblazer in terms of improving diversity and inclusion within the federal courts, including among its judges and court staff as well as the practicing bar, throughout the course of the judge's legal career. The judge has been asked to serve on the board of an organization that is being formed to advocate improvements in diversity and inclusion in the state court system of the state in which the judge presides. The organization's advocacy will not be directed at the federal courts, and the organization will not engage in any litigation in state or federal court. The judge will not be a member of the organization's executive team that meets weekly but instead will participate in quarterly board meetings, which generally occur after normal business hours and last no longer than two hours. Such board meetings are generally held via video conference, and the judge will join these meetings from home. The organization's stated purpose is only to highlight the need to improve diversity among the practicing bar in the state courts, as well as in the state court system itself.

May the judge serve on the board of this organization? If so, why? If not, why not?

A. Yes, because such service would not appear to undermine the judge's independence, integrity, or impartiality.

B. No, because the organization is focused on the courts of the state in which the judge presides, even if the organization's efforts are directed toward the operation of the state courts.

C. Yes, because the matters are strictly related to the state courts, over which the judge has no jurisdiction.

D. No, because the judge's impartiality with respect to issues of diversity and inclusion might reasonably be questioned if the judge participates in the activities of this organization.

5. Judge currently serves on the state's highest court. Judge's spouse is running for the office of U.S. Senator to represent the constituents of the state. Judge issues a press release endorsing the spouse's candidacy for the U.S. Senate. Judge was not paid in any way for this endorsement. The statement contained no disclaimer that it was being made only in Judge's personal capacity and not in any official, judicial capacity.

Is Judge subject to discipline for endorsing his spouse?

A. Yes, because Judge's endorsement should have included a disclaimer that it was being made in Judge's personal capacity.

B. No, because the spouse qualifies as a close family member for which such endorsements are permitted.

C. Yes, because Judge should not have made any such endorsement.

D. No, because Judge is a state court judge, while Judge's spouse is a candidate for a federal elective position.

6. A judge handling a complicated mass torts action often works with her deputy, a member of her staff, to handle and oversee negotiations between the parties. The deputy and the judge routinely discuss confidential matters regarding the case, including the judge's thoughts regarding how she might rule on important procedural matters, and they review material submitted under seal to the court which includes trade secrets of the companies involved in the lawsuit.

Is the judge subject to discipline for sharing confidential information with her deputy?

A. Yes. The judge is supposed to maintain all information handled by chambers as confidential, especially her own thought processes, and should not be sharing any of this confidential information with her deputy.

B. Yes. The judge should have obtained consent to share any confidential information from the parties before her.

C. No. The judge is entitled to share whatever confidential information is in her possession with anyone she deems necessary in order to discharge her judicial duties.

D. No. The judge is permitted to share confidential information with court staff in discharging her judicial duties.

7. Jane Jacob is being discussed as a potential nominee to the state's highest court, an appointed position, named by the state's governor.

From which of the following entities is she barred from seeking an endorsement of herself as a nominee?

A. The state's non-profit bar association.

B. The political party of the state's governor.

C. A non-partisan, non-profit organization that conducts screening interviews of judicial appointees.

D. The non-partisan judicial nominating commission which is an arm of the state legislature.

8. Lawyer is a former judge on the state's highest court who retired when she reached the age of seventy, in accordance with state law applicable to the position. Lawyer now works as a partner in a local firm that handles cases on appeal that have been litigated by other law firms. Lawyer is retained to work on a case, *Smith v. Jones*, in which she had joined in the majority opinion as a judge of the state's highest court, although she did not write the opinion. The losing party in that case now seeks to appeal to the U.S. Supreme Court because there is an issue that gives rise to the Supreme Court's jurisdiction over the matter that was decided by the state's highest court. Without seeking or obtaining the informed consent of any affected client, Lawyer wants to argue the case before the U.S. Supreme Court, defending the opinion of the state's highest court.

Is it ethical for Lawyer to argue the case before the U.S. Supreme Court?

A. Yes, because the case is no longer in the state court system in which she was a judge.

B. Yes, because she is not arguing the case before the same court on which she was a judge.

C. No, because she likely has confidential information about the matter that creates a conflict of interest, even though she did not write the opinion.

D. No, because a lawyer may not represent a party in connection with a matter in which the lawyer participated personally and substantially as a judge without the consent of all affected parties.

8.2 Formative Assessment Quiz

Use these questions to test what you have learned in this chapter.

9. Judge Judy is fairly new to the bench. She has been assigned a complex class action case filed against a series of pharmaceutical companies regarding what is alleged to have been an illegal scheme involving the marketing and sale of opioids. The case is a national class action, and the plaintiffs are seeking a large damage award. Judge Judy is concerned that her inexperience will lead her to make incorrect procedural decisions throughout the course of the litigation. She plans to consult with a retired law professor, whom she knows has studied numerous large national class actions regarding asbestos, for procedural pointers on how the judges in those cases handled such complex matters. Before seeking the professor's advice, she confirms that the professor has no active or potential conflicts of interest. In a written memorandum, the retired professor makes several recommendations to Judge Judy as to how she can manage the case. After receiving the memorandum, Judge Judy shares it with the lawyers for all parties and affords them an opportunity to comment on and object to, in writing, the retired professor's suggestions regarding how the matter should progress procedurally.

Was it improper for Judge Judy to consult with the retired professor in the manner in which she did?

A. Yes, because it was improper for Judge Judy to have consulted with a retired professor on the matter regardless of any notice and comment procedures she utilized.

B. Yes, because the parties should have been afforded advance notice of Judge Judy's intent to consult with the retired professor and given a reasonable opportunity to object.

C. No, because the retired professor was cleared of any conflicts of interest prior to Judge Judy seeking the retired professor's advice.

D. No, because Judge Judy gave notice to the litigants of the retired professor's memorandum and afforded them an opportunity to submit their comments and objections in writing.

10. Pat is a judge in the state's highest court. Pat's spouse, Sam, is running for election for an open seat in the U.S. Congress, which will be decided in a partisan fashion. Pat wishes to make a political contribution to Sam as a candidate for this position. When she does so, Pat identifies herself and her current position on public filings but does not disclose her personal relationship to Sam.

Is Pat subject to discipline for making a contribution to Sam's campaign?

A. Yes, because a judge may not make a political contribution to any candidate for partisan, elected political office.

B. No, because Sam is Pat's close family member.

C. No, because Sam is seeking a position in the federal government as opposed to the state government.

D. Yes, because Pat failed to disclose the familial relationship with Sam when making the contribution.

11. A judge has been a distinguished member of the federal bench for nearly twenty years. The judge has been a leader and trailblazer in terms of improving diversity and inclusion within the federal courts, including among its judges and court staff as well as the practicing bar, throughout the course of the judge's legal career. The judge has been asked to serve on the board of an organization that is being formed to advocate improvements in disability access in state government facilities. The organization will engage in frequent litigation in state and federal courts. The organization's advocacy will not be directed at addressing disability access in any federal buildings, however. The judge will not be a member of the organization's executive team that meets weekly but instead will participate in quarterly board meetings, which generally occur after normal business hours and last no longer than two hours. Such board meetings are generally held via video conference and the judge will join these meetings from home.

May the judge serve on the board of this organization? If so, why? If not, why not?

A. Yes. Such service would not appear to undermine the judge's independence, integrity, or impartiality because the organization's advocacy only impacts state and not federal buildings.

B. No, because the organization's advocacy will result in frequent litigation in the federal court, and the judge would have to recuse.

C. Yes, because the organization is engaged in protected political speech.

D. No, because the judge's impartiality with respect to issues of disability access might reasonably be questioned as a result of the judge's participation in the organization's activities.

12. Judge is invited to join the board of an organization that strives to educate the public about the importance of using the judicial system to resolve disputes between neighbors. Judge intends to engage in all activities of the organization, including the solicitation of financial contributions on behalf of the organization. Judge intends to seek such contributions only from the following individuals and entities: close family members, judges over whom Judge has no supervisory authority, and members of the local county bar association who routinely appear before her in her judicial capacity.

Which of the following accurately describes the judge's proper course of action with respect to these fundraising activities?

A. The judge may solicit funds from her immediate family members and the other judges but not from the county bar association.

B. The judge may engage in all of the fundraising activities.

C. The judge may not engage in any of the fundraising activities.

D. The judge may solicit funds from her immediate family members but not from other judges and not from the county bar association.

Chapter 9

Summative Assessment Quiz

Use this chapter's questions to assess your knowledge of the subject of lawyer professional responsibility as a whole.

1. Lawyer is handling a complex toxic tort case for which he must enter a jurisdiction in which he is not admitted to practice law to defend a deposition that should take no more than five hours to complete. Lawyer is admitted to practice in the jurisdiction in which the proceeding is otherwise pending. During the course of travelling to the deposition, Lawyer accidentally leaves his briefcase behind in the train station. In the briefcase was a file with confidential and incriminating information related to his client. Lawyer knew that the information was sensitive when he decided to take it with him and was reminded by a colleague to safeguard it when he departed his office in the morning. As the Uber pulls away from the train station, Lawyer discovers the oversight. He rushes back to find that a police officer had already been alerted to the abandoned case and opened it, revealing the confidential information and incriminating evidence.

Is Lawyer subject to discipline for any of the conduct described above?

A. Yes, because he should not have defended the deposition in a jurisdiction in which he is not admitted.

B. No, because he is permitted to engage in the provision of limited services in a jurisdiction in which he is not admitted that are related to other work he is performing.

C. Yes, because he failed to act competently in preserving the confidences of the client.

D. No, because leaving the file behind was inadvertent and Lawyer took immediate, if unsuccessful, steps to rectify the problem.

2. Lawyer represents Seller of a condominium unit. Buyer of the unit was represented by counsel throughout the negotiations of the contract of sale. A week before the scheduled date of the closing, Buyer contacts Lawyer to inform Lawyer that Buyer is no longer represented by counsel. Lawyer believes that it is in the best interest of Lawyer's client to go ahead with the sale even if Buyer is not represented by counsel. Lawyer also believes in good faith that it is in Buyer's best interest to proceed with the closing as well, even without representation. Buyer, aware that Lawyer represents Seller, asks Lawyer whether it is a good idea to proceed with the closing even if Buyer is not represented by counsel. All of the documents for the transaction have been prepared already, and there is very little left to do at the closing other than sign all the documents. Lawyer responds, truthfully, that Lawyer believes it is in Buyer's best interest to proceed without counsel because of the expense and delay associated with the Buyer's seeking new counsel, but Lawyer informs Buyer that Lawyer cannot give any other advice to Buyer.

Has Lawyer acted improperly in any way in Lawyer's dealings with Buyer? If so, why? If not, why not?

A. No. Lawyer honestly believed that it was in the Buyer's best interest to proceed with the closing and advised Buyer accordingly.

B. No. Lawyer was merely representing his client's best interests, and there was no risk that Buyer misunderstood that Lawyer was an interested party in the transaction.

C. Yes. Lawyer should not have had any communications whatsoever with an unrepresented party.

D. Yes. Lawyer should not have shared with Buyer the honest belief that it was in Buyer's best interest to proceed to the closing without a lawyer.

3. Lawyer represents Client, a plaintiff in a personal injury action. Client has authorized Lawyer to settle the matter for $25,000. At Client's deposition, the lawyer for the defendant asks very personal questions and is quite abrasive in his dealings with Client. After the deposition, the lawyer for the defendant informs Lawyer that he is authorized to settle the case for $25,000. Lawyer brings this offer back to Client, believing Client will be willing to settle for this amount. Client states that she no longer is willing to accept a settlement at this amount because of the treatment she received at her deposition. She now insists that she will not settle the matter for less than $40,000.

Is Lawyer subject to discipline should Lawyer accept the defendant's offer of $25,000, which is consistent with the Client's original authorization?

A. Yes, because Client is permitted to revoke the authorization to settle the matter at any time.

B. Yes, because opposing counsel treated Client poorly at the deposition, Lawyer should have refused to engage in settlement negotiations with the defendant.

C. No, because Lawyer could act in accordance with Client's first authorization to settle the matter.

D. No, because Client's behavior was unreasonable and Lawyer is not required to follow such an unreasonable directive.

4. Lawyer is consulting with a former intern regarding that intern's application to the state bar in the jurisdiction in which Lawyer practices. Lawyer has provided formal legal advice and assistance to the intern during the course of the intern's attempt to gain admission. One potential barrier to the intern's admission to the bar is an incident involving a physical altercation with the intern's neighbor that occurred several years before the intern went to law school. The intern has shared confidential information with Lawyer about the incident in order to get Lawyer's legal advice on how to describe the incident as part of the intern's application for admission. Lawyer has been asked to provide information to the state committee that is considering the intern's application for admission to the bar. Lawyer refuses to share the information related to the incident that the former intern shared with the Lawyer.

Is Lawyer subject to discipline for failing to respond with full candor to the committee assessing the intern's application for admission to the bar? If so, why? If not, why not?

A. Yes, because a lawyer is obligated to be completely candid with regard to an individual's application to the bar when the lawyer has information that is relevant to the admission application.

B. Yes, because the intern has shared information with Lawyer that should raise a substantial question as to that intern's likely fitness to practice law.

C. No, because the information the intern shared with Lawyer is protected by the attorney-client privilege.

D. No, because no one is obligated to share information related to an application for admission to the bar if that individual chooses not to share it.

5. Lawyer represents Client in a matrimonial matter pending in family court. During the course of the representation, Lawyer discovers that Client has been lying to Lawyer about the source of Client's income in an attempt to shield many of the Client's assets from the court to reduce his liability to his spouse. Several court filings submitted by the Lawyer include factual inaccuracies as a result of Client's misrepresentations about his assets. Lawyer informs Client that he will have to withdraw as Client's counsel if Client does not agree to correct the court filings that contain such inaccuracies. Client refuses to let Lawyer correct the court filings. Lawyer withdraws as Client's counsel because continuing to represent him would require Lawyer to violate his professional responsibilities. Lawyer takes no further action on Client's behalf.

Has Lawyer acted improperly by withdrawing from representing Client in this fashion?

A. Yes, if Lawyer was required to obtain court approval prior to withdrawing from the representation.

B. No, because the Lawyer's services were used to further a fraud on the court.

C. No, because Lawyer warned Client of the fact that he would withdraw if Client did not agree to correct the fraud on the Court.

D. Yes, because Lawyer's services were not used to further a fraud on the court.

6. Lawyer is entrusted with the responsibility of managing a settlement fund created by one of Lawyer's corporate clients (Client). The purpose of the fund is to distribute the proceeds of the settlement to all members of a class with claims against Client. When the deadline by which the claimants must come forward to claim their portion of the fund passes, Lawyer is permitted to subtract Lawyer's fee from the settlement account and refund the balance of whatever is left to Client. Lawyer sends written notice to Client that the settlement account contains $1 million and that Lawyer intends to take $400,000 of that amount as Lawyer's fee and return the rest to Client. Client responds that the amount Lawyer intends to withdraw as the fee is not what the parties agreed to in writing. Lawyer disagrees and believes, in good faith, that Lawyer is owed the full $400,000. Client contends that Lawyer is only entitled to $300,000. Lawyer insists on the full $400,000 as the fee and informs Client that Lawyer will hold the entire $1 million in escrow until the fee dispute is resolved.

Is Lawyer subject to discipline for retaining the entirety of the settlement fund pending resolution of the dispute over fees? If so, why? If not, why not?

A. No, because Lawyer has a good faith belief that Lawyer is owed the $400,000 and thus is entitled to maintain a lien with respect to the entirety of the fund until the dispute is resolved.

B. No, because until the dispute over the fee owed to Lawyer is resolved, Lawyer is not permitted to release any funds from the account.

C. Yes, because Lawyer is obligated to return the entirety of the balance that is not in dispute—that is, Lawyer is permitted to withdraw the amount the Client agreed Lawyer is owed and only maintain custody over the disputed amount in escrow.

D. Yes, because Lawyer is obligated to return the entire $1 million until the dispute is resolved, at which point Client will have to pay Lawyer whatever amount is determined to be owed.

7. Lawyer works as an attorney in the consumer frauds unit of the State Attorney General's Office. During the course of her work at that office, Lawyer conducted a confidential investigation of Big Corp. for a potential fraud claim involving a product. The Attorney General's Office had reason to believe that Big Corp. had defrauded its customers by selling a product that it knew was not an effective disinfectant, yet it sold the product anyway. Many customers of Big Corp. purchased the product. It is likely that those customers relied on the advertised qualities of the product to their detriment. The Attorney General's office chooses not to pursue the investigation further, however, despite Lawyer's firm belief that the office had uncovered serious misconduct on the part of Big Corp. Lawyer leaves the employment of the Attorney General's office, partly because she was upset that this investigation was discontinued. Lawyer goes to work at a firm that is putting together a class action lawsuit against Big Corp. for false advertising involving the disinfectant. Lawyer never represented Big Corp. in any way. In fact, Lawyer was leading the investigation of Big Corp. on behalf of the State Attorney General's Office. Lawyer was exposed to confidential information about Big Corp. by virtue of the company being the subject of the Attorney General's investigation. Such information would be relevant to any subsequent suit by private parties against Big Corp. related to the sale of the disinfectant. Lawyer's new firm will timely screen Lawyer from the Big Corp. matter and Lawyer will be afforded no fee from the representation. In order that Big Corp. and the Attorney General's Office do not receive advance notice that the firm is handling this matter, the firm will notify neither Big Corp. nor the Attorney General's Office of the screening arrangement involving Lawyer.

Is Lawyer's new firm subject to disqualification in an action brought by the firm against Big Corp. involving the disinfectant? If so, why? If not, why not?

A. Yes, because Lawyer worked personally and substantially on the Big Corp. investigation involving the disinfectant, no screening mechanisms could shield the new firm from disqualification.

B. No, because Lawyer never represented Big Corp. during the Attorney General's investigation, Big Corp. is thus not a former client of Lawyer.

C. Yes, because neither the Attorney General nor Big Corp. received timely notice of the screening measures and were given no opportunity to object to them.

D. No, because the screening measures in place at the firm are adequate to avoid the firm's disqualification, even without notice to any impacted parties.

8. Lawyer Marge is the managing attorney with supervisory responsibility for overseeing the work of Lawyer Linda. Though Linda is a relatively junior attorney, she is an excellent trial attorney. Linda won several national mock trial competitions as a law student and has tried several cases as a practicing attorney that have all led to very large judgments on behalf of her clients. Marge is consulting with Linda and learns that in one of these trials, a witness Linda had presented appears to have offered perjured testimony. The time to re-open the trial court's judgment or to appeal it will expire in three days. It is unlikely that, without this information regarding the witness's perjury, the opposing party will appeal the case or seek to re-open the judgment. Marge and Linda agree that there was no way anyone could have reasonably known that the witness would offer perjured testimony.

Is Marge subject to discipline if the firm takes no action to alert opposing counsel of the witness's perjured testimony?

A. No, because no reasonable attorney would have been aware that the testimony was perjured at the time it was proffered.

B. Yes, because at the time Marge became aware of the perjury, there was still time to mitigate the potential consequences of that testimony.

C. No, because Marge's supervision of Linda was adequate under the circumstances.

D. Yes, because Marge failed to prevent the witness's submission of perjured testimony.

9. Lawyer receives a call from an individual who has been his client for a long time. Client is a musical artist, and Lawyer has handled all of her contract work for the last ten years. The call from Client comes at midnight on a Friday evening. Client is frantic because she has just been pulled over for a moving violation. She is afraid that if she submits to a test of her blood alcohol content, she will fail it. She had consumed a few drinks over the last few hours and does not know whether her body has metabolized enough of it so that she will pass the test. She felt fine driving and does not believe she was speeding or engaged in any other violation. Client wants to know if she can refuse to take the blood alcohol test that the police officer wants to administer to her on the side of the road. Lawyer, who is not a criminal defense attorney, asks if he can have a few minutes to consider the question and to contact a colleague of his who would know the answer. Client says there is no time for that and that the police officer is insisting that Client give the officer an answer. In the jurisdiction, someone with the knowledge of a general legal practitioner would know that a driver can refuse a blood alcohol test and that refusal cannot be used against her should she face prosecution later. Unaware of the applicable law, Lawyer tells Client that she must subject herself to the test. She takes it and fails it, but by only the slimmest of margins. Had she delayed the test even by an hour, which she could have done had she received appropriate guidance, she would have passed it, with no legal consequences for having initially refused to take the test.

Is Lawyer subject to discipline for advising Client that she had to submit to the blood alcohol test?

A. Yes, because Lawyer provided incompetent service to Client.

B. Yes, because Lawyer failed to consult with someone who was capable of providing competent service.

C. No, because Lawyer was guilty of a lapse of judgment only, which cannot subject him to discipline.

D. No, because Lawyer gave limited advice in an emergency situation.

10. Lawyer represents a former prisoner in a case involving the prisoner's alleged mistreatment while in custody at a local prison. The action is filed against, among others, the warden of the facility, a correctional officer commander who was responsible for supervising the correctional officers accused of taking part in the mistreatment of the prisoner, and the correctional officers immediately charged with the abuse of the prisoner. Lawyer knows that there were several correctional officers who witnessed the incident, and Lawyer wants to communicate with them outside the presence of the lawyers representing the defendants. There are three potential witnesses Lawyer wants to interview, none of whom are named parties to the action. The first, Officer 1, was present during the incident; was on duty; and, according to the rules governing the operation of the facility, had a responsibility to intervene to stop the incident while it was occurring, but Officer 1 took no action to do so. The second, Officer 2, had just completed his shift and was exiting the facility when he witnessed the altercation between the plaintiff and several correctional officers; as he was officially off-duty at the time of the incident, the rules governing the operation of the facility no longer required him to intervene. The third, Officer 3, was a line supervisor at the time of the incident, meaning that he was responsible for overseeing a small group of officers, including those who are defendants in the action. Officer 3, who is embarrassed by the publicity the incident involving the plaintiff has received, has since retired from service and is no longer an employee of the prison system. Officer 3 witnessed the incident, was on duty at the time it occurred, and, like Officer 1,

had a duty to intervene to stop the incident but took no action to do so. Officer 3 is not a named defendant in the action, however. The warden, who is a defendant, was not on the premises at the time of the incident but is still legally responsible for everything that happens in the prison. Lawyers from the State Attorney General's Office for the state in which the prison is located are representing all defendants, including the State Department of Corrections, which is responsible for the prison and all of its employees, including the warden, the correctional officer commander, and the named correctional officers. Defendants' lawyers will not consent to the plaintiff's lawyer having direct contact with these witnesses without a defense lawyer present.

Which of the following individuals, if any, may Lawyer interview outside the presence of the lawyers for the defendants and without the consent of those lawyers?

A. Officer 2 only.

B. Officer 1 and Officer 3 only.

C. Officer 2 and Officer 3 only.

D. None of the individuals.

11. Lawyer enters into an agreement to represent Client. Client agrees in writing to pay Lawyer's going rate of $500 an hour to represent her in securing a patent for her invention. This is consistent with what a lawyer of similar skill and ability would charge for this service in the community based on Lawyer's assessment of the complexity of the case at the time she agreed to handle the matter. Lawyer begins to represent Client in the matter. Lawyer puts in roughly ten hours per week on Client's application and does so for about four months. After this four-month period, Lawyer begins to realize several things about the case. First, the patent application is far more complicated than she believed it would be when she agreed to take on the case. Second, the commercial value of Client's invention, should she be able to secure a patent for Client, is extraordinary. Lawyer feels the company could be the next Silicon Valley darling. Indeed, she thinks it could be a "unicorn" in the parlance of the business, that is, a company worth more than $1 billion. In light of these realizations, she thinks the rate she is charging is far less than what Client can and should pay. She contacts Client and tells Client that she is going to send over a new written retainer agreement that doubles Lawyer's hourly fee. She says, correctly, that this higher fee is consistent with what a client would typically pay in the community for work involving a potentially high-value invention like the one at issue in Lawyer's representation of Client. Lawyer advises Client in writing on the basic terms of the agreement, which are fair. Lawyer also informs Client in writing that Lawyer is not representing Client on the agreement to change the fee. Lawyer further advises

Client, again in writing, on the desirability of having separate counsel with regard to this new retainer and gives Client the opportunity to consult separate counsel prior to signing the agreement. Client is excited that Lawyer assesses the invention as being potentially very lucrative. Client takes a day to consider the arrangement and whether Client wants to obtain separate counsel. Client ultimately gives consent to the arrangement by signing the new written retainer. The new retainer spells out the generally fair terms of the agreement and that Lawyer is not representing Client in the transaction. Client does not seek separate counsel prior to signing.

Is Lawyer subject to discipline for her actions?

A. No, because Lawyer afforded Client all of the protections required in changing the fee structure.

B. No, because Lawyer's two fee arrangements, both the original rate and the new rate, were each reasonable under the circumstances.

C. Yes, because a lawyer is not allowed to change the fee structure once a representation has commenced, even if the client consents to the change, as the client did here.

D. Yes, despite the fact that the Lawyer's fee arrangements were both in writing.

12. Lawyer represents Employer in a case alleging that Employer created a hostile work environment for its employees. Employer's defense is that Lawyer had provided critical training to all employees that should have helped to prevent the hostile work environment. Employer alleges that, despite these best efforts, several rogue employees were responsible for the hostile environment, and the employer should not be held liable for those employees' actions. Lawyer will likely be asked to serve as a witness as to the training Lawyer provided to the employees in question. The content of the training, about which Lawyer will testify, is at the center of Employer's defense, but the fact that the training occurred and the content of Lawyer's testimony regarding the training will not be contested issues at the trial.

Will Lawyer be disqualified from handling the matter at trial on behalf of Employer because Lawyer will likely have to give testimony about the training Lawyer provided to Employer's employees?

A. Yes, because Lawyer cannot handle the matter if she has a conflict of interest.

B. No, because the disqualification of Lawyer will work a substantial hardship on the client.

C. No, because the issues about which Lawyer will testify will not be contested.

D. Yes, because the disqualification of Lawyer will not work a substantial hardship on the client.

13. Lawyer has served one four-year term as a justice on the state's highest court but has decided to not ask for her term to be renewed, preferring instead to settle back into her practice. Prior to her appointment to the court, she had a highly lucrative practice representing media companies. She is excited to get back into practice because she believes the media landscape has changed dramatically and expects her work will be remarkably interesting. She authored several decisions on the rights of social media companies, and she expects to be able to secure her old clients and probably attract new clients (from so-called "new media") immediately because of the prominence of her decisions, many of which were quite favorable to these new media companies. Lawyer sends out a written announcement to her old clients to inform them that she has returned from her position on the state's highest court and is resuming her practice. This announcement reaches several of her former clients who now are represented by other lawyers. She also advertises her return to practice in a magazine that is popular with new media companies. The advertisement accurately states that she is a former member of the state's highest court. Both communications contain her name and contact information.

Are either of these two communications unethical: the notice to former clients or the advertisement in the magazine?

A. The communications to former clients are unethical, but the advertisement in the magazine is ethical.

B. The communications to former clients is ethical, but the advertisement in the magazine is unethical.

C. Both communications are unethical.

D. Both communications are ethical.

14. Lawyer represents Client, who is charged with having released toxic substances into the local water supply. During the course of the representation, Lawyer learns through confidential communications with Client that the authorities are not aware of the full range of substances Client released into the water supply. These additional toxic substances make the dangers to the local population much more significant than originally thought, particularly with respect to people with certain pre-existing conditions. Locals are aware that the release is likely to cause substantial bodily harm to certain people, and perhaps even death, but they do not understand the true scope of the danger because they are not aware of the additional toxic substances, and thus they underestimate how much of the population is at increased risk of suffering harm. Lawyer wants to reveal this newly discovered information to the authorities so as to avoid even greater illness and potential loss of life than that for which the local community is currently prepared.

Which statement most accurately reflects Lawyer's duty in this situation?

A. Lawyer may reveal this information in order to prevent further loss of life or substantial bodily harm.

B. Lawyer must reveal this information if it might prevent further loss of life or substantial bodily harm.

C. Lawyer is not permitted to reveal this information because it is confidential and was acquired during the course of representation.

D. Lawyer is not permitted to reveal this information because disclosure would only help to prevent injuries that are different in degree rather than different in kind from those risks which are currently known.

15. Lawyer is concerned that Client is about to engage in the willful destruction of evidence in a case involving insider trading. Upon learning this information, Lawyer admonishes Client not to destroy such evidence. Client asks Lawyer, "Why am I even paying you? You're not a fighter!" and hangs up on Lawyer. Lawyer immediately files a motion under seal with the court in Client's case stating that "ethical concerns" have caused Lawyer to seek withdrawal from the representation immediately. Since the case is about to go to trial, the judge is concerned that allowing Lawyer to withdraw at this time will prejudice not just Lawyer's client, but the entire proceeding. The judge directs Lawyer to appear before him in chambers to reveal the basis for the withdrawal without opposing counsel present. Without inquiring into the content of confidential attorney-client communications or the substance of the proceeding itself, the judge receives a brief report from Lawyer. Lawyer again states that "ethical considerations" require Lawyer to seek withdrawal. Opposing counsel is unaware of this motion or the conversation related to it. Lawyer is not comfortable saying more, but the judge considers this articulation of Lawyer's position to be inadequate. The judge denies the motion, admonishing the Lawyer as follows: "Until you come back here with more information as to why you should be able to withdraw, let us never speak of this issue again." Since the motion was denied, the judge does not notify the opposing party of the withdrawal request. The judge is concerned that to do so might give the opposing party an unfair advantage in negotiations with Lawyer, which are ongoing.

Was the ex parte communication in this instance improper in any way? If so, why? If not, why not?

A. Yes, because, at a minimum, the judge should have alerted opposing counsel after the communication and afforded opposing counsel an opportunity to respond.

B. Yes, because the judge should not have heard the matter in an ex parte fashion.

C. No, because the ex parte communication was authorized by court order when the judge directed Lawyer to appear in chambers for this matter.

D. No, because the judge ultimately denied the motion to withdraw.

16. Prospective Client approaches Lawyer with the hope that Lawyer will represent Client in a proceeding in which Client is charged with securities fraud. Lawyer generally tends to handle other types of so-called "white collar" crimes but has never handled a securities fraud case itself. Lawyer reviews the charges against Client, which are fairly straightforward. Lawyer believes that, with a minimal amount of preparation, she can become competent in representing Client and agrees to take on the case.

Is it professional misconduct for Lawyer to agree to represent Client if she has never handled a securities fraud case before?

A. No, because Lawyer has handled similar types of cases before.

B. Yes, because Lawyer has never handled this type of case before.

C. Yes, because Lawyer is not competent to handle this type of case.

D. No, because Lawyer can become competent to represent Client with a reasonable amount of preparation.

17. Lawyer represents Client, a former employee of a large investment bank. Client attended only two years of law school and was never admitted to practice law. Client alleges that he was discriminated against while employed by the bank, in violation of federal law. Because of Client's legal training and the fact that he studied discrimination law extensively as a law student, Client wants the Lawyer to argue several novel theories of recovery. Lawyer does not believe such claims are frivolous but is worried that the claims might be dismissed and that Client might come back and sue Lawyer for malpractice if they are. Lawyer wants Client to enter into a written retainer agreement in which Client agrees to waive any claims of malpractice against Lawyer should the claims be dismissed. Lawyer advises Client on the benefits of obtaining independent counsel regarding the retainer agreement and affords Client an opportunity to obtain such counsel. Nevertheless, Client declines to consult with independent counsel prior to entering into the retainer agreement and readily agrees to waive any malpractice claims against Lawyer because Client understands that the legal theories he wants the Lawyer to pursue are untested, creative, and likely to get dismissed.

Is Lawyer subject to discipline for entering into this retainer agreement with Client? If so, why? If not, why not?

A. No, because Client had legal training, understood the nature of the waiver, and gave informed consent in writing to the arrangement.

B. Yes, because a lawyer can never enter into an agreement with a client in which the client waives claims of malpractice in advance.

C. Yes, because Client was not independently represented in the execution of the retainer agreement.

D. No, because Client understood that the claims were novel and wanted the Lawyer to assert them anyway.

18. Lawyer is sitting in a coffee shop consulting with a Client when a neighbor of Client, Nestor, who is enraged about some running conflict between Nestor and Client, comes in and assaults Client. There are no other patrons in the coffee shop at the time of the assault, and the coffee shop workers did not see the assault take place. Client asks Lawyer to represent her in the personal injury case against the neighbor even though it is likely that the Lawyer will be called as a witness in the action. Lawyer says that she cannot represent her but that Lawyer's firm may do so. After subsequent investigation into the matter, Lawyer realizes that another lawyer at her firm, Laura, previously represented Nestor in a separate matter when Laura was employed by a different firm, but that representation has come to a close and is unrelated to the present conflict.

Is Lawyer's firm subject to discipline if it represents Client?

A. Yes, because if any lawyer at the firm is prohibited from representing Client, all lawyers in the firm are prohibited from doing so.

B. No, even though Lawyer is a likely witness in the proceeding and another lawyer at her firm used to represent Nestor in an unrelated matter.

C. No, unless Nestor and Client did not give informed consent to the representation.

D. Yes, because the firm cannot handle the matter if Lawyer is likely to be a witness in the proceeding and offer material contested evidence.

19. Lawyer has a worker compensation practice in a town dominated by a local employer that serves as a shipping hub for a large internet-based retail company. Workers are regularly injured there, so Lawyer has a booming practice dealing with cases just from that company. In fact, Lawyer has represented roughly two hundred employees in such cases against this company alone. In each of these two hundred cases, which are heard by the local worker compensation tribunal, the same attorney has represented the company. In addition, the same human resources professional, Peter, an employee of the company, has served as both a company representative and the sole company witness at each hearing. Peter is familiar with all of the health and safety protocols deployed by the company and testifies against the employees in their cases seeking worker compensation benefits before the tribunal. One day, before the company's attorney has arrived for the next scheduled hearing between one of Lawyer's clients and the company, Lawyer and Peter are both standing in the waiting room outside the room in which the worker compensation proceedings are held. Peter wants to strike up a conversation related to the case that is about to be heard. Peter initiates the conversation with Lawyer and says he has the company's consent to discuss the matter with Lawyer. Peter offers a letter, signed on company letterhead, in which the Chief Executive Officer of Peter's company confirms her consent to Peter speaking with the Lawyer about the matter. Peter continues speaking to Lawyer and suggests that they try to settle the case. Peter states the company's settlement position. Lawyer listens and says he will have to discuss the matter with his client.

Is Lawyer subject to discipline for communicating with Peter in this way?

A. Yes, because Lawyer's knowledge that Peter was represented by counsel could be inferred from the circumstances.

B. Yes, because Lawyer did not state that he was disinterested.

C. No, because Lawyer had client consent, confirmed in writing, to communicate with Peter.

D. No, because Lawyer did not initiate the conversation.

20. Lawyer A is supervised by Lawyer Z. Lawyer A's client, whom Lawyer A represents in a civil matter, has informed Lawyer A that she intends to make a statement at trial that Lawyer A reasonably believes is false. Lawyer A investigates the matter and is unable to secure any information that confirms or refutes the information Client intends to offer under oath. Lawyer A also believes that it is unlikely that opposing counsel will be able to obtain information that could impeach Client's testimony. Lawyer A cannot establish that the testimony Client intends to give is false, however. No further facts surrounding the issue would indicate—or even help shed light on—whether the statement will constitute perjury. Lawyer A consults with Lawyer Z on the right course of action. Lawyer Z states that Lawyer A may refuse to offer the testimony because Lawyer A has a reasonable belief that it would constitute perjury even if Lawyer A does not know that it will, and even though such knowledge cannot be inferred from the facts and circumstances surrounding the matter.

May Lawyer A proceed in accordance with Lawyer Z's direction without being subject to discipline? If yes, why? If not, why not?

A. No, because Lawyer Z's resolution of the matter is unreasonable in light of the clear professional duty in this instance.

B. Yes, because Lawyer Z is the supervisory lawyer, and Lawyer A, as the subordinate attorney, must always follow Lawyer Z's direction.

C. Yes, because Lawyer Z's resolution of the matter is reasonable in light of the relevant professional duty.

D. No, because all lawyers are responsible for their actions in every situation, whether they are acting under the guidance of a supervisory lawyer or not.

21. Lawyer represents Client in a contract dispute that is about to go to trial. In preparing for trial, Lawyer discusses the potential testimony of a witness in the case with that witness. The witness will testify at trial that Client delivered the required supplies to Client's adversary in a time and manner consistent with the contract, and thus the adversary is required to pay Client according to the contract. In discussions with the witness, a former employee of Client's adversary who was there when the supplies were delivered and will testify to that fact, Lawyer learns that the adversary had fired the witness for cause. Lawyer discusses the matter with the witness, who says that she had been accused of stealing from the company and that she denies the accusations. Lawyer has no way of verifying or disputing the witness's account of the facts related to the termination but is nevertheless afraid that this issue is likely to come out on cross-examination. In her professional judgment, Lawyer correctly determines that anything that would undermine the credibility of Lawyer's witness would ultimately undermine Client's case. Lawyer decides not to call the witness, and Client loses the case because Client is unable to secure the testimony of anyone who can corroborate Client's factual contentions that Client complied with the contract. Client sues Lawyer for malpractice for failing to call the witness. Interviews with several jurors after the trial indicate that the jurors would have ruled in Client's favor had there been any witnesses, even one, who could corroborate Client's factual allegations regarding the timely delivery of the supplies in accordance with the contract.

Is Lawyer subject to discipline for failing to call the former employee of Client's adversary in support of Client's case? If so, why? If not, why not?

A. Yes, because Lawyer was under an obligation to present the testimony that could have swayed the jury.

B. Yes, because Lawyer did not know that the witness was lying about the reasons for her termination.

C. No, because Lawyer's knowledge that the witness was lying about the terms of her termination could be inferred from the facts, and so Lawyer was within her rights to choose not to call the witness.

D. No, because in Lawyer's professional judgment, the witness's testimony could have undermined the case were the adversary to bring up the alleged grounds upon which the former employee was terminated.

22. Lawyer works at a large international firm, the Seita Firm (Seita), that takes on large multi-national clients. Lawyer decides to leave Seita to go work at a small boutique law firm, the Hirokawa Firm (Hirokawa). The boutique law firm sometimes sues some of Seita's clients. One such client, Agro, learns that Lawyer has joined Hirokawa and seeks to disqualify the firm. The suit against Agro involves charges brought by several farmers for alleged patent infringement. When Lawyer worked at Seita, she did not work in the intellectual property division there, which mostly handled matters on behalf of Agro. The intellectual property department was based in New York City, while Lawyer was based in Chicago. Lawyer handled only corporate business transactions while working at Seita, none of them involving Agro. Lawyer had no access to confidential information related to Agro and did not communicate with any of the lawyers working on any Agro client matters. Upon joining Hirokawa, no screens are put in place and confidential information about the farmers is shared with Lawyer.

Is Hirokawa disqualified from representing the farmers against Agro?

A. Yes, because timely screens were not imposed at Hirokawa to shield Lawyer from confidential information about the Agro case.

B. Yes, because the farmers did not consent to the representation.

C. No, because Lawyer did not have access to confidential information about Agro when she worked at Seita.

D. No, because Lawyer only worked on business matters while at Seita and did not handle intellectual property cases.

23. Lawyer represents a criminal defendant in a pending proceeding. Lawyer learns that the local police chief has held a press conference in which she reports on the progress of the investigation in the case in which the defendant is accused. Lawyer has a reasonable belief that one of the factual statements made by the police chief, which is widely reported, is incorrect and prejudicial to his client. The trial is still many months away. Lawyer holds his own subsequent press conference to refute what Lawyer reasonably believes was the factually incorrect statement made by the chief of police and to share information related to the scheduled date for the next pre-trial hearing, the occupation of Lawyer's client, and the time and place of the original arrest of the client.

Is Lawyer subject to discipline for any of the statements made to the press? If so, which?

A. Lawyer is not subject to discipline for any of his statements to the press.

B. Lawyer is subject to discipline for all of his statements to the press.

C. Lawyer is subject to discipline for the statement to the press about the occupation of the defendant but is not subject to discipline for any of the other statements.

D. Lawyer is subject to discipline for his statement to the press about the information related to the arrest of his client but is not subject to discipline for any of the other statements.

24. Lawyer is representing Client in negotiations over a personal injury suit arising from an incident at Client's restaurant, where a patron slipped on what she alleges was a wet floor outside the bathroom of the establishment. During the course of the negotiations with opposing counsel, the following occurs: (1) Lawyer states that Client is going to make an "excellent witness" even though Lawyer knows Client often forgets critical facts no matter how many times the Lawyer goes over them with Client; (2) Lawyer states that the insurance limit for personal injuries on the premises is $100,000, when in actuality it is $200,000, and Lawyer's adversary never asks to see the insurance policy that sets forth the actual limit; and (3) Lawyer says that Client will agree to pay the plaintiff in the action $120,000, an amount which Lawyer falsely claims is the Client's "bottom line," when in actuality Lawyer knows that Client does not care if the settlement reaches $200,000, the true insurance policy limit.

Is Lawyer subject to discipline for any of the statements made during the course of the negotiations?

A. Lawyer is subject to discipline for all of the statements.

B. Lawyer is subject to discipline for misrepresenting that the Client will make an excellent witness, but not for any of the other statements.

C. Lawyer is subject to discipline for the statement about the insurance policy limit, but not for the other statements.

D. Lawyer is not subject to discipline for any of the statements.

25. Lawyer Linda has been retained by Lawyer Dan in a judicial proceeding in which Dan is seeking to challenge his potential temporary suspension from the practice of law for allegedly embezzling funds from his clients. Having conducted substantial research into Dan's banking records as a part of her representation of Dan, Linda believes Dan is innocent of these charges. At the same time, as a result of this research into Dan's records and files, she has uncovered what she believes is evidence that two years ago, Dan assisted in a scheme to launder roughly $1 million on behalf of a Latvian drug lord through a fraudulent real estate transaction.

Is Linda required to report Dan for professional misconduct?

A. Yes, if she has a reasonable belief that Dan has engaged in conduct that reflects poorly on his fitness to practice law.

B. Yes, because the conduct raises a substantial question as to Dan's fitness to practice law.

C. No, because she discovered the information about the allegedly fraudulent scheme during her representation of Dan for professional misconduct.

D. No, because the conduct does not raise a substantial question as to Dan's fitness to practice law.

26. Lawyer represents a corporation that is under investigation by the state tax authorities in the jurisdiction in which Lawyer practices. Lawyer is representing the corporation itself as a part of the investigation, which could lead to civil penalties. The investigation also involves scrutiny of the actions of the corporation's Chief Executive Officer (CEO). Lawyer has reviewed the allegations against the CEO and believes there is a potential conflict between the CEO's interests and those of the corporation, particularly if the corporation is found liable for the acts and omissions of the CEO. At this stage in the investigation, it is not clear that the conflict will arise; however, even if it does, Lawyer believes the interests of the CEO and the company would still be significantly aligned because she believes the best course of action is to show, through the course of the representation, that the corporation and the CEO engaged in no wrongdoing. Lawyer believes she can make a strong case to establish their collective innocence. Moreover, she believes she can be a zealous representative for both the CEO and the corporation, even if a conflict were to arise. She counsels both the CEO and the corporation fully on the possibility of the conflict, and each consents in writing to the conflict.

Is Lawyer subject to discipline for continuing to represent the CEO and the corporation in the state investigation?

A. Yes, because a conflict exists between the CEO and the corporation.

B. No, because the parties have consented to the representation and Lawyer believes she can be a zealous advocate on the parties' behalf even with the conflict.

C. No, because no conflict exists at present between the interests of the CEO and those of the corporation.

D. Yes, because the parties were not separately advised by independent counsel on the agreement to waive the conflict.

27. Pat is a judge in the state's highest court. Pat's spouse, Sam, is running for election for an open seat in the U.S. Congress, which will be decided in a partisan fashion. Pat wishes to endorse Sam as a candidate for this position. When she does so, Pat does not identify herself as a sitting judge but rather states that the endorsement is being made only in Pat's personal capacity.

Is Pat's endorsement of Sam unethical?

A. Yes, because a judge may not endorse any candidate for elected political office.

B. No, because Sam is Pat's close family member.

C. No, because Sam is seeking a position in the federal government as opposed to the state government.

D. Yes, because Pat failed to properly identify herself as a sitting judge.

28. Lawyer represents Client in a civil action tried before a jury in which Client testifies in support of his case. After the trial concludes and Lawyer's client is victorious, Lawyer's opposing counsel sees her in the hallway and tells her that he plans to appeal the verdict, which he has a right to do, and will file his appeal within days, well within the time frame set for the appeal. At a celebratory lunch Lawyer and Client are having later that day, Client jokingly refers to his testimony as "a pile of lies." He begins to brag to Lawyer about all of the ways in which his testimony was fabricated. He thanks Lawyer, informing her that he is grateful for her service and regrets that their relationship must end now that the trial is over by operation of the express terms of the retainer the parties signed. That retainer explicitly says that the relationship would end when the verdict was rendered in the trial. He tells her he knows she is being considered for a partnership at her firm, and he will make sure to put in a good word with the head of the firm, who is a golfing buddy of his. Lawyer cannot finish her lunch because she is sick to her stomach and heads back to her office to review her records. As she goes through the evidence, she begins to see how Client's testimony was clearly fabricated. She's not sure how she missed it, but, in fairness to her, Client was an effective liar; no lawyer would have picked up on the anticipated perjury or anticipate it. Because the jury reached its verdict, however, Lawyer decides that she has no duty to report that Client had offered perjured testimony at trial.

Is Lawyer subject to discipline for failing to report Client's perjury after the close of the trial?

A. No. The duty to report the perjury does not extend beyond the termination of the attorney-client relationship.

B. No. Although Lawyer became aware that Client's testimony was perjured, she did not know it at the time it was offered and thus was under no obligation to report it after the trial had concluded but prior to the appeal being filed.

C. Yes. The duty to report the perjury has no statute of limitations.

D. Yes. Lawyer still has a duty to report the perjury given the procedural posture of the case.

29. Lawyer is on "intake" one day at the legal aid office in which she works. The office employs ten attorneys and handles matrimonial matters, among other practice areas. Lawyer does not handle matrimonial cases but does handle intake screening for all cases. Lawyer interviews a prospective client, Paul, at intake, who provides limited confidential information to Lawyer about his case for the sole purpose of determining whether a conflict of interest exists, among other types of information also related to determining whether the office could represent him. Paul informs Lawyer that the action is against Sarah Smith. Smith is Sarah's married name. Lawyer searches the office's conflict-checking software for a Sarah Smith and finds no one with that name in the client database. Lawyer believes, as a result of this search, that there is no conflict with the office's representing Paul. Lawyer later learns that a Sarah Jones has also applied for representation from the legal aid office. Sarah Jones and Sarah Smith turn out to be one and the same person. The office has already agreed to represent Sarah Jones (aka Sarah Smith) and wants to continue to represent her, so it will screen Lawyer from the representation and will not represent Paul. There will be no fees associated with the representation.

May Lawyer's office continue to represent Sarah Jones/Smith in the case involving Paul?

A. Yes, but only if both Paul and Sarah give informed consent to the representation, confirmed in writing.

B. Yes, if, in addition to the office's screening Lawyer from the representation, Lawyer takes reasonable measures to protect against the disclosure of confidential information, Lawyer does not earn any fees from the representation, and Paul is given prompt, written notice of the representation.

C. No, because there is a conflict of interest.

D. No, because Lawyer cannot be effectively screened from the representation in such a small office.

30. Lawyer represents a family-owned company that has been the subject of significant public scrutiny because several whistleblowers have come forward and spoken to the press about the company's marketing of its powerful opioid medication. It is alleged by these whistleblowers that the company's leaders, members of the Sickler family who hold a controlling share in the closely held company, knew of the likely addictive qualities of this medication but did not adequately warn prescribing physicians to carefully monitor their patients' use of the medication. A consortium of state attorneys general issues a joint press release announcing its plans to launch a joint investigation of the Sickler family's practices that, it is argued, is likely to lead to civil and even criminal charges being filed against the Sicklers. The consortium announces that it will "follow the evidence where it takes us, even if that means criminal charges against individual family members if they broke the law." The leaders of the consortium also state that the formal investigation has yet to begin because the group is waiting for the attorneys general from other states to join, so that they can all present a united front in the matter. Lawyer has a meeting with the Sickler family representatives who control the actions of the corporation, and they ask whether they are within their rights to destroy documents and records related to their marketing of the medication in question, since no litigation has yet commenced against them and the investigation has not even started. Lawyer advises them that as long as no investigation has commenced and no court action has been filed, they are free to take such action as

they wish with respect to the documents and records they want to destroy.

Is Lawyer subject to discipline for the advice regarding the documents and records? If so, why? If not, why not?

A. Yes, because Lawyer knows that these records reveal evidence of a crime.

B. No, because the group of state attorneys general had not yet commenced litigation against the defendant.

C. No, because the group of state attorneys general had not even commenced a formal investigation into the company practices.

D. Yes, because the material has potential evidentiary value in an action the commencement of which is reasonably foreseeable.

31. Lawyer represents Client in an antitrust matter at a reduced rate because Client is in desperate financial straits. Lawyer has long coveted Client's classic 1971 Mustang, one of a fleet of classic muscle cars from the 1970s that Client, who runs a car dealership, maintains. As interest in such gas-guzzling muscle cars has dried up, Client has fallen upon hard times and is considering selling the Mustang at a deep discount. Lawyer tells Client to check the market price for the car because Lawyer will top it, no matter what it is. Client advertises the car with a list price of $20,000, a significant discount from the car's original list price of $40,000. Client receives a few inquiries but no offers. Lawyer not only knows that Client has fallen on hard times but also that Client will not be able to pay the outstanding bills for Lawyer's services, which are considerable, if Client does not prevail in the antitrust case. Lawyer is concerned that if Client goes bankrupt, Lawyer will no longer be able to pursue the antitrust action on behalf of Client. Lawyer agrees to pay the full $40,000 list price for the car. Lawyer communicates the terms of the transaction in writing, informs Client that Lawyer will not serve as the lawyer for Client in the transaction, recommends Client obtain outside counsel, and gives Client an opportunity to secure such counsel. Because Client operates an automobile dealership, Client is familiar with the standard paperwork that needs to be filed with the Department of Motor Vehicles to authorize the transaction, which is all that is needed to complete the transaction in this case. Client declines such outside counsel, prepares the standard paperwork as Client has done many

times before in this type of transaction, and completes the sale.

Is Lawyer subject to discipline for any aspect of the car purchase from Client?

A. Yes, because Lawyer failed to require Client to obtain outside counsel.

B. No, because the product sold to Lawyer is one that the Client generally markets to others.

C. No, because the sale did not require the preparation of any specialized legal documents, since this was a standard sale of a good within the Client's domain and expertise.

D. Yes, because even though the transaction was for the purchase of a product Client generally markets to others, the transaction could be seen as impermissible financial support of a client.

32. Lawyer intends to file a medical malpractice action against a local doctor who has a long history of providing incompetent service to the community. Lawyer's client experienced several acts of what Lawyer believes were inappropriate treatment by the doctor. First, Client received inadequate counseling prior to the doctor's performing a medical procedure; second, the treatment itself was performed in an inappropriate way; third, the post-operative treatment also constituted malpractice. Lawyer is aware that the first two claims arose outside the statute of limitations and are thus time-barred. Lawyer is also aware that the third claim, although not time-barred, is no longer valid under recent precedent of the state's highest court, and Lawyer can make no good faith arguments to support that claim's validity. Lawyer believes in good faith that Client was wronged by the doctor, however. The first two claims are otherwise particularly strong, and Client would have been able to recover over $500,000 for the pain and suffering that resulted from the actions that gave rise to the claims but for the fact that those claims are now barred by the statute of limitations. Lawyer has no good faith basis for arguing that the statute of limitations should not apply. Lawyer files an action raising all three claims, believing in good faith that she can obtain a settlement for Client that would at least partially compensate Client for the damages she suffered as a result of the doctor's misconduct. Lawyer will withdraw the claims if the matter proceeds past the discovery phase, before she has to assert them at a trial.

Is Lawyer subject to discipline for her actions?

A. Yes, because the claims do not have merit.

B. No, because Lawyer believes in good faith that she can obtain a settlement on behalf of Client and will not take the case to trial if she cannot.

C. Yes, because once Lawyer files the case, she has to be willing to see the matter through to its conclusion.

D. No, because Client was clearly harmed by the doctor, and if the doctor is willing to settle the matter, it would indicate the claims had some merit.

33. Lawyer runs a small firm that handles immigration matters. Much of the work is fairly routine, and she employs several paralegals to process the paperwork for the various types of applications that form the heart of her practice. Generally, the paralegals receive a fair amount of training from Lawyer before they start working at the firm, but occasionally Lawyer asks more experienced paralegals to train new paralegals as they are hired. One of the newly hired paralegals who received little direct supervision or training from Lawyer fails to file a form in a timely fashion as a result of this inadequate training. A client is being threatened with deportation as a result of this paralegal's error. Lawyer rushes to court to get an injunction to prevent the deportation and to allow her office time to file the proper forms. Immigration officials allow Lawyer to file the paperwork and the threat of deportation is removed.

Is Lawyer subject to discipline for these actions?

A. Yes, because the client faced the threat of deportation as a result of the paralegal's actions.

B. Yes, because Lawyer did not have proper procedures in place to ensure the provision of competent services by all non-lawyer staff.

C. No, because the threat of deportation was lifted and the client did not suffer any adverse consequences as a result of the paralegal's actions.

D. No, because Lawyer is not responsible for the inadequate supervision provided by other non-legal staff.

34. Lawyer represents Able, Baker, and Charlie (Defendants) in a criminal case in which they are accused of engaging in a conspiracy to distribute pirated DVDs of newly released Hollywood films. Defendants are all indigent, and Lawyer has been assigned as counsel to represent all three. At the trial court level, during pre-trial conferences in the case and throughout the trial, no one raises the issue of potential conflicts of interest among Defendants that might arise due to the joint representation. The case proceeds, and all three are convicted and receive lengthy sentences. During the trial, Defendants presented a united legal front, and Lawyer represented them to the best of her ample abilities, raising novel and creative defenses, objecting at appropriate times, and serving them zealously. As is common in trials like this, none of Defendants testified on his or her own behalf, although Lawyer called several witnesses in defense of Defendants. Defendants' defense was not impacted adversely by the joint representation. Although the jury deliberated for several days, it ultimately found against Defendants. Seeking to overturn their convictions, Defendants now raise the issue, for the first time on appeal, that the representation was constitutionally ineffective.

What is the likely outcome of the request to overturn the convictions based on ineffective assistance of counsel?

A. The convictions will be overturned because the court failed to inquire into the possibility of a conflict of interest prior to holding the trial.

B. The convictions will be overturned because one can assume that the joint representation constituted a conflict of interest and that such conflict of interest must have had an actual impact on Lawyer's representation of Defendants.

C. The convictions will be upheld because Lawyer provided competent, conflict-free representation to Defendants that was not adversely affected by the joint representation.

D. The convictions will be upheld because Defendants failed to raise the conflicts issue at the trial court level.

35. Lawyer is the managing attorney at a small law firm (Firm) and is responsible for overseeing all of the activities of its subordinate lawyers and non-legal staff. Lawyer is also in charge of ensuring that Firm's systems, which are all operating on the cloud in light of social distancing protocols, are protected from cyber security breaches. Firm has long contracted with a company, IT Solutions (ITS), to provide information technology support to Firm, including cyber security assistance. Lawyer feels loyalty to ITS because it helped Firm install its first computer mainframe back in the 1980s. For decades, ITS has been the "go-to" technology company that many lawyers in Firm's geographic area utilize, and many even use the same system that Firm uses. Lawyer attends a training on cyber security threats for law firms and gets nervous about the integrity of Firm's system. Lawyer contracts with a "white-hat hacker," a company that specializes in consulting on cyber security threats, to assess Firm's vulnerabilities. The contractor identifies several vulnerabilities in Firm's system. Lawyer acts on the contractor's advice to have ITS take immediate action to close those vulnerabilities, which it does. Some of the vulnerabilities were quite severe, but it does not appear, based on the contractor's review, that they had been exploited by any nefarious actors. The contractor also informs Lawyer that many law firms use similar systems and have the same vulnerabilities.

Is Lawyer subject to discipline for utilizing a system that was subject to such severe vulnerabilities? If so, why? If not, why not?

A. Yes, because Lawyer failed to act competently in light of security threats.

B. Yes, because Lawyer is strictly liable for not protecting Firm against any possible threats to its system.

C. No, because Lawyer acted competently by utilizing the contractor to analyze the vulnerabilities in Firm's system and then addressing those vulnerabilities promptly upon learning of them.

D. No, because Lawyer is not a technology specialist and does not have a special duty to know about internet security threats to Firm.

36. Lawyer, who works in the Capital Region of New York State, handles employment discrimination cases. In a widely and publicly distributed daily newspaper, Lawyer places a print advertisement that contains the following statement, attributed to Lawyer: "I have won three of the largest jury awards in Albany County in workplace discrimination lawsuits, with each jury award totaling over $1 Million." A statement at the end of the advertisement contains the disclaimer "Prior outcomes do not guarantee future results." The statements are technically true. What Lawyer does not reveal in the advertisement is that one of the three jury awards was reversed on appeal, with the client in that case receiving no compensation.

Is this advertisement unethical?

A. Yes, because the omission of the fact that one of the judgments was overturned on appeal renders the advertisement misleading.

B. Yes, because a lawyer cannot advertise the size of the awards he or she has won on behalf of prior clients, even with a disclaimer.

C. No, because the advertisement is not false on its face.

D. No, because the communication was not made through live, in-person communications.

37. Lawyer formerly represented Big Pharma, an incorporated trade association made up of pharmaceutical companies, including a company by the name of Adage. Lawyer handled Big Pharma's efforts to challenge in court several new government regulations related to antitrust issues in the pharmaceutical industry. During the course of Lawyer's representation of Big Pharma, Lawyer was given confidential financial information about each of the companies that made up Big Pharma. After Big Pharma dissolves as a corporate entity and Lawyer is no longer retained to represent it, Lawyer is approached by InnoVent, a plucky upstart that claims it is going to disrupt the pharmaceutical industry. InnoVent starts to market a generic, over-the-counter alternative to a prescription drug sold by Adage. Adage brings a lawsuit against InnoVent, and InnoVent wants to assert as a defense that Adage is engaging in anti-competitive behavior to maintain its market control of this particular drug. Lawyer has knowledge of Adage's confidential financial information because of his former representation of Big Pharma, and this information is relevant to the proceeding involving InnoVent. Lawyer wants to use that information in his representation of InnoVent. Adage brings a motion to disqualify Lawyer from representing InnoVent.

Will Lawyer be disqualified from representing InnoVent in the action brought by Adage?

A. Yes, because Lawyer can never serve in a representational capacity in an action against a former client.

B. No, because Adage was never Lawyer's client.

C. No, because Lawyer no longer represents Big Pharma or Adage.

D. Yes, because Lawyer obtained confidential information about Adage relevant to the representation of InnoVent.

38. Lawyer has been asked to represent Client in negotiations for the sale of his business to a competitor. Client provides Lawyer with confidential information about the recent profit trends with respect to the business and the markets that Client attempts to target through his business. Client, an experienced businessperson, understands these are essential pieces of information any purchaser would need to know prior to purchasing the business. During the course of negotiations on behalf of Client, Lawyer reveals this information to the competitor in an effort to finalize the deal, but the negotiations fail. After those negotiations fail, Client's competitor begins utilizing strategies to target the markets Lawyer had identified during negotiations as markets Client was serving through Client's business.

Is Lawyer subject to discipline for revealing confidential information about Client's business practices to the competitor?

A. Yes, because Lawyer did not have express consent to reveal such confidences.

B. Yes, because the information was embarrassing and damaging to Client's business.

C. No, because Lawyer had implied consent to reveal this information.

D. No, because Lawyer's zealous advocacy on behalf of Client required him to reveal the information.

39. Lawyer provided excellent service to a group of plaintiffs who brought a personal injury action alleging that a large company had polluted a local water supply. Lawyer was working for a contingency fee, one in which he stood to claim one-third of the plaintiffs' recovery if the case were successful. Plaintiffs sought $10 million in actual damages and an additional $90 million in punitive damages. The jury returned a verdict for the plaintiffs, awarding them the full $100 million sought in the action. The attorney's fee award is thus $33 million, bringing Lawyer's rate to roughly $1,000 an hour.

Which of the following should *not* be a factor in determining whether Lawyer's fee is ethical?

A. Whether the clients were aware that the fee might ultimately amount to the equivalent of $1,000 an hour.

B. Whether Lawyer had to turn down other work to accept the case.

C. The fee customarily charged in the jurisdiction for a similar case.

D. The experience, reputation, and ability of Lawyer.

40. Lawyer is asked to serve as counsel to a defendant facing multiple criminal charges for bribery of a U.S. government official. The prospective client, Paul, is the subject of other investigations around the world, and much of his assets are tied up in litigation in other countries. Paul does not have access to these assets, including his many off-shore bank accounts. Lawyer states that she is worried Paul will not be able to pay her for her services. Paul says that he has an expensive sports car, a classic MG from the 1940s, in the United States that is not the subject of any legal action. Lawyer has long coveted such a car, and Paul's is in mint condition. An independent assessor recently assessed its value at $100,000. Lawyer agrees to represent Paul with the understanding that Paul will sell the car to Lawyer and Lawyer will use the proceeds to pay herself. Lawyer and Paul enter into a retainer agreement. Lawyer then prepares a document that will transfer title to the sports car. Lawyer explains in writing all aspects of the terms of the sale transaction in a manner in which Paul can understand them. She also advises Paul in writing to seek outside counsel on the transaction and also affords him an opportunity to seek such counsel. Paul says he does not need independent representation and goes ahead with the transaction. Lawyer then states that she will put the $100,000 fee in her escrow account as security against future earnings. She agrees that she will return any unearned portion of the funds. She then begins to represent Paul. Lawyer charges Paul a reasonable fee, sends him monthly billing statements, and withdraws the funds she has earned from the escrow account. Paul is satisfied with the representation he receives from

Lawyer; she handles his matter effectively and zealously, and the criminal charges are withdrawn by the prosecutor's office after lengthy negotiations and various pre-trial maneuvers.

Is Lawyer subject to discipline for her actions?

A. Yes, because Lawyer did not require Paul to obtain outside counsel in the sale of the sports car.

B. Yes, because the manner in which Lawyer retained the proceeds of the sale of the sports car in her escrow account could constitute an unreasonable restraint on Paul's right to terminate her as counsel.

C. No, because the manner in which Lawyer conducted the sale and her management of the escrow account were both proper.

D. No, because Lawyer paid the full price for the sports car as determined by an independent appraiser.

41. Lawyer is a prominent intellectual property lawyer who represents Lougle, a large internet company, in an action claiming that it stole the intellectual property of a competitor. Lawyer is informed by employees at Lougle that a professor at a local university had first published material setting forth the theory of the search engine Lougle and its competitors use long before the competitor filed its patent, meaning the patent should never have been issued by the U.S. Patent and Trade Office. Lawyer is shown evidence of this publication, has no reason to doubt its veracity, and represents this fact before the court in oral argument on a motion for summary judgment made by Lougle's competitor. Based on this fact, the judge denies the motion. After the denial, one of Lawyer's paralegals discovers potentially conflicting information about the paper's publication date. Lawyer engages in a good faith investigation into the matter and cannot determine definitively that the paper was posted fraudulently. Lawyer confronts Lougle's representatives, who strenuously deny fabricating the posting date of the paper and have credible arguments to support their position. The case proceeds to trial on other points related to Lougle's actions, and the issue of the publication date of the paper is never revisited by the competitor's lawyers or the court.

Is Lawyer subject to discipline for failing to divulge the new facts that raise questions about the paper's publication date?

A. Yes, because Lawyer should never have made the false statement in the first place.

B. No, because Lawyer reasonably believed the statement was true at the time it was made.

C. No, because Lawyer's knowledge of whether the paper's publication date was fabricated cannot be inferred from the circumstances.

D. Yes, because Lawyer's knowledge of whether the paper's publication date was fabricated can be inferred from the circumstances.

42. Lawyer represents a large, publicly traded company. Lawyer learns that the materials she prepared on behalf of the company for its securities filings were based on fraudulent information, which means those filings are invalid and should be withdrawn so that investors and potential investors do not rely on them. Lawyer brings this information to the attention of the highest authority in the company and insists that the company disavow the filings and submit amended ones. The company refuses to do so. Lawyer feels that she must withdraw as counsel to the company. She withdraws and publicly disavows the securities filings that she prepared so that investors will no longer rely upon them, which results in the company suffering significant negative financial repercussions.

Is it professional misconduct for Lawyer to withdraw from representing the company in this way?

A. No, because Lawyer was permitted to withdraw in this context and to disaffirm the securities filing.

B. Yes, because the withdrawal had negative financial repercussions for the company.

C. No, because Lawyer had reported the matter to the highest authority in the company.

D. Yes, because the disavowal consisted of Lawyer revealing confidential client information.

43. Lawyer Able represents Aidan, an individual involved in the dissolution of a business partnership. The negotiations with Aidan's former partner have been largely amicable to this point, as there are sufficient partnership assets that could be distributed between the partners in a way that satisfies both. The conversations up to this point have largely centered around a fairly even distribution of the proceeds. Lawyer Baker represents the other individual in the business partnership, Beck. Lawyer Baker contacts Lawyer Able to say that, despite prior settlement discussions, Beck is now insisting that he receive no less than seventy percent of the overall value of the partnership's assets. Lawyer Baker is aware that Aidan wants to resolve the matter of the distribution of assets quickly so as to avoid missing out on a new potential business opportunity. Beck knows of this potential business opportunity because he and Aidan were both presented with it; however, Beck has decided not to pursue the opportunity. Lawyer Baker only knows the information related to the business opportunity and Aiden's eagerness to settle in light of it because of a communication between Beck and Baker that is protected by the attorney-client privilege. Beck instructs Lawyer Baker to use this knowledge about Aidan in the settlement negotiations as leverage to secure Beck a higher settlement amount.

Is Lawyer Baker subject to discipline for his behavior in the negotiations? If so, why? If not, why not?

A. Yes, because Lawyer Baker should not have used information learned through confidential client communications in the settlement negotiations.

B. No, because Beck consented to Lawyer Baker's using the information otherwise protected by the attorney-client privilege in the settlement negotiations, and Baker owed no duty to Aidan to preserve that information as confidential.

C. Yes, because Baker used the fact of Aidan's eagerness to settle the dispute as a means of obtaining a higher settlement amount.

D. No. Though possibly technically improper, Lawyer Baker's actions do not raise a substantial question as to his fitness to practice law.

44. Lawyer represents Corporation. Corporation's board of directors, the entity's main decision-making body, has hired Lawyer to investigate whether employees of Corporation have been sharing insider information with institutional investors about new products that Corporation intends to launch. Corporation fears that it will be subject to charges of insider trading if it is revealed that its employees were engaging in these activities. In the course of Lawyer's investigation, Lawyer discovers that senior employees of Corporation, individuals whose actions can be attributed to the company, did, in fact, engage in this sort of illegal activity. Such information would certainly damage Corporation were Lawyer to reveal it to the authorities. Lawyer reveals the investigation's findings to the board of directors, the most senior body within the entity that can act on this information, but the board takes no action. Because the board refuses to act on the information, Lawyer reports the illegal activity to law enforcement officials.

Is Lawyer subject to discipline for sharing the confidential information about the actions of the company's senior officials? If so, why? If not, why not?

A. No, because Lawyer had a duty to report this activity to law enforcement officials once Corporation's board of directors took no action.

B. Yes, because Lawyer learned of this information during the course of an investigation conducted at the behest of the Corporation's board of directors.

C. No, because the information consisted of evidence of a crime.

D. Yes, because Lawyer's services were used in furtherance of a crime.

45. Lawyer is representing a defendant in a criminal proceeding. Soon after the client is indicted, and several months before the case is to go before the jury, Lawyer holds a press conference. At the press conference, Lawyer does the following:

- She provides the scheduled date of the trial.
- She states that her office is available to be contacted if anyone has any information about the incident that forms the basis of the charge against her client.
- She supplies the identity of one of the witnesses who is likely to testify at trial.
- She supplies the identity of the officer who arrested her client.

Which of these statements, if any, are more likely than not to have a material prejudicial effect on the proceeding?

A. None of these statements.

B. The statement seeking assistance with information about the incident.

C. The statement concerning the identity of one of the witnesses likely to testify at the trial.

D. The identity of the arresting officer.

46. Lawyer serves in a "Lawyer for the Day" program and volunteers his time at the local housing court helping tenants who are facing eviction. Lawyer enters into a limited retainer providing that Lawyer will only attempt to negotiate settlement agreements on behalf of tenants regarding their eviction cases, and that if any tenants have a personal injury claim against a landlord, Lawyer will not handle such matters. Such limited-scope retainers are common in this jurisdiction, both as they relate to Lawyer's agreeing only to handle negotiations as well as the restriction on personal injury claims. If the case cannot settle and the matter must go to trial, Lawyer states in the limited retainer that Lawyer is not able to represent the tenant in that situation. If a client has a personal injury claim, the client is given a contact list of attorneys who do handle such claims. Any prospective client is made aware of these restrictions on Lawyer's ability to represent the tenant should the matter not settle. Such tenants who wish to proceed with the representation through a limited-scope retainer provide informed consent to the arrangement in writing. Such tenants who do not consent to the arrangement understand that they are declining Lawyer's assistance.

Is Lawyer subject to discipline for offering clients retainers containing either of the limitations described?

A. Lawyer is subject to discipline for neither limitation.

B. Lawyer is subject to discipline for both limitations.

C. Lawyer is subject to discipline for the limitation related to negotiations, but not for the limitation related to personal injury matters.

D. Lawyer is subject to discipline for the limitation related to personal injury matters, but not for the limitation related to negotiations.

47. Parent reaches out to and secures the representation of Lawyer to defend her adult son who is accused of identity theft. Parent is of high income and pays for Lawyer's services. She tells Lawyer that she wants a "regular report" of how the representation is going. Lawyer and Parent enter into an agreement between themselves indicating that Lawyer should provide Parent with updates on the progress of the case on a monthly basis. This is a side agreement to a separate retainer agreement Lawyer enters into with the adult son only. Lawyer begins an investigation and learns that the son has been a prolific hacker, having hacked even Parent's credit cards. Lawyer discovers that the son has stolen roughly $1,000 from Parent. This theft is not a subject of the criminal charges against the son which Lawyer is currently handling on the son's behalf. The son asks Lawyer not to inform Parent of the theft. As far as Lawyer can tell, this conduct occurred well in the past, long before Lawyer agreed to represent the son, and the son has agreed he will never do it again. As part of Lawyer's monthly report to Parent, Lawyer informs Parent of the credit card theft by her son.

Is Lawyer subject to discipline for any of these actions? If so, why? If not, why not?

A. No. The agreement between Parent and Lawyer explicitly states that Lawyer should provide monthly updates to Parent, and all other actions by Lawyer were ethical.

B. No. Lawyer could exercise professional judgment in revealing client confidences to help mitigate the financial harm Parent has suffered at the hands of Lawyer's client.

C. Yes. Lawyer should not have accepted a fee from someone other than the client.

D. Yes. Lawyer is required to preserve the client's confidences and not communicate them to Parent.

48. Lawyer is handling a personal injury action on behalf of a plaintiff injured in a car accident. Lawyer learns that a key witness in the case, a bystander with no connection to either the plaintiff or the defendant but who will likely offer harmful eyewitness testimony in the case on behalf of the defendant, has a "YouFace" social media account that likely contains damaging information about that witness in the private portion of the site. Lawyer wants to access and use that information to undermine the witness's credibility. Lawyer asks one of his paralegals to pose as a former high school classmate of the witness and send a "Buddy" request that would give the firm access to the private portion of the witness's YouFace account.

Is Lawyer subject to discipline for seeking to obtain access to the witness's private social media page?

A. No, because Lawyer is not seeking such access himself but instead is having a paralegal attempt to do so.

B. No, because Lawyer is not having direct contact with the witness.

C. Yes, because Lawyer is using various forms of deception in contacting a witness.

D. Yes, because Lawyer is not permitted to have any contact with a potential witness for the opposing side without seeking the approval of opposing counsel.

49. Lawyer is a prominent criminal defense attorney who has begun to wind down her practice, preferring to spend much of her time hunting and fishing in rural Wyoming rather than staying involved in the rough-and-tumble of criminal practice. Recently, her next-door neighbor, a Silicon Valley billionaire, has found herself in legal trouble. The neighbor asks Lawyer to represent her in her upcoming criminal trial. Lawyer says that she will handle negotiations on the case but will not continue to represent her if an acceptable plea arrangement cannot be reached. Lawyer informs the neighbor that the case is quite complicated and that she will have to drop all of the few cases she still handles in order to take on the neighbor's case. Lawyer enters into a written agreement providing that Lawyer will only represent the neighbor through the initial negotiations phase of the representation and that if negotiations fail, the neighbor will have to find another lawyer. Lawyer also agrees that if she is able to secure an acceptable plea arrangement, whereby neighbor pleads to a misdemeanor charge or is absolved of all charges, she will accept $1 million as her fee, but if the plea negotiations fail, neighbor owes Lawyer nothing.

Is Lawyer guilty of misconduct?

A. Yes, because the scope of representation is unreasonable.

B. No, because the scope of representation is reasonable.

C. No, because Lawyer agreed to take no fee if she is not successful in obtaining the legitimate goals of the client.

D. Yes, because the fee arrangement in this setting is improper.

50. Lawyer has been retained by a foreign business entity that wants Lawyer to assist it in navigating through American export/import controls and U.S. customs laws. The CEO of the company does not speak English and neither does the company's general counsel, who is an employee of the company. Lawyer does not speak any languages those company representatives speak. Lawyer, CEO, and the company's general counsel conduct a video conference call to discuss the company's plans. Participating in the video conference session is a company-provided interpreter who is employed by neither the company nor Lawyer's firm. The interpreter translates the communications between Lawyer, CEO, and general counsel. During the course of the conversation, the CEO and general counsel seek guidance to ensure that they are not misrepresenting the nature of the products the company is importing into the United States. Some of their products have potential use for military purposes, and they want guidance on abiding by U.S. export/import controls on such products. After this discussion, the company agrees to import only some of their products as to not run afoul of those controls. Any products that would be subject to such controls will not be imported to the United States.

Are the communications between Lawyer, CEO, and the company's general counsel protected by the attorney-client privilege? If so, why? If not, why not?

A. Yes, because all confidential information is protected by the attorney-client privilege.

B. Yes, because the communications were for the purpose of obtaining legal advice.

C. No, because the communications were in furtherance of a crime or fraud.

D. No, because there was a third party present during the conversation.

51. Lawyer represents a tenant who resides in a building that the local city administration believes is unsafe for human habitation and must be demolished immediately, which will displace the tenant. Lawyer knows the building is unsafe but is afraid that if her client is displaced by the city's actions, the tenant will become homeless. Lawyer learns that the city issued an emergency vacate order and the building is scheduled for demolition that afternoon. Lawyer rushes to court to get an emergency stay of the demolition so that she might have a few days to find her client suitable, alternate housing. Lawyer believes in good faith that the building is not unsafe for the client to inhabit for the next few days until suitable housing can be found for her, but an engineer hired by her client has informed Lawyer that there are serious structural problems with the building. Both the engineer and city officials have determined there is a significant risk of imminent collapse within the next forty-eight hours. Lawyer believes that she can find suitable alternate housing for the client within twenty-four hours. Lawyer proceeds in an ex parte fashion before the court, without a lawyer for the city being present, to seek the temporary stay. Lawyer reports to the court that the client is facing imminent risk of homelessness should the demolition occur. Lawyer admits that the building likely needs to be demolished "in the near future" but does not inform the court of the serious structural problems the engineer and city representatives believe could precipitate the building's imminent collapse.

Did Lawyer engage in any misconduct in the manner in which she sought the stay from the court?

A. Yes, because she should not have proceeded in an ex parte fashion in seeking the stay.

B. Yes, because she was under an obligation to inform the court of the structural problems with the building, including the immediate risk of collapse, even if doing so went against her client's interests.

C. No, because she was being a zealous advocate for her client and was not obligated to reveal any facts adverse to her client's interests.

D. No, because she did not make any material misrepresentations to the court.

52. Lawyer represents homeowners in challenges to their local property tax assessments. Lawyer monitors efforts in a ten-county radius to keep track of when a locality or county government engages in reassessment of property values. Whenever such a reassessment occurs, Lawyer sends written correspondence by regular mail to the owners of properties in those areas to determine if they might want to challenge the assessment. Lawyer addresses each correspondence to the "Property Owner," but never identifies the individual owner or owners of the property. The mailing offers Lawyer's services to the property owner and states that Lawyer will only receive payment if the property owner's tax assessment challenge is successful. The mailing also states that Lawyer's payment will only constitute a portion of the tax savings the property owner receives as a result of a successful tax challenge. Lawyer further advertises that if a homeowner is indigent and is having trouble paying the bills, Lawyer will provide financial assistance to the homeowner to ensure the homeowner does not lose the home while the tax challenge is pending. The communication is in writing and indicates Lawyer's name and contact information. It also indicates that Lawyer is a "certified specialist in legal negotiations like these."

What actions, if any, would subject Lawyer to discipline?

A. The direct solicitation of potential clients without addressing the communication to a specific individual.

B. The direct solicitation of clients for pecuniary gain and the failure to identify the entity that certified Lawyer as a specialist.

C. The failure to identify the entity that certified Lawyer as a specialist and the statement about the availability of financial assistance to indigent homeowners.

D. Lawyer is not subject to discipline for any of these actions.

53. Lawyer represents Client in a medical malpractice action and is discussing Client's planned testimony in the matter. Client suffers a range of maladies as a result of the alleged medical malpractice. Lawyer believes Client's case is strong, but Client is nervous about the possibility he will not prevail in the action. Client explains the pain and suffering he is experiencing and that he suffers from sciatica. Lawyer knows the sciatica arose before the medical malpractice is alleged to have occurred and also knows the sciatica was not exacerbated by the alleged medical malpractice. Lawyer counsels Client that he must not testify that health problems that might have arisen prior to the malpractice and were not exacerbated by the defendant's actions were the fault of defendant. Lawyer knows that if Client is asked about the sciatica, Client will testify falsely about it and allege the defendant is at fault for that condition. Lawyer also knows she has to call the client to testify in the action, but she wants to limit the testimony only to those medical conditions that are related to the medical malpractice that is the subject of the lawsuit.

Is Lawyer subject to discipline if she calls Client to testify in the proceeding but does not inquire as to the nature or cause of the sciatica?

A. Yes, because Lawyer has a reasonable belief that Client could testify falsely.

B. Yes, because Lawyer will not be able to control Client if Client is cross-examined and asked to testify about the sciatica.

C. No, because Lawyer has a reasonable belief that Client will testify truthfully.

D. No, because Lawyer can limit the testimony to those matters about which Client will testify truthfully.

54. Lawyer represents Plaintiff in a personal injury action. On the eve of trial, the defendants in the case make an offer of settlement that would award Plaintiff less than what she feels she could obtain by taking the case to trial. Lawyer disagrees, believing that the jury will either return a verdict against Plaintiff or award her less than what the defendants are offering. Lawyer and Plaintiff discuss the settlement offer, and Plaintiff chooses to reject it over Lawyer's advice, preferring instead to take the case to trial. At trial, Lawyer performs competently, even admirably, but Plaintiff is awarded far less than she wanted, and certainly less than the amount defendants had offered to settle the matter. After the verdict is rendered, Plaintiff decides not to seek a new trial or to appeal the case. Instead, she insists that Lawyer reach out to the defendants to try to get the deal that was offered before the trial in order to avoid Plaintiff's filing an appeal. Lawyer reaches out to the defendants, but they turn down Plaintiff's request. They believe their case is strong and will vigorously oppose any appeal, should Plaintiff bring one. Instead of filing the appeal, Plaintiff commences a malpractice action against Lawyer alleging that Lawyer's advice to her regarding the settlement offer was negligent and constituted malpractice. Plaintiff argues that Lawyer should have advised her to accept the settlement when the defendants were offering it. Lawyer is incensed because she did advise Plaintiff to accept the settlement and avoid a trial. Lawyer plans on introducing her own testimony regarding the advice she gave to Plaintiff to accept the offer and Plaintiff's refusal to follow that advice. Plaintiff has hired a new attorney to bring the malpractice action against Lawyer, and that new attorney seeks to preclude Lawyer from introducing any evidence or testimony regarding Lawyer's advice to Plaintiff as well as any response by Plaintiff to that advice on the ground that such communications are covered by the attorney-client privilege.

Can Lawyer ethically present the evidence regarding her advice to Plaintiff about the settlement and Plaintiff's response to that advice?

A. Yes. This information is considered neither confidential nor privileged material.

B. Yes. Lawyer can utilize one of the exceptions to the prohibition on the disclosure of this information, even without Plaintiff's consent.

C. No. This material is covered by the attorney-client privilege and there are no applicable exceptions to the prohibition on disclosure of such information.

D. No. Plaintiff does not consent to the introduction of this confidential information in the case brought against the Lawyer.

55. Prosecutor brings several criminal charges against Accused for alleged violations of the state criminal code for several actions it is alleged Accused took while supposedly participating in a protest action. Accused is charged with having engaged in the destruction of property, for allegedly throwing an improvised explosive device through a storefront window during the protest. Accused claims to have been a mere bystander at the protest who took no violent action in support of it. The protest organizers' professed purpose was to intimidate certain members of the community so that they would not exercise their right to vote. Prosecutor believes it is necessary to press the most serious charges against Accused in order to deter others from engaging in similar actions in the future and to pressure Accused to accept a plea deal on lesser charges. The charges Prosecutor has filed include the following: Charge 1, use of force to intimidate others in order to prevent them from invoking their civil rights; Charge 2, attempted murder, although there was no one in the building or in the surrounding area at the time of the action; and Charge 3, disorderly conduct. Prosecutor does not believe there is probable cause to bring either Charge 1 or Charge 2, but he does believe in good faith that it is necessary to bring these charges against Accused to pressure Accused into accepting a plea deal on at least Charges 1 and 3. Prosecutor only has probable cause to bring Charge 3 but correctly believes that he may be able to obtain a conviction on both Charges 1 and 3 given the makeup of the jury pool, which is likely to be hostile to Accused. If Accused will not accept a plea deal and the matter has to go to trial, Prosecutor intends to withdraw Charge 2 but not Charge 1 or Charge 3.

Is Prosecutor subject to discipline for bringing any, some, none, or all of the charges against the defendant?

A. Prosecutor is subject to discipline for bringing Charges 1 and 2.

B. Prosecutor is subject to discipline for bringing Charge 2 only.

C. Prosecutor is subject to discipline for bringing all charges.

D. Prosecutor is not subject to discipline for bringing any of the charges.

56. Lawyer represents a large big-box store in the community, PriceCutter, in its worker compensation hearings, defending the company against claims when workers assert they have been injured on the job. Lawyer is gregarious and friendly, so whenever she attends these hearings and waits in the halls of the government offices where they are held, Lawyer routinely ends up entering into conversations with unrepresented workers who are waiting for their own hearings. Whenever this happens, invariably the conversation begins to broach subjects related to worker compensation law. Because she is sympathetic to many of the workers' claims, Lawyer tries to counsel them on how to represent themselves in their upcoming hearings. Lawyer generally asks whether a worker is an employee of PriceCutter before providing such advice. If it turns out that an unrepresented worker is an employee of PriceCutter, she identifies herself as PriceCutter's counsel and advises the individual to secure their own counsel.

Is it unethical for Lawyer to provide any of the advice she gives to workers awaiting their worker compensation hearings?

A. The advice to those individuals who are employees of PriceCutter is unethical but the advice to the individuals who are not employees of PriceCutter is ethical.

B. All of the advice Lawyer provides to these unrepresented individuals is unethical.

C. None of the advice Lawyer provides to these unrepresented individuals is unethical.

D. The advice to the employees of PriceCutter is ethical, but the advice to the individuals who are not employees of PriceCutter is unethical.

57. Two Lawyers, Able and Baker, are engaged in litigation in which they each represent plaintiffs in separate actions against the plaintiffs' employer, a large multinational corporation. During the course of the representation, the lawyers for the multinational corporation make a settlement offer that would result in a large award for each plaintiff. This award is much larger than the plaintiffs are likely to receive should their individual cases go to trial, but there is a catch. The company is insisting on a non-disclosure agreement that will govern not just the plaintiffs but also the lawyers. The company is afraid that more potential plaintiffs will come forward if there is a sense that new litigants could secure similar settlements from the company. Able wants to take the settlement offer to her client, while Baker does not. Baker says that although he thinks his client will accept the settlement offer, he does not believe it is fair to him for the client to take it. Neither plaintiff has expressed any desire to recruit other employees to sue the employer, and both have long stated a desire to resolve their respective cases quietly and move on with their lives. Both Able and Baker believe the settlement offer is a good one for their clients generally, but because Baker wants to file more cases against the company, he does not want to be bound by a non-disclosure agreement. Baker wants to use the settlement in advertising to recruit other clients. The company informs Able and Baker that the non-disclosure provision is an essential component of any settlement. Baker informs the company that the settlement offer is being rejected, without having taken it to his client to accept or reject the offer. This necessarily impacts Able because the company stated that the offer was "all or nothing": either both plaintiffs accept the offer or it will be withdrawn.

Is Able subject to discipline for not reporting Baker for appropriate discipline for failing to communicate the settlement offer to Baker's client? If so, why? If not, why not?

A. Yes, because Baker's behavior raises a substantial question regarding Baker's fitness to practice law.

B. Yes, because Baker's behavior was questionable.

C. No, because Baker was acting with the client's interests in mind, even if Baker was also thinking about his own interests.

D. No, because Baker was under no obligation to share the settlement offer with the client if Baker thought it was not in the client's best interest to accept it.

58. Lawyer is a solo practitioner who represents Client, a real estate developer that purchases distressed residential properties at a low price, rehabilitates them, and then resells them at a substantial profit. Client pays Lawyer a fee of five percent of the net proceeds from every building sold by Client. Client also has an escrow account maintained by Lawyer for the purchase and sale of properties targeted by Client. The account contains a fairly consistent amount of $1 million that functions as an operating fund. Lawyer is directed to purchase a property and uses the proceeds of the fund to do so. When a property is sold, the proceeds of the sale go into the fund. Lawyer and Client agree that once the proceeds of a sale are deposited into the account, Lawyer is deemed to have earned Lawyer's fee for a transaction and is permitted to withdraw from the fund the fee earned from that particular property sale. One day, Lawyer's in-house bookkeeper reports that the proceeds from a particular sale have been deposited into the account. This was an error resulting from negligent management of the account on the part of the bookkeeper. Based upon the belief that the sale had been finalized, the funds were in the account, and Lawyer was entitled to withdraw the fee, Lawyer withdraws the fee for the sale of that property. The next day, Lawyer learns that the sale was not finalized and the proceeds of that sale had not yet appeared in the account. Lawyer refunds the account a sum equal to the amount withdrawn plus a small amount of interest, representing the interest that would have been earned had the money withdrawn stayed in the escrow account.

What conduct, if any, could subject Lawyer to discipline with respect to the maintenance of Client's operating fund?

A. Only Lawyer's withdrawal of the funds when such funds had not yet been earned.

B. Only the negligent recordkeeping that led Lawyer to withdraw the fee when that fee had not yet been earned.

C. None of Lawyer's conduct.

D. Both the negligent recordkeeping and Lawyer's withdrawal of the unearned funds.

59. Sam met Carroll through Sam's position as an associate at the firm. Carroll is an inventor, and Sam's firm is representing Carroll with regard to obtaining several patents that could prove quite lucrative. Sam and Carroll fall in love and have sexual relations. Sam informs the firm of the relationship. Sam is re-assigned and no longer represent Carroll, though the firm continues the representation. Sam is screened from any knowledge about the representation and is awarded no fee from the representation.

Is Sam's firm able to continue the representation of Carroll?

A. Yes, if Carroll gives informed consent to the continued representation.

B. Yes, because any conflict caused by the relationship between Sam and Carroll does not affect whether the entire firm has a conflict with the representation.

C. No, because the conflict affects the entire firm.

D. No, because Sam's behavior was unethical.

60. Lawyer is handling protracted litigation on behalf of Plaintiff in a personal injury matter. Defendant's counsel requests a brief postponement of an upcoming deposition of Defendant's representative due to Defendant's counsel's having a recent illness. The postponement will not adversely affect Lawyer's ability to represent Plaintiff and will not result in any overall delay of the proceeding. Lawyer does not confer with Plaintiff before informing Defendant's counsel that she will grant the postponement.

Is it professional misconduct for Lawyer to have agreed to the postponement of the deposition?

A. Yes, Lawyer should have consulted with her client prior to agreeing to the postponement.

B. Yes, because Lawyer must act with reasonable diligence in representing the client.

C. No, because Lawyer has absolute discretion in scheduling matters.

D. No, because the request was reasonable and did not prejudice Lawyer's client.

Chapter 10

Short Answers

Chapter 1: The Attorney-Client Relationship

1.1 Admission to the Bar

1. B
2. C

1.2 Forming the Attorney-Client Relationship

3. B
4. A
5. C

1.3 The Attorney's Duty of Care

6. D
7. A
8. C
9. B
10. A
11. B

1.4 Communication with Clients

12. B
13. C

1.5 Allocation of Authority Between Lawyers and Clients

14. A
15. A
16. D
17. A
18. B
19. C
20. B

1.6 Duties of Supervisory and Subordinate Lawyers

21. B
22. C
23. D
24. B

1.7 Unauthorized Practice of Law

25. D
26. C
27. C

1.8 Partnerships with Non-Lawyers and Rules Related to Law-Related Services

28. B
29. B

1.9 Declining or Withdrawing from Representation

30. C
31. B
32. D
33. C
34. B
35. C
36. B
37. A
38. D
39. A

1.10 Formative Assessment Quiz

40. B
41. A
42. C
43. D
44. C
45. B
46. C
47. A
48. B
49. D
50. B
51. D
52. A
53. B
54. C
55. D
56. C
57. D
58. B
59. D

Chapter 2: Conflicts of Interest

2.1 Client Conflicts Generally

1. A
2. C
3. B
4. C
5. B
6. A
7. A

2.2 Specific Conflicts Issues

8. B
9. C
10. A
11. A
12. C
13. D
14. D
15. D
16. A
17. D
18. C

2.3 Conflicts of Interest with Former Clients

19. A
20. C
21. D
22. C

2.4 Conflicts and Government Lawyers

23. C
24. C
25. B
26. A
27. B
28. A

2.5 Formative Assessment Quiz

29. C
30. D
31. C
32. B
33. A
34. D
35. D
36. B
37. B
38. A
39. A
40. C
41. D
42. B
43. C
44. C

Chapter 3: Confidentiality

3.1 Understanding Confidentiality

1. B
2. A
3. D
4. A
5. D
6. C
7. B
8. C

3.2 Attorney-Client Privilege

9. C
10. D
11. A

3.3 Grounds Permitting Disclosure

12. D
13. C
14. C
15. A
16. B
17. B

3.4 Competence, Supervision, and Confidentiality

18. A
19. A

3.5 Specific Issues related to Organizational Clients (MR 1.13)

20. B
21. D
22. B
23. A
24. C

3.6 Duties to Prospective Clients (MR 1.18)

25. C
26. B

3.7 Formative Assessment Quiz

27. A
28. B
29. B
30. C
31. D
32. A
33. D
34. D
35. B
36. D
37. C
38. B
39. D
40. A
41. A
42. C
43. A

Chapter 4: Attorney's Fees

4.1 Understanding Attorney's Fees

1. C	3. D	5. A	7. B
2. D	4. C	6. A	

4.2 Assessing Reasonable Attorney's Fees

8. C	9. A	10. B	11. C

4.3 Formative Assessment Quiz

12. C	14. D	16. C	18. C
13. C	15. A	17. D	

Chapter 5: Ethics in Advocacy

5.1 Meritorious Claims and Contentions

1. B	2. D	3. A

5.2 The Duty of Candor to the Tribunal

4. A	7. B	10. C
5. B	8. C	11. A
6. A	9. D	12. C

5.3 Preserving Potential Evidence

13. B	14. B	15. C

5.4 Lawyer as Potential Witness

16. D	17. D	18. B	19. C

5.5 Special Responsibilities of a Prosecutor

20. A	21. B	22. C

5.6 The No-Contact Rule

23. D	25. D	27. C	29. C
24. B	26. D	28. D	

5.7 Dealing with Third Parties

30. A
31. C
32. D
33. C
34. B

5.8 Clients with Diminished Capacity

35. C
36. A
37. B

5.9 Safekeeping Client Property

38. A
39. B
40. C
41. B

5.10 Sale of a Law Practice

42. D
43. B
44. B

5.11 Formative Assessment Quiz

45. C
46. D
47. B
48. D
49. C
50. B
51. A
52. D
53. C
54. B
55. C
56. A
57. B
58. B
59. C
60. B
61. C
62. A
63. C

Chapter 6: Addressing Misconduct

6.1 Identifying Misconduct

1. B
2. B

6.2 Reporting Misconduct

3. C
4. D
5. B
6. B
7. A

6.3 Misconduct Related to Diversity and Inclusion

8. C
9. D

6.4 Formative Assessment Quiz

10. B
11. D
12. B
13. C
14. B
15. C
16. C
17. A

Chapter 7: Attorney Free-Speech Rights

7.1 Attorney Advertising

1. C
2. A
3. B
4. C
5. B
6. B
7. B
8. A
9. D
10. B
11. C

7.2 Attorney Communications with the Media

12. B
13. C
14. A
15. C
16. B
17. D

7.3 Formative Assessment Quiz

18. B
19. C
20. D
21. D
22. B

Chapter 8: Judicial Ethics

8.1 Judicial Misconduct

1. C
2. A
3. B
4. A
5. C
6. D
7. B
8. D

8.2 Formative Assessment Quiz

9. B
10. A
11. B
12. A

Chapter 9: Summative Assessment Quiz

1. C
2. D
3. A
4. C
5. A
6. C
7. D
8. B
9. D
10. C
11. A
12. C
13. D
14. A
15. A
16. D
17. C
18. B
19. A
20. C
21. D
22. C
23. A
24. C
25. C
26. B
27. A
28. D
29. B
30. D
31. D
32. A
33. B
34. C
35. C
36. A
37. D
38. C
39. A
40. C
41. C
42. A
43. B
44. B
45. C
46. A
47. D
48. C
49. D
50. B
51. B
52. C
53. D
54. B
55. A
56. C
57. A
58. D
59. B
60. D

Chapter 11

Answers and Explanations

Chapter 1: The Attorney-Client Relationship

1.1 Admission to the Bar

1. B. *See* MR 8.1(b). There is nothing in the fact pattern to indicate that the information is confidential. The lawyer is not in an attorney-client relationship with the law student. In accordance with MR 8.1, the lawyer must reveal what she knows about the government investigation, especially since the law student has indicated that he engaged in no illegal behavior.

2. C. Rule 8.1(b) provides that the failure to disclose a fact necessary to correct a misapprehension in the course of an application for admission "does not require disclosure of information otherwise protected by Rule 1.6," that is, information that is covered by confidentiality rules, including information protected by the attorney-client privilege, and this information qualifies for that protection against disclosure. The information shared with the lawyer was in furtherance of the lawyer's representation of the applicant and thus covered by the attorney-client privilege. As such, it was not necessary to disclose it. There will be much more on confidentiality in Chapter 3.

1.2 Forming the Attorney-Client Relationship

3. B. Here, the information the lawyer provided was general and not particularized to the individual patron, Pat. Because the lawyer simply recommended that Pat speak to a lawyer about her case, there would be no reasonable basis upon which Pat could believe an attorney-client relationship had been formed. Moreover, because the lawyer never even identified herself as such, Pat would again have no reasonable basis for thinking that an attorney-client relationship had been formed. At the same time, if a lawyer's actions would lead an individual to the reasonable belief that an attorney-client relationship has been formed, then those actions will typically lead to the formation of that relationship, particularly if the client relies to their detriment on the belief that the relationship has, in fact, been formed.

4. A. See MR 1.2(c), which provides that a reasonable limitation on the scope of a given representation is appropriate if the client gives informed consent to that limitation. Here, the lawyer's restriction was reasonable and the client gave informed consent. There is no requirement under the rule for independent counsel in executing such an agreement.

5. C. Once again, we look to the permission structure under MR 1.2(c). Here, the limitation was reasonable, particularly given the lawyer's competencies. In addition, the client gave informed consent to the arrangement.

1.3 The Attorney's Duty of Care

6. D. Comment 2 to MR 1.3 provides that "[a] lawyer's work load must be controlled so that each matter can be handled competently." It does not matter that the lawyer believes her incompetent representation is still better than the representation the clients might get from other lawyers. Here, by not managing her workload to provide competent services to her clients, the lawyer did not meet the standard of care.

7. A. Comment 3 to MR 1.1 provides as follows: "In an emergency a lawyer may give advice or assistance in a matter in which the lawyer does not have the skill ordinarily required where referral to or consultation or association with another lawyer would be impractical. Even in an emergency, however, assistance should be limited to that reasonably necessary in the circumstances, for ill-considered action under emergency conditions can jeopardize the client's interest." Normally, the level of skill required in a non-emergency situation is that of a "general practitioner." (Comment 1 to MR 1.1) While the lawyer did not know all of the particular elements of immigration practice relevant to the client's situation, the lawyer's exercise of care here was certainly consistent with that of a general practitioner. In a non-emergency situation, an argument could certainly be made that the lawyer should have known what an expert would know, but in an emergency situation, some leeway is afforded the attorney, and here the lawyer acted in good faith and in a manner consistent with the level of care appropriate to the situation.

8. C. Comment 4 to MR 1.1. provides that "[a] lawyer may accept representation where the requisite level of competence can be achieved by reasonable preparation," as was the case here.

9. B. Comment 4 to MR 1.3 provides that a client may assume that a lawyer still represents the client if the lawyer "has served a client over a substantial period of time on a variety of matters." Doubt should be resolved "preferably in writing" by the lawyer, but the notification is not required to be in writing.

10. A. Rule 1.6(c) requires that "[a] lawyer shall make reasonable efforts to prevent the inadvertent or unauthorized disclosure of, or unauthorized access to, informa-

tion relating to the representation of a client." Comment 18 to MR 1.6 explains that "Paragraph (c) requires a lawyer to act competently to safeguard information relating to the representation of a client against unauthorized access by third parties and against inadvertent or unauthorized disclosure by the lawyer or other persons who are participating in the representation of the client or who are subject to the lawyer's supervision." In addition, Comment 8 to MR 1.1 provides that a lawyer must keep "abreast of changes in the law and its practice, including the benefits and risks associated with relevant technology, engage in continuing study and education, and comply with all" CLE requirements. Here, Lawyer took the reasonable measures required to protect her client's confidences and is not strictly liable for any breach when such reasonable measures are taken.

11. B. Rule 1.3 provides that "[a] lawyer shall act with reasonable diligence and promptness in representing a client." At the same time, Comment 3 to that rule states that "[a] lawyer's duty to act with reasonable promptness, however, does not preclude the lawyer from agreeing to a reasonable request for a postponement that will not prejudice the lawyer's client." Thus, Comment 3 to MR 1.3 advises that, in this situation, the lawyer can deny the extension if granting it is not in the client's best interest, even if the attorney for the restaurant has reasonable grounds for seeking the extension and it is standard practice in the community to grant such extensions.

1.4 Communication with Clients

12. B. Rule 1.4(a)(2) and Comments 3 and 5 to that rule provide that a lawyer should keep the client reasonably informed of developments in the case and confer with the client in meaningful ways, particularly as such communications relate to fundamental matters over which the client has control, like communication about a settlement offer. The lawyer was thus obligated to take reasonable steps—like contacting the client's surrogate—when the lawyer could not reach the client.

13. C. This is a problem of inadequate client counseling. A lawyer can follow guidance from a client that might lead to client harm if the client chose and gave consent to the lawyer's taking that course of action after being apprised by the lawyer of the potential harm that might occur by choosing that particular strategy. Such consent was not present here.

1.5 Allocation of Authority Between Lawyers and Clients

14. A. Even if the lawyer did not believe it was in the best interests of the client to accept the plea deal, the proper course of action was to follow the client's wishes, even if to do so was contrary to the wishes of the individuals paying the lawyer's

fee. Such individuals should not interfere with the operation of the attorney-client relationship between the client and the lawyer. That the client gave consent to share the confidential information with the parents means those actions were not unethical. We will further explore some of the issues that can arise when a third party pays a lawyer's fee in Chapter 2.

15. A. While the lawyer generally controls the "means" of the representation in accordance with MR 1.2, the lawyer must still consult with the client about those means, and here the client's objective of having an expedited case will be frustrated by the course of action the lawyer has chosen. If the lawyer believes she cannot provide competent representation, she should instead seek to withdraw from the case in a manner consistent with MR 1.16 rather than proceed with the depositions.

16. D. We again see the application of the principles surrounding limited-scope retainers as set forth in MR 1.2(c). In such circumstances, the scope of the retainer itself must be reasonable, and the client must give informed consent to the limited nature of the representation. The fact pattern does not seem to identify any harm to the client resulting from the limited scope of the representation, the limited nature of the representation is common in the community, and the client has given informed consent to the relationship. For these reasons, the limited nature of the representation is appropriate.

17. A. Even if a lawyer believes in good faith that a settlement is in the client's best interest, they must still obtain the consent of the client before entering into any settlement. MR 1.2(a) ("A lawyer shall abide by a client's decision whether to settle a matter.").

18. B. No good-cause requirement exists for a client who wishes to terminate the attorney-client relationship. Yes, there is a cost associated with changing attorneys at this juncture in the matter, but this is a cost the client is willing to absorb. The client controls the representation and is willing to face the consequences of terminating the relationship.

19. C. Here, the client has the ultimate authority over the representation, and the lawyer cannot take that away from the client in this fashion. MR 1.2. It is certainly possible that a lawyer could condition their representation on whether the client will take the case to trial or not, if such a limitation was reasonable and the client consented to it in accordance with MR 1.2(c). A lawyer and client might agree that if the time comes to consider a settlement and the client should choose to settle, the lawyer will withdraw and a new counsel can be selected to facilitate the settlement. The reverse is also possible: the lawyer can agree only to handle a settlement, and if the client wants to take the case to trial, an accommodation will be made that the client will have an opportunity to find trial counsel. Here, no such explicit limitation on the representation was undertaken as required by MR 1.2(c).

20. B. *See* Comment 3 to MR 1.2. When a client gives a lawyer, in advance of negotiations, the parameters of the terms of a settlement the client might accept, the lawyer may rely on the advance authorization "absent a material change" in circumstances in the matter. Here, the denial of the motion to dismiss the creative claims changes the leverage the plaintiff has and would therefore constitute such a material change. The lawyer should have returned to the client to discuss that change so that the client could consider whether to revise her settlement parameters.

1.6 Duties of Supervisory and Subordinate Lawyers

21. B. Rule 5.1 sets forth the basic requirements imposed on supervisory lawyers and states that such lawyers "shall make reasonable efforts to ensure that the [office in which the lawyer holds that role] has in effect measures giving reasonable assurance that all lawyers in the [office] conform to the Rules of Professional Conduct." Answer B sets forth the appropriate standard under the relevant rule, and it was not sufficient for the lawyer to have gone with a "gut feeling" and assume the new attorneys knew rules related to timely filings. The rule itself speaks of the supervisory lawyer's "firm," but in accordance with the definitions section of the Model Rules, MR 1.0(c) defines a "firm" or a "law firm" as including "a lawyer or lawyers in a law partnership, professional corporation, sole proprietorship or other association authorized to practice law; or lawyers employed in a legal services organization or the legal department of a corporation or other organization."

22. C. This question explores the application of MR 5.2. Rule 5.2(a) states that all lawyers are "bound by the Rules of Professional Conduct notwithstanding that [a] lawyer acted at the direction of another person." When a complex issue of professional responsibility presents itself and requires some degree of professional judgment to resolve, MR 5.2(b) provides that a supervised lawyer "does not violate the Rules of Professional Conduct if that lawyer acts in accordance with a supervisory lawyer's reasonable resolution of an arguable question of professional duty." Here, the course of conduct, with respect to the taxes, would appear legitimate given the verb tense of the question. The course of conduct with respect to the asbestos, however, cannot be considered an "arguable" question of the lawyer's duty for which the subordinate attorney can follow the guidance of a supervising lawyer. This would be a clear misrepresentation, illegal under applicable law. The subordinate lawyer would not be free to follow the guidance of the senior lawyer on this point and escape professional discipline for that subordinate lawyer's actions.

23. D. This question asks you to identify the proper standard that should be applied to determine the propriety of the supervisory lawyer's conduct in overseeing the subordinate lawyer. Rule 5.1 requires only that supervisory lawyers "make rea-

sonable efforts to ensure that the firm has in effect measures giving reasonable assurance that all lawyers in the firm conform to the Rules of Professional Conduct." Answer D accurately captures the standard against which the supervisory lawyer's conduct will be measured.

24. B. You probably need more information to correctly answer this question, notably whether there is a legal obligation to turn over this information. This question is testing whether the supervisory lawyer's action can be assessed as a "reasonable resolution of an arguable question of professional duty," as stated in Answer C, which is the appropriate standard to apply here (*see* MR 5.2(b)). You have to read this question carefully. The difference between Answer A and Answer C is that A says "if," whereas C says "because." That's a big difference. You do not know whether C is correct because we do not know whether there is a legal duty to respond to the subpoena. Cynthia could be right here, but the proper course of action would be to object to, not to ignore, the discovery demand. Therefore, if there *is* a *clear* legal duty to turn over the information, Jane cannot simply ignore it, and Cynthia's advice would not be reasonable. As a result, Answer B is correct.

1.7 Unauthorized Practice of Law

25. D. Rule 5.5(a) provides that a "lawyer shall not practice law in a jurisdiction in violation of the regulation of the legal profession in that jurisdiction, or assist another in doing so." Even though the lawyer is admitted in the jurisdiction, it is improper for the lawyer to assist others in the unauthorized practice of law, which is what the lawyer is doing here by knowingly assisting the tenant organizers in this way, even if doing so means the otherwise unrepresented tenants will get some help. That factor cannot justify supporting the unauthorized practice of law. This is an evolving area of law, however, and worth watching.

26. C. Comment 2 to MR 5.5 provides that the "definition of the practice of law is established by law and varies from one jurisdiction to another." Although the definition does vary by jurisdiction, many jurisdictions consider the provision of tailored, customized legal advice to a particular person or entity regarding their specific legal situation to constitute the practice of law. Here, there was no individualized guidance tied to a specific client's needs. The only legal service, if any, which was competently provided, was the assessment that the individual could use the non-profit's resources to meet her legal needs, and that assessment was carried out by a lawyer admitted to practice in the jurisdiction. The question did not ask whether the lawyer provided legal services or created an attorney-client relationship.

27. C. Rule 5.5(c) provides that "[a] lawyer admitted in another United States jurisdiction, and not disbarred or suspended from practice in any jurisdiction, may provide legal services on a temporary basis in this jurisdiction that: (1) are un-

dertaken in association with a lawyer who is admitted to practice in this jurisdiction and who actively participates in the matter." Here, there are no indications that Portia actively participated in the matter, and no other exceptions appear to apply that would permit the representation.

1.8 Partnerships with Non-Lawyers and Rules Related to Law-Related Services

28. B. Rule 5.4(b) prohibits a lawyer from forming "a partnership with a nonlawyer if any of the activities of the partnership consist of the practice of law," which is exactly what happened here.

29. B. Rule 5.7 provides that a lawyer is subject to professional responsibility rules when engaged in law-related services that are not distinct from the provision of legal services, as is the case here.

1.9 Declining or Withdrawing from Representation

30. C. Rule 1.16(b)(1) provides that a lawyer may withdraw from representing a client when to do so will not adversely impact the client. Even with an enforceable retainer that is limited as this one is, if the lawyer can withdraw without its having a materially adverse impact on the client, the lawyer is permitted to do so. Here, there is no tribunal from which the lawyer needed to obtain consent to withdraw as would be required under MR 1.6(c) ("A lawyer must comply with applicable law requiring notice to or permission of a tribunal when terminating a representation. When ordered to do so by a tribunal, a lawyer shall continue representation notwithstanding good cause for terminating the representation."). Rule 1.0(m) defines a "tribunal" broadly, as "a court, an arbitrator in a binding arbitration proceeding or a legislative body, administrative agency or other body acting in an adjudicative capacity. A legislative body, administrative agency or other body acts in an adjudicative capacity when a neutral official, after the presentation of evidence or legal argument by a party or parties, will render a binding legal judgment directly affecting a party's interests in a particular matter."

31. B. An attorney-client relationship can be formed through overt and express acts, like signing a retainer, the lawyer's undertaking the provision of legal services to a client, or the lawyer's taking actions that would lead a reasonable person to believe an attorney-client relationship has been formed. None of that happened here. Just speaking to a prospective client about their case does not, without more, create an attorney-client relationship.

32. D. Rule 1.16(b)(4) provides that when a fundamental disagreement arises between a lawyer and client, the lawyer has grounds to *seek* withdrawal, and, here, it was

not unethical to do so, even if the court ultimately denied the request, which it has the authority to do. *See also* MR 1.16(c).

33. C. Comment 2 to MR 1.16 provides as follows: "The lawyer is not obliged to decline or withdraw simply because the client suggests [an illegal] course of conduct; a client may make such a suggestion in the hope that a lawyer will not be constrained by a professional obligation." Here, the lawyer has grounds to seek to withdraw but is not obligated to do so if he is able to convince the client to refrain from illegal conduct.

34. B. This question tests your knowledge of how to apply MR 1.16(c), which provides that if a matter is before a tribunal as defined in the rules (*see* MR 1.0(m)), and the rules of that tribunal require permission from the tribunal to withdraw, the lawyer must obtain that permission prior to withdrawal, even if ample grounds exist to withdraw. Indeed, even if there is a situation that gives rise to a right to withdraw under 1.16(a), a withdrawal under subpart (a) is still conditioned on compliance with subpart (c) if that subpart applies, that is, if consent of the tribunal to withdraw is required (as Answer B indicates it was).

35. C. Comment 9 to MR 1.16 provides as follows: "Even if the lawyer has been unfairly discharged by the client, a lawyer must take all reasonable steps to mitigate the consequences to the client." The proper course of action in a contingency fee case is for the transfer of the representation to occur with the lawyer's receiving a fee proportional to the work the lawyer performed on the case, but only if the contingency occurs. The lawyer cannot interfere with, or hold up, the transfer of the case for a fee if the contingency on which that fee is based has not yet occurred.

36. B. Comment 10 to Rule 1.2 provides as follows: "In some cases, withdrawal alone might be insufficient. It may be necessary for the lawyer to give notice of the fact of withdrawal and to disaffirm any opinion, document, affirmation or the like." This is sometimes referred to as a "noisy withdrawal." In this situation, because the client disavowed the legal opinion, is no longer asking anyone to rely on it, did not sell any of the tanks, and has no plans to do so, the lawyer is under no obligation to make such a noisy withdrawal, and there do not appear to be any grounds upon which the lawyer *must* withdraw. It is certainly possible that the lawyer has grounds to withdraw in this situation if the lawyer feels that the client failed to satisfy a fundamental obligation of the relationship (*see* MR 1.16(b)(4): a lawyer may seek to withdraw when a client "insists upon taking action that the lawyer considers repugnant or with which the lawyer has a fundamental disagreement"). Here, the failure to provide accurate information seems innocent, and no harm will come from the tanks because they have been pulled from the market. There are no grounds *requiring* the lawyer to withdraw, which is what at least one part of the question asked.

37. A. Rule 1.16(b)(6) provides that the lawyer is permitted to seek to withdraw in this situation because the representation had become unreasonably difficult, even if a prior dispute had been resolved.

38. D. Here, no attorney-client relationship was formed. If an attorney-client relationship were formed, it might have required Leslie to take action on behalf of Cam. Leslie chose not to assess the claim and she was not obligated to do so. Thus Answer A is incorrect because Leslie made no assessment of Cam's rights.

39. A. Comment 10 to MR 1.2 provides as follows: "In some cases, withdrawal alone might be insufficient. It may be necessary for the lawyer to give notice of the fact of withdrawal and to disaffirm any opinion, document, affirmation or the like." Because the lawyer's services were used in drafting the faulty agreements and they were still being used, this permits the lawyer to engage in what is known as "noisy withdrawal," which involves informing parties of the reason for the withdrawal (referred to in the Question 36 explanation, above). Thus, there is nothing wrong with the lawyer's engaging in this conduct, and she is not subject to discipline for doing so.

1.10 Formative Assessment Quiz

40. B. A lawyer is not permitted to enter into a partnership with a non-lawyer if the services rendered by the partnership constitute the practice of law. MR 5.4(b).

41. A. The information provided was general and not particularized to the individual. Moreover, the lawyer simply recommended that the litigant speak to a lawyer. There would be no reasonable basis upon which the litigant could believe an attorney-client relationship was formed between the litigant and the lawyer. Informing the litigant about the statute of limitations in this manner is not particularized legal advice.

42. C. The lawyer had an obligation to obtain advanced consent or to approve each settlement individually before entering into it. MR 1.2.

43. D. While the lawyer's limitation on the representation might have been reasonable under the circumstances, such limitation was not clearly communicated to the client and the client was not afforded an opportunity to give informed consent to such limitation. *See* MR 1.2(c).

44. C. *See* MR 5.5(a). Even though the lawyer is admitted in the jurisdiction, it is still improper for him to assist others in the unauthorized practice of law. At the same time, it appears that the lawyer did all that he could do to avoid the organizers' engaging in the unauthorized practice of law, yet, despite the lawyer's guidance, they went ahead and did it anyway.

45. B. A lawyer may take on a matter that the lawyer is not competent to handle, provided the lawyer can obtain such competence in a reasonable time, which oc-

curred here. MR 1.1. There are no issues of waiving future malpractice claims raised in the fact pattern.

46. C. *See* MR 5.1. Here, the supervision was reasonable under the circumstances. The supervising lawyer was always present to oversee the work and was able to catch any of the subordinate lawyer's errors and correct them in an effective way.

47. A. Comment 4 to MR 1.3 provides as follows: "Unless the relationship is terminated as provided in Rule 1.16, a lawyer should carry through to conclusion all matters undertaken for a client. If a lawyer's employment is limited to a specific matter, the relationship terminates when the matter has been resolved. If a lawyer has served a client over a substantial period in a variety of matters, the client sometimes may assume that the lawyer will continue to serve on a continuing basis unless the lawyer gives notice of withdrawal." Even if a lawyer did have a reasonable belief that a client would not be harmed by the non-representation, the lawyer would not be relieved of the obligation to inform the client of the lawyer's wish to no longer continue the representation.

48. B. See Comment 3 to MR 1.2, which covers advance consent to settlements but requires that the lawyer consult with the client in the event that the material circumstances surrounding a matter have changed, such that the client should be afforded an opportunity to assess the circumstances and potentially change the parameters of the settlement the client will accept. Here, there were changed circumstances warranting a consultation with the client prior to the lawyer's continuing to negotiate based on the client's prior settlement parameters. The lawyer's understanding of Company 3's claims changed, and this should have been communicated to the client. Even if a client has given advance consent to a particular settlement, that client should be advised of any new and material information and offered an opportunity to reconsider the client's settlement position.

49. D. *See* MR 8.1(b). Here, the lawyer has an ethical obligation to correct the misapprehension of the committee about the applicant's past. This information was not protected by the attorney-client privilege, and there is no exemption because the jurisdiction to which the applicant has applied is not a jurisdiction where the lawyer is admitted to practice.

50. B. Rules 5.1 and 5.3 provide that supervisory lawyers must have in place systems that provide reasonable assurance that lawyers and non-lawyer staff can comply with a law office's ethical obligations. Those supervisory lawyers are responsible when those systems are inadequate, as they were here, and they are held accountable for the acts of the lawyers and non-lawyer assistants they supervise. The supervisory lawyer's failure to direct the student to not give any advice the student was not competent to dispense demonstrates that the supervisory lawyer did not have adequate measures in place to satisfy their own obligations to provide oversight of the student's work.

51. D. Comment 8 to MR 1.1 provides that lawyers "should keep abreast of changes in the law and its practice, including the benefits and risks associated with relevant technology, engage in continuing study and education and comply with all continuing legal education requirements to which the lawyer is subject." MR 1.6(c) (which we will review in Chapter 3) provides that "[a] lawyer shall make reasonable efforts to prevent the inadvertent or unauthorized disclosure of, or unauthorized access to, information relating to the representation of a client." The software fix was not onerous and the failure to update the software in light of the known risk was unreasonable.

52. A. The limitation was reasonable and common in the jurisdiction. In addition, the clients always gave informed consent to the arrangement. *See* MR 1.2(c).

53. B. Rule 5.5(c)(1) permits a lawyer admitted in another U.S. jurisdiction, and who is not disbarred or suspended from practice in any jurisdiction, to provide services in another jurisdiction on a temporary basis when the lawyer "undertakes" such services "in association with a lawyer who is admitted to practice in [that] jurisdiction and who actively participates in the matter." Since the lawyer appeared to work with another lawyer admitted in the jurisdiction in providing the legal services described, such service was not inappropriate.

54. C. Rule 1.2(d) provides as follows: "A lawyer shall not counsel a client to engage, or assist a client, in conduct that the lawyer knows is criminal or fraudulent, but a lawyer may discuss the legal consequences of any proposed course of conduct with a client and may counsel or assist a client to make a good faith effort to determine the validity, scope, meaning or application of the law." While it appears that the client *is* asking for guidance on how to engage in illegal conduct, the lawyer does not offer such guidance. The advice is consistent with what is proper under the rule.

55. D. See MR Rule 5.2(b), which states, "A subordinate lawyer does not violate the Rules of Professional Conduct if that lawyer acts in accordance with a supervisory lawyer's reasonable resolution of an arguable question of professional duty." The subordinate lawyer's knowledge of the perjury can be inferred from the facts. Moreover, the duty of candor toward the court trumps the duty of confidentiality. Even if the information is confidential, the lawyer has a clear duty to disclose it and thus cannot rely on the supervisor's direction here.

56. C. Comment 8 to Rule 1.1 provides that a lawyer must "maintain the requisite knowledge and skill" to practice competently and, as a result, the lawyer "should keep abreast of changes in the law and its practice, including the benefits and risks associated with relevant technology, engage in continuing study and education and comply with all continuing legal education requirements to which the lawyer is subject." Here, the lawyer's inability to keep up with the changes in technology necessary to practice competently rendered the work incompetent, both in terms of missing the court date and failing to file a timely motion to vacate the default. In accordance with Comment 3 to MR 1.3, a lawyer must also

manage her workload to prevent herself from engaging in misconduct, which the lawyer clearly did not do here (that is, the lawyer failed to manage her workload in such a way that would prevent her from committing malpractice due to the burdens of the work).

57. D. The issues around materially adverse impact on the representation (MR 1.16(b)(1)) only apply to the lawyer's withdrawal. Here, the lawyer is terminated and substitute counsel has been found for the client.

58. B. See MR 5.2(b), which sets forth the subordinate lawyer's obligations when acting under the guidance of a supervisory lawyer to resolve an "arguable" question of professional ethics. Here, the actions with respect to the taxes are not arguably appropriate. The statement that the taxes were paid would be a lie, while the statement about the asbestos would be consistent with the truth and thus appropriate.

59. D. See MR 1.2(d), which states, "A lawyer shall not counsel a client to engage, or assist a client, in conduct that the lawyer knows is criminal or fraudulent, but a lawyer may discuss the legal consequences of any proposed course of conduct with a client and may counsel or assist a client to make a good faith effort to determine the validity, scope, meaning or application of the law." This counseling and these communications are not inappropriate.

Chapter 2: Conflicts of Interest

2.1 Client Conflicts Generally

1. A. Rule 1.7(b)(3) prohibits representation of two parties when the representation will involve the "assertion of a claim by one client against another." The fact that the case may be in the process of being settled does not remove this barrier to the representation.

2. C. It does not appear that a conflict impacted the representation in any way, let alone "adversely," as is required by the case law on the intersection of conflicts of interest and ineffective assistance of counsel. If the issue of conflicted representation is not raised, then the defendant must show that the representation was adversely affected, and defendants cannot do that here.

3. B. Comment 29 to MR 1.7 applies to this situation. Here, the lawyer may have to withdraw from representing both clients because the confidential information that the lawyer is required to preserve once the client asks the lawyer to do so (even in the face of a waiver) is useful to the other client. Maintaining the lawyer's obligations to Bernie means the lawyer cannot represent Arliss with zeal. The lawyer must withhold information that would be useful to Arliss's case and harmful to Bernie's interests. Withdrawal from representing both clients while preserving Bernie's confidences is the right course of action.

4. C. This question explores when, for conflicts purposes, a lawyer might be deemed to also represent a subsidiary of a parent company the lawyer represents, even though it might appear that the two entities are distinct corporate entities. Here, YO will be deemed a client of the lawyer for conflicts purposes because of the harm that could come to Xen should Acme win a damages award against YO. This creates a conflict for the lawyer since the lawyer may not wish to take aggressive action on behalf of Acme because it could ultimately harm Xen. The fact that there are different lawyers working on the Xen and Acme matters within the firm is irrelevant because the representation involves concurrent representation, that is, the representation is simultaneous. Some different questions can arise in successive conflict issues, which we will explore in Section 2.3 below.

5. B. In any potential conflict situation, the first issue to consider is whether the lawyer believes she can be a zealous advocate for the clients on both sides of the potential conflict. If the lawyer does not believe she can be zealous, that should end the inquiry, and the lawyer need not consider the other elements of MR 1.7(b) that might otherwise permit the conflicted representation. *See* MR 1.7(b)(1).

6. A. Comment 31 to MR 1.7 examines the issues related to this question in some detail. It provides that "common representation will almost certainly be inadequate if one client asks the lawyer not to disclose to the other client information relevant to the common representation." Because of this, it counsels the lawyer to "at the outset of the common representation and as part of the process of obtaining each client's informed consent, advise each client that information will be shared and that the lawyer will have to withdraw if one client decides that some matter material to the representation should be kept from the other." At the same time, it also provides that "[i]n limited circumstances, it may be appropriate for the lawyer to proceed with the representation when the clients have agreed, after being properly informed, that the lawyer will keep certain information confidential. For example, the lawyer may reasonably conclude that failure to disclose one client's trade secrets to another client will not adversely affect representation involving a joint venture between the clients and agree to keep that information confidential with the informed consent of both clients." Thus, as is the case here, the advance consent to withhold trade secrets from jointly represented clients is acceptable.

7. A. This question also explores the potential impact of having confidential information about two jointly represented clients where the information from one client could be used to the advantage (or disadvantage) of another client. Comment 31 to MR 1.7 provides that the lawyer "has an equal duty of loyalty to each client, and each client has the right to be informed of anything bearing on the representation that might affect that client's interests and the right to expect that the lawyer will use that information to that client's benefit." Because the duty of

confidentiality for one client conflicts with the duty of advocacy for another, the lawyer cannot represent both clients simultaneously.

2.2 Specific Conflicts Issues

8. B. Rule 1.8(e) generally prohibits a lawyer from providing "financial assistance to a client in connection with pending or contemplated litigation" except in limited circumstances, including as provided in subpart MR 1.8(e)(1), which permits a lawyer to "advance court costs and expenses of litigation, the repayment of which may be contingent on the outcome of the matter." The other subparts to MR 1.8(e) also offer other exceptions to the general rule, including that when representing an indigent client, a lawyer "may pay court costs and expenses of litigation on behalf of the client" (MR 1.8(e)(2): A lawyer "representing an indigent client pro bono, a lawyer representing an indigent client pro bono through a nonprofit legal services or public interest organization and a lawyer representing an indigent client pro bono through a law school clinical or pro bono program may provide modest gifts to the client for food, rent, transportation, medicine and other basic living expenses."). Even where a lawyer can give this sort of assistance, strict prohibitions accompany its provision. The lawyer may not "promise, assure or imply the availability of such gifts prior to retention or as an inducement to continue the client-lawyer relationship after retention," "may not seek or accept reimbursement from the client, a relative of the client or anyone affiliated with the client," and "may not publicize or advertise a willingness to provide such gifts to prospective clients." (MR 1.8(e)(3)(i–iii).) At the same time, such assistance "may be provided even if the representation is eligible for fees under a fee-shifting statute."

9. C. Because the representation had concluded, the lawyer was free to negotiate to purchase client's literary rights but had to do so in compliance with MR 1.8(a), which governs business transactions with a client. Here, the client was not given an opportunity to seek outside counsel nor was he advised on the value of such counsel. Even though the representation *had* concluded, the relationship was long-standing and the lawyer still needed to follow MR 1.8(a).

10. A. Rule 1.8(c) provides that "[a] lawyer shall not solicit any substantial gift from a client, including a testamentary gift, or prepare on behalf of a client an instrument giving the lawyer or a person related to the lawyer any substantial gift unless the lawyer or other recipient of the gift is related to the client." It provides further that the term "related persons" under the rule includes "a spouse, child, grandchild, parent, grandparent or other relative or individual with whom the lawyer or the client maintains a close, familial relationship." Since the rule recognizes "close, familial" relationships as being exempt from the prohibition on preparing a will for a client in which the lawyer receives a substantial gift, this arrangement was not inappropriate.

11. A. Rule 1.8(e)(2) generally prohibits this type of financial assistance and the exceptions provided in MR 1.8(e)(3) do not apply here because the lawyer is not representing the indigent client "pro bono," "through a nonprofit legal services or public interest organization," or representing the "indigent client pro bono through a law school clinical or pro bono program" which might create an exception for this financial assistance. MR 1.8(e)(3); see also the explanation accompanying Question 8, above.

12. C. When a lawyer changes a fee arrangement, the renegotiation of the fee arrangement is treated like a transaction with a client and must follow the provisions of MR 1.8(a).

13. D. Rule 1.8(g) provides as follows: "A lawyer who represents two or more clients shall not participate in making an aggregate settlement of the claims of or against the clients, or in a criminal case an aggregated agreement as to guilty or nolo contendere pleas, *unless each client gives informed consent, in a writing signed by the client. The lawyer's disclosure shall include the existence and nature of all the claims or pleas involved and of the participation of each person in the settlement*." (Emphasis added.)

14. D. Rule 1.8(h)(1) makes it a requirement that the client must have independent legal counsel in consenting to such a waiver.

15. D. See MR 1.8(e)(2), which permits a lawyer to pay the court costs for an indigent client.

16. A. Rule 1.8(j) prohibits sexual relationships between lawyers and clients that do not predate the formation of the attorney-client relationship.

17. D. *See* Comment 1 to MR 1.8. The rule regarding business transactions with clients (MR 1.8(a)) does not apply to "standard commercial transactions." Yes, the lawyer knew about the desperate straits of the client but did not appear to use that to the client's disadvantage. He paid the full list price, albeit discounted, but such a discount was available to any customer of the client's company and was publicly advertised as such. Even someone who did not know of the client's situation would have been able to pay this price. The lawyer did not haggle or apply pressure on the client due to his knowledge of the client's economic situation.

18. C. Rule 1.8(h)(2) provides that the client must be advised in writing about the wisdom of securing independent counsel and given an opportunity to do so. Just giving the waiting period without an express statement about securing independent counsel is inappropriate. The rule explicitly mentions this as a duty owed to a client or a former client.

2.3 Conflicts of Interest with Former Clients

19. A. Rule 1.9(b) applies to this situation. That rule provides that a lawyer "shall not knowingly represent a person in the same or a substantially related matter in which a firm with which the lawyer formerly was associated had previously represented a client," when the interests of that client "are materially adverse to that person" and the lawyer "had acquired information protected by Rules 1.6 and 1.9(c) that is material to the matter; unless the former client gives informed consent, confirmed in writing." Critically, Comment 3 to MR 1.9 provides that "[m]atters are 'substantially related' for purposes of this Rule if they involve the same transaction or legal dispute or *if there otherwise is a substantial risk that confidential factual information as would normally have been obtained in the prior representation would materially advance the client's position in the subsequent matter*." (Emphasis supplied.) Here, the matters are substantially related because the confidential information shared with the lawyer renders her conflicted in the client's litigation, even if she did not formally represent the team directly.

20. C. No confidential information in the prior representation was shared with the lawyer that was relevant to the second matter, so they are not substantially related and there is no conflict. *See* Comment 3 to M.R. 1.9.

21. D. The matters here are not substantially related, and the lawyer owes no duty to share confidential information with a former client about a current client.

22. C. The lawyer has no confidential information about the prospective client's case by virtue of the lawyer's former representation of the local government, and thus the matters are not substantially related. If the matters are not substantially related, the barriers to representation under MR 1.9 do not apply.

2.4 Conflicts and Government Lawyers

23. C. Under MR 1.11, since the lawyer did not participate in the suit against the bank while employed at the prosecutor's office, there is no barrier to the representation and the screening requirements set forth in the rule do not apply.

24. C. Under MR 1.11, the information obtained was "confidential government information" and it could not be used against the factory. The screening put in place when the lawyer came on board was neither "timely" nor "effective" as required under the rule because he shared the information with the firm prior to those protections being put in place.

25. B. Under MR 1.11, the lawyer participated "personally and substantially" in the prior matter. Whether the lawyer can be screened is irrelevant, and the question does not ask about screens. The question only asks whether the lawyer is precluded from representation in the matter. The lawyer's involvement, even as a supervisor, because she was exposed to the confidential information in partic-

ular, is critical here. Moreover, the lawyer's exposure to BioCar's confidential information, which she obtained by virtue of her position as a government attorney, even if she never represented BioCar, was disqualifying. *See* MR 1.11(c).

26. A. Under MR 1.11(c), the critical and applicable distinction here is that the information is "confidential government information" and does not entail the lawyer's representing a private client against the government agency for which the lawyer used to work. Here, screening is required, and the lawyer cannot share in the fee from the representation. However, since this does not entail the representation of a party against the government per se, no notice is required to be given to the agency, and no consent of the party about whom the information was shared is required either.

27. B. Under MR 1.11, since the information upon which lawyer will now depend is all in the public record, there is no barrier to representation.

28. A. According to MR 1.11, the lawyer's not being involved "personally and substantially" in this matter is dispositive, negating any question of conflicts. Just because the lawyer is familiar with the regulations involved in the action does not disqualify him from working on the subsequent matter. The lawyer was involved in the other two matters and that involvement is disqualifying.

2.5 Formative Assessment Quiz

29. C. Rule 1.7 provides that a lawyer can obtain the consent of the client to a conflict if the conflict is disclosed and there is no other prohibition on the conflict. Here, one of the conflicts—that the partners have given instructions to go easy on Huli—was not disclosed, even if the lawyer believed in good faith that the lawyer could still be a zealous advocate for the client. This is not a consent-to-future-conflicts situation.

30. D. This is not a formal former-client/present-client conflict. It is a personal conflict of the lawyer, so no consent of a "former client" is necessary, even a government one. Once the lawyer determined that she could handle the case, the representation was not precluded by law, and the client consented to the arrangement (even when it is not even clear there was a conflict), the representation satisfied the requirements of M.R. 1.7. In such a situation, getting the client to consent to the representation is generally good practice.

31. C. Under MR 1.8(j), the representation is not improper if the consensual sexual relations predated the representation.

32. B. Under MR 1.7(b)(1), the lawyer must reasonably believe she will be able to handle the matter competently and diligently. Consent of the client does not cure that problem.

33. A. Comment 14 to MR 1.7 is helpful in resolving this issue. This problem raises the question of "consentability" to a conflict, and such questions must be resolved

as to each client. The lawyer cannot be a zealous advocate for the client, and thus the fifth client cannot waive the conflict.

34. D. Under MR 1.8(a), any business transaction with a client requires fair and reasonable terms, fully disclosed in writing in a manner that can be understood, and the client must be advised in writing of the desirability of seeking, and given a reasonable opportunity to seek, the advice of independent legal counsel. The client must give informed consent in a signed writing to the essential terms, including the lawyer's role in the transaction and whether the lawyer is representing the client in the transaction. The lawyer followed all of these steps, and the client need not be represented by independent counsel.

35. D. Under MR 1.8(e)(2), financial assistance to a client is permissible when paying the costs and expenses of an indigent client. There are also other instances under MR 1.8(e)(3) where financial assistance to an indigent client might be permissible, but the example given here falls squarely under the MR 1.8(e)(2) exception.

36. B. The "nature of the action," which is the standard articulated in Answer D, is not the correct standard. Two matters can be different in terms of the types of claims involved but still be substantially related if confidential information obtained in the first matter is relevant in the second. *See* Comment 3 to MR 1.9 ("Matters are 'substantially related' for purposes of this Rule if they involve the same transaction or legal dispute or if there otherwise is a substantial risk that confidential factual information as would normally have been obtained in the prior representation would materially advance the client's position in the subsequent matter.").

37. B. Under MR 1.8(g), in an aggregate settlement situation, the lawyer just needs to explain the details of the agreement and get each client's informed consent, which the lawyer did here.

38. A. Possessing confidential information about an entity by virtue of representing a consortium of which that entity is a part can create a conflict of interest even if a lawyer does not have a separate attorney-client relationship with the individual entity. Here, however, no such information was shared that might create a situation where the matters were substantially related, which would have warranted disqualification.

39. A. Under MR 1.8(h), when seeking to enter into an agreement with a client that purports to secure the client's prospective agreement to limit the client's ability to bring a malpractice claim against the lawyer, the client needs independent representation in reaching such an agreement.

40. C. The question of the *new* client's consent is irrelevant. Only the government consent matters in this situation under MR 1.11.

41. D. It does appear that a conflict impacted the representation and did so adversely, at least for Charlie, and thus the conviction is likely to be overturned.

42. B. Under MR 1.8(h)(2), when a lawyer settles a claim of malpractice, the client must be advised in writing of the desirability of seeking, and must be given a reasonable opportunity to seek, the advice of independent counsel. Unlike in a waiver of *future* malpractice claims, under MR 1.8(h)(1), which requires that the client is "independently represented in making the agreement," such independent representation is not required in settling a past claim of malpractice under MR 1.8(h)(2).

43. C. Under MR 1.10(a)(1), this sort of personal conflict is not imputed to the other members of the firm. The firm does not seem materially limited by the lawyer's presence within it during the course of the representation, and there are no additional restrictions imposed when a lawyer has such a personal conflict, including no requirement of client consent.

44. C. While the "personally and substantially" language appears in M.R. 1.11(a), that standard would generally apply if the lawyer were handling a case against the Attorney General's Office. Here, the problem deals with "confidential government information" about a third party, and thus the prohibition in MR 1.11(c) is more directly relevant and provides the most direct guidance. It is thus a closer fit for this situation, and, through its application, the lawyer is disqualified.

Chapter 3: Confidentiality

3.1 Understanding Confidentiality

1. B. Rule 1.6(a) provides that a lawyer "shall not reveal information relating to the representation of a client unless the client gives informed consent, the disclosure is impliedly authorized in order to carry out the representation or the disclosure is permitted by paragraph (b)." (We will explore MR 1.6(b) in depth throughout this chapter—know that no exception under MR 1.6(b) would cover this situation). Here, the lawyer revealed information harmful to the client and should not have done so without the consent of the client.

2. A. Rule 1.6(b)(1) provides that a lawyer *may* reveal otherwise confidential information in order to prevent reasonably certain death or substantial bodily harm. But it is not improper to withhold such information as the provision is merely permissive. Indeed, Comment 17 to MR 1.6 provides that "[a] lawyer's decision not to disclose as permitted by paragraph (b) does not violate this Rule." We may not like this answer, but it is consistent with the rules and comments.

3. D. While a lawyer is generally permitted to share confidential information in order to understand the lawyer's obligations under the rules (MR 1.6(b)(4)), the lawyer here shared client confidences simply to "blow off steam." Yes, an argument could probably be made that, perhaps, the lawyer needed to do this to think

clearly, ensure the adequate representation of the client's interests, and act ethically, but that's reading too much into the fact pattern.

4. A. A lawyer is permitted to share confidential information with other lawyers in the firm. *See* Comment 5 to MR 1.6.

5. D. Rule 1.6(c) provides that a lawyer must make reasonable efforts to prevent inadvertent or unauthorized disclosure of, or unauthorized access to, information relating to the representation of a client. Here, the lawyers had used state-of-the-art equipment. There is no strict liability for data breaches.

6. C. The language of MR 1.6(b) regarding disclosure of information in self-defense is only permissive. It does not require disclosure. There are some lawyers, particularly criminal defense lawyers, who will not divulge client confidences even when clients sue them because they want to send a signal to other clients and potential clients that they are not the type of lawyer who divulges client confidences unless absolutely compelled to. Here, there is nothing compelling the lawyer to divulge this information.

7. B. The lawyer's services were used in a way that caused substantial financial injury to another, but the lawyer is under no obligation to divulge information to prevent or mitigate that harm. The authority to release confidential information through MR 1.6(b)(2) is merely permissive. The lawyer could have shared this information precisely because his services were used but is under no obligation to do so, even when the lawyer's lack of disclosure causes harm.

8. C. MR 1.9(c). A lawyer cannot divulge confidential information of a former client unless it has become generally known. Even though the information may not have been covered by the attorney-client privilege, it was still confidential, even after the death of the client.

3.2 Attorney-Client Privilege

9. C. The communications fall under the "crime-fraud" exception to the attorney-client privilege. In addition, MR 1.2(d) provides that "[a] lawyer shall not counsel a client to engage, or assist a client, in conduct that the lawyer knows is criminal or fraudulent, but a lawyer may discuss the legal consequences of any proposed course of conduct with a client and may counsel or assist a client to make a good faith effort to determine the validity, scope, meaning or application of the law." What the lawyer is being asked to do here is give information to the client as to how to break the law, not merely provide guidance on the "validity, scope, meaning, or application of the law." In addition, the interpreter, even though a third party, was present on the call to facilitate the representation, and thus it was not improper for the interpreter to have participated in the communications.

10. D. While one might, as a defense to a discovery request, object to having to turn over publicly available records because it is burdensome, and although the information here was obtained during the course of representation and *is* covered by the duty of confidentiality, the neighbor's lawyer has made a lawful request for the information and therefore the lawyer must turn it over, even though it is confidential. At the same time, the settlement position is covered by the attorney-client privilege, and the lawyer should not turn that over and is not obligated to do so. Similarly, the records in client's possession are not covered by the attorney-client privilege because they are not "communications." While they, too, might be considered confidential, they are not a communication shared between the lawyer and the client for the purposes of obtaining legal advice. Certainly the purpose of sharing those records was to obtain legal advice, but the underlying documents are merely confidential and not privileged, meaning they must be turned over in the face of an appropriate discovery request. Only that portion of the discovery request that seeks the settlement position of the client is inappropriate, and the client must respond to that demand for any responsive information that is not privileged.

11. A. It was reasonable for the lawyer and client to assume that their conversations were confidential because Company advertised them as such. Based on that reasonable expectation of privacy, the lawyer is not at fault and the privilege will be preserved.

3.3 Grounds Permitting Disclosure

12. D. Here, the lawyer is appropriately exercising her rights under Rule 1.6(b). First, the lawyer can talk to an ethics expert. Second, the lawyer is not obligated to report this information, even if the expert suggests that she do so. In other contexts, willfully ignoring the guidance of an expert where the duty is clear and consistent with that advice could certainly get the lawyer in trouble. Here, however, there is no duty to turn over the information and the lawyer has the full discretion to do so or not, even when an expert advised the lawyer that she is "within her rights" to disclose. That is the accurate statement of the rule in this instance. The lawyer is permitted, but is under no obligation, to disclose.

13. C. The lawyer may introduce even privileged matter to the extent necessary to interpose a defense to a claim brought against her, and this type of claim would qualify. It does not require the client's consent. MR 1.6(b)(5). At the same time, the information that is not related to the lawyer's defense may not be introduced where, as here, it is clearly confidential. The rules permitting disclosure generally permit the lawyer to reveal information related to the purpose that a particular sub-part of the rules is designed to achieve. For example, while a lawyer may reveal information to prevent reasonably certain death from occurring, the

lawyer may reveal only that information necessary to do so. *See, e.g.*, Comment 6 to MR 1.6.

14. C. The activities of the lawyer were in furtherance of the alleged fraud that caused financial harm. This means the lawyer is within his rights to disclose this information to mitigate the harm of that action. *See* MR 1.6(b)(2) and (3).

15. A. Since it was standard in the industry to divulge utility costs, the lawyer had implied consent to share such information under MR 1.6(a). The client was aware that it was standard in the industry to share such information.

16. B. Under MR 1.6(b)(4), the lawyer is allowed to share confidential information in order to obtain information about the lawyer's ethical obligations. Here, there is no indication that the disclosure was broader than it needed to be to secure such advice.

17. B. Answer D is incorrect because even something that is merely embarrassing is still considered confidential. Nevertheless, with a court order, the lawyer may (and usually must) turn over such information. M.R. 1.6(b)(6).

3.4 Competence, Supervision, Confidentiality

18. A. The lawyer must undertake reasonable efforts to preserve the clients' confidences, which is all that is required. MR 1.6(c); Comment 18 to MR 1.6; and Comment 3 to MR 5.3.

19. A. Lawyers have a duty to act competently to preserve confidences and keep abreast of changes in technology. Comment 8 to Rule 1.1. Comment 18 to Model Rule 1.6 provides that "[p]aragraph (c) [of MR 1.6] requires a lawyer to act competently to safeguard information relating to the representation of a client against unauthorized access by third parties and against inadvertent or unauthorized disclosure by the lawyer or other persons who are participating in the representation of the client or who are subject to the lawyer's supervision." Similarly, under MR 5.1, supervisory/managing lawyers with responsibility for a firm's operation as a whole have a particular duty to put "reasonable" systems in place that provide "reasonable assurances" that the lawyers are upholding their ethical obligations, including preserving confidences. Here, the new threats warrant, at a minimum, upgrading the system that has not been updated for 18 months, especially when such an upgrade is not expensive.

3.5 Specific Issues Related to Organizational Clients (MR 1.13)

20. B. Rule 1.13(b) provides, in relevant part, that "if a lawyer for an organization knows that an officer, employee or other person associated with the organization is engaged in action, intends to act or refuses to act in a matter related to

the representation that is a violation of a legal obligation to the organization, or a violation of law that reasonably might be imputed to the organization, and that is likely to result in substantial injury to the organization, then the lawyer shall proceed as is reasonably necessary in the best interest of the organization." If the lawyer believes it is "in the best interest of the organization to do so," the lawyer is obligated to "refer the matter to higher authority in the organization, including, if warranted by the circumstances to the highest authority that can act on behalf of the organization as determined by applicable law." Then, MR 1.13(c) provides that if that authority takes no action, that inaction is "is clearly a violation of law," and the lawyer has a reasonable belief "that the violation is reasonably certain to result in substantial injury to the organization," then the lawyer *may* reveal information "relating to the representation whether or not Rule 1.6 permits such disclosure," but only to the extent necessary "to prevent substantial injury to the organization." At the same time, in accordance with MR 1.13(d), the permission under MR 1.13(c) does *not* apply "with respect to information relating to a lawyer's representation of an organization to investigate an alleged violation of law, or to defend the organization or an officer, employee or other constituent associated with the organization against a claim arising out of an alleged violation of law." Here, the lawyer was permitted to divulge this information pursuant to Rule 1.13. In this situation, the use of the lawyer's services is not required as it is in several provisions of MR 1.6(b).

21. D. Under MR 1.13(f), when dealing with a constituent of an organization, the lawyer shall explain the identity of the client when interests are adverse with a constituent.

22. B. First, the lawyers have been hired to investigate the matter, and thus Rule 1.13(d) provides them relief from having to report the behavior to any authority. More importantly, even if there were no such relief, such reporting is merely permissive. Neither lawyer is required to report this behavior. See MR 1.13(c)(2), which states only that the lawyer "may" reveal such information. Sam's advice is sound in this context.

23. A. Rule 1.13(d) covers this situation and the lawyer is not permitted to reveal it under MR 1.13(c).

24. C. Although a lawyer represents an organization acting through its duly authorized constituents (MR 1.13(a)), under MR 1.13(f), a lawyer "shall explain the identity of the client when the lawyer knows or reasonably should know that the organization's interests are adverse to those of the constituents with whom the lawyer is dealing." By not revealing her conflict, the lawyer is under an obligation to preserve the information as confidential. The lawyer may have to withdraw from representing the employee and the corporation.

3.6 Duties to Prospective Clients (MR 1.18)

25. C. Rule 1.18(c) provides protections to prospective clients only where a lawyer has received information harmful to the prospective client, and here, the lawyer did not obtain any such information.

26. B. The firm followed the procedures set forth in MR 1.18(d)(2) to allow it to continue to represent Client B.

3.7 Formative Assessment Quiz

27. A. Rule 1.6(b)(1) provides no restriction on the release of information merely because it is of a different degree and/or kind. The MR 1.6(b) provision does not provide any limit on the release of the information if it is learned during the course of an investigation. That restriction only applies to a release strictly pursuant to MR 1.13. If a lawyer is permitted to release information under one of the MR 1.6(b) exceptions, the fact that it was uncovered through a lawyer's investigation of the matter is not a bar to the lawyer's revealing that information. The lawyer might feel that it is better not to reveal this information because it might discourage the client from asking the lawyer to investigate matters in the future, but the discretion to disclose always resides with the lawyer. If the lawyer fears the client will no longer turn to the lawyer, then that could be a factor the lawyer considers when determining whether to exercise that discretion to release such information.

28. B. The communications do not appear to be in furtherance of an alleged crime. The lawyer's services were not used to create the financial harm on the small investors, and thus no exception to the duty of confidentiality exists. *See* MR 1.6(b)(2) and (b)(3).

29. B. Rule 1.6(b) prohibits revealing information to the disadvantage of a client, and MR 1.8(k) extends that to all lawyers in the firm. Rule 1.6 would not permit the release of this information because the lawyer's services were not used to further the crime. Answer A is wrong because sharing information within a firm is common, and, without explicitly saying that the lawyer could not share the information within the firm, such consent to share such information is implied.

30. C. The question does not ask whether the lawyer can reveal the information to prevent reasonably certain death or substantial bodily harm, it only asks whether the lawyer could share such information to understand the lawyer's ethical obligations. The issue of whether information that is the subject of an investigation can be shared pertains only to investigations under MR 1.13. An argument could be made that this investigation would qualify as one covered under MR 1.13, but that provision only pertains to the "report up/report out" obligations of MR 1.13. It does not apply to disclosures pursuant to MR 1.6(b).

31. D. A lawyer's disclosure of confidential information, when permitted, is only authorized when it is designed to accomplish a specified purpose allowed under the rules. This authority permits the lawyer to disclose only that information that is designed to accomplish that purpose. It is not a blanket permission to release all confidential information possessed by the lawyer. Here, his self-defense only requires information related to the decision not to file the frivolous action. *See* Comment 16 to MR 1.6.

32. A. Rule 1.18(d) offers two options to permit representation in this context, one in which consent is required and one in which it is not. These are offered in the alternative. Here, the firm followed the MR 1.18(d)(2) option, and thus the ongoing representation of the current client is still permissible even without the consents. This question is testing whether you know that there are two options under MR 1.18(d), either of which could be followed (and that one does not require consent).

33. D. The lawyer's services are not being used to perpetrate the fraud and no other exception to the confidentiality rules applies. *See generally* MR 1.6(b).

34. D. Under MR 1.6(b)(2), the lawyer can reveal confidential information if to withhold it is "reasonably certain to result in substantial injury to the financial interests or property of another and in furtherance of which the client has used the lawyer's services."

35. B. In accordance with MR 1.13(b), a lawyer does not need to report conduct to the highest authority in the organization if the lawyer believes it is not in the organization's best interest to do so. Here, sharing such information would actually have the potential of harming the organization because the leadership of the entity might have some liability should it learn of the illegal acts of the subordinates.

36. D. Here, the lawyer is properly invoking the exception under MR 1.6(b)(5): disclosing information in self-defense.

37. C. Under Comment 9 to MR 1.6, a lawyer can share confidential information to secure advice on how to comply with rules, even when doing so may permit the advisor to identify the identity of the client about whom lawyer is seeking assistance.

38. B. In this context, under MR 1.13(d), when the lawyer learns of information during the course of an investigation, such information should remain confidential, unless some other exception is available to the lawyer under MR 1.6(b) to reveal such information, and even there, the release is merely permissive.

39. D. The lawyer did not have the consent of the client to share this information. Answer C is close to the correct answer but does not provide an accurate statement of the rule: a lawyer is permitted to reveal confidential information in certain circumstances when such consent is implied by the nature of the representation.

40\. A. Generally speaking, even if a basis exists under MR 1.6(b)(5) to reveal confidential information in self-defense, the lawyer is only permitted to reveal that information which is necessary to carry out the purposes of the exception. Here, the client is not objecting to the fee charged related to the investigation, so the lawyer is not permitted to reveal information related to that work. *See, e.g.*, Comment 10 to MR 1.6 ("Where a legal claim or disciplinary charge alleges complicity of the lawyer in a client's conduct or other misconduct of the lawyer involving representation of the client, the lawyer may respond to the extent the lawyer reasonably believes necessary to establish a defense.") *See also* Comment 16 to MR 1.6 ("Paragraph (b) permits disclosure only to the extent the lawyer reasonably believes the disclosure is necessary to accomplish one of the purposes specified.").

41\. A. Just because the information is confidential (because it is embarrassing or damaging to the client's case) does not mean the lawyer is not obligated to turn it over. The emails do not involve a communication with the lawyer in furtherance of the fraud, so they are not exempt on that basis. If material is "merely" confidential, and not also subject to the attorney-client privilege, it must be turned over in response to a lawful discovery demand. *See* MR 1.6(b)(6). This information was not subject to the attorney-client privilege.

42\. C. This ties into Chapter 2, which deals with conflicts of interest. Even though formal representation had not commenced, the proper course of action would have been to screen Stark from the prospective representation in a "timely" fashion, that is, once the firm determined that it might represent the bank. MR 1.10(a)(2)(i). A timely and effective screen would have prevented the firm from mining Stark's knowledge of Lannister's confidential information in order to gain an advantage in the subsequent representation. A firm cannot circumvent this requirement and access this otherwise confidential information simply by saying that the firm hadn't been retained yet.

43\. A. This question implicates the mechanisms set forth in MR 1.18(d). Here, the only option is MR 1.18(d)(1), which permits the representation when both parties provide informed consent. The lawyer cannot invoke a second option, embodied in MR 1.18(d)(2), because precautions were not taken to ensure that only information related to determining whether a conflict existed was gathered.

Chapter 4: Attorney's Fees

4.1 Understanding Attorney's Fees

1\. C. This requires the application of MR 1.5(c), which provides that a contingency fee agreement "shall be in a writing signed by the client and shall state the method by which the fee is to be determined, including the percentage or percentages that shall accrue to the lawyer in the event of settlement, trial or appeal; litigation and other expenses to be deducted from the recovery; and whether such expenses are to be deducted before or after the contingent fee is calculated." It must also "clearly notify the client of any expenses for which the client will be liable whether or not the client is the prevailing party." While contingency fee agreements are generally permissible (except in limited circumstances, set forth in MR 1.5(d)), they must be in writing. The rate was otherwise consistent with prevailing approaches in the community.

2. D. A lawyer cannot charge a contingency fee in a criminal matter. MR 1.5(d).

3. D. Rule 1.5(b) provides as follows: "The scope of the representation and the basis or rate of the fee and expenses for which the client will be responsible shall be communicated to the client, preferably in writing, before or within a reasonable time after commencing the representation, except when the lawyer will charge a regularly represented client on the same basis or rate. *Any changes in the basis or rate of the fee or expenses shall also be communicated to the client*." (Emphasis added.) This arrangement was not subject to the requirements of MR 1.8(a) because it would not be treated as a business transaction with a client since the prior representation had terminated and there was no outstanding retainer (see Chapter 2). Nevertheless, the lawyer effectively communicated the change in the rate to the client.

4. C. While a third party can pay a lawyer's fee, the third party cannot be privy to confidential communications between the attorney and client without the client's consent. The client revoked such consent here.

5. A. Initial retainer fees are acceptable, but if the representation terminates before the lawyer has earned the entire amount of the retainer charging the lawyer's normal and agreed-upon rate, the lawyer must return the unearned portion of the retainer.

6. A. Comment 9 to MR 1.16 provides that even where a lawyer has been unfairly discharged, the lawyer must "take reasonable steps to mitigate the consequences to the client." Moreover, the fact that the lawyer was working on a contingency fee basis means she cannot get paid until the contingency comes to pass, if at all.

7. B. In accordance with MR 1.5(b), the change in the fee structure for this case was contrary to the retainer, and any such change should have been communicated to the client.

4.2 Assessing Reasonable Attorney's Fees

8. C. Rule 1.5(a) provides that a lawyer "shall not make an agreement for, charge, or collect an unreasonable fee or an unreasonable amount for expenses." It also set forth a range of factors "to be considered in determining the reasonableness of a fee," including "(1) the time and labor required, the novelty and difficulty of

the questions involved, and the skill requisite to perform the legal service properly; (2) the likelihood, if apparent to the client, that the acceptance of the particular employment will preclude other employment by the lawyer; (3) the fee customarily charged in the locality for similar legal services; (4) the amount involved and the results obtained; (5) the time limitations imposed by the client or by the circumstances; (6) the nature and length of the professional relationship with the client; (7) the experience, reputation, and ability of the lawyer or lawyers performing the services; and (8) whether the fee is fixed or contingent." Here, the higher fee is justified given the time involved and the results obtained. It is not an unreasonable fee.

9. A. In a contingency fee case, it is common to consider the amount earned in relation to the hours worked by the lawyer on the case to come to an assessment of what the lawyer earned on an hourly basis to determine whether the fee is reasonable. Once that is established, one can compare that hourly rate to rates charged by lawyers in similar circumstances in the community. Here, the question asks which of the answers was the *least* important in this case. The factors set forth in MR 1.5(a) indicate that the items identified in Answers B, C, and D would matter more than those set forth in Answer A.

10. B. Charging a high fee, even one that is "somewhat higher" than that which is typically charged in the community, is not, in itself, unreasonable. Here, the high risk in the representation and the fact the lawyer had to turn down other clients meant the higher fee was not unreasonable. MR 1.5(a).

11. C. *See* MR 1.5(a). Given the risk involved in the practice, including that the lawyer was likely to receive a lower fee than is normal in the community (and did, in some instances), it was not unreasonable for the lawyer to receive a higher fee than is normal in the community for this type of representation.

4.3 Formative Assessment Quiz

12. C. Charging a high fee, even one that is "significantly higher" than that which is typically charged in the community, is not, in itself, unreasonable. Here, the high risk in the representation and the fact the lawyer had to turn down other clients meant the higher fee was not unreasonable. MR 1.5(a).

13. C. In accordance with MR 1.5(a), the fee arrangement is appropriate "if [it is] apparent to the client that acceptance of the particular employment" will preclude the lawyer from taking on other cases.

14. D. The method of calculating the award in relation to the expenses should have been communicated through the retainer. *See* MR 1.5(c). It does not matter what community practices might be (unless, of course, the lawyer's practices could be considered unreasonable in light of community standards). Here, however, the problem is the communication to the client, not necessarily the unreasonable nature of the approach in light of community standards.

15. A. Rule 1.5(c) provides that "[a] contingent fee agreement shall be in a writing signed by the client and shall state the method by which the fee is to be determined, including the percentage or percentages that shall accrue to the lawyer in the event of settlement, trial or appeal; litigation and other expenses to be deducted from the recovery; and whether such expenses are to be deducted before or after the contingent fee is calculated."

16. C. A lawyer may only withdraw fees as they are actually earned. *See* MR 1.5(c); *see also* MR 1.15 (handling client property).

17. D. The limitation on the scope of representation is reasonable and the client agreed to it. MR 1.2(c). The fee arrangement is essentially a contingency fee in a criminal matter and thus barred. MR 1.5(d)(2).

18. C. Rule 5.4(c) provides that "[a] lawyer shall not permit a person who recommends, employs, or pays the lawyer to render legal services for another to direct or regulate the lawyer's professional judgment in rendering such legal services."

Chapter 5: Ethics in Advocacy

5.1 Meritorious Claims and Contentions

1. B. MR 3.1. A lawyer defending a client in a criminal proceeding may "so defend the proceeding so as to require that every element of the case be established." To attempt to undermine the trespass element of the crime, the lawyer is free to cross-examine the eyewitness as to his account, even if the lawyer knows that the client was present at the time of the robbery.

2. D. Under MR 3.1, a lawyer is prohibited from "bring[ing] or defend[ing] a proceeding, or assert[ing] or controvert[ing] an issue therein, unless there is a basis in law and fact for doing so that is not frivolous, which includes a good faith argument for an extension, modification or reversal of existing law." Here, the lawyer had a good faith basis for bringing the claims even if she ultimately lost the case. She researched the backgrounds and prior rulings of recent appointments to the Supreme Court and appears to have believed in good faith that she could convince them of her arguments. Conducting such research and having a good faith basis for one's argument after doing so should be sufficient to ensure compliance with the applicable rule.

3. A. Under MR 3.3(a)(3), a lawyer may refuse to offer evidence the lawyer reasonably believes is false, and thus the lawyer was permitted to not proffer this evidence. The rule does not require the lawyer to know such information is false. The standard for deciding not to submit evidence the lawyer believes is false is lower than the standard required to have an obligation to take "reasonable remedial measures" when a witness has committed perjury, which may include disclosure to the tribunal of the fact that the witness presented perjured testimony, when to do so is necessary to correct the record. There, the lawyer must

"know" the witness provided such perjured testimony. *See* MR 3.3(b) and the next section.

5.2 The Duty of Candor to the Tribunal

4. A. Rule 3.3 provides that a lawyer must not "fail to correct a false statement of material fact or law previously made to the tribunal by the lawyer."

5. B. The evidence is not material, and the lawyer did not present any material evidence that was perjurious. The requirement of the duty of candor contained in MR 3.3 applies only with respect to material evidence. The lawyer's reasonable belief that the witness would present perjured testimony is sufficient grounds for the lawyer to discontinue to present the testimony or to refuse to call the witness in the first place.

6. A. Rule 3.3(a)(2) provides that a lawyer may not "fail to disclose to the tribunal legal authority in the controlling jurisdiction known to the lawyer to be directly adverse to the position of the client and not disclosed by opposing counsel." Answer C is incorrect because a lawyer does not have a duty to disclose any authority, just adverse authority.

7. B. The MR 3.3(a)(3) duty to take reasonable remediable measures when a witness presents perjured testimony attaches even if the lawyer is not the one who elicited the perjured material and even if the information is otherwise protected by the attorney-client privilege. *See* MR 3.3(c).

8. C. Rule 3.3(b) provides that "[a] lawyer who represents a client in an adjudicative proceeding and who knows that a person intends to engage, is engaging or has engaged in criminal or fraudulent conduct related to the proceeding shall take reasonable remedial measures, including, if necessary, disclosure to the tribunal." The lawyer is not involved in Bertrand's trial and thus has no affirmative obligation to report the information.

9. D. Comment 6 to MR 3.3 states that a lawyer should generally try to persuade a client from providing false testimony if the lawyer believes the client intends to do so. At the same time, if the client insists on providing such testimony, "the lawyer must refuse to offer" it, and if "only a portion of a witness's testimony will be false, the lawyer may call the witness to testify but may not elicit or otherwise permit the witness to present the testimony that the lawyer knows is false."

10. C. Under MR 3.3, the lawyer's duty of candor extends to the conclusion of the proceeding, which would include the time during which an appeal could be filed in the case. *See* Comment 13 to MR 3.3. There is also no exception to the duty of candor, even if the lawyer believes in good faith that any revelations about misstatements of fact would not change the outcome of the proceeding. Moreover, the client admitted that his testimony was "fiction," and thus we can infer the lawyer had knowledge of the perjury from that statement, even if the

client refused to fill in the details about the testimony. The lawyer had an affirmative duty at that point to probe further to determine the extent of the perjury and to advise the client that he has an affirmative obligation to correct the record. If the client refuses to do so, the lawyer must then make an affirmative disclosure of the perjury to the tribunal as long as the obligation exists (and the obligation still exists in this fact pattern).

11. A. Rule 3.3(d) provides that in ex parte proceedings, "a lawyer shall inform the tribunal of all material facts known to the lawyer that will enable the tribunal to make an informed decision, whether or not the facts are adverse." In such situations, since there is no adversary by virtue of the fact that the proceeding is ex parte, the lawyer's obligation to serve as not just an advocate but also an officer of the court requires the lawyer to present all evidence necessary for the court to make an informed decision, even if it means disclosing facts that are unfavorable to the lawyer's position.

12. C. A lawyer is not ineffective as counsel to a criminal defendant if the lawyer convinces the client not to commit perjury, and the lawyer can even threaten to withdraw as counsel in an effort to ensure the client does not do so. *See Nix v. Whiteside*, 475 U.S. 157 (1986).

5.3 Preserving Potential Evidence

13. B. Under MR 3.4(a), a lawyer shall not "unlawfully obstruct another party's access to evidence or unlawfully alter, destroy or conceal a document or other material having potential evidentiary value" and "shall not counsel or assist another person to do any such act." This applies not only to evidence in cases that are already underway but also in cases that have not yet been filed but will reasonably foreseeably be. *See* Comment 2 to MR 3.4.

14. B. Here, again, we see the application of Comment 2 to MR 3.4. The proceeding was reasonably foreseeable, and thus it was improper to not preserve the material that would likely have potential evidentiary value.

15. C. Again, the question tests the issue of potential evidentiary value in a reasonably foreseeable proceeding. *See* Comment 2 to MR 3.4. Answer D speaks to the standard for the scope of discovery. Comment 2 to MR 3.4 addresses the idea that much substantive law makes it a requirement to generally preserve evidence when a proceeding is foreseeable, as this one was, even if possibly unlikely.

5.4 Lawyer as Potential Witness

16. D. Rule 3.7(a) provides that a lawyer "shall not act as advocate at a trial in which the lawyer is likely to be a necessary witness unless: (1) the testimony relates to an uncontested issue; (2) the testimony relates to the nature and value of legal

services rendered in the case; or (3) disqualification of the lawyer would work substantial hardship on the client." The issue about which the lawyer will testify is not contested, even if "necessary" to the litigation.

17. D. Under MR 3.7(a), a lawyer shall not act as an advocate at trial where the lawyer is likely a necessary witness unless "disqualification of the lawyer would work substantial hardship on the client." Here, the client would not be affected adversely because alternate, suitable counsel are readily available from the lawyer's firm and there does not appear to be any issue that would adversely affect the alternate representation (like a conflict of interest related to the fact that a colleague is testifying in the action).

18. B. Under MR 3.7(b), "[a] lawyer may act as advocate in a trial in which another lawyer in the lawyer's firm is likely to be called as a witness unless precluded from doing so by Rule 1.7 or Rule 1.9." Lawyer B's knowledge creates a potential conflict between the lawyer's relationship to Lawyer A and Lawyer B's loyalty to the client, meaning the 3.7(b) exception which would otherwise allow this arrangement cannot be invoked.

19. C. The lawyer is not acting as an advocate, and a lawyer from the lawyer's firm may handle the matter provided the associated lawyer is not precluded from doing so by MR 1.7 or 1.9. You were given no information to suggest that a conflict of interest under 1.7 or 1.9 would preclude the associated lawyer from taking the case. See MR. 3.7(b).

5.5 Special Responsibilities of a Prosecutor

20. A. Under MR 3.8(a), a prosecutor in a criminal case "shall ... refrain from prosecuting a charge that the prosecutor knows is not supported by probable cause."

21. B. Rule 3.8(b) provides that a prosecutor shall "make reasonable efforts to assure that the accused has been advised of the right to, and the procedure for obtaining, counsel and has been given reasonable opportunity to obtain counsel." In addition, under MR 3.8(c) a prosecutor shall "not seek to obtain from an unrepresented accused a waiver of important pretrial rights, such as the right to a preliminary hearing." Here, under either provision, the important right is the right to have a lawyer present during questioning. The prosecutor took no reasonable steps to protect the rights of the accused regarding access to counsel.

22. C. Under MR 3.8(g), "[w]hen a prosecutor knows of new, credible and material evidence creating a reasonable likelihood that a convicted defendant did not commit an offense of which the defendant was convicted," the prosecutor is required to do the following: "(1) promptly disclose that evidence to an appropriate court or authority, and (2) if the conviction was obtained in the prosecutor's jurisdiction, (i) promptly disclose that evidence to the defendant unless a

court authorizes delay, and (ii) undertake further investigation, or make reasonable efforts to cause an investigation, to determine whether the defendant was convicted of an offense that the defendant did not commit."

5.6 The No-Contact Rule

23. D. Rule 4.2 provides that "[i]n representing a client, a lawyer shall not communicate about the subject of the representation with a person the lawyer knows to be represented by another lawyer in the matter, unless the lawyer has the consent of the other lawyer or is authorized to do so by law or a court order." Because the elements of MR 4.2 that would require opposing counsel's consent to speak to Harry seem to be met here, only consent by Harry's lawyer would make the communication permissible.

24. B. Under MR 4.2, a lawyer can communicate directly with those employees of an adverse party whose statements would not bind the party because their job responsibilities are unrelated to the incident that gave rise to the liability. Lawyers can also communicate with "former constituents" of the entity (that is, former employees), even if the subject matter of the communications are within the former employee's job responsibilities. *See* Comment 7 to MR 4.2, and *Niesig v. Team 1*, 76 N.Y.2d 363 (1990).

25. D. The lawyer did not have permission to listen to the opposing party's message just because the opposing party ignored the instructions of the lawyer's outgoing message. This was not an inadvertent message.

26. D. The language of MR 4.2 speaks of "matter" and that the lawyer must know the opposing party is represented by counsel. Here, that knowledge can be inferred because a single law firm handles these types of cases in the community, including representing the particular landlords that are the targets of the investigation. Further, the matter in question does not have to be litigation per se, although here, the expectation is that the investigation will lead to litigation. Nevertheless, even an investigation can be a matter requiring consent from the opposing counsel.

27. C. This crane operator was a mere witness whose testimony would not bind Steel, and thus the lawyer is not prohibited from speaking to her. *See* Comment 7 to MR 4.2, and *Niesig v. Team 1*, 76 N.Y.2d 363 (1990).

28. D. Rule 4.2 only covers communications about the subject matter of the representation, and these communications were unrelated to the subject matter of the representation.

29. C. The food service worker is a "mere witness," so no duty to intervene applies. Officer 2 is a "former constituent." See Comment 7 to MR 4.2, which provides that "[c]onsent of the organization's lawyer is not required for communication

with a former constituent" even where the former constituent's scope of work means their statements can be binding on a party. *See also Niesig v. Team 1*, 76 N.Y.2d 363 (1990).

5.7 Dealing with Third Parties

30. A. Rule 4.3 provides that when a lawyer is communicating with an unrepresented party, the lawyer "shall not state or imply that the lawyer is disinterested," that is, the lawyer should inform the party that the lawyer represents another party that may be adverse to the unrepresented person. It provides further that "[w] hen the lawyer knows or reasonably should know that the unrepresented person misunderstands the lawyer's role in the matter, the lawyer shall make reasonable efforts to correct the misunderstanding." In addition, the lawyer is prohibited from "giv[ing] legal advice to an unrepresented person, other than the advice to secure counsel, if the lawyer knows or reasonably should know that the interests of such a person are or have a reasonable possibility of being in conflict with the interests of the client." Here, the lawyer no longer had an interest in representing Stark and only gave Baker information necessary for Baker's self-representation. The lawyer had no interest in the matter and thus had no duty to reveal the lawyer's former representation of Stark.

31. C. Under MR 4.4(b), a lawyer who receives inadvertent information shall "promptly notify the sender." The rule is silent as to whether the lawyer can or cannot read the email, which means she is under no obligation to not do so and thus "may" read the email.

32. D. As provided in Comment 2 to MR 4.3, the rule "does not prohibit a lawyer from negotiating the terms of a transaction or settling a dispute with an unrepresented person," provided the lawyer "has explained that the lawyer represents an adverse party and is not representing the person." In such situations, "the lawyer may inform the person of the terms on which the lawyer's client will enter into an agreement or settle a matter, prepare documents that require the person's signature and explain the lawyer's own view of the meaning of the document or the lawyer's view of the underlying legal obligations."

33. C. An attorney can give basic advice to individuals to assist them in representing themselves. This is consistent with MR 4.3 and does not violate the provisions related to the unauthorized practice of law. *See also* MR 5.5.

34. B. Under MR 4.1, which covers "truthfulness in statements to others," a lawyer should not misstate the finding of the appraiser, even though she paid for it. The purpose of the independent appraiser was to find an objective sale price for the yacht, and the lawyers agreed to the use of the appraiser to identify such a price. The statements regarding the client's bottom line are consistent with the normal conventions of practice, however, and are thus not prohibited.

5.8 Clients with Diminished Capacity

35. C. In accordance with MR 1.14(c), such disclosure is not improper because the lawyer believed the client was suffering under a diminished capacity and because the lawyer only revealed confidential information for the purpose of protecting, and only to the extent necessary to protect, the client's interests. Consent to disclose such information is considered to be implied under the rules.

36. A. Under MR 1.14(a), even when the lawyer may fear that the client is acting under some diminished capacity, "the lawyer shall, as far as reasonably possible, maintain a normal client-lawyer relationship with the client." As long as the lawyer believes the client can still act in her own best interest, no further action is required at this time.

37. B. Rule 1.14 creates a permission structure for the lawyer to take reasonable action to protect the client's interests. Here, the client was clearly suffering under a diminished capacity, and, as such, the lawyer shared such confidential information as was necessary to protect the client's interests. The rule explicitly provides that a lawyer is deemed to have implied consent to reveal this information if necessary to protect the client's interests. MR 1.14(c).

5.9 Safekeeping Client Property

38. A. Rule 1.15 does not require that the lawyer provide weekly accountings to the client. The lawyer's other actions with respect to the clients' funds are appropriate under that rule.

39. B. Rule 1.15(c) provides that "[a] lawyer shall deposit into a client trust account legal fees and expenses that have been paid in advance, to be withdrawn by the lawyer only as fees are earned or expenses incurred." A lawyer is generally not permitted to take an advance on fees not already earned from proceeds the lawyer is safekeeping for the client.

40. C. Rule 1.15(e) provides that when "a lawyer is in possession of property in which two or more persons (one of whom may be the lawyer) claim interests, the property shall be kept separate by the lawyer until the dispute is resolved." At the same time, the lawyer must "promptly distribute all portions of the property as to which the interests are not in dispute." Thus, if fees are in dispute, they should be maintained in escrow until the dispute is resolved. It does not matter that the lawyer committed to returning any fee the court determines is excessive.

41. B. Under MR 1.15(e), the lawyer must "promptly distribute all portions of the property as to which the interests are not in dispute." Accordingly, the lawyer should retain only the portion that is in dispute ($20,000) and distribute those portions of the proceeds ($40,000 to each client) that everyone agrees should go to the clients.

5.10 Sale of a Law Practice

42. D. Rule 1.17(b) provides that a firm can only sell the entirety of its practice or an entire practice area. There are no special exceptions or provisions for situations where a client's work may be "split" between two practice areas.

43. B. Under MR 1.17(c), the sale of an entire law practice requires written notice of the proposed sale to the seller's clients regarding the following: the fact of the proposed sale, the clients' right to retain other counsel, and the clients' right to take possession of files. The fact of consent to the transfer of files is presumed after ninety days without objection. If a client cannot be given notice, the lawyer must seek a court order to permit the transfer. Here, all clients here received notice, so their consent can be presumed after ninety days even without a court order. The court order is only required when a client cannot be given notice.

44. B. Rule 1.17(b) provides that a firm can only sell the entirety of its practice or an entire practice area. Here, the firm did not sell the entire practice area. While withdrawal and transfer of the cases would have been appropriate, their sale would not.

5.11 Formative Assessment Quiz

45. C. The crane operator is a "former constituent" under the rules and not covered by the "no contact" rule. *See* Comment 7 to MR 4.2, and *Niesig v. Team 1*, 76 N.Y.2d 363 (1990).

46. D. Under MR 3.3(a)(1), a lawyer cannot knowingly "fail to correct a false statement of material fact or law previously made to the tribunal by the lawyer."

47. B. Under Comment 2 to MR 4.1, and under the normal conventions of negotiations, a lawyer is not obligated to truthfully state the client's "bottom line" when asked.

48. D. Under MR 1.15(e), a lawyer may distribute proceeds as between two parties when the amount to be distributed is not in dispute, even if other portions are still in dispute. Both parties agree they should, at a minimum, receive $200,000 apiece. It's the remaining $50,000 that is in dispute, and that portion alone should be withheld. An argument could be made that the lawyer could distribute $225,000 to Able and withhold only $25,000 because Baker appears to want, at a minimum, the proceeds to be divided equally. The lawyer would, in that situation, withhold only $25,000 and distribute $200,000 to Baker. Answer D is the option that most accurately reflects the lawyer's obligations.

49. C. The lawyer did not communicate about the subject matter of the litigation and thus did not trigger the consent requirements of MR 4.2. The lawyer's communication with the marina only related to the routine maintenance of her boat, which bears no relation to the pending litigation matter.

50. B. Under Comment 2 to MR 3.1, a lawyer may file a claim even if the lawyer does not think the claim will prevail, if the lawyer has a good faith basis for the claim.

51. A. Rule 3.7(a)(3) permits a lawyer to serve as an advocate on behalf of a client and to testify as to a contested issue where the lawyer's disqualification would materially prejudice the client.

52. D. Rule 4.3 provides that "[w]hen the lawyer knows or reasonably should know that [an] unrepresented person misunderstands the lawyer's role in the matter, the lawyer shall make reasonable efforts to correct the misunderstanding." In addition, "the lawyer shall not give legal advice to an unrepresented person, other than the advice to secure counsel, if the lawyer knows or reasonably should know that the interests of such a person are or have a reasonable possibility of being in conflict with the interests of the client." Even if the lawyer does his best to give "objectively accurate" advice, he still should have identified himself as representing the tenant's landlord and refrained from giving any advice other than the advice to seek representation.

53. C. In accordance with Comment 13 to MR 3.3, the practical time limit on the duty to disclose is "when a final judgment in the proceeding has been affirmed on appeal or the time for review has passed." Here, that time for review had not closed, and thus the lawyer still has an affirmative duty to take remedial action to correct the perjured testimony.

54. B. *See* MR 3.4(c). The refusal to act in accordance with the judge's direction was not done in an open fashion even though it was based on an assertion that no valid basis existed for the direction.

55. C. Under MR 3.3, there is no exception to the duty of candor before a tribunal for information learned during the course of a representation or to defend a proceeding. The same considerations apply whether the person committing the perjury is a client or a witness.

56. A. Under MR 3.3 and MR 1.0(f), a lawyer's knowledge that testimony is false can be inferred from the circumstances. And under Comment 8 to MR 3.3, "although a lawyer should resolve doubts about the veracity of testimony or other evidence in favor of the client, the lawyer cannot ignore an obvious falsehood." Here, the lawyer understood that it was "impossible" that the client could achieve the large return on the investment without adding additional funds to the account, so, at a minimum, the lawyer's knowledge of the perjury could be inferred from the circumstances.

57. B. Under MR 3.8(a), probable cause is the standard necessary to bring a charge, and it applies even if the prosecutor does not think the charges will prevail.

58. B. Comment 1 to MR 3.1 provides that "[t]he question" as to whether a lawyer's action is appropriate "is whether a competent lawyer acting in good faith would regard the course of action as having some substantial purpose other than de-

lay." It provides further that "[r]ealizing financial or other benefit from otherwise improper delay in litigation is not a legitimate interest of the client."

59. C. Under MR 3.3(a)(3), a "lawyer may refuse to offer evidence, other than the testimony of a defendant in a criminal matter, that the lawyer reasonably believes is false."

60. B. In accordance with MR 3.9, the lawyer must state that she is testifying on behalf of a client, even if she has some other grounds upon which she might testify. Here, the client explicitly asked the lawyer to testify on behalf of the client's interests, and the lawyer had a duty to disclose that role.

61. C. Under MR 4.2, the lawyer cannot communicate with someone the lawyer knows is represented by counsel unless opposing counsel gives consent to such a communication. Only opposing counsel can give such consent; the opposing client cannot.

62. A. Under MR 4.3, a lawyer is obligated only to identify herself and advise unrepresented, adverse parties of the desirability of obtaining their own counsel. There is no obligation that the lawyer actually afford those parties time to secure counsel.

63. C. Comment 7 to MR 4.2 provides that consent from opposing counsel is not required for a lawyer to speak to a former constituent of a represented party, but it also states that the lawyer "must not use methods of obtaining evidence that violate the rights of the organization," which would have included probing the privileged communications between the employer's lawyer and the supervisor when the supervisor was employed by the employer.

Chapter 6: Addressing Misconduct

6.1 Identifying Misconduct

1. B. Rule 8.4(a) prohibits lawyers from violating the rules "or to do so through the acts of another." Here, Lawyer A directed Lawyer B to do something that Lawyer A could not do, that is, violate MR 4.2. Even if Lawyer B were not a lawyer and Lawyer A asked him to take action that Lawyer A could not take on her own, it would still constitute a violation of Lawyer A's professional obligations.

2. B. According to MR 8.4(c), which provides it is misconduct to "engage in conduct involving dishonesty, fraud, deceit or misrepresentation," any such improper conduct can be attributable to a lawyer, even if not related to the lawyer's practice of law.

6.2 Reporting Misconduct

3. C. Allie's repeated, self-disclosed actions against the wishes of the client raise a substantial question about her fitness to practice law, and thus the lawyer is required to report Allie under MR 8.3.

4. D. According to the terms of M.R. 8.3(c), the reporting requirement "does not require disclosure of information otherwise protected by Rule 1.6 or information gained by a lawyer or judge while participating in an approved lawyers assistance program." A lawyer who is facing disciplinary proceedings is entitled to the same right as anyone else to speak to an attorney and have those communications protected by the attorney-client privilege. If it were otherwise, that is, if the lawyer's own attorney would be compelled to report the misconduct, no lawyer would seek counsel when facing such charges.

5. B. Misappropriating client funds certainly raises a substantial question as to opposing counsel's fitness to practice law under MR 8.3(a) even if no one was harmed and the opposing counsel arguably had earned the funds he withdrew in payment for his services. His agreement with his client said that he would be awarded a portion of the fees only after the claims were resolved. While one could argue that the clients were harmed to a certain extent because the funds he withdrew reduced the principal of the trust, meaning the interest on the trust was less than it would have been had the money not been withdrawn, what matters here is the misconduct—misappropriation of funds—and not the extent of any harm. This type of conduct raises a substantial question regarding his fitness to practice law and imposes an obligation on Lawyer to report it.

6. B. Lawyer is not obligated to share this information, even if it raises a substantial question as to his fitness to practice law, because she was retained to represent Tyrion for professional misconduct and the information related to the sharing of confidential information was obtained during the course of that representation. *See* MR 8.3(c) and Comment 4 thereto.

7. A. According to MR 8.3(b), similar to the requirements of MR 8.3(a) regarding attorney misconduct, a lawyer who knows that a judge has committed a violation of applicable rules of judicial conduct that raises a substantial question as to the judge's fitness for office shall inform the appropriate authority.

6.3 Misconduct Related to Diversity and Inclusion

8. C. Rule 8.4(g) states that it is professional misconduct for a lawyer to "engage in conduct that the lawyer knows or reasonably should know is harassment or discrimination on the basis of race, sex, religion, national origin, ethnicity, disability, age, sexual orientation, gender identity, *marital status* or socioeconomic status in conduct related to the practice of law." (Emphasis added.)

9. D. By its express terms, MR 8.4(g) "does not preclude legitimate advice or advocacy consistent with these Rules." The lawyer is involved in a legitimate form of advocacy on behalf of the female inmates strictly on account of their gender and is not required to also represent this other male inmate. Because the advocacy is legitimate itself, it is not a violation of 8.4(g).

6.4 Formative Assessment Quiz

10. B. Under MR 8.3(a), whether a substantial question is raised about the fitness of the lawyer to practice law is the appropriate standard, and Baker meets this standard, which imposes a burden on Able to report Baker. Baker's decision to reject a beneficial settlement offer not just for Baker's client but also Able's (though it is not clear whether that would be an effective rejection of the offer to Able's client) is clearly inappropriate, even if the action was arguably taken in good faith. Baker should have taken the offer back to his own client so that the client could consider the offer, and Baker definitely should not have attempted to reject the offer for Able's client, which it appears Baker did to prevent information about the offer from reaching his own client.

11. D. It is consistent with the conventions of negotiations to not share a client's bottom line in negotiations unless the lawyer feels it is to the client's advantage to do so. There are limited situations in which a lawyer might be obligated to share some specific information during negotiations, as was the case in *Virzi v. Grand Trunk Warehouse & Cold Storage Co.*, 571 F. Supp. 507 (E.D. Mich. 1983), where the lawyer was required to reveal that his client had died prior to settlement of a matter. Without such an independent obligation, Lawyer A's actions do not raise a substantial question about her fitness to practice law.

12. B. Comment 4 to MR 8.3 provides as follows: "The duty to report professional misconduct does not apply to a lawyer retained to represent a lawyer whose professional conduct is in question. Such a situation is governed by the Rules applicable to the client-lawyer relationship."

13. C. The investigation mentioned in Answer B is not relevant to the exemption. Lawyer was not retained by Baker to conduct an investigation. Baker's conduct clearly meets the standard for the duty to report attorney misconduct, that is, it raises a substantial question as to Baker's fitness to practice law. *See* MR 8.3(a).

14. B. Under MR 8.4(a), a lawyer cannot knowingly violate the rules "through the acts of another." Here, the lawyer counseled a third party to seek out information through direct communication with someone protected by MR 4.2, actions which would have been improper if the lawyer carried them out directly. A lawyer cannot use a third party to get around the rules.

15. C. If Opposing Counsel had engaged in any misconduct, that might trigger at least an inquiry into whether the reporting obligations of MR 8.3(a) would require

reporting, that is, if Opposing Counsel's conduct rose to the level of raising a substantial question as to his fitness to practice law. Here, there is no event that would trigger even an inquiry as to whether 8.3(a) mandates reporting. Opposing Counsel's conduct is completely appropriate and thus cannot raise any question about his fitness to practice law, let alone a substantial one.

16. C. Rule 8.4(g) makes it improper to discriminate "on the basis of race, sex, religion, national origin, ethnicity, disability, age, sexual orientation, *gender identity*, marital status or socioeconomic status in conduct related to the practice of law." (Emphasis added.) Refusing to hire someone on the basis of gender identity would constitute misconduct even if the local jurisdiction does not make it illegal, and hiring practices for a law firm are related to the practice of law.

17. A. This question tests your knowledge of the appropriate standard regarding the duty to report attorney misconduct: such conduct must raise a substantial question as to the lawyer's fitness to practice law in order to trigger the reporting requirement. Here, that standard was not met. As a result, there is no duty to report the conduct. *See* MR Rule 8.3(a).

Chapter 7: Attorney Free Speech Rights

7.1 Attorney Advertising

1. C. Rule 7.1 provides as follows: "A communication is false or misleading if it contains a material misrepresentation of fact or law, or omits a fact necessary to make the statement considered as a whole not materially misleading." A lawyer can advertise an area of practice, however, as long as the lawyer does not improperly identify as a "certified specialist" unless authorized to do so. The lawyer here did not help secure the award for the victims of the EquiFacts breach, and thus the advertising is false.

2. A. Under MR 7.1, a lawyer "shall not make a false or misleading communication about the lawyer or the lawyer's services. A communication is false or misleading if it contains a material misrepresentation of fact or law, or omits a fact necessary to make the statement considered as a whole not materially misleading." Even though the rate the lawyer charges may be reasonable, failing to advertise the higher rate that applies after the first hour leaves out a material fact that is necessary to make the advertising not misleading.

3. B. Rule 7.3(b) provides that "[a] lawyer shall not solicit professional employment by live person-to-person contact when a significant motive for the lawyer's doing so is the lawyer's or law firm's pecuniary gain, unless the contact is with a: (1) lawyer; (2) person who has a family, close personal, or prior business or

professional relationship with the lawyer or law firm; or (3) person who routinely uses for business purposes the type of legal services offered by the lawyer." At the same time, even if the conditions of MR 7.3(b) are satisfied, they do not permit the lawyer to engage in in-person solicitation if "(1) the target of the solicitation has made known to the lawyer a desire not to be solicited by the lawyer; or (2) the solicitation involves coercion, duress or harassment." Here, Cersei appears to be someone who routinely uses these types of services, so the prohibition on in-person solicitation does not apply, and no exception under MR 7.3(c) seems to prohibit the solicitation engaged in here.

4. C. Answer D is incorrect because a disclaimer is not enough, standing alone, to immunize a lawyer from improper advertising. Rule 7.2(b)(1) allows a lawyer to pay the normal cost of advertising or solicitation. Lawyers engage in a lot of public speaking in an effort to "get their names out there" to try to attract clients, for example, by participating in public events, writing op-eds, and hosting radio shows or podcasts. There is nothing wrong with any of that provided no attorney-client relationship is formed and it is not considered an in-person solicitation. Those issues were not present here.

5. B. Rule 7.2(c) requires that if a lawyer advertises that he or she is a "certified specialist," the advertisement must contain an indication that the lawyer is such a certified specialist as recognized by an appropriate authority and it must list the name of that authority.

6. B. In *Shapero v. Kentucky Bar Association*, 486 U.S. 466 (1988), the U.S. Supreme Court found that a general prohibition on written solicitation of clients who are known to be in need of legal services was unconstitutional. Later, in *Florida Bar v. Went for It, Inc.*, 515 U.S. 618 (1995), the U.S. Supreme Court upheld a ban on lawyers' soliciting victims of an accident or disaster until thirty days had passed since the incident. The Court found such a ban was appropriate in order to respect the privacy rights of the victims and their families and because the potential clients' rights were generally not jeopardized by the brief delay.

7. B. Rule 7.3(b) prohibits "live person-to-person contact" for the purposes of soliciting clients for pecuniary gain. In addition, Comment 2 to MR 7.3 explains that "'[l]ive person-to-person contact' means in-person, face-to-face, live telephone and other real-time visual or auditory person-to-person communications where the person is subject to a direct personal encounter without time for reflection," while providing also that "[s]uch person-to-person contact does not include chat rooms, text messages or other written communications that recipients may easily disregard." Here, while the real-time, personal outreach could not be performed by a person other than the lawyer if such an effort was done at the behest of the lawyer, these sorts of pre-paid plans are considered appropriate under the rules. *See* MR 7.3(d).

8. A. Unlike with commercial speech, where a state seeking to regulate lawyer speech, including advertising, has to do so in the service of a substantial governmental interest and only through means that directly advance that interest (*see, e.g.*,

Bates v. State Bar of Ariz., 433 U.S. 350 (1977)), the speech in this situation involved political speech and, as a result, is entitled to a higher level of protection. In such situations, the state's interest in limiting the lawyer's speech must be compelling and its means of restricting it narrowly tailored to satisfy those interests. *See In re Primus*, 436 U.S. 412 (1978).

9. D. Rule 7.2(a) permits in-person solicitation that is not for the lawyer's pecuniary gain. The fact that some prospective clients may seek out Lawyer's services in light of her public service does not change the analysis that Lawyer's service is performed for non-pecuniary gain.

10. B. Under MR 7.3(b) and (c), a lawyer cannot engage in solicitation by live person-to-person contact when pecuniary gain is the motive, as was the case here, unless the lawyer has a close relationship with the target of the solicitation, and only until that person expresses a lack of interest in the lawyer's services.

11. C. Rule 7.2(b) provides that "[a] lawyer shall not compensate, give or promise anything of value to a person for recommending the lawyer's services except that a lawyer may: (1) pay the reasonable costs of advertisements or communications permitted by this Rule; (2) pay the usual charges of a legal service plan or a not-for-profit or qualified lawyer referral service; (3) pay for a law practice in accordance with Rule 1.17; (4) refer clients to another lawyer or a nonlawyer professional pursuant to an agreement not otherwise prohibited under these Rules that provides for the other person to refer clients or customers to the lawyer, if: (i) the reciprocal referral agreement is not exclusive; and (ii) the client is informed of the existence and nature of the agreement; and (5) give nominal gifts as an expression of appreciation that are neither intended nor reasonably expected to be a form of compensation for recommending a lawyer's services." Under subpart (b)(4), this arrangement is appropriate.

7.2 Attorney Communications with the Media

12. B. Rule 3.6(a) provides that "[a] lawyer who is participating or has participated in the investigation or litigation of a matter shall not make an extrajudicial statement that the lawyer knows or reasonably should know will be disseminated by means of public communication and will have a substantial likelihood of materially prejudicing an adjudicative proceeding in the matter." Critically, this prohibition only applies to lawyers who are "participating in" or who have "participated in" the matter. Here, since the lawyer was not involved in the matter, the prohibition does not apply to her.

13. C. While a lawyer representing a client should generally refrain from engaging in making public statements that have "a substantial likelihood of materially prejudicing an adjudicative proceeding in the matter" (*see* MR 3.6(a)), here, the lawyer was responding to adverse publicity, even if the lawyer's statement about the confession might be the type of information that might otherwise tend to be improper. *See* MR 3.6(c).

14. A. Comment 5 to MR 3.6 identifies a number of issues that are considered more likely than not to prejudice a proceeding, and thus lawyers should generally try to avoid making them. The statement here is the type of statement that is likely to prejudice the proceeding, and the lawyer is not merely attempting to correct negative publicity presented by others. The prosecutor did not speak about the lawyer's client in his statements; had he done so, it might have triggered the lawyer's ability to respond to adverse publicity engendered by the acts of another, as MR 3.6(c) permits (*see* next question).

15. C. Under MR 3.6(c), a lawyer can make a statement to offset the prejudicial effect of information given by others. During the press conference, however, the prosecutor refers to the witness's polygraph test results, information which Comment 5 to MR 3.6 (related to the results of tests) identifies as having a tendency to be prejudicial. Although MR 3.6(c) does give the lawyer some leeway when responding to adverse publicity generated by someone other than the lawyer or the lawyer's client, that authority is not unlimited. That part of the rule also provides as follows: "A statement made pursuant to this paragraph shall be limited to such information as is necessary to mitigate the recent adverse publicity." In this fact pattern, there is no indication that the results of the polygraph are related to the accusation that the witness was charged with embezzlement, so one could not say that statements made about the tests were reasonably related to address the false publicity directly.

16. B. The fact pattern does not suggest that there was any threat to the proceeding by this statement (*see* MR 3.6(a)), nor does the nature of the statement inherently suggest such a threat is likely. Moreover, it is also appropriate merely to report on scheduling matters (MR 3.6(b)(4)), even if such a statement could prejudice the proceeding. The lawyer was not responding to any adverse publicity, however, so it was not necessary to rely on that provision to justify this statement.

17. D. Once again, the rules related to publicity require that the lawyer has to be involved in the matter for the provisions of MR 3.6 to apply, but these requirements extend to all members of the firm under MR 3.6(d). Like with a disabling conflict that can "infect" the entire firm, the prohibition on extrajudicial statements extends to all members of a law firm.

7.3 Formative Assessment Quiz

18. B. Answer D is incorrect because a disclaimer is not enough, standing alone, to immunize a lawyer from improper advertising. Rule 7.2(b)(1) allows a lawyer to pay the normal cost of advertising or solicitation.

19. C. The lawyer did not engage in direct, person-to-person solicitation of business at the event, and thus her actions were not improper. *See* 7.3(b)(3).

20. D. Although the lawyer is speaking about the admissibility of evidence (noted in Comment 5 to MR 3.6 as more likely to be prejudicial to an adjudicative proceeding), MR 3.6(c) and Comment 7 thereto note that statements that might otherwise be improper are allowed when they are in response to bad publicity initiated by someone other than the lawyer.

21. D. Rule 7.3(c) provides that "[a] lawyer shall not state or imply that a lawyer is certified as a specialist in a particular field of law, unless: (1) the lawyer has been certified as a specialist by an organization that has been approved by an appropriate authority of the state or the District of Columbia or a U.S. Territory or that has been accredited by the American Bar Association; and (2) the name of the certifying organization is clearly identified in the communication."

22. B. This activity, even the in-person solicitation, is protected political speech in accordance with the ruling in *In re Primus*, 436 U.S. 412 (1978).

Chapter 8: Judicial Ethics

8.1 Judicial Misconduct

1. C. Under MCJC R. 2.15(B), the duty to report attorney misconduct is mandatory when a judge has knowledge of conduct that raises substantial questions about a lawyer's fitness to practice law, as these facts indicate. The source of the knowledge is irrelevant, and the conduct cannot merely be unethical. What matters is whether the judge has knowledge of the behavior.

2. A. MCJC R. 2.9 covers ex parte communications, and subpart 2.9(A)(1) allows for such communications in circumstances where it is required "for scheduling, administrative, or emergency purposes, which does not address substantive matters" as long as "(a) the judge reasonably believes that no party will gain a procedural, substantive, or tactical advantage as a result of the ex parte communication; and (b) the judge makes provision promptly to notify all other parties of the substance of the ex parte communication, and gives the parties an opportunity to respond." Here, the communication was proper in light of these provisions and the opposing firm was promptly notified and given an opportunity to respond.

3. B. MCJC R. 4.5(B) provides that "[u]pon becoming a candidate for a nonjudicial appointive office, a judge is not required to resign from judicial office, provided that the judge complies with the other provisions of this Code."

4. A. MCJC R. 3.1 permits a judge to "engage in extrajudicial activities, except as prohibited by law or" by the MCJC. At the same time, "when engaging in extrajudicial activities, a judge shall not: (A) participate in activities that will interfere with the proper performance of the judge's judicial duties; (B) participate in activities that will lead to frequent disqualification of the judge; [or] (C) partic-

ipate in activities that would appear to a reasonable person to undermine the judge's independence, integrity, or impartiality. . . ." It is unlikely that the judge's participation in the work of this group will undermine the judge's "independence, integrity, or impartiality," nor will it "lead to frequent disqualification."

5. C. Under MCJC R. 4.1(A)(3) and Comment 5 thereto, there is no family exception for campaign endorsements made by judges. There is no exception for endorsements of federal candidates by state judges. No disclaimer would make this endorsement ethical.

6. D. According to MCJC R. 2.9(a)(3), "[a] judge may consult with court staff and court officials whose functions are to aid the judge in carrying out the judge's adjudicative responsibilities, or with other judges, provided the judge makes reasonable efforts to avoid receiving factual information that is not part of the record, and does not abrogate the responsibility personally to decide the matter."

7. B. Under MCJC R. 4.3(A) and (B), a judge can only seek endorsements from entities other than partisan political parties. It does not matter that the political party is the same political party as that of the governor who is endorsing the judge.

8. D. This question takes us back to the Model Rules. Rule 1.12(a) provides that "a lawyer shall not represent anyone in connection with a matter in which the lawyer participated personally and substantially as a judge or other adjudicative officer or law clerk to such a person or as an arbitrator, mediator or other third-party neutral, unless all parties to the proceeding give informed consent, confirmed in writing."

8.2 Formative Assessment Quiz

9. B. MCJC R. 2.9(A)(2) states that a judge may obtain written advice of a "disinterested expert" but must first give "advance notice" to the parties of the judge's intent to do so and give them "a reasonable opportunity to object and respond to the notice and the advice received."

10. A. MCJC R. 4.1(A)(4) provides that a judge "may not solicit funds for, pay an assessment to, or make a contribution to a political organization or a candidate for public office." No political contributions may be made by a judicial officer (MCJC R. 4.4(a)(4)) and there is no family exception thereto (Comment 5 to MCJC R. 4.1), even if disclosed. What is more, Comment 5 to MCJC R. 4.1 provides that "although members of the families of judges and judicial candidates are free to engage in their own political activity, including running for public office, there is no 'family exception' to the prohibition in paragraph (A)(3) against a judge or candidate publicly endorsing candidates for public office. A judge or judicial candidate must not become involved in, or publicly associ-

ated with, a family member's political activity or campaign for public office. To avoid public misunderstanding, judges and judicial candidates should take, and should urge members of their families to take, reasonable steps to avoid any implication that they endorse any family member's candidacy or other political activity."

11. B. Under MCJCR. 3.1, since the litigation in which the organization engages is likely to occur in federal court, it would require the judge's frequent recusal, and thus the judge should not serve on the board of this organization.

12. A. MCJC R. 3.7(A) provides that "a judge may participate in activities sponsored by organizations or governmental entities concerned with the law, the legal system, or the administration of justice, and those sponsored by or on behalf of educational, religious, charitable, fraternal, or civic organizations not conducted for profit, including but not limited to ... soliciting contributions for such an organization or entity, but only from members of the judge's family, or from judges over whom the judge does not exercise supervisory or appellate authority."

Chapter 9: Summative Assessment Quiz

1. C. A lawyer must act competently to preserve client confidences. Although this was an inadvertent act and Lawyer took immediate, if unsuccessful, steps to rectify the problem, the sensitivity of the materials contained in the briefcase required more attentive behavior. (*See* Comments 18 and 19 to MR 1.6.) In addition, Comment 10 to MR 5.5 provides that "a lawyer admitted only in another jurisdiction may engage in conduct temporarily in this jurisdiction in connection with pending litigation in another jurisdiction in which the lawyer is or reasonably expects to be authorized to appear, including taking depositions in this jurisdiction." Taking the deposition was itself not improper.

2. D. It was reasonable for the buyer to take such information as legal advice regarding whether to obtain counsel, and the lawyer should have refrained from providing any advice to this adverse party other than the advice *to* obtain counsel. (*See* MR 4.3.) Even though it might appear that the interests of the lawyer's client and that of the buyer are aligned, they are still formally on opposite sides of the transaction, and thus there is a formal conflict that requires the lawyer to refrain from providing any advice to the buyer other than to obtain counsel. Suggesting, even in good faith, that the buyer's interests lie with proceeding without representation is improper.

3. A. Comment 3 to MR 1.2 provides that a client may revoke prior authorization to accept terms of a settlement at any time.

4. C. Rule 8.1(b) provides that information protected by the attorney-client privilege need not be revealed to a bar admissions body; however, if this information *was*

not protected by the attorney-client privilege, the lawyer *would* have a duty to reveal it.

5. A. Rule 1.16(c) mandates that, even where there are permissible grounds for withdrawal, as there were here, an attorney must obtain court approval to withdraw where the court's rules require it.

6. C. Comment 3 to MR 1.15 provides that "[t]he lawyer is not required to remit to the client funds that the lawyer reasonably believes represent fees owed. However, a lawyer may not hold funds to coerce a client into accepting the lawyer's contention. The disputed portion of the funds must be kept in a trust account and the lawyer should suggest means for prompt resolution of the dispute, such as arbitration. The undisputed portion of the funds shall be promptly distributed."

7. D. Under MR 1.11(c), although the lawyer has "confidential government information" about a third party, the lawyer was timely and effectively screened and afforded no fee from the representation. There is no notice requirement under 1.11(c), neither to the former government employer nor to the affected party.

8. B. Rule 5.1(c) provides that "[a] lawyer shall be responsible for another lawyer's violation of the Rules of Professional Conduct if: (1) the lawyer orders or, with knowledge of the specific conduct, ratifies the conduct involved; or (2) the lawyer is a partner or has comparable managerial authority in the law firm in which the other lawyer practices, or has direct supervisory authority over the other lawyer, and knows of the conduct at a time when its consequences can be avoided or mitigated but fails to take reasonable remedial action." Answer B best reflects the situation in this fact pattern and the obligations that arose as a result.

9. D. Comment 3 to MR 1.1 provides as follows: "In an emergency a lawyer may give advice or assistance in a matter in which the lawyer does not have the skill ordinarily required where referral to or consultation or association with another lawyer would be impractical. Even in an emergency, however, assistance should be limited to that reasonably necessary in the circumstances, for ill-considered action under emergency conditions can jeopardize the client's interest." There is no indication that the lawyer offered assistance beyond that which the lawyer believed was necessary under the circumstances, even if wrong. The duty of competence to that of a "general practitioner" is generally relaxed in such situations.

10. C. Officer 1 was responsible for the incident and his communications related to that incident would be binding on the corporation, and thus they are covered by the protections of MR 4.2. *See Niesig v. Team 1*, 76 N.Y.2d 363 (1990). Officer 2 is a "mere witness" and was under no duty to intervene in the incident. *Id.* Officer 3 is a "former constituent" and under Comment 7 to Rule 4.2, "[c]onsent of the organization's lawyer is not required for communication with a former constituent."

11. A. When a lawyer changes a fee arrangement, the renegotiation of the fee arrangement is treated like a transaction with a client and must follow the provisions of MR 1.8(a), as the lawyer did here.

12. C. Under MR 3.7(a)(1), since the testimony the lawyer will give is uncontested, the lawyer will not be disqualified from serving as an advocate in the matter due to providing such testimony.

13. D. The lawyer's statements are truthful, and the prohibition under MR 4.2 on communicating with represented parties only applies to matters where the lawyer represents an interest adverse to the represented party. Here, no such relationship exists. While attempting to "poach" clients from other attorneys may be frowned upon in the community, it is generally not unethical. *See* MR 4.2, and MR 7.1, MR 7.2, and 7.3.

14. A. Rule 1.6(b)(1) provides no restriction on the release of information merely because it is of a different degree and/or kind. At the same time, when the lawyer is permitted to make a release under MR 1.6(b), the information that may be released is limited to that which will accomplish the goal of the provision under which the information is being released. *See, e.g.*, Comment 7 to MR 1.6.

15. A. *See* MR 3.5 and MCJC R. 2.9(A)(1)(a) and (b). Although it could be argued that the communication did not address the substance of the dispute, the fact that the judge was aware that this information would give the adversary an "unfair" advantage means that this is not a non-substantive issue. All affected parties should have been given prompt notice of the communication afterward (at a minimum) and afforded an opportunity to respond, even if the motion was denied.

16. D. A lawyer may accept representation when competence can be achieved with "reasonable preparation." *See* Comment 4 to MR 1.1.

17. C. Under MR 1.8(h)(1), independent representation is required in an agreement that seeks to waive future liability for malpractice.

18. B. Rule 3.7(b) permits the firm to represent the client even though Lawyer may not. Even though the other lawyer at the firm used to represent Nestor, the matters are not substantially related.

19. A. The lawyer was aware that Peter was represented by counsel (at a minimum, such knowledge can be inferred from the facts). It does not matter that Peter initiated the communication, nor does it matter that the CEO gave consent for the communication. Only an opposing lawyer can give such consent. *See* MR 4.2 and MR 1.0(f).

20. C. Under MR 5.2(b), "[a] subordinate lawyer does not violate the Rules of Professional Conduct if that lawyer acts in accordance with a supervisory lawyer's reasonable resolution of an arguable question of professional duty." Here, the subordinate lawyer was free to refuse to offer the testimony based on a reasonable belief that it was perjury (MR 3.3(a)(1)). The lawyer has to "know" that

testimony already offered was perjury for the duty to take reasonable remediable measures, including, if necessary, disclosure, to take effect.

21. D. A lawyer is generally afforded a degree of latitude to exercise professional judgment as to which witnesses to call and what evidence to present. Here, Lawyer made the tactical decision not to call the witness out of fear that allegations about the grounds of the witness's termination could undermine her credibility, regardless of their truth. This is not a "candor toward the tribunal" setting under MR 3.3 because it's not a question of whether the witness will testify truthfully. This is a tactical decision that resides appropriately with Lawyer. In this situation, a lawyer could certainly discuss the question with the client, talk about the risks, and consider the client's perspective on the question of whether to call the witness, but the lawyer would generally have the flexibility to exercise the lawyer's own judgment in this situation.

22. C. The lawyer did not have access to confidential information in the prior representation, and thus she is not precluded from representing the farmers. *See* MR 1.10. The Hirokawa firm is not disqualified. That the lawyer only worked on business matters does not, standing on its own, mean that she was not exposed to confidential information about Agro.

23. A. The lawyer's refutation of the statement made by the chief of police is acceptable under MR 3.6(c). All of his other statements are also acceptable under MR 3.6(b).

24. C. It is consistent with the conventions of negotiations to not share a client's bottom line in negotiations unless the lawyer feels it is to the client's advantage to do so. And a lawyer can speak in glowing terms about the lawyer's witnesses, evidence, or claims, even if the lawyer is not confident in them. A lawyer can even misrepresent that bottom line. A lawyer may not misrepresent the policy limit, however. *See* MR 3.6 and MR 4.1.

25. C. Linda received the information about the alleged fraudulent scheme during the course of representing Dan, and thus she is not obligated to report it. A lawyer's involvement in a money laundering scheme would raise a substantial question as to that lawyer's fitness to practice law because it shows the lawyer's inability to follow the law and willingness to engage in financially improper conduct. Furthermore, the question is framed in terms of a mandatory obligation—it is not asking whether Linda "may" report the misconduct as Rule 1.6 might permit. You have been given no indication that anyone is at imminent risk of death or serious bodily harm for the misconduct, and you have not been told that the lawyer's services are being used to further the fraud. *See* Comment 4 to MR 8.3 and MR 1.6. Even if such information was indicated from the fact pattern with regard to any injuries that might result from Dan's actions, Linda would have been under no *obligation* to report it.

26. B. Under MR 1.7, the representation is appropriate because the clients consent to the conflict and there is no indication this is a non-waivable conflict (i.e., no indication they will be on opposite sides of a lawsuit).

27. A. Comment 5 to MCJC R. 4.1. Not identifying oneself as a judge makes no difference to whether the endorsement is permitted or prohibited.

28. D. Comment 13 to MR 3.3 provides as follows: "A practical time limit on the obligation to rectify false evidence or false statements of law and fact has to be established. The conclusion of the proceeding is a reasonably definite point for the termination of the obligation. A proceeding has concluded within the meaning of this Rule when a final judgment in the proceeding has been affirmed on appeal or the time for review has passed."

29. B. Rule 1.18(d) covers this situation but provides several options to make this representation appropriate, either 1.18(d)(1) *or* (d)(2). Rule 1.18(d)(1) is not controlling because it says a lawyer is disqualified "only if" both parties give informed consent. But this is not how (d)(1) and (d)(2) work. Either could be satisfied, and the office can satisfy (d)(2) according to Answer B.

30. D. Rule 3.4(a) provides that the standard for when evidence cannot be destroyed is when it has "potential evidentiary value," that is, when it could be used in a pending proceeding or one the commencement of which is reasonably foreseeable, as was the case here. Comment 2 to MR 3.4.

31. D. Although the client does market this product to others, the lawyer paid double what could not even be obtained on the open market. This would raise the question whether this was an inappropriate form of financial assistance to the client. MR 1.8(a) and 1.8(e). This is absolutely an MPRE-style question: it has several layers to it and there are several different types of issues that MIGHT be implicated. Your task is to use the FORCE to identify what knowledge is being tested. See Comment 1 to MR 1.8.

32. A. Even if the lawyer intends to withdraw claims she believes do not have merit, such claims cannot be filed in the first place. A lawyer can file weak claims in the hope of exacting a settlement from the other side, but those claims still must have a good faith basis before they are asserted in a filing. MR 3.1.

33. B. Rules 5.1 and 5.3 impose affirmative duties on a supervisory lawyer to ensure that she has proper procedures in place to oversee non-legal staff. Here, the problem is the lack of oversight, not necessarily whether the client was harmed in the end. In a malpractice action, the question would be whether the client was harmed, and one could assume that, if the client knew of the improper filing and the threat of deportation, the client would have suffered some damages because of that looming threat and the fear of uncertainty. Here, the question asked simply whether the lawyer was subject to discipline.

34. C. It does not appear that a conflict impacted the representation in any way, let alone "adversely" as is required by the case law on the intersection of conflicts

of interest and ineffective assistance of counsel. If the issue of conflicted representation is not raised below, the defendant must show that the representation was adversely affected, and the defendants cannot do that here.

35. C. Lawyers have a duty to act competently to preserve confidences and keep abreast of changes in technology. Comment 8 to MR 1.1. Comment 18 to MR 1.6 provides that "Paragraph (c) [of MR 1.6] requires a lawyer to act competently to safeguard information relating to the representation of a client against unauthorized access by third parties and against inadvertent or unauthorized disclosure by the lawyer or other persons who are participating in the representation of the client or who are subject to the lawyer's supervision." Similarly, under MR 5.1, supervisory/managing lawyers with responsibility for a firm's operation as a whole have a particular duty to put "reasonable" systems in place that provide "reasonable assurances" that the lawyers are upholding their ethical obligations, including preserving confidences. Here, the new threats warrant, at a minimum, upgrading the system, which the lawyer did here.

36. A. Under MR 7.1, a lawyer can make no false or misleading statements about services in advertisements. The advertisement is false if it omits facts that are necessary to make the statement not misleading. Even if technically true, the statement is still misleading and improper.

37. D. Comment 3 to MR 1.9 explains that matters are substantially related, and thus create a conflict of interest, "if they involve the same transaction or legal dispute or if there otherwise is a substantial risk that confidential factual information as would normally have been obtained in the prior representation would materially advance the client's position in the subsequent matter."

38. C. Under MR 1.6(a), the circumstances related to the nature of the representation indicate that the client would know this information is the type that would typically be shared in negotiations. As a result, the lawyer had implied consent to share this confidential information.

39. A. Rule 1.5 sets forth the factors that can determine the reasonableness of a fee. Answer A is not one of those factors.

40. C. The lawyer's actions were consistent with her obligations under MR 1.8(a), and she agreed she would refund any unearned amount so the arrangement would not constitute a nonrefundable retainer agreement that would be improper and in violation of MR 1.16(d).

41. C. Under MR 3.3(a)(1), a lawyer cannot "knowingly ... fail to correct a false statement of material fact or law previously made to the tribunal by the lawyer." Nevertheless, here, the lawyer's knowledge that the paper was fabricated cannot be inferred from the facts. See also MR 1.0(f) for the definition of "knowledge."

42. A. This is what is called a "noisy withdrawal," as described in Comment 10 to MR 1.2. As set forth there, the lawyer is permitted to "give notice of the fact of withdrawal and to disaffirm any opinion, document, affirmation or the like."

43. B. Beck shared the information with Lawyer Baker and authorized the lawyer to use the information in the negotiations. There is nothing improper about using the information that an opposing party may want to settle a matter quickly to try to exact a better settlement for the client.

44. B. Rule 1.13(d) governs this situation, and the lawyer's role in investigating the matter restricts the lawyer's ability to release this information. There are no other facts in this fact pattern that would offer any other grounds under Rule 1.6(b) to permit the lawyer to divulge this information, like if the lawyer's services were being used to commit a crime or otherwise cause "substantial injury" to the financial interests of others. There is no evidence the lawyer's services are being used to further a crime.

45. C. Under Comment 5 to MR 3.6, the statements about identity of a witness or expected testimony of a witness or party are more likely than not to have a material prejudicial effect on a proceeding, particularly where the matter is before a jury.

46. A. The limitations are both reasonable and common in the jurisdiction. In addition, the clients always give informed consent to the arrangement. *See* MR 1.2(c).

47. D. While a third party can pay a lawyer's fee, the third party cannot be privy to confidential communications between the attorney and client without the client's consent.

48. C. This behavior likely violates MR 4.3 and MR 4.4, with respect to the rights of third persons, as well as MR 8.4 in many ways (using another to violate the rules, using fraud and deception, etc.).

49. D. Rule 1.5(d)(2) makes it clear that contingency fees are prohibited in a criminal case like this.

50. B. The communications do not fall under the "crime-fraud" exception to the attorney-client privilege. In addition, MR 1.2(d) provides that "[a] lawyer shall not counsel a client to engage, or assist a client, in conduct that the lawyer knows is criminal or fraudulent, but a lawyer may discuss the legal consequences of any proposed course of conduct with a client and may counsel or assist a client to make a good faith effort to determine the validity, scope, meaning or application of the law." What the lawyer did here was give information to the client as to how to *follow* the law, not break it, and it appears the client followed that advice. The lawyer provided guidance on the "validity, scope, meaning, or application of the law." In addition, the interpreter, even though a third party, was present on the call to facilitate the representation, and thus it was not improper for the interpreter to have participated in the communications.

51. B. Rule 3.2(d) provides that in an ex parte proceeding, a lawyer shall "inform the tribunal of all material facts known to the lawyer that will enable the tribunal to make an informed decision, whether or not the facts are adverse."

52. C. Both the failure to identify the certifying entity and the promise of providing financial assistance are improper. *See* M.R. 7.2(c)(1) and M.R. 1.8(e)(3).

53. D. Rule 3.3(a)(3) provides that "[a] lawyer may refuse to offer evidence, other than the testimony of a defendant in a criminal matter, that the lawyer reasonably believes is false." Comment 6 to MR 3.3 explains further that if a lawyer knows a portion of a client's testimony will be false, she may offer the witness's testimony but avoid that portion she knows will be false.

54. B. The lawyer may introduce even privileged matter to the extent necessary to interpose a defense to a claim brought against her, and this type of claim would qualify. It does not require the client's consent. MR 1.6(b)(5).

55. A. Under MR 3.8(a), probable cause is the standard necessary to bring a charge even if the prosecutor believes a charge will prevail at trial.

56. C. According to MR 4.3, only when a lawyer has interests adverse to a non-lawyer must the lawyer not give legal advice other than to consult an attorney. The advice to the individuals who are not employees of PriceCutter is acceptable because it is assistance that will help them represent themselves. The communication with the PriceCutter employees is not improper because the lawyer identified herself and the only advice she gave them was the advice to seek their own counsel.

57. A. Under MR 8.3, the standard for when a lawyer has a duty to report the misconduct of another lawyer is whether that second lawyer's actions or inactions raise a "substantial question" as to that lawyer's fitness to practice law. Baker's self-serving behavior that is contrary to what would appear to be the client's interests raises a substantial question as to Baker's fitness to practice law. Once that substantial question is raised, Able is then obligated to report Baker.

58. D. Some may consider this a close call, but even an honest mistake could lead to discipline for *both* the negligent recordkeeping and the results of that recordkeeping—the withdrawal of funds that were unearned. If there had not been negligent recordkeeping, and, for example, a bank error had indicated that funds had been deposited and then the lawyer withdrew the fee, it would have been the bank's error that led the lawyer to withdraw the funds. Here, we are told that Lawyer's own in-house bookkeeper's negligent recordkeeping is what resulted in the improper withdrawal, and thus it is the poor recordkeeping and the result of that recordkeeping (the withdrawal) that would get the lawyer in trouble here. Under MR 5.3, a lawyer is responsible for the conduct of all non-lawyer staff working under the lawyer. We certainly do not know all of the facts, but the question explicitly asked what conduct, if any, could subject the lawyer to discipline. The only way the negligent recordkeeping would not be the lawyer's responsibility is if the lawyer were not, in fact, responsible for that recordkeeping. But the lawyer is responsible. The question explicitly says the lawyer is a solo practitioner, and thus the lawyer is clearly responsible for any work of non-lawyers employed at the firm.

59. B. Under MR 1.8(k), any conflict that flows from the relationship between Sam and Carroll, contained in MR 1.8(j), applies only to Sam.

60. D. Rule 1.3 requires the lawyer to engage with "reasonable diligence and promptness in representing a client," but that does not preclude the lawyer from agreeing to "a reasonable request for a postponement that will not prejudice the lawyer's client." Comment 3 to MR 1.3.

Index of Authorities

Cases

Model Code of Judicial Conduct

Model Rules of Professional Conduct

Index of Terms